Robert Ferrell

MUSICAL BIOGRAPHY

JEAN SIBELIUS *by Karl Ekman*

CHARLES T. GRIFFES *by Edward M. Maisel*

SERGEI PROKOFIEV *by Israel Nestyev*

THE LIFE OF RICHARD WAGNER *by Ernest Newman*

BRAHMS *by Walter Niemann*

MY MUSICAL LIFE *by N. A. Rimsky-Korsakov*

BOHUSLAV MARTINŮ *by Miloš Šafránek*

DMITRI SHOSTAKOVICH *by Victor Seroff*

ROSSINI *by Francis Toye*

VERDI *by Francis Toye*

MOZART *by W. J. Turner*

HANDEL *by Herbert Weinstock*

TCHAIKOVSKY *by Herbert Weinstock*

These are BORZOI BOOKS, *published by* Alfred A. Knopf

Theme and Variations

BRUNO WALTER

(*photograph by Ernest E. Gottlieb*)

Theme and Variations

AN AUTOBIOGRAPHY

BY

Bruno Walter

TRANSLATED FROM THE GERMAN BY

JAMES A. GALSTON

NEW YORK   Alfred A. Knopf   1946

Late resounds what early sounded,
Good and ill to song are rounded.

GOETHE

PREFACE

THIS is the story of a life filled to the brim with music. Had it been my music, music created by me, I should probably never have written this book; an autobiography of sound would have satisfied my urge to express myself. However, I have made only the music of others sound forth, I have been but a "re-creator."

And so I felt impelled to write down the text of my fading Song of the Earth, so as to preserve my mundane life itself from fading altogether. After a long journey, I suddenly felt like standing still and turning backward my gaze which had always been directed ahead — contemplating the road I had traveled, reflecting. A man of sixty-eight, I decided to take a year of rest in order to remember, to search, and to tell of my life.

I wanted to tell it to myself so that I might comprehend it, might compare achievement with what I had planned and hoped for, might contrast my age with youth, and might, out of the countless variations of my life's experiences, recognize and appraise myself as their theme. But my tale was meant also for those friends of my art who had thus far known me only through my musical activity. I wanted to thank them for their encouraging companionship by opening to them my heart as far as that was possible in words.

In the course of my work I was made to think of even a wider circle, for it seemed to me as if the Odyssey of my life, objectively unfolded before my aging gaze, might be of general human interest.

Thus this book acquired its twofold sense: self examination and a message. But since I made perfect sincerity the basic law of my tale I must point out that I did my writing under somewhat unfavorable circumstances. No notes were at my disposal. Where I could not look up data in newspapers or books, or turn for confirmation to friends, I had to rely solely on my memory. When I first descended into the mine of the past, everything was dark about me. But I did not have to grope long. My eyes became accustomed to the dark — I could distinguish forms and figures, dwellings, streets, schools, conservatories, concert halls, theaters, landscapes, and oceans. I could see my parents, brother and sister, relatives, friends, and enemies. They moved, they spoke. One person would draw another, one event lead to another. Thoughts, feelings, and words that had been slumbering within me rose to the surface. I discovered that the past was not past unless it had never been alive; that it lived way down below in the shadowy part of our inward self's immense domain, ready to rise to the light at the call of memory. As my work progressed, I was often reminded of piano pieces that I had not played in a long time, and which I did not seem able to remember; but no sooner had I started playing than my fingers would run nimbly along their accustomed way. Memory depends upon the intensity with which a person has lived, acted, and felt. I have never wanted in intensity. But since its course is marked by curves, their low points are bound to be shrouded in a fog that the gaze can pierce only with difficulty. Thus it may well have happened that I have erred in details, that my memory has deceived me at times. At any rate, I have endeavored to tell the full truth in everything. Whenever I was not quite sure, I have given expression to my doubts.

It has not been my intention, however, to tell everything. My only resemblance to Bluebeard of fairy-tale fame lies in the fact that in my house, too, there is a chamber I refuse to have opened. True, it does not contain severed heads and a bloodied ax, but only personal experiences and sentiments that I recoil from discussing and that can hardly be of interest to others.

But is a musician's life at all able to arouse general interest? In my youth, I would mournfully have answered the question in the negative. Important in the eyes of the world were the prince, the statesman, the warrior; enjoyable perhaps, but dispensable, and by no means comparable to them in importance seemed the artist. Was not that expressed ever so plainly in the outward circumstances of all those people's lives? The Emperor of Austria lived in the Imperial Palace, the chief of government in the ministerial palace; Schubert and Mozart had dwelled in miserable quarters. The main part of the newspapers and their large headlines were given up to the historical events in the world, proving by their preferential treatment how vastly superior they were in importance to the news of art, to which but a secondary position was allotted. History told of Alexander and Napoleon, of Bismarck, Disraeli, and Metternich. How inferior, in comparison, how unimportant to the world seemed to me the circle comprising my world! Gradually, however, I began to see more clearly. What was left of the deeds of Alexander and Napoleon? What had become of Bismarck's Reich and of the most tremendous historical revolutions? There was a time in my life when the world's history reminded me of the remarkable street-cleaning machine I used to see at night during my first years in Vienna: its rotating brooms swept up the dust and whirled it into the air; but soon it floated down again and covered the street as before.

I have given up entertaining such extreme views. But I have preserved the unshakable conviction that man's spiritual accomplishments are vastly more important than his political and historical achievements. And so, a modest apostle of music and its great works, I venture to record my life because it has served music's timeless power and beauty, and because its transitoriness has been blessed by an alliance with the immortal. For the works of the creative spirit last, they are essentially imperishable, while the world-stirring historical activities of even the most eminent men are circumscribed by time. Napoleon is dead — but Beethoven lives.

Preface

was a time in my life when the world's history reminded me of the remarkable street-cleaning machine I used to see at night during my first years in Vienna: its rotating brooms swept up the dust and whirled it into the air; but soon it floated down again and covered the street as before.

I have given up entertaining such extreme views. But I have preserved the unshakable conviction that man's spiritual accomplishments are vastly more important than his political and historical achievements. And so, a modest apostle of music and its great works, I venture to record my life because it has served music's timeless power and beauty, and because its transitoriness has been blessed by an alliance with the immortal. For the works of the creative spirit last, they are essentially imperishable, while the world-stirring historical activities of even the most eminent men are circumscribed by time. Napoleon is dead — but Beethoven lives.

ILLUSTRATIONS

Theme and Variations

BOOK ONE

I

I CAME into this world on September 15, 1876. The house in which I was born has no place in my memory. It stood in Mehnerstrasse, near Alexanderplatz, in a poor, overpopulated district of the northeastern part of Berlin. During the second year of my life my parents moved to Elsasserstrasse. My earliest childhood recollections go back to that prosaic, unattractive, but clean and rather friendly street in the northern part of Berlin. It contrasted favorably with two neighboring and particularly ugly and noisy cross-streets, which impressed me as being gloomily threatening when, from the corners, I gazed down their lengths with dread and aversion, and yet with a kind of fascination. A person had to pass them and the Borsig Locomotive Works to get to Friedrichstrasse, the great north-south artery leading to Berlin's most brilliant quarter: Unter den Linden, Leipzigerstrasse, and, farther on, Belle-Alliance Platz. Lower middle-class people lived in Elsasserstrasse at that time. Their simple needs were supplied by the street's modest shops. One of the principal means of communication in the Berlin of those days was the horse cars, conveyances rumbling along with a metallic twang, running on tracks, and drawn by two heavy horses. One of these tram lines ran through Elsasserstrasse, and my memory has preserved its high, quick, and energetic tinkling, the deeper, slower, and more jovial ringing of the Bolle milk carts, the hoarse cries of the vendors pushing their vegetable and potato carts through the streets, and the chant of the junk dealers, whose "Rags, bones, paper, old boots!" still sounds in my ear as the leitmotif of that Berlin street's unmelodious symphony.

Our apartment was on the second floor of a tenement house and consisted of the light "company room," the dark dining room, the parental bedroom, and the nursery. The kitchen was ruled by a maid of all work, whose person changed from time to time but whose name persisted in being the ultra-Berlinese one of Minna. The fact of her presence as well as the number of rooms seem to indicate rather comfortable circumstances. The utmost economy was nevertheless practiced at home, and though, then as later, I was spared need and deprivation, I still recall quite clearly the modesty of our mode of living.

At any rate, peace, kindness, and decency prevailed in the modest Jewish family. I do not recall any "scenes" between Father and Mother or any coarse or ugly words in our family life. My Father was at that time a bookkeeper in a large silk concern, in which he was to be active for upward of fifty years, his salary and the importance of his position increasing gradually. He was a quiet man, thoroughly reliable and conscientious, who, out of business hours, lived only for his family. He came originally from the Magdeburg district, whose dialect was still occasionally noticeable in his otherwise good German. A man of poor beginnings and simple upbringing, he was filled with a craving for the better things of life. He was fond of reading lyric literature, the German classics, and Shakespeare. Occasionally, he attended a play or an opera and, at times, one of the "classic" operettas, at that time assiduously cultivated at the Friedrich Wilhelmstädtische Theater. Even in my early youth I joyfully participated in the after-effects and the lingering echoes of these delights. When I was a small child, Father was in the habit of carrying me in his arms while he hummed melodies from operas and operettas. Among them were the beginnings of arias by Mozart, with the German text used at that time, such as "Ah, the fond yearnings of loving hearts" ("*Voi che sapete*") from *Figaro*, "If the champagne makes us flush with desire" ("*Finch' han dal vino calda la testa*") from *Don Giovanni*, and similar operatic fragments. I was told that I was particularly delighted with "Dame Fortune's favors oft are sold" from Rocco's aria in the first act of *Fidelio*. He also let me have a few refreshing and stimulating drops from the spring of classic poetry. He loved to declaim verses, gaining pleasure from their stirring rhetoric, and to sprinkle his conversation with familiar quotations, especially from Schiller's dramas. This usually odious habit did not have an insipid effect in his case because of the warmth with which he always cited his quotations. I recall that the exalted language was pleasing to my ear long before I comprehended its sense.

When my parents conversed in low tones, I sensed that a serious problem or a difficult situation had arisen, and that Father needed Mother's help and advice. My naughtiness would cause occasional outbursts of anger, quickly changed into laughter, however, by my merry pranks. The dominant note of our home life was struck by the peaceful disposition and the serene cheerfulness of the family's provider. I can still see him sitting at Mother's side on the sofa. It is evening, he has just come home from his office and is enjoying his first warm meal of the day. The children, who have had their bread-and-butter and cocoa an hour before, are watching him in the hope that he may leave some of the delicacies for them. In this they are rarely disappointed, for he usually pushes his still half-filled plate away from him, as if he has eaten his fill. The kerosene lamp, hanging down from the ceiling, sheds its light over the table. If it smokes, there is soot in the room. Faded photographs are looking down from the walls, the placid hooded faces of grandmothers and grandfathers with canes. Our parents listen proudly to the children's smart prattling. Father was an early riser and, of a fine Sunday morning in the warm season, loved to take the children for breakfast to one of the nice Tiergarten restaurants "At the Tents" at about six o'clock. How delightful it was to breathe in the fresh morning air under the trees, observe the dew on the grass, and taste the crisp sandwiches, buttered on one side only — we called them *Knueppel* or *Schrippen* — that we had brought along; they were to be accompanied by the coffee Father would order at the restaurant.

Father's sedate cheerfulness was splendidly complemented by Mother's agile liveliness. While he loved art and was reverently devoted to matters of the spirit (without, however, being especially gifted in any one direction) , Mother had an unmistakable musical talent, which she had developed to a certain degree as a student at the Stern Conservatory. She played the piano nicely and sang songs by Schubert and others in an agreeable small voice. Our piano, an upright, was in the "company room," and I can see myself, a little child, standing at its side and listening enchantedly to Mother's music. Another object in that room attracted me mysteriously. A wooden pedestal, lacquered brown and shaped in two steps, supported a mirror, and in front of it on the upper step lay a large conch. Holding it to my ear, I would hear an exciting soughing, rich and deep, and often I would sneak into that room, not only to pick out a familiar tune from the black and white keys, but also to listen again and again to the puzzling sound of the conch. Among the pleasant musical recollections of my early childhood is the blaring of the Prussian military band, sounding up from the street and making me rush to the window. Unfortunately, it gave way at certain intervals to the harsh and dreary sounds of piercing fifes and sonorous drums. They were no less disagreeable to me than the strains of a hurdy-gurdy from the back-yard. Its merriest dance tunes made me as sad as the sight of the Franco-Prussian war invalids who lugged those heavy implements of torture on their backs, put them on a stand they had been carrying in their hand, and ground into the air melodies by Verdi and popular Berlin

[5]

songs. Paper-wrapped coins would come flying through the air from open kitchen windows, a mute, but well understood request to the organ grinder kindly to move on.

I am supposed to have shown an early inclination to wildness, obstinacy, despotism, and violent outbursts. More or less patient victims of my tyrannical moods, but also eager participants in my mischievous infractions of law and order, were my elder brother, my younger sister, and three girl cousins who lived on our floor with their parents, my Mother's sister and her husband. A door in the wooden partition separating our flats furthered our lively intercourse.

My Mother's disposition was fundamentally as cheerful as that of Father, but she was more lively and active than he and at the same time more given to changing moods. A woman of varied interests, communicative and gifted, she knew how to captivate me by vividly told tales and to steer me away from my evil moods and strange outbursts. But her most effective means for taming me was music, for no sooner did she seat herself at the piano than I changed and became quite docile and gentle under the effects of her playing and singing.

My vivacity, which frequently burst out in paroxysms of refractoriness, was also interrupted by moods of a strangely lasting and meditative tranquillity. Mother told me that, spirited though I was, I would suddenly become silent and sit in quiet absorption, as if I were "lost to the world." I myself can recall such a mood in connection with a visual impression, clear before my eyes even now. Two pictures are hanging on the wall — a rather lusterless dull painting on wood depicting two serious old women seated at spinning wheels, and a steel engraving called *Les Pelerins,* showing three figures, one recumbent and the other two propped on their elbows. I used to sit on the floor before these peaceful pictures for long spells, and I can still remember how my contemplations drew me deeper and deeper into their tranquillity and unreality.

The contemplative side of my nature was understood and furthered by a kind of good family spirit. It was my Uncle Emanuel. He was an almost dwarfishly small man with a pointed beard, fine features, frank eyes, and a warm heart. Quite absorbed in a wealth of spiritual interests, he was wholly unsuited for any practical vocation. Once in a while, a newspaper would print an essay he had written, or a periodical publish one of his poems. But after all, it was his task "to look, and not to create." So, from his little room in the adjoining flat, he looked into the world, read and studied, wrote prose and poetry. He was my parents' adviser, the children's playmate, the oracle consulted before decisions, the stand-by in difficult situations, and the source of information for questions of all kinds, from trivial ones of everyday life to complicated ones in the realm of science. From my childhood, and while I was a boy and a youth, I made ample use of this living encyclopedia and never failed to receive valuable instruction. Conscious of his unworldliness, but without bitterness or self-reproach, he patiently and devotedly fulfilled the demands of the part assigned to him by fate: to be consumed in the life of others. I not only owe to him instruction in a number of spheres, as for instance my first introduction to the ideas of Kant, but I also cherish the memory of a comforting, touching, and interesting personality in whom selfless and active goodness were paired with an insatiable thirst for knowledge and a philosophical calm.

Our family life was warmed by a sincere, quiet, but by no means orthodox religiousness. On holidays we went to the synagogue of the reformed Jewish community. It was natural that the beautifully pure choral chants and the solemnity of the strains of the organ had a more powerful effect upon my mind than the religious services themselves. Greatly impressive, however, was the evening of the Passover festival, when the handsomely laid table was lighted by candles stuck in the two silver candelabra inherited from my maternal grandparents, when the two families sat round the festive board, the men with their head covered, when prayers were read and liturgical responses murmured. According to religious usage, one of the children was required to speak a few words, a task that fell to me on several occasions. Singular and touching were the concluding chants, for which I easily found a suitable accompaniment on the piano. The Day of Atonement, too, was observed with fasting, followed by a lavish evening meal. I recall with emotion my parents' "commemorations." Every year, at the anniversaries of my grandparents' deaths, small wicks floating on oil were lighted in a glass and placed in a hollow space of the tiled stove. There were times when, with a sense of awe, I watched my parents whisper before it their prayers in memory of the dead. Except for these special occasions, religion was rarely mentioned at home. The children were required to say their morning and evening prayers, and that seemed to satisfy my parents.

How peaceful ran the course of life during that period of my early childhood! No political passions, no economic crises disrupted Germany's civic life in the 'eighties. The Congress of Berlin had purified the international atmosphere. Old Kaiser Wilhelm I, who was to die a nonagenarian in 1888, was still alive. Bismarck guided Germany's policies. My Father, who voted Liberal and admired

Rudolf Virchow and Eugen Richter, was rather set against the Iron Chancellor, like all Leftists. But the struggle of the political parties was generally waged within moderate bounds, and until far into the 'nineties I heard little, if anything, of politics. The victory of 1871, accompanied by the creation of the Reich and the alliance with Austria, brought about a general feeling of security and a mounting prosperity, so that in the prevailing calm families like ours could live peacefully and attend to the raising of their children.

From my earliest days, my musical inclination was revealed to my parents through the excited fascination with which I listened to every musical sound. Their growing conviction that their strange offspring bore the seeds of an artistic talent within him was confirmed when, in 1881, Father sent his family for a summer holiday to the village of Thal, in Thuringia. I was going on five then. An old *Kapellmeister,* whose name has slipped from my memory, was our neighbor there. He was said to have listened frequently and with mounting astonishment and interest to my singing and then to have assured Mother with a great deal of earnestness that I was destined to become a musician. And as almost every day brought new revelations of my musical inclinations, my parents thought that, as I was six and thus of school age, they might as well get my musical education started too.

And so, life did not present me with that helpful family resistance which in so many instances had fanned into flame the spark of a genuine talent. There was no unappreciative and unartistically inclined father to oppose me, no disconsolate mother to implore me on her knees to renounce a musician's career and to curse me when I remained steadfast — a fate that had actually befallen poor Berlioz. Nor were there any material cares to harass me. My inclinations were perceived and recognized by my parents from my early childhood, and my later development constantly furthered by a self-sacrificing father. So I ought really to regard almost with suspicion the smoothness of the outward course of my years of study. Looking back, however, it is clear to me that my burning zeal, especially during the decisive years of my development, needed no fanning. Later in my life, there was a sufficiency of inward difficulties and outward opposition to keep me "awake and alert," to use Eichendorff's words. There is only gratitude in my mind when I think of the helpful spirit at home during my childhood and youth.

II

I BECAME a schoolboy. In a way, that was a good thing, for my parents had long been unable to satisfy my craving for activity. It was less of a good thing, though, that I had schoolmates, for I came all too readily under the turbulent influence of boys of tender age but tough habits with whom school brought me in contact. The unruliness of the Berlin schoolboy blended harmoniously with my individual mischievousness, and many were the instances of more or less droll obstinacy and refractoriness with which I burdened my Mother's life. One of these instances may be cited here, for I still remember it quite well and it seems characteristic of the then seven- or eight-year-old boy. One Sunday evening, on returning with my parents from a visit, it suddenly occurred to me that I was too tired for walking and that we would have to take a cab. A droshky — even one of the so-called "second class" — meant splendor and luxury, and that's what I happened to be craving. My parents, however, disapproved of my extravagant fancy, and so, in spite of my loud wailings and protests, I had to walk home with them. Grumbling, I went to bed and on the following morning awoke with a renewed feeling of indignation at my parents' callousness. I claimed I had greatly overexerted myself last night and was therefore unable to get up and go to school. Neither friendly persuasion nor reasonable exhortation was of any avail. The upshot was that I was put into my clothes, though a bit forcibly, and, my schoolbag strapped to my back, shoved out the door, which clicked shut behind me. But I, thirsting for satisfaction and firmly determined to be tired, lay on one of the wooden steps, defiance in my heart. Whenever anybody came up the stairs, he had to step across me; and as every one rang our bell and urged that the human obstacle be removed, there was nothing Mother could do but fetch me back again. So far I had remained victorious, but Mother knew how to change the dangerous triumph into a salutary defeat. She explained to me that she would now actually have to put me back to bed because I was obviously tired. There I lay, a prey to a boredom that no book was permitted to relieve, no visitor to interrupt. At noon, I was given some gruel, though I knew that the others were enjoying my favorite dish in the adjoining room. It was afternoon before, without much ado, harmony was restored, a condition that at heart I liked best of all.

I am sorry to disappoint any well-meaning friends who may be inclined to see in the exceptional obstinacy of my defiance the childish form of a subsequent strength of will such as is bound to lead to success in life's struggle. Such a diagnosis would be fundamentally wrong, both with regard to the strength of will and to the success in life's struggle. What fighting spirit and inflexible strength of will were given me were in fact exerted only in the realm of art. There I actually "stuck it out." In the struggle for existence, on the other hand, I frequently assumed a yielding attitude, one of appeasement even, in order to save all my fighting spirit for the uncompromising assertion of my artistic convictions. Indifference and a yielding disposition toward disputes in an artist's personal life seem to me unavoidable if he wishes to husband his strength. In those exceptional cases in which his valor in worldly issues, too, is seen to prevail, the question may be raised whether his artistry is not impaired by what benefits his life-controlling forces. As for myself, I believe that I have been able to muster up sufficient strength for the settlement of life's most important questions, a strength expressing itself in obstinacy; but my highly promising childish defiance did not by any means develop into an indomitably forceful self-assertion in later life, to say nothing of that effortless domination of people characteristic of a strong nature. In short, I did not develop into a fighter. Mine was nevertheless not merely an artistic nature turned away from life and toward art. My case was more complicated, as I propose to show later.

In my childhood, at any rate, my obstinacy and wilfulness grew to such an extent that it caused serious and painful conflicts, especially with Mother, although our fondness for each other was always able to prevent serious dissension.

The Friedrich Gymnasium of Berlin, in whose lower classes I was so successfully initiated into Berlin scampdom, was in Friedrichstrasse, near the point where Elsasserstrasse met it. All I recall of the three years I spent in that preparatory school and of the later schooling I received at the Askan Gymnasium and, still later, at the Falk Real-Gymnasium is that I had little trouble with my studies and my school work. My exceptionally good memory stood me in good stead. I never had to make a real effort to memorize anything. Whatever I heard or read seemed to stick automatically in my memory, provided it interested me. To learn anything by heart I merely had to read it carefully. All in all, I passed through the rather strict Berlin schools without much difficulty. True, I never was a model pupil. My report cards never showed an "Excellent" in any subject except singing. And in that connection, I recall my intense distaste for the then customary unisonal shouting with which the class did violence to popular and patriotic songs to the accompanying scraping of a fiddle.

Theme and Variations

Mother's piano lessons started at the same time I began going to school. Manual facility and quick apprehension enabled me to progress so rapidly that, after one year and a half, she no longer felt competent to teach me and decided to engage a young instructor by the name of Konrad Kaiser. He turned out to be an excellent pianist and a conscientious teacher, and we developed a mutual liking for each other. From him I gained my first exciting impression of pianistic brilliance, which kindled my zeal for technical exercises. So pleased was he with my enthusiasm and talent that after hardly more than a year he proposed to Mother to have me tested by a musical authority. If his own opinion of my exceptional ability were confirmed, a serious musical education on a broad foundation would seem to be indicated. And so came about one of the decisive events in my young life, my call upon Robert Radeke, conductor at the Berlin Royal Opera and co-director at the Stern Conservatory for Music.

Robert Radeke was an old man with thin silvery hair and a long gray beard. He received Mother and me with friendly dignity in his beautiful large music room. From one corner, a marble bust of Beethoven looked down at me. The center of the room was taken up by a Bechstein concert grand. What a highly pleasing, and yet intimidating, sight for a boy of eight, who had never known anything but an upright and was now for the first time to place his hands upon so mighty an instrument!

Every detail of this first examination in my life impressed itself indelibly on my memory. How could it be otherwise? Mother and I attributed decisive importance to it and it fulfilled our every expectation. It has remained unforgettable, too, because of the warming kindness of the old man's friendly eyes, which made my diffidence dissolve, and because of the first praise from an expert's lips. It aroused within me a feeling of faith in my own ability, and was to prove a lasting incentive. My examination proceeded in the following manner: Radeke asked if I had an absolute ear. When Mother said I had, his almost jesting request was: "Well, let me hear you sing an A." After I had sung a clear A, I was told to turn round and call the tones he sounded on the piano behind my back, singly at first, then in consonant chords, and finally in dissonances. After that, he placed before me unfamiliar pieces, which I had to play at sight. Next came works of my own choice. I played a movement from a Mozart sonata and two of Mendelssohn's *Songs without Words*. Finally, I was told to improvise for a few minutes.

This thorough examination over, I was told to go to the adjoining room while the old man talked things over with Mother. When I was summoned back, I was praised and exhorted to keep on striving zealously. He finally wrote me a most gratifying testimonial, concluding with the words: "Every inch of him is music." I still think back with joy on these fine words, meant to testify in a particularly emphatic form to the presence of an elemental musical ability.

When I view the vast wealth of events in a long life and my changing reactions to them; when I think of the many developments and transformations within myself, I find it difficult to retain the consciousness of my own identity, to see myself as a continuity in the confusing multiplicity and contrariety of thinking, feeling, and acting. But to the present day, my close affiliation with music, or rather my being firmly rooted in it, has remained unchanged and unchangeable. Not that I am musically creative; I soon became convinced that I was not endowed with a creative talent. But I believe I may say with all due modesty that from the days of my childhood I have felt music to be the element for which I was born, in which I am at home, and which is the language I understand and am able to speak. In all the doubts of myself, in the frequently harassing results of my self-searching, I have been comforted and reassured by the thought that there is a "quiescent pole in the flight of events," that my unshakable relation to music is the inmost core of my being. This fundamental inclination seems to have manifested itself even in my childish pianistic efforts, as indicated by Radeke's friendly words.

Throughout my life there has been a singing within me — is not every production of music really connected with singing? — and even as a boy, urged on by an inward singing, I was searching for a *legato* and for shadings of touch at the piano, in order to impart to the played melody a songlike character. Mendelssohn's *Songs Without Words* and Chopin's *Nocturnes* must have been eminently suitable to these endeavors, for I played them at home with a passionate devotion. My own dreamy improvisations were also said to have been rather Chopinesque or Mendelssohnesque and to have had a songlike quality.

Naturally, I covered innumerable sheets of music with "compositions" of all kinds, but none of those sonata movements, nocturnes, impromptus, fantasies, and songs seemed in any way remarkable to me when I looked them over later, unless it be for the perseverance with which I filled whole books of music with imitations of my favorite piano pieces and songs. Here and there among the many barren ears there was a fertile one. An interminable ballade entitled *The Horseman and Lake Constance,* for instance, contained a pretty thematic idea that I rather liked even at a later date.

Theme and Variations

How serious my endeavors were is shown by an "invention" that enabled me to grasp with rhythmic precision the synchrony of regular eighths and triplet-eighths such as occur, for instance, in Mendelssohn's *Song Without Words* in E-flat major. I would hurry along the street and, while taking two steps, count aloud and in exactly equal rhythm "one, two, three," my "one" always coinciding with my left foot. Then I would just as exactly count "one, two" while taking three steps, my "one" coinciding alternately with the left and the right foot. Thus the correct execution of a triplet accompaniment to regular notes soon became an effortless habit.

During my early years at school I had developed a passion that seriously competed with my love for music: reading. The poetically inspired profound fairy tales of the Danish poet Andersen and the inexhaustible wealth of Grimm's German fairy tales had occupied my imagination from early childhood, for I knew many of them from having them read or told me before I myself was able to read. Later, a book and myself in blissfully enraptured solitude, I became wholly absorbed in the charmed circle of those fairy tales, teeming with figures and events, now demoniac and now humorous. Throughout my life, a certain mental affinity has attracted me to them again and again. Still later, I was captivated by the fabulous world of Greek mythology. A juvenile edition of *Tales of Classic Antiquity* by Gustav Schwab told me of Heracles and Perseus, of Icarus and Prometheus, Iphigenia, Agamemnon, the rape of Helen and the Trojan War, of the adventures of shrewd Odysseus and his return, of the expedition of the Argonauts and the tragedy of Medea. I am thankful to this day for the three volumes of that juvenile book. Beyond delighting me with its immortal tales and figures, it aroused within me the first faint idea of Grecism, a reverence for the antique, and a continuous desire to draw near to it. As for books about redskins, great favorites in those days with boys of a certain age, the only one I read was Cooper's *Leatherstocking*, but I took a passionate interest in Robinson Crusoe's adventures, which I read over and over again. I also have a vivid recollection of how greatly I enjoyed Grube's *Historical Pictures*, a boy's book containing tales about Hannibal, Charlemagne, Columbus, Cortés, and other explorers and historical figures.

When I was nine or ten, the attraction of my juvenile books began to fade, and I felt drawn toward the treasures in my parents' bookcase. There, behind glass plates, stood Goethe, Schiller, Lessing, Heine, Hauff, Rückert, and others. Shakespeare, too, was there in the excellent Schlegel-Tieck translation. Schiller's *Die Jungfrau von Orleans* was, I believe, the first drama I read. I used to recite in a loud voice Joan's monologues. I was carried away by the solemn rhythm and splendor of the verses, and my violent emotion at the tragic ending was hardly bearable.

I have no doubt that every vivid human being lives from childhood with the figures with whom history or narrative or dramatic literature has brought him in contact. He identifies himself with every protagonist of important actions and sentiments, with every interesting historical or mythological figure. Their speeches, their passions, and their actions become his very own. That was how all the important figures and events in my books affected me. Above all, and to a considerably higher degree, that was how the persons in a drama affected me. I felt as if I were truly the noble-minded, despairing Max Piccolomini, and I answered him in the spirit of the diplomatic Octavio; I was the base scoundrel Wurm and the rapturous Ferdinand, the raging Othello and the innocent Desdemona, Hamlet and Polonius, Tasso and Antonio. I even executed a number of parts in a manner different from that of the author and as I felt I would have acted in their place. In a word, I was even then obsessed by the demon of the theater. Before the drama's vivacity and immediacy, before its direct speech and action, narrative and descriptive literature seemed to pale. Literature reported past events, and the narrator always stood between me and the hero. The drama brought me into his immediate presence.

My early eagerness for and susceptibility to the drama and my inclination to identify myself with its figures clearly indicate a dramatic vein in my mental endowment. No wonder, then, that at the very beginning of my career I was irresistibly drawn toward the opera and felt amphibiously at home in both of its interpretative elements, the dramatic and the musical. I shall speak later about the dramatic requirements in operatic performances and their interrelation with music. I merely wish to point out here the early awakening of the stage instinct of a child who, through the wealth and contrasting quality of the poetic figures sprung into life within him, had become dimly conscious of a certain breadth in his own nature. I wonder today how I managed to read so much, devote myself so assiduously to music, and yet do justice to my schoolwork. For I did not read my books once only; I read them over and over again, so often and so intensively that striking passages are to this day imprinted on my memory.

The emotional exaltation, temperament, and excitability that characterized my musical activities and caused me to plunge into reading, naturally were reflected also in my personal conduct. Gentle and friendly though my general disposition was, my relations to my parents, brother and sister, relatives, acquaintances, teachers, fellow-pupils, and friends, were frequently disturbed by sudden ungovernable outbursts. And yet I can hardly recall an instance when I did not at once try by tenderness to make amends for hurts I had inflicted. Besides, there dwelled within me not only violent commotion, but also its counterpart, a deep calm. The growing boy, too, frequently manifested a strange condition of dreaminess, of absorption or enchantment, when all the wheels, usually turned so violently by the torrent of inward and outward phenomena, were halted and stood still as if they had been disconnected. I still recall how such a calm first manifested itself to me as a melancholy emotion, am still conscious of what I felt at the time, and can still visualize the place at which, a boy of ten or eleven, I experienced that spiritual thrill. I have forgotten how it came about that I was standing alone in the schoolyard — I may have been kept in as a punishment — but when I stepped out into the large square associated in my mind with the noise of playing or romping boys it seemed to me doubly empty and forsaken. I can see myself standing there, overwhelmed by the deep quiet. While I listened to it and the soft wind, I felt an unknown and powerful something clutch at my heart from out the solitude. It was my first dim conception that I was an *I*, that I had a soul, and that it had been touched — somehow — from somewhere.

III

In my account of my craving for reading and my first serious experience, I have run somewhat ahead and I now return to an orderly continuity.

When I was nine years old, my parents moved to Steglitzerstrasse, presumably because Elsasserstrasse had changed considerably for the worse. Among the pleasant street scenes from my early childhood was, for instance, the sight of a bricklayer during his lunch hour, sitting on a beam in front of a new building, his "old woman" at his side, munching the sandwiches she had brought him, and taking hearty swallows from his beer bottle. Such street impressions and others of a similarly cheerful popular character were later amplified by less enjoyable ones, such as the always frightening sight of drunken persons stumbling out of one of the ever growing number of so-called "distilleries," the thumping of vulgar piano music coming through the curtained windows of dance halls in the evening, and the appearance, late in the afternoon, of a strange kind of ladies with large loud-colored hats and painted faces. These indications of mounting activity and declining morals probably caused my parents to move to another part of the city, the "Old

West." Our new flat was three flights up, but we had the use of a rather pretty garden with beautiful old trees and an arbor. This garden, reached through the entrance hall and across the court-yard, served us children as a playground and outdoor reading room. Unfortunately, its quiet enjoyment was occasionally en-croached on by a wholly unprovoked acoustic and moral attack, frequently accentuated by the throwing of missiles of varying hard-ness. The perpetrators were a number of fiendish boys from the adjoining garden. Their scornful faces would suddenly appear on top of the rather high dividing wall, they would shatter the beau-tiful quiet by wild shouts, treat us to an expert selection of the vilest Berlinese invective, and as suddenly disappear again into nothingness. The briefness of these hellish manifestations was probably due to the fact that the horrid boys' muscular endurance was put to a hard test by the height of the wall. The infernal tur-moil was followed quickly and without transition by the old heav-enly quiet. Often in the future, when a lofty mood was brusquely interrupted, I would think of those garden scenes with their abrupt swings between *pianissimo* and *fortissimo,* and feel inclined to take a humorous view of more serious inconveniences of a kindred sort.

My way from Steglitzerstrasse to the Askan Gymnasium in Halle-schenstrasse led through handsome tree-lined streets — or at least they seemed handsome to eyes unspoiled by the Berlin North — and past the ever tumultuous Harbor Square. There, massive boats were loading and unloading their cargoes, which had to be carried down the Spree and through canals; powerful cranes were raising, twisting, and lowering their burdens, and a bridge, which had to be "drawn up" to permit the passage of ships with high deck loads, afforded not only an exciting and interesting sight, but also a valid excuse for being late at school. And round the corner from the Harbor Square stood Berlin's Philharmonic Hall, the place of my boyish yearnings and joys and, decades later, the frequent scene of my own activity.

There is little I can say of the Gymnasium itself beyond the aforementioned fact that I was a "passable" pupil, without particu-larly distinguishing myself. I was "good" only in Latin, which had always been my favorite subject. I have probably to thank the excellent teacher at the Askan Gymnasium for my ready under-standing of the elegance and clearness of that language as well as for my early interest in it. If music had not from the very begin-ning been mistress of my soul, an innate disposition and inclina-tion would likely have led me to philology by way of Latin. I came more and more to recognize in language and its development one of the most admirable accomplishments of human genius. Its ex-

BRUNO WALTER'S FAMILY, 1880

(*sister Emma, father, mother, brother Leo, the author*)

BRUNO WALTER, 1886

(*at the time of his first public appearance*)

ploration seemed a way to the light and to deep insight, a way I should have liked to tread. But I had to content myself with enjoying its wonders as an amateur. I was also fond of mathematics and physics and was said to have been quite proficient in the former. It was schooling itself, however, that pleased me, because I was eager to learn and learning did not give me any trouble. Besides, I enjoyed the companionship of my fellow-pupils, for to a certain degree I was sociably and amiably inclined. When the frequent school excursions came, with marching, singing, and playing of games, I quite naturally became a homogeneous member of the crowd to which I was somewhat alien in other respects because of a feeling of "being different." But I was by no means a "spiritual type" or stay-at-home. On the contrary, in spite of my being different, I was a wild boy, fully up to my fellow-pupils' standard as far as torn trousers, bruised shins, and an occasional broken head were concerned. To be sure, I had little liking, and less aptitude, for physical exercise, and my parents' endeavors to put my boyish wildness to practical educational use by urging me to take part in gymnastics, swimming, and skating met with but moderate success. I liked gymnastics, but was not good at them; I loved skating, but it was to remain an unrequited love; and while my attempt to learn to swim brought me a modest moral victory, it also resulted in a considerable physical defeat. I was still quite small, and the Wilmersdorf Lake's black surface was uncomfortably ruffled by the cool morning wind. I had no great liking for cold water anyway, and when I looked down from the swaying springboard and, secured by a belt and line, was ordered to jump, I was frankly scared. But I knew it had to be, and I jumped. Similar occasions have often occurred in my life, always with the same result. I am not by nature courageous, but I jumped into the water every time. And it may well be asked if the courage of Siegfried, who never learned the meaning of fear, is of higher moral value than the decision to attack the dragon in spite of fear, no matter what may come of it. Unfortunately, my moral courage at Wilmersdorf Lake was ill rewarded. The swimming-instructor, a man of the Prussian sergeant type and obviously given to Spartan ideals, considered it his stern duty to punish me at the second or third lesson for my repeated awkwardness by so loosening the line that I sank below the surface. When the Spartan tautened the line again, it appeared that I had swallowed too much water and was in poor shape. It was all over for me with swimming, for whenever I got into the water thereafter, suspended from a line, I became quite sick. So I was forced definitely to give up this sport. My physical fitness was not altogether neglected, though. I was fond of walking tours and applied myself to them diligently. I even managed to become a rather skilful mountain climber, and was later able to gaze blissfully into far spaces from many a tall Tyrolean summit.

During my first years at the Gymnasium I gradually became aware that in spite of my easy grasp of things the growing volume of subject matter and of corresponding homework pushed me farther and farther away from music. I fought stubbornly, but my double efforts on behalf of school and music had taken on such proportions during the first three years that I felt the fourth form would be too much for me. My passionate entreaties for help finally made my parents agree to interrupt my attendance at school in favor of my musical studies and self-sacrificingly to replace the former by private tuition. A teacher at a gymnasium, my Mother's cousin, undertook to instruct me at his home in the ample and diversified subject matter of the fourth form. He was a serious, friendly man of sound knowledge with an exceptional gift for teaching. Under his guidance I managed to master the two-year Gymnasium curriculum in a shorter period and still have sufficient time for my musical studies. My teacher happened to be a touchingly zealous, though not particularly gifted, violinist. The lesson over, I would at times seat myself at the piano and steer him through a violin sonata by Mozart or Beethoven with a tactfully proportioned mixture of schoolboy respect and musical superiority.

After having privately mastered the fourth form, I had to go back to a public school for the diploma that would secure for me the privilege of serving in the army as a one-year volunteer. But everything within me shouted for freedom when I found myself again chained to a desk in the lower fifth of the Falk Real-Gymnasium. No sooner did I have the diploma in my pocket than I told Father that it would be senseless for me to spend another three years at school only to languish musically. I had no intention of going to a university, and so I needed no upper fifth, no sixth, and no final exams. I wanted to become a musician, and would therefore have to devote myself henceforth entirely to music.

I did not realize what my prematurely leaving school would mean to my general education. At any rate, it seems that nobody tried to dissuade me and that my parents were unable to cope with my impatience and impetuosity. So it came about that I left school at the age of about fifteen, without unfortunately having passed the final examinations and, what seems a greater loss to me, without having laid a solid foundation for my Greek. Private tuition had introduced me merely to its beginnings, and the Falk Real-Gymnasium was not a humanistic school: while it taught Latin, Greek was replaced in its curriculum by English. Much later in life, I made an independent attempt to take up the study of Greek, without, however, making more than modest progress. This deficiency has often pained me, for I have become increasingly convinced that a humanistic education, properly built upon an early foundation, is indispensable to a universal spiritual development. I may say that even at a mature age I strove earnestly to compensate for my youthfully impatient termination of systematic schooling. My impatience has left me with a sense of guilt, a fact that needs recording in this personal account and is hereby repentantly admitted.

While I have no distinct recollection of any details of my years at school, of my teachers and fellow-students, or of any remarkable incidents, I should like to refer to some words spoken by my religious instructor while I was in either the first or second form. They have remained in my memory because of their naïve impressiveness and because they proved helpful later when I was haunted by religious doubts and evil atheistic moods. In speaking of the folly of atheism, the teacher pulled a large silver watch from his vest pocket, opened the lid, and let us look at the busily working movement. "Has this watch made itself by its own effort?" he asked. "Has blind accident made its parts get together so that they can work with one another and measure time? Or has a watchmaker planned and created the watch?" This forceful proof — comprehensible to a child's mind — of the existence of a Creator who has formed a world in which the stars revolve in their appointed courses and in which universal laws govern the grain of dust as well as the solar systems became engraved upon my mind. It naturally grew clear to me later that its simple and plausible conclusiveness failed to touch upon the central problem. For thinking and feeling man is harassed not so much by doubts of the God-Creator as by his doubts of divine kindness. If the Creator is almighty, man ponders, He must also have created evil and suffering, or permitted them to endure. But if evil exists and operates contrary to God's will, He cannot be almighty. These momentous, spirit- and soul-stirring questions, these doubts of either God's omnipotence or His kindness, have been either evaded by philosophy, passed over in silence, or shelved with a more or less outspoken and disappointing *ignorabimus*. As for myself, they kept rising within me again and again for years. That is why I have mentioned them, though this is not the place to discuss them. But let me say this much: increasing maturity has taught me that this form of questioning leads us astray. I have looked for other ways to "harmony with the infinite," ways that have been pointed out by the Christian doctrine, toward which my heart has gradually turned with deep devotion.

At any rate, at the time of that religious lesson I was free from doubt. My optimistic nature made me think that life was wonderful, the world perfect, and only school a bit disturbing because it took up too much time. But I managed to make the best of things, and now I rather like to recall my days at school, though I do so without longing. It seems to me that I attended to school duties in a somewhat casual manner. Except by my Latin teacher, mentioned before, they were surely not made attractive or impressive by any distinguished teaching personality. I regarded these duties as a kind of unavoidable tribute one had to pay to the practical demands of life — which I did not value very highly — so that one could use the rest of the time for "living," by which I meant working at music and satisfying my spiritual hunger in my own particular way by reading and thinking.

IV

THE STERN CONSERVATORY was in Friedrichstrasse, near its southern end, a short distance from Hallesches Tor. During the first months of my tuition, or perhaps even during the first year, we still lived in Elsasserstrasse, which ran into the northern end of Friedrichstrasse. So I had to pass from one end of the city's longest north-south street to the other in order to reach the place of my musical education. But there was fascination in the fact that, instead of the humiliating infantile schoolbag on my back, I, a boy of nine, could now with dignity carry under my arm a grown-up student's case full of music. What was more, Mother gave me two groschen for a bus ride to and from the Conservatory. The unrestricted right of disposal of this restricted capital gave me the chance to do without one ride and spend half of the money, ten pfennigs, on an "applecake with," as they said in Berlin, which meant a piece of applecake with whipped cream. A walk of more than forty-five minutes was quite a trial, but so great was my fondness for sweets that it nearly always emerged victorious from the unequal conflict of emotions. Quite near my goal, at Puttkamerstrasse, was a small and very cozy confectioner's shop in which I used to buy my dainties. Later, some fellow-students and I would stop there occasionally for brief refreshments. Someday, I suppose, the long-overdue panegyric will be written, extolling the historical and cultural importance of the Vienna coffeehouse. I hope that the chronicler will not fail to throw a comparative, laudatory sidelight upon Berlin's old confectionery, the *Konditorei*. It was one of the city's characteristic landmarks. Sweets were sold in these modest, quiet places. Newspapers in frames hung from pegs in the walls. In the narrow twilit room there were a few round-topped tables on which chess was played or at which vital problems were discussed, where coffee or chocolate with a piece of cake was enjoyed, and where one could meet one's young lady friend for a discreet rendezvous. So important and popular was this combination of gustatory enjoyment and heartfelt effusion that the Berliners had coined the particular, though horrible verb *kondietern* in order to define it.

The Conservatory, founded by Julius Stern and conducted after his death by his sister-in-law Jenny Meyer, with Robert Radeke as co-director, occupied at that time the rear part of an old house. It was reached from Friedrichstrasse through a dark hallway and by crossing a courtyard. While the tuition rooms, in each of which stood a Bechstein, Bluetner, or Duysen grand piano, were large and gloomy, the hall that served for recitals, choral exercises, and orchestral rehearsals, besides being used for an additional tuition room, was beautiful, light, and nobly proportioned. On the platform stood two grand pianos, behind which, at the Sunday recitals, the pupils' string group was posted. There were no winds: their parts were played on the piano by one of the pupils of the conductors' class. During my final years at the Conservatory this task was nearly always allotted to me. Only when I was slated to conduct did I relegate the job to one of my fellow-students. With what gratitude do I recall that hall, in which I was permitted to be one of the crowd of attentively listening students (in front of us, in the first row, the imposing group of directors and teachers), and on whose platform I heard my first performances of the works of classic literature — Schubert, Schumann, Chopin, Bach, Handel, Beethoven, Mozart, Haydn, and Brahms. Whatever concertos, solo pieces, sonatas, chamber music, arias, and songs were within the technical scope of advanced students were performed there. The level of perfection, so it seems to me in retrospect, was quite remarkable. I became acquainted with a considerable part of classic music — only the cello and its literature were somewhat neglected — and I shall never forget the feeling of happiness that filled my young heart when I sat there and steeped my thirsty soul in music.

It was not long before I took an active part in those performances. During the first years I played piano compositions. There was a little footbench under the piano with a mechanical contrivance that enabled my short legs to reach the pedals. Later, at the Sunday morning events, I played piano concertos with orchestral accompaniment, and during the final years I conducted concertos, arias with orchestra, and movements from Haydn's symphonies.

I have no recollection whatever of any of my fellow students at the Conservatory, but I can see myself quite plainly as the only child among adults: I was surrounded by people who were commonly referred to as "young folks," surely not a natural or desirable condition. The very fact that I was pampered and spoiled by my grown-up fellow students accentuated the distance between us. That was bound to intimidate me. I *was* intimidated and remained so because, in those important years, I lacked the reassuring contact with children of my own age, a contact that teaches a boy how to stand on his own legs, how to offer resistance, how to carry his point as an equal among equals. The normal conditions prevailing at school could not make up for the damage inflicted by the inequality of years in the more impressive sphere of musical studies. Things improved in that respect during my final period at the Conservatory when, from my fifteenth year, there were other students of my own age. But a similar and even more harmful condition existed at the beginning of my operatic career, when I was seventeen and had to deal with mature professional singers, members of the orchestra and chorus, and other theatrical employees. In those days I felt as if my youth were a catastrophe or a crime — how often I was reproached for it! — and it was probably due to those impressions that throughout my life I felt rather young and unsure of myself, an outsider, and not quite a match for all the self-assured, efficient, practical, experienced, plucky — in short, grown-up people around me.

Radeke's testimonial, by removing the obstacle of my extreme youth and smoothing my way into the Conservatory, had brought about the strangely anomalous condition just described. I had no difficulty in passing the entrance examination. After a brief preparatory period with Franz Mannstädt, I was assigned to the "advanced" piano class taught by Professor Heinrich Ehrlich. He had an excellent reputation as a piano teacher and, being the leading musical critic of the *Berliner Tageblatt,* occupied an important position in Germany's musical life. As for theory, I was naturally assigned to the beginners' class. It was taught by Ludwig Bussler, a distinguished theorist, whose books on harmony and counterpoint were used in many schools of music.

My mind being ever ready to revere, my teachers' personalities made a strong impression on me, although the longed-for meeting with "great musicians" did not materialize. Ludwig Bussler, a broad-shouldered tall man with gray locks, taught me for years. Although he was learned and conscientious, he was a rather dry teacher. I do not know whether he himself scanned the depths of the theoretical problems of music and investigated them. I am inclined to assume that he faithfully clung to tradition rather than have his foundations shaken by disturbing doubts. At any rate, it was not within his ability greatly to interest his pupils in theoretical questions, and I believe I galloped gaily and unsuspectingly over the dangerous and alluring depths of theory like the hero of my early composition, the horseman traversing the deceptive icy cover of Lake Constance, and that, led by my sound musical instinct, I arrived safely on the secure grounds of practical musical execution. Only later, under the influence of the writings of the profound theorist and musical philosopher Heinrich Schenker, I became aware of what I had missed and began to grasp the theoretical problems; or rather, they grasped me, they even fascinated me; but to be absorbed by them, to lose myself in them, was "not in my line." All too irresistibly my nature drew me away from them and toward a vital execution of music.

I was on firm ground in my piano instruction. Heinrich Ehrlich was an excellent teacher and pianist. Moreover, in the course of many years of critical activity, he had again and again heard the most prominent pianists, and I was convincingly impressed by his censures, corrections, and suggestions, based as they were upon insight and experience. He was a well educated, serious, and clear-sighted musician, but he was quite unromantic and rather cool. Whenever he played for me, which happened frequently, I felt enlightened, but hardly warmed or inspired. However, my own exuberance, of which I always felt a bit ashamed in his presence, was not to be restrained, and he was wise enough to give my romantic nature a free rein and not to suppress the intensity of my expression. But I was never able to determine from his quiet words and his reserved attitude if he was moderately satisfied with me or even more profoundly pleased with my playing. At any rate, he frequently, though quite unsolicitedly, gave me private lessons at his home because he considered the time available at the Conservatory insufficient. Thus, his deeds proved what his words and attitude failed to disclose: a serious interest in a zealous pupil.

I also like to recall the charming and temperamental personality of the phenomenal violinist Émile Sauret, the Conservatory's leading violin teacher. Although I did not come in contact with him in his capacity as teacher, I, like everyone else, felt drawn toward him by his sparkling vivacity. Besides, there were several occasions when he came up to me and praised my playing at the evening recitals. How often we pupils crowded around him, begging him to play something for us! Then flageolet runs and double-stop passages would mount into the air like rockets, and when we stared at him with amazement, he would laugh and say in his droll French-

German: "Is nozzing, *mes enfants,* it all lies on the fiddle, only must take!" a dictum that attained the status of a household word at the Conservatory.

My lessons with Radeke in composition and the reading of orchestral scores did not, I believe, begin until I had reached the age of thirteen, when I had brought the helm round, having decided to abandon a pianist's career and devote myself to conducting.

I have nothing to report of other teachers from that epoch, but I must mention the institute's strongest individuality: Jenny Meyer, its director. She was one of the few people I am inclined to call a "moral power," to use the words applied by Goethe to Carlyle. Of majestic appearance — one might have thought of a Judith, had she not been rather stout — she was a veritable source of contagious impulses of strength. It was the first time that reality had brought me in almost daily contact with so idealistic and high-minded a personality. I was plainly aware even then how sublimely her being contrasted with the depressing triviality of most people within my field of vision. Much later, some hints concerning the history of her life reached me. She was said to have been the victim of a romantic, unrequited attachment to the Conservatory's founder, Julius Stern, her sister's husband. After his premature death, she had decided to take over his life-work in order to safeguard its continuation in his spirit. To me, the story seems credible and to furnish a key to her solemn and somewhat melancholy gravity, her exalted sense of duty, and the quiet fanaticism of her tireless devotion to her work. During my latter period at the Conservatory, I frequently played the piano accompaniments at her singing lessons and thus became thoroughly acquainted, musically as well as vocally, with a great many songs and arias from operas and oratorios. She had studied with Marchesi and was said to have been the possessor of a wonderful alto. She had lost her voice early through an illness. An enthusiastic advocate of the Italian style of singing, she took for her model mainly the methods of Lamperti and Marchesi. The only solfeggios sung at her lessons were those by Concone and Bordogni. That she placed the utmost value upon a depressed tongue when singing now fills me with certain misgivings concerning the correctness of her method. At any rate, her interpretative instructions were splendid, noble, and clear. Of even greater importance to her pupils than her frequently very valuable artistic suggestions were her pure principles and her exalted idealism in all questions pertaining to art.

I can still visualize Jenny Meyer, tall and powerful, a large bunch of keys dangling from her hand. I see her somewhat fatigued by the day's work, for she was no longer a young woman, and her beautiful raven hair, held in place and crowned by a tall Spanish comb, was plentifully streaked with gray. The singing lesson, at which I played the accompaniments, over, we would often stand in the anteroom, chatting for a few minutes before she locked up, the last person to leave the premises. While I cannot recall any of our conversations, I do remember that she talked to me, not like a grown-up person to a child, but in a communicative, kind, and friendly way, that she listened attentively to my replies — directed upward, for I was quite a little fellow and she very tall — and that she knew how to bridge the distance between us by making me feel that she trusted and esteemed me. I, too, did my share in bridging the distance, for I felt an upsurge of heartfelt gratitude as well as of deep sympathy, sentiments that brought me quite near her and may have sprung from a deep-seated understanding. Then she would walk up the stairs with a strong firm tread, keys jingling — keeper and guardian of an estate entrusted to her — while I started on my way home, uplifted and full of noble resolutions, finding life a bit sad perhaps, but immeasurably beautiful too.

Under the conscientious and inspired leadership of its director, the Stern Conservatory maintained and added to its established reputation and kept its place in Berlin's musical educational system at the side of the Royal Academy. However, neither Jenny Meyer nor her teachers permitted themselves to be seized by the wave of Wagnerian enthusiasm and, like the highly distinguished conservatories in Leipzig, under Reinecke, and in Cologne, under Wüllner, the institute represented the reactionary tendency. It competed with the Academy, directed by Joachim, not only in the seriousness and thoroughness of its tuition, but also in its antagonism to Wagner, whose name was never mentioned within its precincts.

To be sure, Wagner's works flourished and triumphed, and all operatic stages performed them, practically lived by them. Bayreuth was the guardian of the Grail, the festival plays under Cosima furthered the Wagnerian tradition based upon the master's teachings and directions, and the style-school in Bayreuth endeavored to educate the younger generation of artists to a Wagnerian style of singing, interpretation, and treatment of the language. What would have been more natural than for the older music schools to rally in support of the great cause and to welcome with enthusiasm the reformation and enlargement of their sphere of didactic activities? But the opposite was true. Anti-Wagnerianism had withdrawn into the conservatories, as into so many fortresses, and their gates were closed. While a large new artistic community was filling the operahouses and enjoying Wagner with a glowing enthusiasm never before known in a theater, a considerable part of the public — and by no means its worst part — stood aloof, lined up on the side of the conservatories in an attitude of quiet but determined repudiation. I repeat: by no means its worst part. It consisted largely of those who felt that the purity of music was threatened by the "Art of the Future," and who were backed by the infinitely valuable and truly music-loving circles in whose houses altars to classic music had been erected. Those were not yet the days of mechanical inventions, when the mere turning of a knob would provide a ready-made home delivery of Beethoven's Ninth Symphony or Schumann's Piano Concerto. Life's musical enrichment was a thing to be worked for. The raising of the cultural level through the ennobling influence of music was part of the educational program of almost every middle-class family. Musical appreciation was thus not only a general possession, but also a very personal and highly valued one because it had been gained by years of individual endeavor. The children had masters to teach them the playing of their instruments. They practiced, they were taken to concerts where they heard the leading artists, and they formed groups to play classic chamber music, frequently at fixed dates. But even the opposition of these serious circles would have been powerless if it had restricted itself to a purely negative attitude toward the works of Wagner. They drew vital strength, however, from a positive attitude toward Brahms, around whom they gathered and whom they had raised up as Wagner's counter-idol. I can testify to that, for I grew up in that middle-class, chamber-music-playing, and anti-Wagnerian world and gained my musical education at one of those anti-Wagnerian conservatories.

Johannes Brahms lived at some distance, in Vienna, but Joseph Joachim, his friend and adherent, was in Berlin. In him, wholly admirable though he was in every other respect, the reactionaries had their most influential representative. The nimbus that long years of masterful accomplishments on the violin and the splendid activity of his quartet had gained him was brightened further by the fame that his leadership had brought to Berlin's Royal Academy. His personal friendship with Schumann and, later, Brahms, and the enmity between him and Wagner clearly and effectively indicated his artistic inclinations. A large part of the musical public, especially the "classically" minded public described by me, reverently acknowledged his authority and adopted his likes and dislikes.

Aside from their reactionary tendency, the musical institutes mentioned above were surely deserving of the highest respect and appreciation. Their reputation was known all over the world. From other European countries and from America, a great many students, eager for a thorough musical education and for authentic interpretations and methodics were drawn to the Germany, which at that time was justly considered the "mother-country of music." I remember how interesting I found the Babel of languages buzzing round my ear in the anterooms and corridors of the Conservatory.

My first experience of *Tristan* had wholly put me under the spell of Wagner, though I was still a boy at the time. I heard people speak against my ideal and cite Joachim as their authority. Now as then, however, my admiration for Joachim's personality was in no way diminished by his antagonism to Wagner's creations. I must have felt that his obstinate opposition could no longer do any harm to the cause of Wagner, while, on the other hand, his noble musicianship and his highly principled activity were a blessing to the cause of music generally.

I heard Joachim only once as a soloist in his famous interpretation of Beethoven's Violin Concerto. I also attended one of his last quartet recitals. He was an aged man, and his hand and intonation were no longer reliable. But his simplicity, greatness, and ultimate maturity made a deep, ineradicable impression on me. His sublime absorption at singing phrases, as for instance at the cavatina of Beethoven's B-flat major Quartet, touched my very soul. It has been a model to me throughout my life. So highly was his teaching regarded that, many years after his death, to be "a pupil of Joachim's" was considered the highest recommendation for a violinist wishing to become a member of an orchestra. I also believe that the magnificent violin tone of the Berlin Philharmonic Orchestra and that of the Royal Operahouse Orchestra were largely due to the tradition created by Joachim and continued by his many pupils. Unfortunately, I met Joachim personally but once, when a blind girl, a pupil of Jenny Meyer's, asked me to accompany her at an audition he had granted her. I believe it was a question of getting her his powerful recommendation for a small teaching position. I was about twelve years old and was looking forward to the meeting with eager expectation. Joachim bore himself with quiet dignity, graciousness, and warmth. He listened to the young singer kindly and seemed to be quite satisfied with my accompaniments, for he turned to me with noticeable interest, inquired about my age, the progress of my studies, and my intentions, and said a few words of praise to me. The meeting left me with a sense of happiness and, in spite of his opposition to Wagner, with a growing regret not to have come closer to him in life.

Theme and Variations

V

FROM my first day at the Conservatory, I was said to have proved a zealous and conscientious student. I did not, however, concentrate on my musical studies exclusively. Life seemed to offer all too much of what was interesting to my wide-awake mind, and I was not made to graze merely on the nearest pasturage. But the same healthy instinct within me that made me fight against the onesidedness into which a specific talent so easily slides also saved me from splintering my powers of apperception and thus sliding into superficiality. I believe that I intuitively chose my spiritual nourishment so as to strike a proper balance in the furtherance of my varied interests without placing too heavy a strain on my powers of assimilation.

The results of my endeavors naturally first manifested themselves in my pianistic progress. It must have satisfied my teacher, for one day he surprised me with the announcement that I was to participate in the Conservatory's next public recital, an annual event at the Berlin Singakademie.

The Berlin Singakademie! I see before my eyes the noble edifice visible from Unter den Linden behind the thin growth of trees of the chestnut grove through which an avenue led toward the building's sweeping flight of outside steps. Zelter, Mendelssohn, and other great musicians of the past had held sway in its distinguished old rooms. The acoustics of the magnificent recital hall were ideal. Busts of classics looked down from the walls. On its platform, musicians like Liszt, Rubinstein, Sarasate, Joachim and his quartet — in short, artists of world-renown had performed, And I, a shy boy of nine, was to be permitted to enter those culturally and historically so important rooms, that venerable Mecca of musical believers. There I was for the first time to prove my worth before an audience. I can feel to this day my solemn diffidence in such impressive surroundings. I never set foot in the Berlin Singakademie without a sense of awe. It was an echo of the hymn rising up in the heart of the child when he was first affected by the temple's atmosphere; and it was caused no less by the immediate effect of its beautiful, nobly simple architecture and its forms, eloquent of spiritual history. I have often been profoundly stirred when gazing at stones with a tale to tell, have been agitated by history solidified into permanent form. But such impressions engrave themselves most deeply on the mind of a child, still poor in experiences; and though he is still too immature to grasp their importance, they weigh upon him with a force rarely matched later by similar occurrences.

I believe it was on a Sunday morning when, after mounting with a beating heart one of the two symmetrically arranged inside stairways from the artists' room, I suddenly found myself in the public eye, facing the well-filled hall. Joining the other performers, I took my place on a bench of the steeply rising platform, majestically overtopped by the metal pipes of the organ. I had to wait a long time, and my feverish excitement rose every time a fellow-pupil got up from our bench to show what he could do. But when my turn finally came, I became aware that my excitement had vanished before I had even struck the first note, an experience that was to be repeated almost regularly in the course of my career. I was said to have stated afterward that the many listeners had troubled me as little in my playing as if they had been so many apples or pears. If I am not mistaken, I played Schubert's graceful *Impromptu* in A-flat-minor and Mendelssohn's *Rondo Capriccioso*. The tender romanticism of these pieces executed by the hands of a child was said to have rather convincingly touched the hearts of the audience.

There was a festive sequel to my first public appearance. It took place at the Café Bauer, a resplendent establishment of the old Berlin, on the eastern side of the "Kranzlerecke." That memorable day reached its climax in a cup of chocolate to which my parents treated me. A more important consequence of the event was a letter from Jenny Meyer informing Father that he would no longer have to pay for my tuition. Since, moreover, a number of quite favorable comments had appeared in the newspapers, my parents were overjoyed. Father carried the criticisms about with him for weeks.

It was natural that my longing soon went beyond piano playing and piano literature into the wider realm of music. Father began to take me occasionally to orchestra concerts and at times even to the Opera. His own inclinations running parallel to my desires, it gave him all the more pleasure to further the latter, especially as I was able on the day following a visit to the Opera or a concert to play for him from memory a number of the melodies.

The Kroll Garden was a spacious popular restaurant where, on a fine warm afternoon or evening, the Berliners liked to sit under thickly-leaved trees, eating, drinking beer, and, if memory serves me, listening to a military band. How enjoyable it was there, especially toward evening, when the gas lamps were burning and the wind was rustling the leaves so excitingly and romantically! And yet, the darkening garden gave me but a presentiment of coming happiness, a foretaste of the ascension into a higher world. Evening came at last, and people walked to the far end of the main avenue. There stood the Kroll Theater, the scene of operatic performances. The fifty-pfennig admission fee — or was it but twenty-five? — paid by the garden guests entitled them to standing room in the Opera. A wide semi-circle of standees surrounded the entire orchestra floor, so that the first arrivals could stand way in front near the orchestra, either at the right where the brasses and percussion instruments were or at the left near the wood winds, but at any rate near the stage. Father took me there once in a while. There I heard for the first time Mozart's *Figaro* and *Don Giovanni*, Rossini's *Barber of Seville*, Verdi's *Rigoletto* and *Ballo in Maschera*, and other operas. My most enthusiastic approval was bestowed upon the young and divinely gifted Marcella Sembrich in the parts of the enchanting Susanna or the graceful and scintillating Rosina. Those were the rôles in which she literally sang and played her way into the hearts of the Berliners. More than thirty years later, I called on Marcella Sembrich in New York. It gave me great pleasure to confess to her my long-stored, but by no means withered, boyish enthusiasm and to awaken within her nostalgic memories of those early triumphs. Another performance I shall never forget was D'Andrade's fascinating Don Giovanni, one of the rare instances where an artist seemed to have been predestined for a part by nature. In 1901, in Riga, I conducted a *Don Giovanni* with D'Andrade as guest artist. His voice had noticeably deteriorated, but I was nevertheless gratified to have the ecstatic standee's impression renewed and confirmed from the conductor's desk and through personal contact. I also recall with admiration D'Andrade's brilliant Figaro in *The Barber of Seville*, his exuberant mood, his natural vivacity, his vocal brilliance, his technical mastery of the spoken word, and his aristocratic elegance which, to be sure, was less suited to the Barber than to the Don.

In addition to the evenings at Kroll's, two performances at the Royal Opera Unter den Linden have remained in my memory: Lortzing's fairy opera *Undine,* and, considerably later, Mozart's *Magic Flute.* It seems worth mentioning that, in spite of all the happiness and agitation with which I listened to the music and followed the action, I was again and again aware of a mounting regret whenever the music was interrupted by dialogue, and again, when the dialogue was cut off by music. No sooner did I feel carried away by the warm stream of music than I was disappointingly transferred to the colder zone of the spoken word; and no sooner had I willingly become acclimated to the interesting element that explained and spurred on the action than the dramatic tension was suspended by the music, which frequently, especially in the numbers of the classic opera, put a stop to the action. I enjoyed those evenings at the Opera. They satisfied my craving for music, sustained my eagerness to behold, and gave nourishment to my innate sense of the stage through the performances of gifted artists. But in spite of *Figaro, Don Giovanni,* and *The Magic Flute,* or rather because on those occasions the individual performances impressed me, and not Mozart himself — I was at that time more ardently devoted to absolute than to dramatic music, and no opera spoke to my soul so eloquently as the piano music I played or the symphonies I heard.

Yet, I am conscious also of a more profound reason for this attitude. For one thing, the operas I had thus far seen were largely of the cheerful kind; for another, the interpretation of especially the dramatic and passionate parts, like those in *Don Giovanni, Ballo in Maschera,* and *Rigoletto* left much to be desired. In short, my limited experience had given me the impression that opera as such was lacking somewhat in seriousness. I leaned toward the tragic, and was rather disdainful of the cheerful. It is my belief that young people at that stage of life are more easily impressed by what is heroic and grandiose; that they more readily understand works of art in which passionate feelings are violently uttered in raised accents, and that the lighter sounds of cheerfulness are less impressive to them. Or, to express it more explicitly and in a Schilleresque manner, youth inclines toward the exalted; and the beautiful, in which category lightness in art belongs, discloses itself only to the more mature mind. Thus, Beethoven was my god, and I considered Mozart merely pretty. Schumann's stormy romanticism spoke to me more eloquently than Schubert's blissful melodies. Lessing's *Minna von Barnhelm* and Shakespeare's *As You Like It,* no matter how greatly I was attracted by them, no matter how beautiful and interesting I considered them, were "merely comedies" to me, not grand art like *Emilia Galotti* or *King Lear.* As for my personal disposition, I was cheerful, occasionally merry and even exuberant, and except for intermittent attacks of melancholy, smoothly and equably attuned in my outward behavior. Gradually, however, and ever more consciously, I drew a dividing line between life and art. My everyday life was filled with a spirit of cheerfulness, but from art I demanded and received emotional upheaval and exaltation.

My musical education was furthered also by attendance at the popular concerts in Philharmonic Hall. They were led by Gustav Kogel and took place every Tuesday and Wednesday evening. The charge for admission was quite moderate. People sat at tables and were served beer and food. Serving during the music was fortunately *verboten*. The excellent Philharmonic Orchestra presented practically all the important symphonic works. I remember, by the way, that I often asked Father to leave before the waltz or other piece of popular music with which the program usually concluded. I felt pained by this descent from a higher region. On the other hand, I had no objection to playing dance music in the circle of my family. If we had company, and my brother and sister, our cousins, and their friends wanted to dance, I would sit at the piano for hours, playing and improvising waltzes, polkas, schottisches, and other popular dances. I considered dance music perfectly proper for purposes of entertainment, but my boyishly serious mind was absolutely opposed to mixing art with amusement.

Among the biographies of musicians included in my reading matter I was most deeply moved by the life of Beethoven, his Titanic character, his growing deafness, his disdain of the aristocracy and society, the destruction of his dedication of the *"Eroica,"* the Heiligenstadt Testament, and other facts. But I also read with sympathy whatever biographical tales of Mozart, Schubert, Bach, Handel, Schumann, Mendelssohn, and other creative musicians happened to come into my hands. I was startled and perplexed to learn that in almost every instance the oppressive poverty of these masters' mundane existence contrasted shockingly with the richness of their creative gifts. Mozart kept servilely begging a few gulden from an old benefactor; he and his wife danced about their unheated room just to keep warm on a cold November day; worse even, he suffered moral degradation inflicted upon him by the Archbishop of Salzburg. And while these things happened, his soul conceived the tremors of the beyond in the music of the Statue, he sang the message of human love in Sarastro's Sacred Halls, and he wept the *Lacrymosa* of his Requiem. What fateful connection between the inescapable triviality of mundane everyday life and the exalted processes of inspired artistic creation so tragically burdened the artist's existence? Not that, as a boy, I put the question to myself in that form. But the biographies — there were not among them serious works like Jahn's *Mozart* or Spitta's *Bach,* but rather anecdotal juvenile books — always recorded in addition to the artistic triumphs the contrast between inward blessedness and outward distress. At the same time I felt that the blessed themselves not infrequently inclined with a human, all-too-human, side of their being toward the world of the trivial, that the contrast between exalted creation and lowly living ran parallel with a similar contrast in the artists' own soul. Even I, within my still narrow province, began early to suffer from such a conflict — from the

BRUNO WALTER, 1903

THE AUTHOR'S WIFE, ELSA, 1900

workaday world and my own triviality, which adjusted itself all too readily to that workaday world, and from the contrast of both to the life of the spirit for which I felt I was born. I experienced the first visitations of *Weltschmerz*. I felt that from these growing sufferings and doubts, which were feelings rather than trains of thought, a chilling wind was blowing over me. In the course of time, it actually caused me to catch a life-long cold. Well, we can live and work even with a cold. Why, a popular saying has it that it protects us from serious illness.

At any rate, a gift for which I am deeply grateful to fate provided a better protection even than a cold: a sense of humor. Early in life, I felt inclined to view happenings and experiences from an angle and distance that revealed their comic side. That was why I became so particularly fond of humorous literature. The acrimonious humor of Swift, the lovable one of Dickens, and the demoniac one of E. T. A. Hoffmann aroused the most grateful echo in my soul. My love of Sterne came later. I was twenty when Jean Paul rose as a new star in my firmament, where he was to outshine everything for a long time. My inclinations toward the humorous enabled me to overcome with greater ease much of the evil that befell me, though of course not the heavy blows dealt me by fate.

While during the days of my growth the inward warmth and heartfelt laughter of Dickens were balm to my soul, I was actually obsessed with Hoffmann. I had been afraid of ghosts as a little child, and Hoffmann's wild imagination once more aroused the terrible shudders of old. Too, I was warmed by his love of music. I saw in his *Kapellmeister* Kreisler a musician's nature akin to mine. Even my dreams were affected by his now diabolical, now friendly, now mad humor, by his profusion of figures, and by his exuberant enjoyment of telling stories. What gratified me most, however, was the climate of his imagination, the fiery element in which his salamander nature felt at home.

It was of course Hoffmann the romanticist who so enthralled me. He possessed to a specially high degree the tension and high-mindedness that are common traits of all romanticists, setting them apart most decisively from humdrum affairs, even from normality. The romanticist is the very antithesis of the Philistine. In that fact lay the main reason — of which I was hardly conscious — for my passionate devotion to Hoffmann's writings and for the powerful influence they exerted on my youth. Even prosaic Berlin appeared to me in a somewhat romantic light through his charming tale *Adventure of a New-Year's Night*. True, the wine tavern of Lutter and Wegner on Gensdarmenmarkt was quite hopeless. It would never be anything but an emphatically normal Berlin wine restaurant, in spite of the fact that it used to be honored by the author's frequent visits. Repeated attempts in later years to visualize Hoffmann's ghost in its rooms were put to naught by their prosiness. They may have been more primitive at the time when the poet drank his punch there, but I doubt that they could ever have looked Hoffmannesque. And by the way, the brilliant man caused me a disappointment too. Hoffmann, one of the favorite poets of almost all musicians, the hero even of an opera, Offenbach's *Tales of Hoffmann,* whose truly ingenious music has a number of features reminiscent of the poet himself, had actually written an opera of his own — *Undine* — and I found it to be a weak work lacking in originality. Astonishingly, there was in its feeble words and tunes nothing of the demoniac firebrand whose profound affinity with music was manifest in so many of his writings.

My Sunday afternoons were frequently devoted to playing chamber music and to occasional group readings of dramatic works, each part being assigned to a different person. My own longing for chamber music and that of my music-loving comrades was insatiable. We would gather immediately after the noonday meal and play violin and cello sonatas, piano trios, quartets, or quintets. We never seemed to be able to get enough of them. Warned repeatedly of a waiting, cold supper, we would tear ourselves away with difficulty; still chewing our last bite, we would rush back to our instruments until the thought of tomorrow's school or, worse, some unfinished homework would force us to stop. In those days, home music of that kind was a source of enjoyment not only to future musicians like ourselves. As I said before, the large numbers of amateurs and music lovers of all ages were the very ones who spent their leisure hours in the enjoyment of jointly played music.

I also liked to take part in the group readings, usually choosing for myself the passionate and, at times, the particularly demoniac or evil characters. The fiendish Moor in Schiller's *Fiesco* suited me splendidly; I practiced my diabolics on the President of the same poet's *Intrigue and Love;* but parts like those of Tasso, Marquis Posa, Max Piccolomini, and other high-minded spirits were the ones whose verses I really loved to recite.

As a matter of course, the cold season was more favorable to such endeavors than the warm months. Summer held other attractions for me and affected me by forces that powerfully drew me away from studying and reading, from practicing and striving, and pointed a way leading to myself and, dimly, to the universe. Next to music, nature, which spoke to me most eloquently during the warm season, has always been the strongest power in my life. And it surely did not penetrate into my soul merely through my vision, no matter how fervently I enjoyed the sight of beautiful mountains, valleys, lakes, sunny days, and moonlit nights. I was vouchsafed also a more immediate access; I felt akin and attached to the thicket and the ocean, to the rocky solitude and the thunderstorm, to the humming of insects, and to the noonday quiet. Saturated with nature, and feeling part of it, I was able early to enter into the sense of Faust's verses:

> This glorious Nature thou didst for my kingdom give,
> And power to feel it, to enjoy it.
> 'Twas not the stranger's short permitted privilege
> Of momentary wonder that Thou gavest;
> No, Thou hast given me into her deep breast
> As into a friend's secret heart to look;
> Thus teaching me to recognize and love my brothers
> In still grove, or air, or stream.

Berlin, with its meager surroundings, offered scant joy to the nature-loving wanderer. The country was flat and dreary, although the lakes of the Havel and the scrubby pine woods on their sandy soil had a peculiar charm, especially at sunset. But the gentle moon in a blue and cloudless sky was shining even upon the Berlin backyards, the wind also rustled in the treetops of the Tiergarten, and if one were to be out in the open on a fine evening, the starry sky would expand one's soul, filling it with the overpowering sense of the infinite. In winter, I also learned to love the snow, crunching underfoot, the ice ferns on the windows, the whirling snowflakes, the white-blanketed trees, and the wide snowy plains. It was fortunate that Father was able to send his family into the country every summer, usually spending a few days there himself. For several summers, the Isle of Rügen in the Baltic, reached by a charming steamer trip from Stettin or by ferry from Stralsund, was the scene of our vacations. There I became acquainted with real forests, for along the coast and deep into the interior of the island magnificent beech woods extended. We wandered through them, or I blissfully lay in their shade. From the tall cliffs of Stubbenkammer I would look down upon the sea deep below, feeling a fierce joy at the sight of the eternally undecided mythical struggle between the surf and the rocks. Cairns on the heath reminded me of prehistoric human life, and the reading of local myths called forth a dawning understanding of the effect such a landscape might have on a poet's imagination.

Other summers were spent by us in Thuringia, with its charming valleys and gentle mountains. There a noble medieval past rose before my vision from the Wartburg and its romantic surroundings. A stain on the wall of a small room recalled the prodigious life of Luther, who had hurled his inkwell at the devil. Above all, however, it was there, on the summit of the Kiekelhahn near Ilmenau, that I first entered into a spiritual alliance with Goethe, who, according to an inscription, had long before stood at the same spot in the deep of the night, sanctifying the place with the verses *"Über allen Wipfeln ist Ruh'"* ["O'er all the treetops reigns quiet"]. I found traces of the young Johann Sebastian Bach at Eisenach. Our stay in Thuringia thus furnished more fuel than my torch of life could consume.

Some of our three- or four-week summer vacations were spent in the Harz Mountains. The wild Bode Valley between Rosstrappe (Horse Trap) and Hexentanzplatz (Witches' Dancing Ground) were well suited to the fairy tales suggested by the names of the mountains. The Brocken, with the dismal districts round Elend and Schierke, through which I passed amidst wafting fogs, seemed in that wretched weather the proper place for the Walpurgis Night and Witches' Sabbath described by Goethe in *Faust*.

In giving a picture of my spiritual development during those boyhood years, I ought to attribute a greater importance to my walks and wanderings than to my studies and reading. Studying is the absorption and digestion of knowledge; reading, as Schopenhauer correctly says, is "thinking with other people's thoughts." During those summers, in addition to a wealth of impressions from outside, thoughts of my own came pouring forth. There began a direct relation between me and the world, in short, there occurred a spiritual growth from within me and toward the world. It seems that the Muses — and perhaps more severe goddesses too — prefer to bestow their feminine favor upon wanderers and roamers, shunning the stay-at-homes and the hurrying mortals who rush about in automobiles. Would anybody venture to assert that Beethoven could have written his symphonies or Goethe his poems without the inspiration that came to them on their wanderings?

The desire to broaden the foundation of my education induced my parents to make me acquainted also with works of art, and I was quite ready to use my eyes as well as my ears. I visited the museums of Berlin on many a Sunday morning: the Old Museum behind the Lustgarten, the New one still farther behind, and the National Gallery. The solemn forms of the Egyptian temples with their strange hieroglyphics struck me with astonishment, but also filled me with awe. Surprised and bewildered, I stood before Schliemann's Pergamon excavations. I admired the beauty of the paintings of the Italian Renaissance and found the Dutch interesting. But in spite of frequent visits and subsequent serious endeavors I was long to be unsuccessful in establishing close relations with the visible arts. I lived by the ear. The gift of beholding had not been bestowed on me by nature, and only in later years, when my cultural background had grown richer, was I fortunate enough to learn to love the works of the visible arts.

Back at the Stern Conservatory, where I was still zealously preparing for a pianistic career, Ehrlich's musical guidance had kept me firmly in the serious direction indicated by my nature. Technically, too, I had progressed considerably, thanks to his pianistic method. True, he did not attempt to develop a brilliant virtuosity, though it would have been within my natural gifts; he would probably not have been the right teacher for that anyway. I became conscious of that for the first time when the excellent Felix Dreyschock, a son of the famous Russian pianist Alexander Dreyschock, substituted for his former teacher Heinrich Ehrlich and took over his class for a few weeks. Now I heard the perfect playing of thirds and octaves and saw with admiration the working of a splendidly developed wrist. I began of my own accord to practice exercises aiming at virtuosity. Dreyschock was a brisk young man. His unconstrained attitude and cheerful readiness to play for me gave me sincere pleasure. He, too, seemed to enjoy the lessons, and so a cordial relation resulted between the interesting and distinguished artist, a man half-way in his thirties, and the boy who looked up at him with devotion. I also remember his charmingly handsome young wife, her premature death, and the tragic change in Felix Dreyschock's bearing and appearance because of the terrible loss.

Although at thirteen I was not as yet the possessor of a brilliant technique, my teacher considered me pianistically and musically mature enough for a public appearance. He sent for Mother and discussed with her his intention to introduce me to the public in an inobtrusive manner that would not disturb my future development.

Hermann Wolff was at that time the leading German concert manager, representing the world's foremost artists. An efficient, enterprising, sensible, and witty man, he was a sincere friend and adviser of the artists he managed. He played a truly important part in the musical life of Berlin. His correspondence with Hans von Bülow, who was as brilliant and straightforward as he was difficult and unpredictable, shows Wolff in his true colors. In Bülow's letters, now witty and friendly, now impatient and disgruntled, there was always a noticeable undercurrent of esteem for and confidence in his impresario. On Wolff's side, there was artistic understanding and personal frankness and firmness, qualities by means of which he had gained the confidence of Bülow and other artists.

Heinrich Ehrlich, who was on friendly terms with Wolff, induced him to have me come to his home and give me an audition. In the handsome drawing-room, which seemed to me furnished with the utmost luxury, I met Hermann Wolff, his prepossessing, temperamental wife, the later "Queen Louise" of Berlin's musical life, and my teacher Heinrich Ehrlich. They were having tea. If I am not mistaken, I played for them Schumann's *Kreisleriana*. Many years later, when Louise Wolff and I were in close professional contact — she had inaugurated the "Bruno Walter Concerts" with the Berlin Philharmonic Orchestra and managed them for years — she told me that she could clearly remember how shy and silent I had been, but also how greatly pleased with my playing they all had been. At any rate, Wolff seemed interested and proposed to my teacher that I be introduced to the public at one of the popular Philharmonic concerts.

And so, in February, 1889, I played Moscheles's E-flat-major Concerto with the Philharmonic Orchestra. The success I won was quite encouraging. Somewhat less encouraging had been the orchestra rehearsal on the day preceding the concert. After I had gone through my piece and, so I believed, imparted the necessary brilliance to the bravura passages, my place at the piano was taken by Teresa Careño, Eugen d'Albert's second wife, who also had to rehearse for an impending concert with the orchestra. Here was a true virtuoso. I could hear the thunder of her onrushing octave runs, the sparkle and brilliance of her passages. If my crest had been inclined to rise, I now stood "in the crushing feeling of my nullity," although — I remember it distinctly — I was fascinated much rather than crushed.

At any rate, the evening at Philharmonic Hall had furnished proof of my ability as a pianist. My parents were against a prodigy career, both because of my physical delicacy and because my systematic development must not be interfered with. But we — teacher, pupil, and parents — had definitely adopted the principle of a pianistic career. At about that time I heard Josef Hofmann, a child prodigy of twelve. He came from Russia, where his amazing technical ability and precocious musicality had caused a veritable sensation. His brilliant Berlin success, which I witnessed, and his exceptional performance encouraged me in my own plans and hopes and kindled my zeal.

But my dream of a future great career as a pianist began to fade on the day when, from a seat way up on the platform behind the kettledrums, I heard and saw Hans von Bülow conduct the Philharmonic Orchestra in a classic program. At the popular Philharmonic concerts under Kogel as well as at the operatic performances I had witnessed, I had paid hardly any attention to the conductor. Now, however, I saw in Bülow's face the glow of inspiration and the concentration of energy. I felt the compelling force of his gestures, noticed the attention and devotion of the players, and was conscious of the expressiveness and precision of their playing. It became at once clear to me that it was that one man who was producing the music, that he had transformed those hundred performers into his instrument, and that he was playing it as a pianist played the piano. That evening decided my future. Now I knew what I was meant for. No musical activity but that of an orchestral conductor could any longer be considered by me, no music could ever make me truly happy but symphonic music. Before the evening was over I told Father that I would be glad zealously to continue my piano studies and be publicly active as a pianist later, just as Bülow was, but today the die had been cast, today I had recognized what I had been born for. I had decided to become a conductor.

VI

No sooner had I begun to realize my good fortune, no sooner had I started to plan the necessary broadening of my studies, than another event pierced my soul with the rapidity and force of a bolt of lightning. It set me aflame and wholly revolutionized my inward life. The event was a performance of *Tristan und Isolde*, the consequence "heaven-born enravishment." This is how it happened. There was, as I have said, a deep-rooted antagonism to Wagner at the Conservatory, at my parents' house, and among the people with whom I associated. They were all "classically" minded. Brahms was considered the man to carry on the traditions of great music, and Wagner was the destroyer and corrupter from whom to guard the ear and the soul. To be sure, *Lohengrin* and *Tannhäuser* were beautiful. That was admitted not only by my relatives and acquaintances, but also at the Conservatory, while the true Wagnerites were already beginning to speak of these early works somewhat condescendingly. But the *unisono* of the chorus was to the effect that after *Lohengrin* Wagner had gone astray. On the other hand, there was my spirit of contradiction and my tendency toward hero worship. Bismarck was criticized, and those around me were against him — so I was inclined to consider him a great man. Everybody within earshot was speaking against Wagner —

so I felt impelled to take his part. But I did not know him, and so was lacking in effective weapons. When I said uncertainly that it was impossible that a composer who had written two operas of so much beauty could all at once utterly lose his power, I had to listen to scornful references to *"Wagala weia"* and *"Hojotoho."* Besides, the corrupter of the language had corrupted also the music, had abandoned all moderation and form, and had vitiated the sound of the orchestra by the augmentation of brass and percussion instruments. Such noise could not be borne by any cultivated ear and, more than that — it was added in a low voice — there was another wicked and impure element in Wagner's music, one that was still beyond me. I knew quite well that they were referring to sensuality, which I found rather interesting and by no means wicked. My position with regard to Wagner's tendency to coin new words was weak, for I actually rather disliked it. But my interest in him had mounted mightily. I longed to hear his orchestral sound and found his lack of moderation most attractive. So I rose up in arms and declared at home that now I wanted to become acquainted with one of Wagner's works. I must have been earning some money then, for Father would certainly not have contributed to the corruption of my soul by the purchase of a ticket. There I sat in the topmost gallery of the Berlin Operahouse, and from the first sound of the cellos my heart contracted spasmodically. The magic, like the terrible potion that the deathly ill Tristan curses in the third act, "burst raging forth from heart to brain." Never before had my soul been so deluged with floods of sound and passion, never had my heart been consumed by such yearning and sublime blissfulness, never had I been transported from reality by such heavenly glory. I was no longer in this world. After the performance, I roamed the streets aimlessly. When I got home I didn't say anything and begged not to be questioned. My ecstasy kept singing within me through half the night, and when I awoke on the following morning I knew that my life was changed. A new epoch had begun: Wagner was my god, and I wanted to become his prophet.

The next question was how best to approach the god. What way should I take to penetrate into the wholly unfamiliar world of Wagner? More than anything else, I needed time, and I didn't have any, for the greatly increased studies of the budding conductor consumed almost every bit of time left me by my schooling, which was private at the time. But even if I had been able to manage a free hour now and then, in what manner could I have utilized it for the benefit of my Wagnerian yearning? The Conservatory ignored Wagner, owned none of his works, and I did not have the money for such costly purchases. Patience and a yielding disposition are not among the virtues of youth. They were surely not among mine, least of all when my flaming heart was so sorely beset. I must become acquainted with Wagner and get intoxicated with his music: that brooked no delay. I found a way to make some money by playing accompaniments for young singers, coaching them. Of course, I had but little time for this activity, and my fee of fifty pfennigs per hour did not fill my pockets rapidly. At any rate, I earned enough to hear an occasional Wagner performance from the amphitheater, the name given to the top gallery, in which a seat cost one mark, standing room sixty pfennigs. I thus was able to dedicate myself ever more passionately to my raptures.

I have no clear recollection of individual singers of that time. One picture only, deeply affecting, stands before my vision: the noble figure of Rosa Sucher, perfect in beauty and inspiration, pledging Tristan with the raised goblet, waving the veil, flourishing the torch. I am sure that in my enthusiasm I had "that drink within me, which sees a Helen in ev'ry woman." But I was not the only one to whom "the Sucher" was beautiful and majestic, who admired the heroic style of her expression and gesture. It was fortunate indeed that my conception of a heroic character and of tragic greatness was not confounded by a banal personality. Josef Sucher, the singer's husband, was at that time the Wagner conductor at the Berlin Opera. I gratefully remember the man whose honest and warm-hearted musicianship I had come to appreciate. As a matter of fact, I considered everything and everybody magnificent. But with the exception of Rosa Sucher, the artists faded before the works themselves. They filled my soul with ecstasy.

Gradually, so far as that was possible through my attending performances, I got to know all of Wagner's works but *Rienzi* and *Parsifal* and became acclimated to their sphere. I also studied with earnest endeavor the great man's writings. There were ten volumes: *Mein Leben* appeared only much later. His essays from the first Paris epoch entertained and moved me. The considerable trouble I had with his theoretical investigations I naturally attributed to my own insufficiency. There were but two essays, in fact, to which I owed profound and lasting impressions: "Of Conducting," a mine of information in connection with the plans I then entertained, and "Beethoven," that magnificent piece of writing in which one creative genius reverently probes the essence of another. My choice between Wagner and Brahms, which ought to have been painful to me because of the milieu in which I had been brought up and was living, was actually quite easy. I did not choose, I just loved both of them without trying to reconcile what, according to the opinion of so many high-principled people, was plainly irreconcilable. True, I was more devoted to Wagner at that time than to anybody else. He dominated my life. But though he brightly outshone all others, he was unable to banish from my heart any of the classic composers. In explanation of my diverse inclinations I may assume the existence within me of a certain dualism, of a Dionysiac and an Apollonic side of my nature, which seemingly had enough breadth to grant both sufficient room for mutual tolerance.

In addition to the coaching lessons, I had found other modest sources of income for the financing of my Wagnerian dissipations and of some inconsiderable personal requirements. Although I had given up my pianistic plans, there were occasional opportunities, especially in vacation time, for brief concert tours with women singers. If my parents considered them trustworthy, I set out with them to accompany their songs and arias and do some solo playing in between.

My pleas at the Conservatory had brought about my admission to the conductors' class headed by Robert Radeke. The future conductors were taught thorough-bass, reading and playing of orchestral scores, the principles of form, composition, and instrumentation. They were required to be present at chorus practice and orchestral rehearsals and gradually to take part in them. It was furthermore recommended that we drop in on instrumental or singing lessons, though this was very sensibly left to our choice. In addition, I took lessons in counterpoint with Bussler and was diligently writing fugues and double fugues. The burden of my tasks would have been almost too heavy had it not been for the fact that everything came to me so easily. I recall that the reading and playing of orchestral scores gave me hardly any difficulty. No sooner had the meaning of the treble, alto, and tenor clefs been explained to me than I was able to play without trouble the chorales written in four clefs; and no sooner had I understood the principle of the transposing instruments than I read and played by sight scores by Haydn, Mendelssohn, or Beethoven as if they were piano pieces or accompaniments to songs. I even remember that, as a joke, I transposed orchestral scores, just as I frequently transposed songs at Jenny Meyer's singing lessons. Under Radeke's guidance, I studied with great interest the forms of sonata and symphonic literature, followed his instructions and classical examples in orchestrating my own and other composers' piano pieces, and composed sonatas, quartets, overtures, and choruses. The fact that everything came to me so easily, that everything turned out so unproblematically, disturbed me. I also felt oppressed morally, for between me and Radeke, whom I respected highly personally, stood my secretly entertained "modernism." I did not keep my love of Wagner to myself from cowardice or a want of candor, but because of the clearly felt senselessness of any discussion. Radeke could never have pointed out to me the way beyond the territory with which he was familiar. The Conservatory's curriculum and instructive material contained nothing that transcended the tradition of the institute, and the more diligently I studied, the less trouble I had in mastering my task, the surer I was in my conviction that my studies would never lead me to the works that agitated my soul, nor to their interpretation, and that in spite of all the honest thoroughness of the Conservatory's tuition I would never get beyond a certain preliminary stage. How, for instance, could I have had any confidence in my orchestration lessons, if, filled with the magnificent sound of Wagner's orchestra, I was told that it was in bad taste to use the trumpet in any but its natural tones? How, at the composition classes, could I trustingly submit to the rigorous commandments and interdictions concerning harmony, while the *Tristan* chromatics sounded in my ear? To make matters worse, it seemed to me as if I were untaught even in connection with classic music. I felt everything more elementally, more simply, but also more passionately, powerfully, and personally than it was being taught. At the same time, I respected superior knowledge and experience; and so, altogether, I felt more uncertain every day. While I apparently made rapid progress, and the Conservatory expected much of me, I thought that my development was being impeded. I hesitated, doubted, and finally despaired when I saw no way out of my difficulties.

Then, suddenly, everything was set going by a strange fellow student from the conducting and composing class. He was a young German-Russian from one of the Baltic provinces, a light-blond youth of about sixteen or seventeen, with a gentle, high-pitched, broadly Baltic manner of speaking. He had become greatly attached to me, and we spent many an hour in conversation and the joint playing of music. How great was my astonishment on learning that the outwardly so modest, soft-spoken, and well-mannered lad was musically an extreme heretic and rebel, yes, almost a nihilist. I had made known to him in a confidential conversation my enthusiasm for Wagner, my problems posed by the teachings of the Conservatory, and the new world which had been revealed to me. To this he answered very quietly and gently that the teachings of the Conservatory were no whit more unsatisfactory and outmoded than the subject to which they were directed: classic music. I could take his word for it that Bach and Handel were old fogies who could no longer interest anybody. Mozart, although he had written pretty melodies, was boring. Beethoven, while interesting, had no inventive power. In short, we at the Conservatory were definitely living in the past, in a museum whose windows were closed and whose air was not fit to breathe. Wagner, to be sure, had opened new ways to music, but he had written for the theater, and the theater appealed only to the coarse masses. The only really great musician of our century was Berlioz; we had to cling to him and to the thoroughly modern principle of program music. The gentle iconoclast was unable to shake my faith. His indignation made no impression upon me, but his enthusiasm did. We happened to find the familiar numbers from Berlioz's *Damnation de Faust* on the program of the next popular concert at Philharmonic Hall. We went, and though I was not profoundly touched, I was nevertheless carried away by the magic of the orchestration. When I complained to my friend that the new attraction had done nothing but add to my uneasiness, because I saw no chance to occupy myself with it and search out its character, he advised me with a conspiratorial look to thumb my nose at the Conservatory and go to the Royal Library, where all music could be obtained. There I could study the orchestral scores.

Here, at last, was the redeeming word. It fell upon my languishing soul as a spark falls upon dry powder. On the very next day — I must have left the Falk Real-Gymnasium by that time — I took the daring step that relieved me of the fetters I had worn. I became my own tutor. With all the uninformed shyness of my fifteen years I entered the magnificent music department of the Royal Library. Dr. Kopferman, the librarian, looked at the young visitor with considerable surprise. I stammered my request to be allowed to look at scores that had been unavailable to me and that I needed for my education. The kind man gave his permission, and a time of feverish studying began. My memory has retained but few details, but I remember having copied the *Tannhäuser* Overture, the *Tristan* Prelude, the *Parsifal* Prelude, the Kyrie from Beethoven's *Missa Solemnis,* and much else. I likewise recall having written down excerpts from Berlioz's theory of orchestration, and having pored over the orchestral scores of Wagner and Berlioz, but also of classic composers. I also recall an invention of mine, to which I owe a wealth of information. In order to fathom the secrets of Wagner's orchestration, I noted on an endless number of slips of papers the text words coinciding with chords of an interesting or unusual orchestration. Beneath the respective word, I wrote down the chord and its orchestration. The pockets of my coat and trousers filled with these slips, I stood or sat on the top gallery of the Operahouse under the red lamp of the emergency exit and endeavored by means of the well-ordered notations and by listening most intently to impress upon my mind the sounds whose component parts I had written down. Now, at last, I felt that I was headed in the right direction. I was fully aware of the fact that, while I owed to the Conservatory the preparatory schooling that enabled me to make use of the vast new material of study, I was only now learning autodidactically what was indispensable to my life-plans.

Those hours at the library gave me a strange feeling of happiness such as I had never experienced before. When I closed the tall oaken door to the music department behind me, I felt darkly as if I had shut out the confusion of the present and was now surrounded by a quiet, well-ordered, and powerful past. After entering the hall, and before becoming immersed in my score, I used to prowl around softly, gaze at the backs of the countless rows of music and books, and enjoy the silence of the spacious room with its many readers absorbed in their studies. Now as then, I am quite susceptible to the solemnity of a library hall, where the spirit of centuries is collected, where the thoughts and works of the most exquisite minds lie saved from corruption, and where succeeding striving generations find a source of inexhaustible instruction and elevation. In that tranquil shade there exists no loud Now, no exciting Tomorrow, but only a definite and immeasurable Yesterday of the spirit, containing, at the same time, the imperishable seeds of future thinking and creation. Even as a boy I felt something of the encouragement that invigorates my heart today when I look at my books on their shelves and think: my friends!

Soon I began to reduce my work at the Conservatory in favor of my studies at the library as much as I could without arousing attention or hurting anybody's feelings. It is moreover likely that but a short time elapsed before I finally admitted my "sin," for I can well remember the amazing event when Jenny Meyer permitted a young English baritone, who like myself was partaking of the fruits of the forbidden tree, to have his way and sing to her class the "Lilac Monologue" from *Die Meistersinger*. Then she turned toward the pupils who had formed a circle round us and said with friendly dignity: "I do not like this music and would not care to make a habit of hearing it here, but," and here she looked at me at the piano "I wanted to give pleasure to our Bruno."

Thus I felt absolved, and frankness reigned, a condition without which I was unable to feel comfortable. Now, too, my work seemed to have sense, for it carried me forward in the desired direction. And so the sky was blue, a fresh wind filled the sails, and my ship was at last gliding along smoothly and swiftly.

VII

AFTER that orchestra concert at Philharmonic Hall, I had chosen Hans von Bülow as my model. My thoughts revolved around the great conductor, by whose work I meant to be guided and whom I hoped to emulate. I desired to study the musician and would have liked nothing better than to know the nature of the man. In my search for personal characteristics and utterances I was not impelled merely by childish curiosity. A healthy instinct told me that the art of so emphatically subjective a musician could not be fully grasped without a knowledge of the man himself. His very appearance aroused my interest. Had he been taller, the sight of the lean man with the high forehead and the graying pointed beard might have reminded one of Don Quixote. His eccentricity, his combative idealism, and the chivalry manifested in his life and foretold by his bearing would have suited that picture well. But he was short of stature, and the vivacity of his gestures, the exalted spirituality of his forehead, and especially his fitful moods pointed to another and more intimate relationship: to Hoffmann's *Kapellmeister* Kreisler, of whom some characteristic trait of perhaps every true musician will remind us.

At the time when I first heard Bülow, he was considered the undisputed ruler of German orchestral music, and his authority in the interpretation of the classic symphonic literature was firmly established. The public was moreover interested in his combativeness, his capricious irritability, and his imaginative wit. Hardly any other musician enjoyed a popularity equal to his. Unfortunately, he no longer conducted very often in Berlin. Physical and mental suffering had undermined his vitality, and the number of his concerts grew less every year. I believe I was present at almost every one of the comparatively few occasions when he conducted. Thus I had the good fortune of listening to authentic interpretations of part of the classic literature and of many a valuable later work. There were, above all, the Beethoven symphonies, but also Mozart, Schumann, Schubert, Brahms, Weber, and others. As far as I remember, he no longer played Wagner, to whose service his entire former life had been devoted. But ever since the parting of the ways, when his friend had taken his wife away from him, a radical estrangement, personal as well as definitely artistic, had existed.

I do not feel justified in talking about the quality of Hans von Bülow's musical activity. I was a boy with no experience when I first met the great musician. I knew no other prominent conductors and was lacking in personal conceptions, and there were no bases for comparison. Thus I can speak only of the convincing power of his performances and — in spite of the subjectiveness of his playing, sensed even by a boy — report the inescapable impression of authenticity. At any rate, a sublime artistic purity shone from his interpretations. They were never marred by disturbing liberties. The seriousness of his musicianship and his reverential attitude toward the work would not permit that. Every individual playing of music, however, savors of the Ego, and should savor of it; and if the Ego is complex and a stormy life has deeply scarred it, even an utterly "faithful" performance will reveal the peculiarities of the interpreter's personality. Thus it is quite possible that, especially in his last years, Bülow's moods and whims occasionally went so far as to influence many a less essential detail of his performances. I heard repeated references to that subject at the time, but as for myself, I always found his performances simple and great, and felt his subjectivity merely as a personal charm and fascination. However, there is much I could report about his whimsical unpredictability, which manifested itself, if not in the music itself, in connection with it. I remember, for instance, that, before playing the Funeral March in a powerful performance of Beethoven's *"Eroica,"* he had the utterly mad idea of putting on black gloves. At the end of that, or perhaps some other performance of the same work I heard his famous utterance to the effect that, while Beethoven had crossed out the symphony's dedication to Napoleon, "we ourselves will dedicate it to Bismarck, the greatest living German." When thereupon part of the audience, perhaps because of enmity toward Bismarck, or perhaps as a protest against a political demonstration in a concert hall, began to hiss in disapproval, Bülow drew out his handkerchief and dusted his shoes with a demonstratively flourishing gesture: See, how I am shaking the Berlin dust off my feet! After that symbolic act, he quickly left the platform. I am unable to say, by the way, whether he actually declined to conduct in Berlin again after that. I am amazed to this day by his undertaking to play Beethoven's Ninth Symphony twice in succession at the same concert. It was probably meant as a rebuke aimed at a certain narrowminded part of the public, which still resented the daring features of the work. But I recall that, in spite of my respectful assent to all of my paragon's extravagances, I felt somewhat rebellious when, after the jubilation of the choral finale, the beginning of the first movement plunged me again into darkness.

As a pianist, too, Bülow occupied an important position in Germany's musical life. On his English, Russian, and American concert tours arranged by Hermann Wolff, he had succeeded in making an unparalleled impression. I remember especially his masterful

Beethoven recitals, but should like to mention nevertheless that a certain didactic element in his playing may have deprived it of some of the spontaneity manifested in his orchestral work. Yet, classic piano music was also his domain; here, too, he was a torch bearer, spreading clearness, throwing light into the depths, and kindling enthusiasm. His pianistic ability lent luster to the general conception of the reproductive musician, but musical history will nevertheless have to mention him primarily as the first great conductor. He was the founder and pioneer in a realm of musical interpretation hardly touched upon before him.

As mentioned before, I tried to form an idea also of Bülow's personality. I had heard much of the gradual waning of his power of resistance to saddening experiences. Old mental upheavals, a growing nervous irritability, and an innate Hoffmannesque whimsicality had beclouded his lofty spirituality and ethical purity. Weirdly impressed though I was at times by the oddities and unpredictabilities of his behavior, I felt impelled to probe them, searching for anecdotes illustrative of his encyclopedic knowledge, wit, and power of repartee. Many of his puns — witticisms frequently indulged in by musicians, but rarely with his pregnancy and spirit — had become famous. The following little story shows that he had at his disposal also a more profound variety of wit. Told of the venality of the critic T., whose approval could be bought by means of very moderately priced lessons, he said: "That isn't so bad; he charges such small fees that you might call him almost incorruptible." But, above all, his wit and quickness at repartee were used in support of his combative spirit, for Bülow was a *frondeur,* a fighter whose courage and love of fighting remained in evidence until his death. In his earlier years he had been fighting for the cause of Wagner, while he later championed Brahms. At every opportunity he entered the lists in behalf of genius and against whoever was hostile to his ideals. Those who wish to look into his heart would do well to read his letter to Cosima, written after the great catastrophe in his life. If a man loses what was dear to him, it is a terrible misfortune; if he is struck by disgrace, it is still more terrible. Both blows fell upon Bülow at the same time. When he discovered that his friend and his wife had deceived him, he was not only sneered at, but despised. People in Munich spread lies about him. Perhaps there were even those who believed that he had actually known of the affair and acquiesced because of the hope of professional advantages. His letter to Cosima reveals that in that epoch of deepest despair and shame he was able to reach admirable heights of understanding and forgiveness. His life was shattered, and he never recovered from the blow. But he bravely kept on living, working, and fighting, and he is entitled to a place of honor not only in the annals of music but also in the history of the human heart.

A pianistic experience of those days affected me both as a man and as an artist. My teacher, Heinrich Ehrlich, had long withdrawn from public activity. He was teaching, and writing for the *Berliner Tageblatt*. What he taught and wrote was plausible, well founded, and ingenious; but because he had not appeared as a pianist for a great many years and musically never really came out of his shell during lessons, we pupils, while admitting the sound musicianship and teaching ability of the taciturn man, considered him old, devitalized, and barren. How greatly surprised we were when the director announced one day that a special occasion was being arranged at which Professor Ehrlich would play for the students of the Conservatory Beethoven's op. 106, the *"Hammerklavier"* Sonata. The man who had settled in the frozen calm of bitter resignation because of all manner of excitement and suffering must have been driven by a violent emotional upheaval to seek refuge in his old, better self. A public controversy with the pianist Moriz Rosenthal had done considerable moral harm to his reputation and undermined his time-honored position with his paper and in the musical life of Berlin. His wife had died of cancer of the eye after years of suffering. Life around him had become empty. He wanted to find refuge in a serious and important task such as he had frequently mastered in days long gone by. He suddenly began to practice on the piano, disciplining his old stiff fingers — for the last time, probably — to give him the necessary technical service once more. The evening came, and there he sat at the piano, a small shrivelled figure with sunken, but still intellectual features. But no decay, no dryness, coolness, stiffness, or didactic tendency could stem the mighty spiritual sluice-break that evening. A strong innate musicianship, partly obliterated by professional toil, partly forgotten through lack of practice, came into its own once more, urged on by some violent distress and wafted to our ears by hands that had regained their eloquence. Deeply moved, we became reverently conscious of the magnitude of the moment. I never heard Heinrich Ehrlich play again, but the ultimate maturity of his rendition of the prodigious work left me with an ineradicable impression and the conviction that I was fortunate indeed to have had the privilege of his tuition.

While the picture of the revered old teacher and benefactor, whose newly fanned musical flame soon died down again, pales before my backward gaze, a promising youth advances, his brilliance to be recognized by the musical world. I remember well the radiant fame achieved by young Eugen d'Albert in his rapid rise. I shall never forget the Titanic force in his rendition of Beethoven's Concerto in E-flat major. I am almost tempted to say he didn't play it, that he personified it. In his intimate contact with his instrument he appeared to me like a new centaur, half piano and half man. I thought that Liszt and Rubinstein, whom I had unfortunately not been privileged to hear any more might have played thus. The performances, too, of the young pianists Moriz Rosenthal and Leopold Godowski made a fascinating impression on me by their fantastic display of brilliance and dash. But I was even more strongly impressed by a young composer-conductor whose name was Richard Strauss. I had been told that the tall, thin young man had been forced to go to Italy some years before to seek relief from a pulmonary affliction. He had come back with a symphony entitled *Aus Italien*. Hans von Bülow had liked it and had given further expression to his high opinion of Richard Strauss's creative talent by proposing to have his new work, *Tod und Verklärung* performed at a Philharmonic Concert and by inviting the composer to conduct its first Berlin performance. I was present at the performance and felt perplexingly overwhelmed by it; but in spite of the intoxicating splendor of the orchestration and the dramatic force of the conception I was excited and disturbed rather than deeply moved and uplifted. However, the impression stayed with me for a long time, and I felt convinced that I had witnessed a memorable event.

Expressions of a fundamentally different kind of youthful creativeness were coming from Italy at about that time. A prize composition launched by the Italian publishing house of Sonzogno had been responsible for presenting the theater with two new operas that gained world-wide success: Mascagni's *Cavalleria Rusticana* and Leoncavallo's *Pagliacci*. The advent of *verismo* in opera coincided curiously with the beginning of a naturalistic epoch in literature. Starving weavers and their economic problems were put on the stage by Gerhart Hauptmann; Sudermann dramatized the "stylish" front of Berlin houses and their "vulgar" rears; Wildenbruch surprised his public by a proletarian milieu; and Ibsen had forsaken the exalted sphere of *Peer Gynt, Brand,* and *Emperor and Galilean,* and gone over to the prose of the society drama in such plays as *A Doll's House* and *An Enemy of the People*. The verses of Arno Holz and Johannes Schlaf moved in a similar direction. The actors endeavored to be natural on the stage, though their naturalism bordered at times upon the ridiculous. A feeling of being surfeited with an elevated style must have been in the air at the time. Under these circumstances it was not surprising that the attempt to portray earthbound bluntness on the operatic stage, too, was gratefully received. The sudden fame of those first veristic operas was also due to the fact that they abounded in musical ideas and dramatic feeling, especially *Cavalleria Rusticana,* a hit if there ever was one.

Angelo Neumann, the director of the Prague Opera, had become famous through his daring and successful tour with Wagner's *Ring.* He had proved his skill as an impresario by the choice of his conductors: Nikisch, Mahler, and Muck, to be followed later by Bodanzki and Klemperer. Now he undertook to make capital of the sensational success of *Cavalleria Rusticana.* To fill an evening at the theater, he needed another opera. His choice — as astonishing as it was meritorious — fell on Cornelius's *Der Barbier von Bagdad,* which to my knowledge had never been performed in Berlin. Eugen Gura, an excellent singer and actor, famous also for his rendition of Loewe ballads, was engaged for the leading part.

To provide for the contingency of Gura's falling ill, Josef Arden, the highly gifted basso-buffo of the Bremen Opera was engaged. That's where I got my chance. Arden, who had studied with Jenny Meyer before my time, had heard of me. He asked me to help him study *Der Barbier von Bagdad.* That was my first opportunity to coach a professional opera singer, and when he later studied Alberich, Beckmesser, van Bett, and other roles with me, I actually felt as if I were almost an operatic conductor.

The Cornelius opera wholly won my heart and has had a secure place in it to this day. What other *opéra-comique* can compare with its lovely melodic charm, its characteristic humor, and its wealth of musical ideas? What work with a fairy-tale background is more fragrantly flavored with the spirit of the Arabian Nights or more aptly portrays their atmosphere than that of Cornelius?

Peter Cornelius, though a friend and disciple of Wagner, was musically and spiritually influenced by Schumann's romanticism. His poetic inclinations were dominated by Eastern poetry and the linguistic art of Rückert. I count him among the most eminent post-Wagnerites. Had he lived before Wagner, his noble talent might have opened the gates of the world to him. The dramatic tempest unleashed by the Titan drowned out his gentler voice. He was vouchsafed at least a great posthumous success in Germany. I was able to keep his charming humorous-romantic work on the repertory of the operahouses at which I was active, but I was fortunate of course in having Richard Mayr in Vienna and Paul Bender in Munich at my disposal for the role of Abu Hassan.

Angelo Neumann's Berlin enterprise was a great success. The performances under the musical direction of Muck were excellent.

Cavalleria was enthusiastically acclaimed. I, too, was strongly impressed by its dauntlessness and its fiery musical eloquence. *Der Barbier von Bagdad* had won a great many hearts. Opera houses blessed with gifted bassos were beginning to include it in their regular repertory.

As for literary nourishment, I had long before given up my reading mania and turned to a well-ordered and more profound cultivation of authors I loved. Thus I had at last found my way to Goethe, whose *Wilhelm Meister* and *Dichtung und Wahrheit* had implanted in me a passionate desire for self-education and for the systematic development of my talents. I was hoping fervently that this desire might soon bear fruit. True, I did not as yet know what steps to take, but a seed had found its way into my mind and a direction had been indicated to me.

It is understandable that I lost myself completely in *Faust* for a considerable time and that, as a consequence, I turned to philosophical subjects for the first time. I had managed to procure Windelband's *History of Philosophy,* and though the Greek philosophers' systems, of which the author gave me concise excerpts, were still beyond my power of conception, they opened the world of philosophic thinking for me and awakened within me an interest in their problems. I soon exchanged the history for philosophy itself and daringly approached Kant's *Critique of Pure Reason.* Without going into detail, I mention this here because Kant's philosophic idealism had a powerful effect not only on my thinking but also on my life, a fact that will be referred to later. Although I did not share the fate of the poet Heinrich von Kleist, whom Kant's theories of time and space had almost driven to suicide, the waning of my cosmic conceptions under the influence of Kant deeply disturbed me in the course of time and effected a lasting change in the fundamental mood of my soul.

In 1891 or 1892 I was the recipient of a Bayreuth *stipendium* entitling me to a free trip to Bayreuth and admission to three performances at the Festspielhaus. I am no more sure of the year than I am of the cause of this mark of honor. The conservatories were probably given these *stipendia* and asked to distribute them. I was chosen because of either my general work or my choral composition with orchestra based upon Goethe's *Calm Seas and Prosperous Voyage* — Mendelssohn's purely orchestral composition of the same name was also inspired by that poem — which I had been permitted to conduct with our own chorus and the Berlin Philharmonic Orchestra at one of the Conservatory's public examinations. According to my later judgment, the composition was wholly lacking in originality, though it was rather effective and well orchestrated. At any rate, it had given me the first opportunity for a public display of my skill as a conductor.

I am still at a loss to understand why Bayreuth should have placed a *stipendium* at the disposal of an institute that, to state it mildly, had never shown much interest in Wagner, or why the Conservatory should have abetted so infernal a seduction. But the miracle did happen, and one morning — for the first time all alone — I left the parental home and Berlin and rode straight into adventure. I arrived in hallowed Bayreuth in the evening. There stood the Festspielhaus on the hill. People crowded the streets, a Babel of voices beat against my ear — it was all one big magic garden of Klingsor in which I wandered about, delighted and stunned. But there was a heavy burden oppressing the soul of the "pure fool." I still had no place to spend the night, and though I knew entire scenes from Goethe's *Faust* almost by heart and consorted with Kant's ideas, I had not as yet attained enough spiritual maturity personally to approach a hotel manager or a rooming-house keeper. I was as shy and unsure of myself as any fifteen-year-old among grownups, and the fact that I finally forced myself to pull the bell of an ugly house and apply for the vacancy proclaimed by a sign was a moral accomplishment of about the same magnitude as my dive into Wilmersdorf Lake on a former day. The attitude of the fat Bavarian woman in charge and the airless room with its window facing the landing were exactly what inexperience and shyness might have expected of the rough world. I remember that at the sight of the house's interior and its keeper Mignon's words came to my mind: "There dwells in caves the dragon's savage brood." But never mind the dragon! Never mind the cave! The day and the evening belonged to me. I prowled around the Villa Wahnfried, stood at Wagner's grave, watched the impressive line of carriages approaching the hill — Cosima and her children were in one of the vehicles — and finally found myself in the Festspielhaus. Out of the darkness and the "mystic abyss" softly rose the Supper Theme. How wonderful, how unforgettable it was, how unspeakably moved and happy I was! I heard *Parsifal* and *Tristan* under Hermann Levi's direction, and, unless I am mistaken, *Der fliegende Holländer* under Felix Mottl. I returned to Berlin, deeply attached to the world of Wagner and confirmed in my serious intentions and the rooted belief in my own artistic mission.

I was now all the more diligent in my endeavors to broaden my musical education. Neither classic composers, nor romanticists, nor Wagner, close though they were to my heart, could stop me from impartially adding to my knowledge. I studied with interest German, Italian, French, and Russian operas as well as symphonic music of every kind, played and practiced the piano with insatiable and enthusiastic devotion, familiarizing myself with its extensive literature and penetrating even into the realm of the virtuoso. I also played Liszt Rhapsodies and others of his brilliant piano pieces, but my pianistic — and musical — affection was naturally centered upon the older classic composers and the works of Schumann, Chopin, and Brahms. Among my favorite compositions were Schumann's Sonatas, *Carnaval,* and *Symphonic Etudes,* Chopin's F-minor Fantasy and Sonata in B-minor, and Brahms's Ballads and F-minor Sonata. I spent hours of violent agitation at the piano. There were times when I felt restrained within my own limitations by the magnitude of the creative artists; times when I was filled with bliss by a feeling of affinity with those exalted friends. This latter was especially the case when I became "enthralled" by Schumann's C-major Fantasy and through it gained a profound insight into the composer's soul. Even today, that composition is dear to me; even today, I am able to find among Schumann's songs the most intoxicating blossoms of musical lyricism, especially among the compositions based upon Eichendorff's poems. What a mysterious affinity of souls between the musician and the poet! Are not Eichendorff's poems Schumann music put into words, and is not Schumann's whole creative work fragrant with Eichendorff's poetry? Schubert, too, had in the meantime become my mental property. Not only had his songs sung their way into my soul, but his instrumental melodies made me conscious of a very particular kind of floating blissfulness, such as no other composer's inspiration was able to impart. Those were the days, too, when I laid the foundation of my life-long attachment to Beethoven's *Missa Solemnis.* It is gratifying to recall that in spite of my immaturity this masterwork among masterworks spoke to me at once as with a prophet's voice. Mozart only, who was later so thoroughly to dominate me and fill me with a blissful happiness, was still somewhat alien to me. I was still unable to sense the seriousness in his charm, the loftiness in his beauty.

What was I to do to bring about a realization of my desire to become an operatic conductor? There were any number of theatrical agencies in Berlin but, from all I had heard, they were interested mainly in singers. Directors of court and municipal theaters called on them and gave auditions to young singers, engaging those they liked. It was not uncommon for me to be present on such occasions, for some of the fledgling nightingales — or less melodious fowl — from Jenny Meyer's class would ask me to accompany their warblings. I was especially pleased if in that way I was able to give at least musical expression to one of my frequent romantic fancies — as fervent as they were shy and unspoken — for a future poetic Agathe or a charming Susanna. But though there were instances when a manager or director would show interest in the expert accompanist, and though Herr Drenker, the head of the agency, used to say when introducing me that "the young man is the pride of my office," there never seemed to be an opening for me. There was nobody to do anything in my behalf, and I considered it undignified to offer my services.

Then it happened that Robert Radeke, my old benefactor, left the Stern Conservatory for reasons unknown to me. His place was taken by Arno Kleffel who, up to that time, had been the leading conductor at the Cologne Opera, and whose services had been greatly appreciated there. I presume that he was my teacher in composition and in the various departments of the conductors' class during my last year at the Conservatory, but he soon acted as adviser rather than as teacher of his greatly advanced pupil. I have but a faint memory of that time. I know that I was "professionally" active on a number of occasions, giving piano lessons, coaching singers, and going on small concert tours. In addition, I did some composing, guided by the advice of Kleffel. Secretly, however, I was working on an opera, *Agnes Bernauer,* based upon Hebbel's tragedy, which a young man of my acquaintance, whose literary ambition rather exceeded his talent, had worked into a libretto. I believe that I managed to finish two acts and that certain details of the third act were sketched. While the score contained a few pretty lyric episodes, the whole thing was thoroughly immature and, strange to say, quite un-Wagnerian.

Kleffel was interested in me and seriously discussed with me my future. He was definitely in favor of a career as an operatic conductor, and I heaved a sigh of relief when he said that he didn't see why my youth should prevent me from making a start. He furnished an active proof of his confidence in my ability by writing a very detailed letter to the management of the Cologne Opera, recommending me highly as a coach. The incredible and hardly hoped for happened. Director Hofmann, the head of the Opera, sent me a contract which bound me to the Municipal Opera of Cologne for one season, beginning on September 1, 1893, at a monthly salary of one hundred marks.

Thus ended the first phase of my apprenticeship. I looked forward with hope and confidence to the next phase — my first professional activity. I wanted, as Eichendorff said, "to accomplish things in the world," and while there was no doubt about my good intentions and the high goal I had set for myself, my ability had still to stand the actual test of practical use.

Theme and Variations

The world was still at peace. It was one of those epochs of which Jacob Burckhardt wrote in his *Force and Freedom (Weltgeschichtliche Betrachtungen)* that just as there were preëminently political and preëminently religious epochs, there were those, too, "which seem to live particularly for the sake of cultural purposes." My youthful years, described in these pages, were spent in one of the "cultural" periods. I remember that a sense of duty made me read the political sections of the newspapers, though my guileless mind was hardly interested in them. But I devoured anything that appeared in the sections devoted to the realm of the intellect. It was there that I one day read a scornful criticism of Gustav Mahler's First Symphony. It aroused my desire to become acquainted with that eccentric work and its daring author, a desire fate was later to fulfill most abundantly. In the meantime, a certain change of key in the world of politics — a change to the minor — might have been dimly foreseen. The brusque dismissal of Bismarck in 1890, and some of the other actions and speeches of the young Emperor began to cause unrest and anxiety in Germany as well as abroad. Faint sheet-lightning on the horizon indicated a coming atmospheric disturbance.

BOOK TWO

I

THE *German Stage Almanac* appeared every year. It contained a list of all the country's court and municipal theaters and stated the names of the people connected with them. It furnished an imposing picture of the extent and importance of theatrical life in the Germany of those days. Regular performances were given in almost all towns, large, small, and even smallest. In the smaller ones, the performances were generally confined to plays, but there was an astonishingly large number of small towns cultivating opera, or at least operetta. The fact that towns like Rostock, Oldenburg, and Trier had opera houses and that concert-life was flourishing there gives one an interesting idea of the spiritual attitude of those times.

To be sure, the register also listed quite a number of so-called *Schmieren,* low theaters which in their comical wretchedness surpassed even Mr. Crummles's group of strolling players in *Nicholas Nickleby.* I remember, when leafing the pages of the *Almanac,* having come across a little theater — it was in a small Bavarian town, if I am not mistaken — whose director, cashier, actors, and technical employees, with but two exceptions, all bore the name of Piltz, indicating that a single family administered the theater, put up the scenery, and portrayed kings and beggars, lovers and villains, tragic rôles and comic ones. At that, they probably led a jolly, though rather poor life. I loved to scan the dry lists and try to visualize the proud picture of the mighty Royal Theaters, with the general manager resplendent in a court uniform, the staff of officials, the famous singers and actors, the large orchestras and choruses, and then, in contrast, to imagine the theater of the Piltzes, where the director-cashier had to rush off to the dressing room at a bell signal from the *Frau Direktor,* so that, majestically costumed and made up, he might ring up the curtain, shake the thunder apparatus, and declaim with rolling r's Schiller's verses on the stage, while his wife, sons, daughters, cousins, and relatives, to say nothing of the two wretched outsiders, similarly lent a helping hand between pathos on stage and work off it, in an effort to conjure up before their Bavarian audience the illusion of a higher existence. And yet I felt that the anachronistic Director Piltz and his Bavarian group of strolling players belonged in the same category as the entirely up-to-date General Director Count Seebach of the Dresden Court Theater; that the *Almanac*, by its printed contiguity, had brought a long historical development down to its lowest common denominator. I was made happy by the thought that, someday perhaps, I might usefully employ my own efforts on behalf of a further continuation of that historical line.

So there was on the one side the considerable number of small theaters with their touching and comical conditions, dimly indicated in the lists of the *Almanac,* and on the other the luxurious and dramatic stages of Berlin, Vienna, Dresden, and Munich. More eloquent, however, of the powerful share of the theater in the nation's cultural life was the large number of stages in towns of middle size. There were such court theaters as those of Stuttgart, Karlsruhe, Mannheim, Wiesbaden, and Hannover, and the somewhat smaller court stages of Weimar, Meiningen, Darmstadt, Altenburg, and Schwerin; there were, moreover, the leading municipal theaters of Hamburg, Frankfurt am Main, Leipzig, Cologne, Breslau, Düsseldorf, and Bremen; the less important, but by no means negligible theaters in Nürnberg, Kassel, Königsberg, Danzig; and a great many others. Every one of them had an honorable past, whose well recorded history testified to valuable contributions toward the national total of theatrical accomplishment. The bulky volume of the *Stage Almanac* thus demonstrated the genuine popularity of the theater among the various social strata of the nation, for such large numbers of theaters, in so many towns and cities, could exist only if they satisfied a genuine popular need. They were able to have a powerful influence on the public only because they corresponded to its spiritual hunger as well as its cultural level. In the larger towns, opera and drama were cultivated either in separate houses or on the same stage, alternating with each other. In Munich, where I was director for ten years, operatic performances were given in three theaters: the National Theater, where Wagner and "grand opera" were played; the Residenz Theater, devoted to Mozart and suitable works by other composers; and the Prince Regent Theater, which had originally been planned only for the summer Wagner festivals, but was later used also for other performances. As a rule, the drama had its home at the Residenz Theater, while the National Theater was the scene of operatic performances. Once or twice a week, though, there was an exchange. Frankfurt had a repertory opera house of its own and a playhouse with an equally varied daily program. Similar conditions prevailed in Stuttgart. In addition to the court and municipal theaters, every sizable town had a number of individually owned so-called private theaters. They were either dramatic repertoire stages or given to the performance of operettas. In many of the medium and smaller theaters both operas and operettas were performed. Special casts were frequently maintained for the latter genre, though a performer had occasionally to be borrowed from the operatic personnel. The smallest theaters probably played six or seven months a year, while the season of the large ones usually lasted ten months or more. There was a daily change of performances. German, French, Italian, and Russian operas were staged. The dramatic repertoires were similarly varied.

General managers administered the theaters as the representative of the Court. At the time when I joined the stage, the directors were for the most part individuals who leased the theater from the city. This type gradually disappeared; the cities appointed a board, which chose a director or manager. Neither courts nor cities ever expected their theaters to show a profit or even to be self-supporting. The financial administration set aside a certain sum to cover the unavoidable deficit. It was one of the manager's or director's tasks to make this sum do, or to justify an occasional overdraft. At any rate, the princes and city administrations considered it their matter-of-course duty to make financial sacrifices for the sake of the cultivation of art, and even in the days of the lessee the town administration frequently helped matters along by making no charge for lighting or for the use of city-owned costumes and scenery.

An inside view reveals the fact that the German theater of that epoch stressed the accomplishments of individual artists of talent and ability rather than ensemble art. The day had not yet come when stage directors and conductors welded groups of artists into a harmonious whole in support of the work. The actors or singers were still supreme. As late as 1901, the programs of the Vienna Court Opera stated the names of the singers in any given performance, but not the name of the conductor, a fact that clearly demonstrated the assumed superiority of individual performances to ensemble art; and this in spite of the fact that in the year when I started my activity at the Vienna Court Opera its leading conductors were Hans Richter and Gustav Mahler.

The theatrical development that I experienced and in which I was permitted to collaborate led from brilliance to seriousness, from virtuosity to art, from performances in which individual artists tried to draw from their parts whatever effects they would yield to those in which all forces were subordinated to a universal intention inspired by the work itself, the governing idea being the enthronement of the author or the composer in the realm of the theater. The administrators of the works of art — the stage director of a play, the stage director and conductor of an opera — wanted to secure for the creative artist the ruling position that was legitimately his due, but which had been usurped by re-creative performers. The latter were to be shown gently but firmly that they must recognize a more justifiable order of rank.

The stage is the hunting ground of the re-creative artist, and who will begrudge him his triumphs or to fail to enjoy his freedom and the occasional trespasses springing from an inspired gift of representation? The best method of theatrical guidance is surely not the restriction and subordination of exuberantly gifted artists, but rather their coördination and adjustment. There have been splendid examples to prove that a great dramatic or musico-dramatic work of art may be produced by means of a well-balanced joint execution in which all individual performances become effective with the appearance of utter freedom and spontaneity. The way to such a goal was more difficult and complicated in operatic performances than in dramatic ones. In the latter, the relation between leadership and cast was simple and natural. There was one man to lead and take charge of the rehearsals: the stage director. The cast was chosen with an eye to individual representative talent, adaptability to a certain part, linguistic technique, suitable appearance, and so on. Thus, on the dramatic stage, the development of ensemble art had to overcome no fundamental obstacles. Nothing stood in the way of the regisseur who had a superior conception of his task, who was able to penetrate deeply into the spirit of the plays, and who had learned how to inculcate his will upon the actors.

Matters were different in opera. How much more complicated the relation between leadership and cast, and how one-sided and unsatisfactory the principle underlying the engagement of singers! Instead of a single person, there were two to conduct the rehearsals: the regisseur and the musical director. This very fact makes obvious the difficulty in the way of an effective method of work; indeed, it seems to make even the possibility of such a method questionable. Moreover, a one-sided and unnatural principle governed the engagement of singers. Following the famous example of Montecucculi, who considered three things essential for the conduct of war: money, money, and again money, the men in charge of opera, and the public too, demanded voice, voice, and again voice. They were quite ready to overlook a lack of acting ability, an unfavorable stage appearance, and even the absence of musical talent. This one-sided overvaluation of the voice was a constant threat to the conductor, for he could not put on a satisfactory performance with a merely vocal display and without the finer shadings of musicality; it was bound utterly to defeat the stage director, whose success depended largely on the singers' acting ability. It is obvious, therefore, that opera was a long way from unified, musico-dramatic ensemble art and that serious fundamental obstacles stood in the way of its development.

While this emphasis on the vocal principle had so unfavorable an effect on the artistic management of opera houses, exceptional personalities were nevertheless able to cover up many shortcomings. Theatrical directors whose instinct, good fortune, or superior feeling for art enabled them to find singers gifted both vocally and histrionically, and singers who by their own effort were able to do justice to the vocal as well as the dramatic requirements of their parts, lent luster to opera. The hearts of the audience were captivated by the brilliant performances of great singers, but the general application of faulty principles still militated against a full appreciation of the intrinsic value of the operas themselves. In fact, opera could never have survived had it not been for the fascination emanating from strong artistic personalities endowed with musical and dramatic talent and with magnificent voices. The occupants of orchestra stalls as well as the gallery gods realized that *Der Freischütz*, let us say, could never be performed like a concert and that Weber's music lost its sense unless Kaspar was a demonic villain, Agathe a loving bride, Ännchen a merry and good-natured creature, and unless the three of them did more than merely sing their arias and ensemble numbers correctly.

Even the most excellent individual accomplishments, however, could not make the more cultivated part of the audience forget the weakness and colorlessness of the performance as a whole, and the broad masses, too, were dimly aware of essential deficiencies. Opera as a work of art was not taken seriously. The prevailing mixture of strangely balanced styles was readily accepted. People were satisfied if occasionally there were fine singing and temperamental playing of music; grateful for some particularly successful histrionic or scenic accomplishment; and almost indifferent to the general incompetence in acting and to dramatic senselessness. After all, it was "only opera."

Of the two generals who had jointly to plan and carry into effect the strategic action, the conductor was in a considerably more favorable position. The voice, for the sake of which the singer had been engaged, was after all a musical instrument, and its use came within his domain. But what could the stage director do with it if its owner was lacking in other artistic qualifications? The vitalization and inspiriting of stage events, matters which the regisseur had to see to, depended on talents that were given little or no thought when singers were being engaged. The director was therefore often compelled to try to realize his dramatic ideas — provided he had any — with singers who, try as they might, were unable to do what was asked of them. Frequently, too, when it came to casting an opera, he had to forego the use of an efficient actor-singer in favor of one with more ample vocal material. There were singers who could not or would not do some effective piece of acting for reasons of breath control or tone production. If, in addition, the difficulties in making chorus scenes dramatically credible are considered, it will be understood that stage directors were inclined to envy Sisyphus the easy job fate had imposed on him. No wonder, then, that there were hardly any operatic stage directors who took their work seriously, or that those who did soon changed. Aging singers whose vocal faculties had declined switched over to directing. If their own distinguished past had left within them some superior artistic conceptions and desires, they were able at best to give acting hints to talented and ambitious singers or occasionally to realize some idea of staging. But if they wished to avoid becoming all too unhappy and bitter, they had above all to gain mastery of the art of opera directing, nine-tenths of which consisted in "doing without." Those aging singers, on the other hand, who were not burdened by reminders of an artistic past or whose directing was not inspired by ambition, were satisfied to employ methods that had gradually become a firmly rooted tradition. They saw to it that the singers came on stage or left it at the proper place, they arranged the prescribed action in accordance with the libretto — or occasionally deviated from or ran counter to it — they shouted at the chorus, treated modest artists roughly and immodest ones politely, and let things generally run their course. At all events, however, they were at loggerheads with the conductor. There was still another type of operatic regisseur. He came from the dramatic stage and was frequently able to make a singer understand some of the finer points of acting; but he was bound to fail in his attempt to apply methods of the dramatic stage to opera, whose arias and ensemble numbers, whose vocal difficulties, and whose musical peculiarities demanded entirely different principles of stage direction.

A decided change for the better was gradually brought about by Bayreuth, where Wagner had created a new style of operatic interpretation, watched over and continued by Cosima and her aides. The Bayreuth example had a vitalizing and instructive effect on opera in Germany. Wagner performances were benefitted first and foremost, but not exclusively, for singers and directors were made aware of a new way leading generally toward a deeper dramatic seriousness. Later, when Gustav Mahler was at the head of the Vienna Court Opera, higher operatic aims were introduced there. Mahler's deeds and suggestions fruitfully influenced the activities of directors and conductors of other stages. A new generation of them was inspired by his example. As for myself, I believe that I contributed to the best of my ability — in Munich as well as in Berlin, in Salzburg as well as in Vienna — to a further development and increased use of those re-creative principles on the operatic stage.

II

I LEFT Berlin at the end of August 1893. Accompanied by my parents' wishes and anxious thoughts, I started on my travels. They led me first to "ancient sacred Cologne," immortalized by Heine and Schumann in the *Dichterliebe*. From the mighty span of the bridge over the Rhine, across which my train was carrying me, I beheld the Cathedral and was captivated by it. Without unpacking, I hurried from the furnished room I had hired back to Cathedral Square, to face the gigantic edifice and submit to its overwhelming effect. I had never before seen a Gothic building; now Gothic art entered my life. Deeply stirred, I succumbed to the magnitude of the impression. I wandered around the structure and finally entered the solemn dusk of its interior — a forest of stone, so it seemed to me. I told myself with growing consternation that I would never be able fully to comprehend that sublime and varied mystery of forms, and I promised myself to submit to its influence every day, childishly confident that, as I could not rise up to the spirit of the wonderful edifice, it would condescend toward me. I soon realized that I had succumbed not so much to the wealth and expressive power of the language of Gothic forms, which I gradually came to see more clearly and to understand, as to the simultaneousness with which the gigantic edifice assailed the eye and the soul. The wonders of music and poetry affected me differently. To be sure, they, too, were full of the creative secret; but not only did I feel that the essence of music was disclosed to me and that I was able to live in the world of Shakespeare, but music and poetry were more accommodating, as it were, in that they progressed with time, whereas architecture's ponderous existence in space overwhelmed my capacity of perception. My musicianship was of course to blame for the distress I felt, for my eyes had not been attuned to seeing as my ears had to hearing. The poet Siegfried Lipiner, of whom I shall speak later, once told me, when referring to art, that one's attitude toward its great works should be similar to that prescribed by the court ceremonial for intercourse with persons of princely rank: don't speak; wait until they speak to you. That was instinctively my attitude toward Cologne Cathedral. I believe that throughout my stay in Cologne I paid it daily, or almost daily visits, at times even nightly ones. Gradually it unbent to my silent contemplation, but, like every other Gothic structure, it always impressed me by its severe aloofness. In spite of the friendly, even good-natured, grimaces of certain ornaments, it seemed to be turned toward heaven rather than toward man.

"De Dom, de Rhing un' dat köl'sche Wasser!" That was how in the attractive Low German of Cologne the charms of the city were summed up. The second of these charms, the much-sung Rhine, did not come up to my expectations. The broad quiet stream flowing past Cologne reminded one in no detail of the lively young mountain river rushing through Switzerland, to say nothing of the "raging demigod" in Hölderlin's poem. It had no doubt spent the last of its fierceness in the magnificent Falls of Schaffhausen. Far behind, too, lay the dreamy romanticism of the mountains and castles mirrored in its waters, and the singing of the Lorelei no longer mingled with the rushing sound of the stream. On the other hand, it had not as yet attained the majestic breadth with which it approaches the sea in Holland. Here, at Cologne, the Rhine was serious, efficient, and industrious. It carried freighters and excursion steamers, it served and worked; and though I liked to look at it from the bank or from a bridge, my attitude toward it was largely one of indifference. As for the city's third charm, Cologne Water, which the popular saying so unfeelingly mentioned in the same breath with the Cathedral and the Rhine, I was most favorably impressed by the place from which it spread its fragrance, the pretty Jülichsplatz, the home of the *eau de Cologne*. I tarried there occasionally on my rovings through the narrow streets and wide squares of the old city, past its innumerable differently-styled churches, and across its crowded market places. I was struck ever more forcibly by the startling difference between Protestant, historically uninteresting Berlin and Catholic Cologne, pregnant with history, whose peculiar attraction grew upon me in the course of my tireless ramblings.

On the morning after my arrival, I went to the old Municipal Theater — the magnificent Cologne Opera had not as yet come into existence — to make my introductory bow. It was wonderfully exciting to be privileged for the first time to enter a theater by its stage door. In the office, I recognized with interest several singers whose professional pictures I had studied in the windows of a bookstore the evening before. I had the gratifying feeling of being a fellow-artist. Director Hofmann received me pleasantly, referring in a few nice words to the favorable things Kleffel had written about me. His frank friendliness, so reassuring to the newcomer, never varied throughout the season. True, there never was any close association between us, but then, how could a young coach expect anything but casual friendliness from the head of the theater? There were occasions, nevertheless, that plainly proved his confidence in my ability and sound judgment. His wife, an imposing brunette whose very appearance suggested a fine rich contralto — throughout my life, similar first impressions have rarely deceived me — displayed a greater warmth of understanding on the few occasions when we met in the course of my Cologne engagement. Twenty years later, when I was General Musical Director of Bavaria, I met her again in Munich, where she taught singing. She told me how proud her husband had been of having "discovered" me, that he had from the first prophesied that I would go far as a conductor, and that she could clearly remember the disturbing impression my mixture of sensitiveness, enthusiasm, and shyness had made on her.

Hofmann was a born impresario. He had the gift of discovering talented artists, of placing and exploiting them. In my time, to be sure, the outstanding singers among the artistic personnel were few: Charlotte Huhn, a contralto of exceptional caliber, Baptist Hoffmann, a powerfully voiced baritone, and Meta Kalman, a charming soubrette. Hofmann's great discovery had been the tenor Emil Götze, a singer with a fine stage presence and a really magnificent voice. At the time when I was in Cologne, he appeared only occasionally as a guest artist, but he was still the public's idol. I have a vivid recollection of his Lohengrin, who actually seemed to come "from bliss and splendor." It was said that Hofmann had made a fortune through his contract with Emil Götze, but had squandered it by rather recklessly enjoying life's pleasures. A man of medium height, stoutish, with a wine drinker's reddish face from which gazed a pair of merry blue eyes, he was a sympathetic epicurean, remarkable for his theatrical enthusiasm, his genuine enjoyment of talent in others, and his optimistic, enterprising spirit. Cologne surely owes him a debt of gratitude for his operatic leadership.

The conductors, at my time, were Wilhelm Karl Mühldorfer, whom I recall as a capable *routinier,* and Josef Grossmann, a young, gifted, and temperamental Viennese who, however, seemed to be lacking in seriousness and weight. At any rate, his performances of the *Ring* so satisfied my fervent Wagner enthusiasm that he could have made me his staunch adherent, had he cared to do so. Unfortunately he was not interested in me, and he displayed toward me the intimidating manner of a superior. But what was the conductor's thinly disguised, though mild, antipathy compared to the roughly despotic unmannerliness and coarse incivility of Chief Stage Director O.? I can still see myself high above the stage, perched on the organ bench to which I had to climb by using a kind of iron ship's ladder. I was to play the organ accompaniment to the Intermezzo from *Cavalleria Rusticana*. And there was my enemy, a rather uncultured, gigantic fat man of about sixty, pantingly dragging his weight up a wooden structure. A small baton in his big fist, he was beating the time which, through a hole in the wing, he took from the conductor. When he saw how smoothly I did my job, he felt impelled, when climbing down, to give expression to his disappointment by a disdainful grunt. I had no difficulty in understanding the metaphysical cause of his antipathy and his craving to express it. That I was a good musician and an optimist, and considered beautiful things beautiful, might have been bearable to this dweller in a rawer spiritual region, but together with my youth these qualities assumed the proportions of an insult. Ah, that youth of mine! It seemed as if I could see all about me the features of Steerforth's man Littimer, whose every word and look said to the intimidated David Copperfield: "You are very young, sir! You are exceedingly young!" The director and the conductors, the singers and office employees, the stage directors and stagehands, even the waiters in the restaurants and the railway porters — they all had the manner which plainly said: "You are very young! You are exceedingly young!"

The boorish type, still frequently in evidence in those days of despotic managers, stage directors, and conductors, has gradually disappeared in the course of years, and so has despotism. The contracts entered into at that time gave the directors the one-sided right to terminate them after the first year. Only prominent artists were able to have this paragraph struck out or to insist upon the mutual right to terminate the contract. There were even contracts that gave the director the right of dismissal within the first four weeks of a season. I often witnessed with dismay and pity the despair of those who had been so summarily discharged. It may easily be imagined what chances of despotism and rudeness these conditions offered, and how they led to presumptuous arrogance on the one side and to suffering and servility on the other. I mentioned before that the principle of leasing a theater was gradually abolished in favor of appointing a director who was responsible either to the city or to the theater's administrative department. His rights, similar to those of a court theater's general manager, were so clearly circumscribed that many incentives for despotic excesses of authority were removed. The Union of Members of German Theaters succeeded in abolishing the four-weeks dismissal clause and in having the mutual right of notice embodied in theatrical contracts. These facts and the considerable increase in the minimum wages paid to soloists, orchestra players, chorus members, and stagehands were gratifying proof of the German theater's social and economic advancement which was aided considerably by the helpful attitude of the corporation of general managers and directors, the Stage Association.

When, at the start of my Cologne engagement, I entered the world of the theater, I was a wholly innocent and inexperienced young musician of seventeen looking forward to wonderful experiences in its adventurous fairyland and to a glorious solution of all the allotted tasks, but who at the same time was humbly determined to carry out his duties to the very best of his ability. In the chaos of new impressions and situations, I had no opportunity to compare my youthful dreams with the prosaic activity into which I had been plunged. There would be an ensemble rehearsal of *Il Trovatore* in the morning; in the midst of it, I might be summoned by the stage manager to conduct the backstage trumpets at an orchestra rehearsal of *Lohengrin;* in the afternoon, I would have to rehearse a soprano cast for the Forest Bird in *Siegfried;* a *Freischütz* rehearsal with Agathe and Ännchen would follow; then I would have to test the voice of a young woman so that I could tell the director whether she was able to sing the shepherd boy in *Tannhäuser;* the score of a new opera was under my arm, for the director wished to have a report about the work within two weeks; I had to play the organ in a performance of *Cavalleria;* a chorus lady was standing in the wings awaiting my sign for the scream that would announce the death of Turiddu. This very appearance of confusion had a steadying effect on me in the whirling strangeness of my new surroundings, for whenever music was involved I was professionally sure of myself. I felt amateurishly unsure only in connection with the many personal contacts brought about by my work. However, my unconquerable shyness has never really hampered or harmed me seriously in my professional activities. Even in that critical early period I managed to assert myself artistically. Soon after entering on my duties, for example, I had to rehearse the first act of *Die Meistersinger* with a number of soloists. Every time I corrected a false note or a rhythmical inexactness, or called attention to one of Wagner's dynamic instructions, I could feel the singers' dissatisfaction and restlessness grow, until the Pogner said to me: "Young man, you are dealing with mature artists. Don't give us any instructions, and never mind your corrections" — or words to that effect. To my surprise I heard myself reply quietly and without shyness that it was my duty to correct musical mistakes and inexactnesses; I would have to continue to do so, and I begged him not to make things difficult for me. Well, I had my way and kept up my energetic rehearsing. I was even buoyed up emotionally by the resistance I had experienced. At the end of the rehearsal, my former antagonist, a rather mediocre singer, threw his arms about me and assured me of his and his colleagues' utmost approbation. From that moment, I was on the best of terms with the artists. I had the impression that in that quarter even my youth had been forgiven. Soon there was quite a number of singers, especially among the younger ones, who asked me to rehearse with them. I was filled with satisfaction and hope by my ability to make myself useful. The fact that I did not approach the singing parts purely from the standpoint of the conductor, but from that of the singer and of singing gained me the approval and loyalty of the soloists. I had early adopted the habit of demonstrating by my own singing how the thing ought to be done. I never demanded of the singers what lay beyond their vocal possibilities, but I did demand everything that lay within their power, and insisted that they do justice to their parts musically and dramatically.

The fact of my friendly relations with the majority of the singers was to prove a source of aggravation and dissatisfaction to me. The details I had worked out with them and the intensity of expression I had developed disappeared at the stage rehearsals and performances because of the conductor's excessively fast tempi, crumbled because of his dragging the music, or were rendered ineffective by the stage director's instructions. I began to suffer from the dramatic and musical indifference of the performances and from my powerlessness against the prevailing spirit of routine. As far as I can remember, by the way, the vocal and dramatic parts of the performances under Grossmann were more seriously affected by lassitude than the orchestral part, which frequently impressed me quite strongly. I can still see myself backstage, stirred to my very depths by the funeral music from *Götterdämmerung,* whose overwhelming floods of sound came up to me from the orchestra pit while stagehands were rushing about and I was standing at the side of a horn player waiting to give him his cue.

All the sufferings and joys of my existence as a coach were forgotten, however, when I listened to the performances from the artists' box. Let me say here a brief, heartfelt word of praise of that artistic and humane arrangement, universally adopted by the largest court theaters as well as by the smallest municipal theaters. It was humane because it represented an act of kindness toward the artists of the house without offering any advantage to the management — with sold-out houses, the two reserved boxes meant even a loss — and it was artistically valuable because if presented to younger members of the staff opportunities to gain experience through the performances of mature artists, to learn the works in their entirety, and generally to familiarize themselves with the spirit of the theater. Every theater had two of these reserved boxes, one for women and one for men, usually on opposite sides of the house. There were times when Eros would succeed in distracting the stageward gaze and turning it seductively toward a charming vis-à-vis. But on the whole, and during the many years of my eager use of that pleasant institution, I derived a great deal of satisfaction from the serious interest with which the younger artists, and some of the older ones too, watched, studied, and discussed the performances.

My own interest was by no means confined to operatic performances, though I was always in attendance unless I was needed backstage. I enjoyed and watched with meticulous attention also the excellent and spirited dramatic performances that alternated regularly with opera. Occasionally there were interesting dramatic guest appearances, two of which deeply impressed themselves upon my memory: those of Adolph Sonnenthal and Friedrich Mitterwurzer. I saw the former as Wallenstein in Schiller's *Wallenstein's Death,* and was struck by the nobility of his bearing and by an elocutionary art such as I had not previously encountered. I was moreover aware that the great artist represented Europe's most exalted dramatic tradition, that of the Vienna Burgtheater. That was my first, rather indirect, contact with Vienna, but I rejoice to this day in the knowledge that even then that message of an old culture struck a familiar chord within me and kept it sounding. Mitterwurzer, to be sure, represented no tradition; or rather he did: that of genius. I found in him a new type of actor, a Proteus. I saw him, too, in the part of Wallenstein, in that of Mephisto, in a Bendix comedy whose name escapes me (I think it was called *A Comedy*), and as Striese, the theatrical director, in *The Rape of the Sabine Women.* It would have been impossible to recognize the same man in the four parts. He was a fundamentally different person in each instance, representing in his every gesture, tone, and attitude nothing but the character he was portraying. It was a complete change

of personality, achieved, so it seemed, not through the putting together of individual features, but through a single act of being
transformed into a clearly defined and profoundly conceived person. For the first time in my life, I had come in contact with the
mysterious ability to be *I* and *you* at the same time, an ability upon
which is based all artistic interpretation, especially in music.

Hofmann had gradually gained a favorable opinion of my abilities. He began to assign me tasks at the conductor's desk that, while
they would have been below the dignity of a regular operatic conductor, could well be demanded of a young coach. It goes without
saying that I warmly welcomed them as my first opportunities to
conduct. I still remember two of the pieces over which I presided.
One, *From the Cradle to the Grave,* was a cross between pantomine
and ballet. The music by Reinecke was, as far as I can recall, pretty,
well orchestrated, and written in a style resembling that of Mendelssohn. The other, a fairy extravaganza called *Lumpazivaga-
bundus,* was a sheer delight to me, not because of its rather insignificant music, but because the spirit of Vienna spoke to me once
more from the imaginative work of the brilliant Nestroy. The
Austrian mixture of amiability and a sharp tongue, levity and profundity, good nature and pertness, seemed somehow familiar to me
as though I were experiencing a feeling of pre-stabilized harmony.
I had frequent occasions to recall it later when I had taken root in
Vienna.

The day came when the director decided to entrust an opera to
me. I was to take charge of the revival of Lortzing's charming *Der
Waffenschmied.* I performed it in February or March 1894. What
must I have felt when, a lad of not yet eighteen, I conducted my
first opera? I recall most clearly what I did *not* feel: I felt no uncertainty whatever and was not worried. I had the score in my
head, the singers' parts had become familiar to me in the course of
many rehearsals, and the fact that instead of a piano I now had at
my disposal an orchestra was not an unaccustomed burden but a
source of joy. My hand knew automatically what to do: it had the
ability to hold the orchestra together and keep the soloists and the
chorus in harmony with it. My careful coaching of the singers in
their arias and ensembles had provided for enough precision —
without robbing the performance of its freedom and vitality — to
prevent my innate technique from being confronted with unexpected problems. In every art innate technique is an essential and
proof of talent. It anticipates an ability that must be gained step by
step, often with a great deal of trouble. But before it is gained, it is
miraculously there already, imparting to the performer a deceptive
feeling of sureness which, with growing maturity, is subjected to

many a severe trial. And so I, too, felt entirely sure of myself. Even when, at a subsequent performance of the same opera, a singer's sudden illness made the recasting of an important role necessary, my hand and my brain felt quite capable of meeting any contingency. Without embarrassment or noticeable upset, I led that performance, too, to its successful conclusion. I was naturally much too immature to have even a faint idea of the real difficulties of conducting. On the other hand, I did not feel that I deserved special praise because of my sureness. It was to me a matter of course. But I seem to remember that I was made happy by the thought that a movement of my hand could unleash the forces of the orchestra, send waves of music into the theater, command the brilliance of the brasses and the power of the tympani, make the strings play a gentle accompaniment to the solos of the woodwinds, and correspondingly support the latter's crescendo. I delighted in maintaining a firm tempo suitable to the course of the music and the events on the stage, in using a look or a gesture to spur the orchestra on to an intensification of sound and expression, or in softening a dynamic excess by a deprecatory gesture with my left hand. This enjoyment of immediate power, of which I could have been but darkly conscious at the time, was accompanied by real pleasure in the charming and gay light opera and by a feeling of gratification in seeing my zealous and enthusiastic rehearsing bear fruit in a musically clean and vital performance. In spite of the lifelessness of the stage direction, I had managed to light a little fire even in the dialogue by studying secretly with members of the cast who were well disposed toward me. The general aftereffect of my first performance was the encouraging feeling of having stood in the place for which I had been destined.

Not only had the technical direction of the opera rested lightly on me, but none of the other tasks assigned to the coach or the budding conductor had given me any difficulty. Therein lay the grave danger of underestimating the importance of artistic tasks and of overestimating myself. Nowhere near me did I see a musician I considered superior to me. I felt unable to be highly appreciative of the theater's conductors, in spite of Grossmann's excellent technical command of the orchestra. Concerts in the *Gürzenich,* led by Franz Wüllner, father of the subsequently world-famous singer and rhetorician, Ludwig Wüllner, seemed to me dry and stiff. I think that, for a time, I was headed straight for conceit.

Why did everything seem so easy to me? Partly, of course because I was a true musician, both by instinct and training. But I should hardly have felt justified in taking pride in my musical facility. No, I was proud of the ease with which I was able to master something new to me: the specific demands made by an operatic enterprise. I did not understand that I was confusing one thing with another, that an operatic enterprise was something on a lower plane and more earthbound than art, whose demands I thought I was fulfilling. I was no longer occupied with Beethoven's *Fidelio* itself, but with the *Fidelio* of the Cologne Opera, an object of theatrical routine. I had no idea at the time — how could my inexperience have given me such an idea? — that someday my main task in life would be the removal of the varnish of routine and the consigning to oblivion of the conventional, with the aim of penetrating again to the core of the work itself and of producing it as if it were having its world *première*. That was no easy task. It was made more complicated by a simultaneous careful self-cleansing from unconsciously acquired habits. At that time, however, in Cologne, I succumbed to the allurement of the facility with which routine knows how to smoothe the rough spots of art and change the works of the masters into theatrical enterprises. I began to be proud of the ease with which I achieved everything asked of me by the leaders of the theater. For it is the atmosphere of theatrical routine that breeds vanity, the professional disease of artists, while the atmosphere in the realm of art calls forth a sense of reverence. I do think, though, that I may claim never to have seriously yielded to vanity, that a still small voice of dissatisfaction with myself persisted in asking me whether I was still in contact with my better self. I presume that my readers will have gathered by now that I had a Faustian feeling about myself and that I therefore rejected satisfaction — and consequently self-satisfaction too — as being hostile to my ardent spirit of inquiry and my craving for enlightenment. That was why the easily gained professional satisfaction, no matter how flattering at first, was bound to become highly suspect, and finally even repulsive to me.

The press had been very kind about my debut. I believe that Otto Neitzel, the highly regarded critic of the *Kölnische Zeitung*, said something about a pronounced talent for conducting. A Herr Wolf in the *Kölnische Volkszeitung* prophesied great things for me. Only one paper referred to my youth by the not particularly brilliant remark that I should have been "given the bottle" between the acts.

Verdi's *Falstaff* had been published that year, and Director Hofmann had acquired the right of production. Newspaper reports of performances in other places called *Falstaff* an old man's work, bearing the marks both of masterly skill and of a decline in creative inspiration. I had borrowed the piano score and spent blissful days in the atmosphere of the work. Hofmann, who, as I said before, had gradually come to place confidence in my musicianship, asked for my opinion. When I told him that, contrary to the notices in the papers, I could see in *Falstaff* not the end of a great life-work but rather the beginning of a higher style of the *opéra-comique,* and that it was marked by unbelievable freshness as well as by the noblest maturity, he gratefully pressed my hand and confided to me that his conductors had almost succeeded in discouraging him by their adverse judgment and that he was delighted to have his own impression confirmed by so gifted a young musician.

This led to somewhat closer relations between us. I was asked to have tea at his home, where the composer Spinelli was to play his opera *A Basso Porto.* It was of the *verismo* type, like *Cavalleria* and *Pagliacci,* and seemed to me superior to both in dramatic force and melodic invention, a judgment that proved entirely correct when I myself conducted the opera in Riga six years later.

The Cologne performance of *Falstaff* was conducted by Grossmann and scored but a moderate success. I still remember how disappointed I was when, after weeks of enjoyable piano rehearsals with the singers, I found everything distorted by an unappreciative and unfeeling interpretation and, above all, by unsuitable tempos. My memory is still burdened by the wholly arbitrary *andante maestoso* of the concluding fugue, *"tutto nel mondo è burla, l'uom è nato burlone."*

Spinelli's homicidal and lustful opera, on the other hand, which I had also prepared for production, was highly successful. I believe that its performance found favor even in my judgment, presumptuous though it had grown in the meantime.

When, to my disappointment, the director's friendly disposition toward me did not lead to the expected intensification of my activity, I decided boldly to try my luck elsewhere. I am no longer able to say how my departure from Cologne and my engagement in Hamburg came about. I suppose Hofmann could give me no hope of an improvement in my position as coach, and it is possible that my enemy, Chief Stage Director O., opposed my advancement. An agent who had heard favorable reports about me from Cologne singers may have procured the Hamburg engagement for me. At any rate, I left my first position with increased confidence in myself and no mean store of practical theatrical experience.

Before bidding farewell to Cologne, I wish to record two meetings, one with a tenor, the other with a nightingale. The tenor's name was Bruno Heydrich. He sang Tristan, Siegmund, and the Siegfrieds, and had a voice that, though robust, was without charm and no longer quite fresh. He was musically reliable and quite adequate as an actor. A tall ungainly man, he was, rightly or wrongly,

considered a somewhat questionable character by his colleagues.
I heard a few years later that he had left the stage and assumed the
management of a music school in Halle. The Nazi hangman of
Prague, Reinhard Heydrich, who was laid low by a Czech William
Tell, was the man's horrible son. Whenever I read the name of that
sadistic brute, I had to think of the mediocre singer with the disagreeable voice who, himself wholly lacking in fiendish attributes,
was destined by fate to spawn a devil.

Before leaving Cologne, I was privileged to hear a voice more
beautiful than that of the fiend's father. There are nights whose
memory clings to us, not because of some event, but rather because
its very atmosphere has excluded the world and made human
events fade into distance. It was such a moonlit night of which
Goethe sang:

Flooded are the brakes and dell
With thy phantom light,
And my soul receives the spell
Of thy magic might.

I had gone to Bonn with the opera company. My services were
not required during the second act, and I thought I'd pay a visit
to the beautiful park. There, for the first time in my life, I heard
a nightingale. It was one of those happy moments when we forget
all agitation and are given up to restful quiet. The friendly call of
the bird, half dolorous and half enticing, sounded to me like a beautiful message. I have recorded so quiet and eventless a moment because I like to recall gratefully that in this world of ours, though
it has room for a Heydrich and others of his kind, there are moonlight nights, too, and nightingales. Should we not bear in mind the
beautiful whenever the pressure of evil relents and we are spared
its sight? Is such a mental tendency sentimentality, or is it not rather
a healthy leaning toward thoughts and feelings that strengthen our
vital energy?

III

"YES, there is a Providence!" Leonore exclaims in *Fidelio,* and that
was what I said to myself when a generous fate presented me with
a contract from the hand of the by no means generous Pollini,
director of the Hamburg Stadttheater. This served to bring me in
contact with Gustav Mahler, a fact that decisively influenced my
artistic development and my whole life.

Hamburg was considered the second city in Germany, but in
the opinion of Hamburgers it ranked first. There was a rivalry

between the two large cities, which looked down upon each other. In a comedy by Blumenthal, a Hamburg senator says to a young man who has told him that he was born in Berlin: "Ah, well, a fellow's got to be born some place." The great seaside town was considered tedious by the Berliners, while the capital was judged an upstart by the people of Hamburg. At any rate, Hamburg, as a city, had a personality, which was more than could be said of Berlin. It had been drawn by history, and there was character in the splendid districts adjoining the Inner and Outer Alster, the Jungfernstieg's brisk traffic, the mighty harbor, the confusion of the seamen's amusement center in St. Pauli, the beautiful Elbe resorts of Blankensee, the *Luehe,* and many other sights. All these features told of the life of a Hanse town looking out upon the sea and the world, while the majority of the German cities were affected by an inland complex. What was more, Hamburg was not only a city, it was a state. As such, it attached great value to its equality with other German states, especially with powerful and unpopular Prussia. Its citizens were known for the pride and dignity of their bearing. The cultivation of the arts was a subject of particular attention on the part of the city's officials because they recognized the representative value of Hamburg as a center of culture. But the theater did not owe its eminent position in the city's spiritual life to civic pride alone, but rather to a wide-spread genuine enthusiasm for the arts. Hamburg was what at the time was known as a theater city, a city in which the theater and its artists enjoyed genuine and heartfelt popularity. The operatic and dramatic offerings of the municipal stages and the other theaters — the Thalia Theater with its excellent dramatic performances foremost among them — were dear to the hearts of the Hamburgers and were discussed with interest among the broad masses of the population.

The Stadttheater management was also responsible for a number of operatic and dramatic performances at the Altona Theater, an old gaslit house in the neighboring little town of Altona, which was reached by way of St. Pauli. There are two reasons why I shall never forget a performance of Leoncavallo's *Pagliacci* that I conducted there: first, that my vigorous conducting made me continually scorch my fingers on the hot chimneys of the gaslamps at the side of the conductor's desk, and second, that, whenever I turned toward the second violins, I could see a lady seated in the first row at my right knitting away at a stocking. She would lean across the handrail from time to time and, disregarding my conducting, ask me in a friendly tone if the performance would be over soon. I am afraid she had no very high opinion of an operatic conductor's importance. Altogether, the reaction of the Altona public to our artistic endeavors required the exertion of a considerable part of our sense of humor.

In Hamburg itself it was different. Whenever an outstanding performance was announced, which was frequently the case, a capacity house was assured. All cultural institutions were required to be worthy of the old dignity and the present importance of the city, and the people took pride in the facts that Hans von Bülow had been the conductor of the Hamburg Symphony Concerts and that Gustav Mahler, the former director of the Royal Opera in Budapest, was at the head of the Hamburg Opera. That Hamburg's interest in the theater reached far back into the past may be seen from Lessing's classic critical masterpiece, the *Hamburger Dramaturgie*. In the north German and somewhat gloomy city — dark skies with rain and fog were called Hamburg weather — opera occupied a far more serious position than, for instance, in Rhenishly serene and sunny Cologne. The importance of the Hamburg theater was, as a matter of fact, readily recognized in Berlin. The capital's newspapers were in the habit of sending their leading critics to Hamburg to review important first performances. It was not surprising, then, that I looked forward eagerly to my engagement. But the focal point of my expectations was Gustav Mahler, the composer of that exceptionally interesting symphony which the critics had treated so scornfully. The thought that a musical poet of so extravagant an imagination — I pictured him to myself as something of a new Berlioz — was the conductor of the Opera at which I was to work was indeed exciting, and so I was looking forward with a feeling of awe and hope to meeting a creative genius of such magnitude.

My first impression after my arrival in Hamburg did not tally with my conception of the usually rather sober district round the railway station of a big commercial town. When I stepped out of the Klostertor Station, will-o'-the-wisps were dancing above me, colorfully illuminating the night sky. It was the Hamburg Electric, which seemed to celebrate my arrival with running fireworks of sparks from its overhead wires, Hamburg having been among the first German cities to electrify its street railways. The merry, scintillating sprites accompanied me on my first extended walk through the city's wide streets, across the mighty bridge at the Dammtor, and around the beautiful Inner Alster. Looking into the show-window of Bieber's studio on Jungfernstieg, my gaze was attracted by a photograph. The head impressed me at first sight as being that of a musician, and I presently became convinced that it was that of Mahler. Nobody but the composer of the "Titan" Symphony could look like that. His actual appearance confirmed my power of divination. For when, on the following morning, I came out of Pollini's sanctum, where I had made my bow to my new boss, one of the first men I saw in the office was Mahler, a lean, fidgety, short man with an unusually high, steep forehead, long, dark hair, deeply penetrating bespectacled eyes, and a characteristically spiritual mouth. Pollini introduced us to each other, and there followed a brief conversation, whose amused report by Mahler was often laughingly repeated to me by his sisters. "So you are the new coach," Mahler said. "Do you play the piano well?" "Excellently," I replied, meaning simply to tell the truth, because a false modesty seemed inappropriate in front of a great man. "Can you read well at sight?" Mahler asked. "Oh, yes, everything," I said again truthfully. "And do you know the regular repertoire operas?" "I know them all quite well," I replied with a great deal of assurance. Mahler gave a loud laugh, tapped me on the shoulder pleasantly, and concluded the conversation with "Well, that sounds swell."

I was soon permitted to prove that I had not exaggerated. Mahler was standing on the stage during a business rehearsal of Humperdinck's *Hänsel und Gretel,* which was the first operatic novelty to be produced that season. I could see how painfully he felt the insufficiency of the accompanist, and I should have loved to jump into the breach. I was to have my wish, for suddenly Mahler's gaze fell on me, and he said, "You told me you could play everything at sight. Would you trust yourself to play an opera you don't know?" When I said I would, Mahler waved off the accompanist, and I seated myself delightedly at the piano, a place I was not to relinquish during all of Mahler's rehearsals.

A short time later, I was asked if I felt equal to directing the chorus. The former chorus master had not come up to Mahler's requirements. I accepted, though I had never before had anything to do with a chorus. And so, one morning, a youth of eighteen, I found myself at the piano in the chorus hall, in charge of a chorus rehearsal of *Lohengrin.* Mahler told me later that when Pollini had asked the leader of the chorus how I had made out, the man had replied, "He's got a lot of experience." To this Mahler added the remark that at the theater talent was frequently taken for experience, and experience for talent, an opinion that was borne out by my own subsequent observations.

Mahler's way of performing music and conducting rehearsals profoundly affected my attitude toward my own tasks. I no longer enjoyed my facility, for I began to understand that what counted were other accomplishments than those which came to me so easily.

It was very difficult to get singers to the point of almost instrumental musical exactitude and at the same time to achieve a full measure of dramatic expression. Passionate feeling tends toward retardations or accelerations and forgets the dot at the side of the eighth note. Precision, on the other hand, chillingly obstructs the way to expressiveness. There was much to learn for a lad of my questionable tendency to neglect musical correctness for the sake of feeling. The object of Mahler's endeavors was to bring music and the many-styled drama into proper correlation. This subject, discussed at length between us, soon began to occupy my thoughts. It became a practical task at my rehearsals. Mahler's piano rehearsals were unforgettably instructive to me because of his imperious and imaginative injunctions to the singers and his deep penetration into the works. At his orchestra rehearsals, his tyrannical personality forced the musicians by intimidation and passionate stimulation into giving their utmost. These experiences put a definite end to whatever feeling of self-satisfaction I might still have harbored. It was splendid to have daily before one's eyes the example of a man who demanded the utmost of himself and of others. I was wholly absorbed by a fascinating spectacle and felt as if my soul were aflame as in a prairie fire. Although I was still young, I had an old enemy: workaday triviality. I was no longer afraid of it. Here was a man against whom it was powerless, who renewed himself every minute, and who did not know the meaning of slackening either in his work or in his vital principles. The oppressive experience that, while art was sublime, life was commonplace, and that an artist's existence must therefore be humiliating was finally brought to naught by a great musician. He knew no trivial moment, he thought no thought and spoke no word that might have meant a betrayal of his soul. In the seventeen years of my friendship with Mahler I always found him at the very peak of his exalted being.

Pollini, the lessee and despotic director of the Stadttheater, had assembled a surprising cast. Gustav Mahler was the brilliant leading conductor, Otto Lohse a gifted second in rank, and a number of rather efficient musicians were assigned to lesser chores. Prominent among the singers were Katharina Klafski, a vocally magnificent Leonore, Isolde, and Brünnhilde in the grand style; the versatile and highly gifted Ernestine Schumann-Heink; Bertha Förster-Lauterer, a poetic interpreter of lyric parts; the Wagnerian tenor Max Alvary, rather unimportant in voice, but exceptionally impressive in appearance and personality; the vocally accomplished tenor Birrenkoven; and the powerful Czech basso Wilhelm Hesch. Here was a group of singers with whom outstanding performances could be achieved. I have retained no recollection of any individual performance under Mahler, but I do know that the Hamburg Opera flourished under his guidance. On the wall of Mahler's study hung the ribbon from a wreath — I believe it was the only trophy he had ever preserved — with the inscription: "To the Pygmalion of the Hamburg Opera — Hans von Bülow." This symbolic tribute paid to Mahler by Bülow made a great impression on me, for it conferred honor upon both men: upon Mahler, whom the beautiful comparison endowed with the power to breathe life into the inanimate; and upon Bülow, whose artistic high-mindedness impelled him to render the other man so ingenious and warm-hearted an homage. The impetuous energy with which Mahler's uncompromising artistic will had swept routine work and indolence out of the theater, and which had led to the introduction of a new operatic epoch exemplified by performances of emotional animation and musical purity must have been a balm to Bülow during his last years of suffering. This is attested by a strange scene that was reported to me. When Bülow stepped to the desk to conduct one of his Hamburg concerts, he saw Mahler in the front row of the hall. Instead of acknowledging the applause with which he had been received he hurried down the steps of the platform and toward Mahler, offering him his baton and inviting him with a courteous gesture to take his place on the platform. When Mahler, embarrassed, declined, Bülow mounted the steps again and conducted the concert. While the two men were but casually acquainted personally, their superpersonal relation, expressed in that strange — and, by the way, once more repeated — scene in the concert hall, manifested itself even after Bülow's death. The first movement of his Second Symphony, surely one of the most powerful symphonic compositions, was conceived by Mahler while under the impression of Bülow's funeral rites.

There was one man who did not share in the general enthusiasm caused by the musically magnificent operatic performances in Hamburg under Mahler's guidance — Mahler himself. He was greatly distressed by the stage direction, whose weakness neither the considerable histrionic talents of a number of the singers nor the dramatic faithfulness of his musicianship was able to cover. He did not at the time discuss with me the fundamental obstacles in the way of stage directing. Their nature may have become clear to him only in the course of his reformatory activity in Vienna. But he did complain in all the dynamic shadings between a good-humored shaking of his head and outbursts of acute despair about the personal shortcomings and absurdities of Chief Stage Director B., whose constructive — or rather, obstructive — coöperation an unkind fate had bestowed upon him. B., a burly tall man, belonged in the same artistic category as his Cologne colleague O., mentioned in the previous chapter, although B. was more mannerly and rather more good-natured. I was fortunate enough not to arouse his antagonism, but he was hostile to Mahler, whose violent demands in artistic and managerial matters he blocked effectively by his indolent immovability. An open break between them was avoided only by the circumstance that B. was too lazy even to fight, or rather, because the mere fact of his ponderous presence was tantamount to an unyielding repudiation. The manner in which B. arranged chorus scenes seems worth telling. First of all, he assigned their positions on stage to the representatives of the four voices. This done, he considered his task practically accomplished. But he never failed to add a few general instructions for good measure. He would, for instance, advise middle-aged Hamburg women to disport themselves in the first act of *Carmen* as if they were playful Spanish maidens; or he would instruct the worthy men in the second act of *Tannhäuser* to stride through the hall of the Wartburg in the courtly attitude of princes and counts. However, he did not care to waste his time in explanations. He confined himself as a rule to calls of: "Lively, folks, lively!" and to demands that the choristers "share in the action." Thereupon a movement would go through the chorus, the men and women would look at the acting soloists, point them out to one another, and relapse into their former lethargy until B.'s renewed exhortations or a loud snapping of his thumb and forefinger caused another outburst of dramatic participation. B. had succeeded in developing finger-snapping into a veritable art, and even during performances he tried to infuse animation into the chorus scenes from his place in the wings by waving to the chorus members and "snapping them to attention." But because he paid scant heed to the course of the performance and frequently produced his favorite snapping sound thoughtlessly, perhaps while telling a joke, it happened at times that the chorus burst into animation rather unexpectedly and unjustifiably. I shall never forget the finale of Hochberg's *Werwolf*, when a number of chorus ladies had to stand solemnly still, angels' wings attached to their backs and palm branches in their hands. Suddenly, a movement went through them, they waved their palm branches in the air, and the scene had lost all of its meaning because of a thoughtless snapping of B.'s fingers. It may easily be imagined what a source of merriment this and similar directional accomplishments were to Mahler and myself. But it is equally understandable that they were unbearable and finally contributed toward making Mahler thoroughly disgusted with his activity.

Pollini soon gained confidence in my ability. I had proved my worth as a coach and chorus master. He was probably impressed, too, by Mahler's favorable opinion of me. After I had helped the theater out of an embarrassing situation by substituting for a conductor who had suddenly fallen ill — I think it was at a performance of *Cavalleria* — he gradually entrusted me with the conducting of one opera after another. At first they were mostly light operas like Lortzing's *Zar und Zimmermann, Undine,* and *Die beiden Schützen,* and Flotow's *Martha.* Pollini preferred giving them the benefit of my youthful zest to handicapping them with the customary condescension of the older conductors. I greatly enjoyed my work — especially the first-named Lortzing opera, with its jovial humor and charming musical invention — and endeavored to put on spirited performances. Verdi's *Il Trovatore* soon followed. My Manrico did not quite come up to my requirements with regard to *bel canto,* but his fabulous high C in the *stretta* was always sure to bring down the house. He was Heinrich Bötel, a native son of Hamburg. One day he had climbed down from the box of his cab to let Pollini hear his voice. The tenor's popularity was assured when the clever impresario introduced him to the public in Adam's *Le Postillon de Longjumeau.* His brilliant high notes won him the applause of the audience, while the expert cracking of his whip brought thunderous approval from many former colleagues who crowded the gallery. Bötel was a friendly and modest man, eager to learn. His ascent to high C had not turned his head. Not only was his stage manner natural and decorous, but he actually had an innate talent for portraying dashing young fellows. I recall with pleasure a performance of Smetana's *Bartered Bride* under Mahler's direction in which he fully held his own beside Hesch's classic Kezal and Förster-Lauterer's charming Marie. I came in frequent artistic contact with Ernestine Schumann-Heink. I was at the desk when she sang Azucena, Carmen, and — during my second year in Hamburg — Amneris, Ulrica, and other parts. But we never got close to each other. Her wilful disposition and her remarkable talent resisted the influence and the efforts of so young a musician. I finally confined myself at our rehearsals to a purely musical understanding, knowing that she could be depended upon to use her great gifts in a thoroughly artistic manner. Hers, too, was an original and folk-like nature, and I shall always remember that she managed to sing Carmen in spite of the plainly visible symptoms of approaching motherhood — a fact that complicated the drama by the addition of a family detail not intended by the author — and that a little more than a week after the generally expected event she was again in harness, in the part of Amneris.

I made an interesting acquaintance in the person of a heroic tenor — Max Alvary. He came of a Düsseldorf family of painters named Achenbach, had grown up among painters, and had, in the face of so decided a hereditary taint, undertaken to become a singer. But the attempted switch from the eye to the ear had not been entirely successful. He was still a painter when singing and acting Tannhäuser or Siegfried. He had a robust voice, but his singing was devoid of beauty, and his acting lacked the dramatic accent. Picturesquely, however, he was eminently satisfactory because of his splendid stage presence. The public loved and extolled him. His affinity with art made him stand out from his surroundings on the stage. He looked like a distinguished visitor from another world who was somewhat out of place but knew how to make people forget his inherent strangeness by the force of his purposeful and firmly rooted personality. His picturesque style, which he had brought to perfection, did not by any means consist merely in coolly striking a pose. In spite of his peculiar deficiencies he had to be given credit for a certain craftsmanship. His at times grotesque manner of singing was too much of an insult to Mahler's ear to permit the establishment of an amicable relationship between the two men, but Alvary's serious musical conscientiousness had a propitiatory effect and served to lessen the abyss between the dramatic musician and the singing painter. What was more, Alvary was an intelligent and cultivated artist. I may say that I gained a higher opinion of his comprehension of his tasks from my conversations with him than from his performances.

The first year of my Hamburg activities has left me no memory of events connected with individual artists. But I acquired a growing experience in my professional intercourse with artists. As a consequence, a dawning comprehension of what, beyond his musical-dramatic task, was a conductor's most important problem: the human problem. The conductor himself produces no music, but does so by means of others, whom he must lead by gestures, words, and the power of his personality, and the result depends upon his ability to handle people. In this respect, too, innate talent is of decisive importance — a talent for asserting one's own personality — and it needs to be developed by constant endeavor and by making the most of daily experiences. He who has been born without authority and is lacking in the essential dynamics originating in the sphere of the will cannot gain a firm footing as a conductor, irrespective of musical talent, ability, or knowledge. He may reach a point at which he will be able to express himself with masterly skill on the piano or the violin, but he will never be successful in welding an orchestra or an operatic company into an instrument of his own. The result of his conducting will be more impersonal, insignificant, and ineffective than that of a musician of lesser ability who has the natural gift of authority.

Thoughts on this subject kept agitating my mind. They disturbed me for very personal reasons. But it grew clear to me in the end that youth was rarely able to carry those personal dynamics into action and that in the scales of authority years unquestionably weighed heavily, at times decisively. At any rate, they weighed too lightly in my case, and I became convinced that those who reproached me with youthfulness were quite right. Moreover, the power and influence of an operahouse's leading conductor happened to be wielded in Hamburg by a man of innate ruling ability, even of tyrannical bent, so that everybody stood in awe of him. What was more natural, therefore, than the desire of both singers and musicians to escape from the intimidating rule of the feared man and find restful relaxation in the presence of a wholly unfearsome youth? I could readily understand that, and so I tried to influence the artists by psychological methods appropriate to and in conformity with my nature. While my efforts were not always successful, they at least afforded me a comforting insight into a side of my nature to which I had paid no attention before: I became aware that I had an educational instinct.

It was natural that the effect on me of Mahler's activity should be both stimulating and, occasionally, depressive. I asked myself if anything I would ever accomplish could hold its own when compared with so exalted a perfection. I remember how happy and encouraged I felt when Mahler's sister Justine confided to me one day that her brother, having listened to my conducting of an act or two of *Aïda,* said to her: "Why, the fellow's a born conductor."

I gained a good deal of experience in conducting. I made it a principle to comply with every request to substitute for an indisposed colleague, and it would seem to me in retrospect that a comradely spirit prompted many a medical report of slight temperatures, so that I might have another opportunity for proving my versatility. I was at all times unhesitatingly ready for an assignment, and the ease with which I mastered my tasks never deserted me. I recall one such occurrence which gave me a great deal of pleasure and was the cause of special approbation. Fortunately, it was not caused by anybody's illness. A *Siegfried* stage rehearsal with orchestra was scheduled, and Mahler had not shown up. Everybody was waiting, and Pollini finally turned impatiently to me, asking me if I trusted myself to conduct the rehearsal. Of course I trusted myself, and a minute later the supreme desire which had agitated my heart for years was fulfilled — I was conducting Wagner. It was the stormy beginning of the third act, the awakening of Erda, whose mythical primordial sound I was privileged to conjure up. My luck lasted until far into the scene between the Wanderer and Siegfried — until the passing through the fire, I believe. A misunderstanding had caused Mahler to be half an hour late, and, instead of relieving me at once, he had good-naturedly proposed to Pollini to let me keep on conducting.

When I had thus furnished repeated proof of my musicianship and of the fact that I felt thoroughly at home at the conductor's desk, my conducting activities began to increase and gradually to conflict with my job as chorus master. I should nevertheless have had to continue the latter during my second year in Hamburg had not Katharina Klafski and her husband, *Kapellmeister* Otto Lohse, jumped their contracts and gone to America in the spring of 1895. We suffered a great artistic and moral loss, and I recall that Pollini fell seriously ill from excitement. Recovered, he asked me to call on him and told me that, both professionally and personally, he had a good deal of confidence in me. He asked me if, young though I was, I dared take over Lohse's position. I gladly accepted, and so, in the autumn of 1895, I became a regular *Kapellmeister* at the Hamburg Stadttheater. In looking for a replacement for the magnificent Klafski, Pollini once more demonstrated the sagacity of a born impresario. He discovered and engaged a beginner, Anna von Mildenburg, a young girl from Klagenfurt whom he had heard in Vienna when she was a pupil of Madame Paumgartner-Papier. She was to become the great tragedienne of the German operatic stage.

It would be an exaggeration to say that my unheard-of advancement affected me deeply. I was made glad by the prospect of doing a considerably increased amount of rehearsing and conducting, and by the fact that my activity would be lent the added authority wielded by a regular *Kapellmeister*. I felt relieved to have the burden of chorus directing and coaching removed from my shoulders — although I voluntarily continued to coach for Mahler — but I aimed at goals higher than a mere advancement in my career. I wanted to gain in discernment and knowledge. I yearned to increase my intellectual status.

How could Providence have bestowed on me, feeling as I did, a greater boon than my association with Mahler? It was of inestimable value to my musical growth that, instead of the Cologne condition of working under the direction of conductors whose worth I was unable fully to acknowledge and to whom I actually felt superior in talent, I was privileged to serve a master of so overwhelming a musical endowment and of so powerful a personality, an institution within whose walls burned a pure and strength-irradiating flame, a temple in which indolence and cynicism, the enemies of artistic endeavor, were unable to gain a foothold. But I gained considerably more than mere musical growth. Soon after our first meeting in the theater's office Mahler had asked me to his home, which he shared with his two sisters. I frequently walked with him there by way of Grindelallee and Rotebaum-chaussee, our conversations embracing the wide realms open to a mind as prolific as his. Just as I unreservedly acknowledged the artistic and mental superiority of the man who was sixteen years my senior, so I was firmly convinced from the beginning that I profoundly understood his demonic nature. No sooner did my initial reserve permit it than I asked him about his creative work. It was he, seated at the piano, who introduced me to his First Symphony, to the work of his impetuous youth, with its flowering early movements, the brilliantly conceived Funeral March, and the tempestuous finale. He played his Second Symphony for me at the time he put the finishing touches to its orchestral score. He showed me *Das klagende Lied* and sang for me songs with piano and orchestral accompaniments. They lay in his desk, still undiscovered. How am I to describe my deep emotion when, guided by him, I wandered through that new land? How am I to report the upheaval caused me by a view into the great man's soul, stirred to its depths by world-woe and the yearning for God?

"Who is right, Alyosha or Ivan?" Emma, Mahler's younger sister, asked me at one of my visits. Seeing my look of surprise, she explained that she was referring to the chapter "The Brothers Get Acquainted" in Dostoyevsky's *Brothers Karamazov.* The subject was so passionately occupying her brother's mind that she took it for granted that he had talked to me about it. That conversation between Ivan and Alyosha eloquently reveals a condition similar to Mahler's mental grief, to his suffering because of the world's afflictions, and to his search for a comforting uplift. Basically, all that Mahler thought, spoke, read, or composed was concerned with the questions of whence, to what purpose, whither? He had moments of believing tranquillity and was fond of Roadmender-Hans's beautiful words in Anzengruber's daring play *Die Kreuzel-schreiber:* "There's nothing that can happen to you." But the atmosphere of his soul was stormy and unpredictable. Cheerful, childlike laughter would suddenly, and without outward cause, give way to an inward spasm, the rising of fierce and desperate suffering.

Mahler showed me the way to Dostoyevsky, who soon took possession of my soul. It was he who aroused my interest in Nietzsche, with whose *Thus Spake Zarathustra* he was deeply occupied at the time. When he noticed my inclination toward philosophy, he made me a Christmas present of Schopenhauer's works, in 1894, and thereby opened to me a world to which I have never since become lost. Mahler was pleased also by my interest in natural science. In his conversations with me he gave me free rein to his imaginative ideas concerning physical theories. For instance, he would replace the attractive power of the earth by a repelling power of the sun and insist that his idea was more effective than Newton's law of gravitation. Or he would animate atomism by explaining atomic energy by a theory of inclination and disinclination. Although every detail in the realm of nature was close to his heart, he was interested mainly in those natural-historical phenomena that furnished philosophy with new material for thought. Friends of his, professionally occupied with natural science, were hard pressed by his deeply penetrating questions. An eminent physicist whom he met frequently could not tell me enough about Mahler's intuitive understanding of the ultimate theories of physics and about the logical keenness of his conclusions or counter-arguments. Today, by the way, the physical fantasies indulged in by Mahler seem by no means more artistically unscientific to me than Gustav Theodor Fechner's philosophic thoughts about the soul-life of plants or doctrine of "The Comparative Anatomy of the Angels." It was a pity that Mahler never made the acquaintance of Fechner. The author of *Zend Avesta* would surely have become his friend. Let me mention here a book I read at Mahler's suggestion. It was Albert Lange's *Geschichte des Materialismus,* a classic work dealing with the oldest ailment of man's cogitative faculty. It put a definite end to any similar inclinations in my own thinking.

But there were other things at Mahler's home beside confessions of the soul, philosophy, and music. There was a good deal of cheerfulness. It was of the Austrian type which, from the first words uttered in the Viennese dialect by Mahler or his sisters, had struck a responsive chord in my soul. And how effective was the wooing power of the Vienna *Mehlspeis,* the tasty sweets, of which an infinite variety was put on Mahler's table by his superbly skilled cook Elis'! Mahler was quite fond of the Austrian cuisine. It was one of his favorite jokes to declare that anyone who did not like a certain dish must be a jackass, and then to ask his guests if they liked it. Mahler had the gift of wit and he appreciated the witticism of others. But he hated to have jokes told or recounted in his presence. To the speaker's chagrin, he never moved a muscle of his face on such occasions. One of our favorite pastimes was playing in duet music by Schubert, Mozart, Schumann, Dvořák, and other composers. There were occasions when Mahler would invent Viennese dialect texts to Schubert marches or dances. They fitted the music as if it had been composed for them.

My first year in Hamburg passed on wings. Summer came, and I returned to Berlin to spend part of my vacation in composing and reading, waiting all the time until the season would permit the fulfillment of my desire to see mountains covered with perpetual snow and to climb them, if possible. My stay in Berlin unexpectedly vouchsafed me a refreshing foretaste of intellectual mountain air. At a home, to which I was attached by ties of the heart, I made the acquaintance of an actor from the Deutsches Theater who had already managed to call general attention to himself. He was Max Reinhardt, a young man of twenty-two. We got into the habit of taking long walks after having seen home the two sisters who were the objects of our affection, discussing problems of art from the standpoint of youth yearning to achieve great things, and talking over theatrical and musical events that agitated us. Reinhardt loved music, was extremely musical, and while rhapsodizing about his theatrical dreams of the future frequently referred to the essentiality of music at all important moments of the spoken drama. He was considered one of the young generation's most gifted portrayers of brief character parts. Later — about 1901 — I had occasion to admire the truly masterly work of the young actor in the parts of Itzig in Beer-Hofmann's *Der Graf von Charolais* and of Mortensgaard in Ibsen's *Rosmersholm*. These figures, strange as their characters were to Reinhardt's own nature, have remained unforgettable to me because of the actor's penetrating and forceful delineation. I shall have more to say about him later.

I proceeded to the Tyrol and rejoiced in the sight of charming Bozen and delightful Meran. I can still recall the exciting thirteen-hour drive in a horse-drawn mail-coach over the dusty Austrian roads, through the blazing heat of the Vintschgau, and up to the icy heights of Sulden, overtowered by snowcapped mountain tops. We arrived there in the evening. An excellent Tyrolean guide instructed me in the rudiments of mountain climbing, and I showed a certain aptitude for scaling rocky heights and traversing glaciers. Leaving the shelter hut in the dark of the night, making our lantern-lit way across moraines, watching the first sunbeam strike the highest of the peaks surrounding us, the first snow beneath our feet, the arduous ascent, and the final arrival at the summit with its magnificent view of majestically lonesome expanse — how unforgettable all that has remained to me! When, worried, I asked my guide at a particularly difficult part of the ascent how we would ever manage to get down again, he answered me with the charming saying, uttered in broad Tyrolean accents: "There's no devil to

help you up, but all the Saints'll help you down." I always thought
the most magnificent moment of a mountain tour had come when
I felt alone with the mountain, when the valley had dropped out
of sight, when no tree or bush or grazing goat reminded of the
familiar earth, and when the sight of moraines and snowy expanses,
and the consciousness of wind and loneliness solemnly touched my
soul as with a lofty greeting from an unearthly realm.

Invigorated, I got back to Hamburg, where a wealth of new tasks
awaited me. Pollini entrusted me with *Aïda* and *Tannhäuser,* and,
unless I am mistaken, also with *Der Freischütz* and *Fra Diavolo.*
The parts of Aïda and Elisabeth were sung by Mildenburg, and I
recall with pleasure the rehearsals with the brilliant woman — the
mighty Isolde of later days — and the rapid progress she made.

Among the dead ore I encountered in the course of my conscientious studies of many new operas I one day struck pure gold. I
happened upon Hans Pfitzner's *Der arme Heinrich.* At first, I was
inclined to see in the initial scenes' deeply moving atmosphere of
illness a powerfully expressive but rather Tristanesque sequel to
Wagner. But the farther I got, the more clearly I recognized the
inspiration and original inventiveness of a creative dramatic musician. Unfortunately, I do not recall how Mahler reacted to my
enthusiastic report. It is likely that my discovery came at the time
when the relations between Pollini and Mahler had become
strained, and that the latter therefore considered a recommendation of Pfitzner's work useless. I suppose that I myself must have
told Pollini about my impression, but without any success, for it was
a full four years later, when I was conducting at the Berlin Opera,
that I was able to produce Pfitzner's youthful work.

A historically important musical event, which took place toward
the end of 1895, must be recorded here: the first complete performance of Mahler's Second Symphony in Berlin. Mahler had grown
tired of "remaining undiscovered like the South Pole" as a composer. So he decided to engage at his own expense the Berlin Philharmonic Orchestra. Rehearsals commensurate in number to the
novelty and difficulty of the work were to precede the performance.
He also succeeded in securing the assistance of the chorus of the
Berlin *Singakademie.* On December 13, this tragic symphonic
dream of man's fate and confident faith was performed at Berlin's
Philharmonic Hall. The work, masterfully conducted by Mahler in
spite of an almost unbearable attack of migraine, had the effect of
an elemental event. I shall never forget my own deep emotion and
the ecstasy of the audience as well as of the performers. While some
of the reviews were adverse, malicious, and scornful, there was no
lack of critical enthusiasm and even of deeply penetrating under-

standing. The most serious report was written by the musical critic of the *Vossische Zeitung,* Max Marschalk, the composer of a charming musical accompaniment to Gerhart Hauptmann's *Hanneles Himmelfahrt* that I had enjoyed conducting during my first year in Hamburg. For years, Marschalk espoused Mahler's cause in his paper. He turned away from him at the time, I believe, of the Fifth Symphony, but found his way back after Mahler's death, through *Das Lied von der Erde.* After I had made the acquaintance of this serious and kindly-disposed man during one of his calls on Mahler, a heartfelt sympathy sprang up between us. It was not clouded by his many years of apostasy and lasted long after he had found his "way home" again. He later established a publishing firm in Berlin and gave me pleasure by publishing a number of songs with piano accompaniment that I had composed in the late nineties. Our last meeting occurred in 1935 or 1936 in Sils Maria in the Engadine, when we discussed recollections of the far distant past.

A growing antagonism, unavoidable because of the difference of the two men, had developed between Pollini and Mahler. Pollini's gloomy reserve and Mahler's fiery impetuosity were bound to lead to an eventual parting of the ways. Mahler longed to be off, and it was but natural that he should dream of Vienna. Whenever his doorbell rang, he would say: "Here comes the summons to the god of the southern zones." He advised me to leave too. My friendship with him, he said, could do me only harm in Hamburg; I had got as far there as circumstances permitted; now I should go "out into the world." I agreed with him more than I dared admit. I realized that his influence had been a blessing to me, but might grow into a danger to my further development. Mahler wrote to Dr. Theodor Loewe, the director of the Breslau Stadttheater, and was told that there was a vacancy for a young conductor. I soon received my contract. Loewe suggested, however, that I change my family name of Schlesinger (literally Silesian) because of its frequent occurrence in the capital of Silesia. That was how I came to adopt Walter as my stage name — thinking of Walter von Stolzing, Walther von der Vogelweide, and of Siegmund in *Die Walküre,* who would have liked to be *Frohwalt* but who had been compelled to call himself *Wehwalt.* When I took Austrian citizenship in 1911, Walter became my legally authorized name.

My second season in Hamburg had drawn to its end. Mahler invited me to spend the summer with him and his sisters in Steinbach on the Attersee in Austria's beautiful Salzkammergut. I had never seen Mahler so unconstrained and communicative as in the midst of that Upper Austrian country with its rocky mountains, its woods, and its large green lake. On the lawn between the house he occupied and the shore of the lake stood his little "composer's hut," one room with windows and a roof. There he wrote the major part of his Third ("Nature") Symphony, that summer. In between, there were long walks, conversations, the playing of music, and reading aloud. Mahler would read *Don Quixote* to us. We laughed with him and at his inspired comments. At the end of the lake lay Berghof, a half-hour's steamer sail away. The place was owned by the family of Ignaz Brüll, whose opera *Das goldene Kreuz* I had conducted in Hamburg. I was received most hospitably at Berghof. Brahms, who used to be a frequent visitor, was not there that summer. He was ill, and unable to leave Ischl, where he spent the summer. Mahler called on him there and told us later how the old man's dark and morose mood had corresponded to that of the first of his group of *Four Serious Songs*.

Mahler reported that he had left Brahms toward evening. As he walked through the dark corridor toward the door, he took a backward look and saw the sick man go to an iron stove and take from its inside a piece of sausage and some bread. Mahler described the grotesque and sad impression that the ill man's frugal solitary supper had made on him. Deeply moved, he kept murmuring to himself: "For all things are but vanity."

Richard Specht, a lyric poet who later became a critic and the biographer of Richard Strauss, lived at Berghof and paid us a number of visits in Steinbach. Other young literary lights lent charm to Berghof's social life. But the most interesting figure of that circle was young Hugo von Hofmannsthal, twenty-two years old, and hailed as a poetical genius by Austria's literarily inclined youth. His poems from that period in his life, which may be conceded an honorable place at the side of those of Goethe and Hölderlin, had stirred my heart deeply. We all saw in him a new Goethe. I felt gratified by the friendly relations that sprang up between us that summer. While they never matured into friendship, they nevertheless were to last a great many years. The development of that splendid poetical talent did not quite come up to the superlative promise of those early years. It would seem to me that his truly magic mastery of the language were to blame for that; that it became more important to him than poetic thinking, which language was meant to serve. He once told me of a poet who lived and loved so intensely that he was rarely in the mood for creative work, because "the covered side of his roots was more widely developed than his spreading top," meaning that life meant more to him than his poetic creations. I am almost inclined to think that the very opposite was true of Hofmannsthal: he was more devoted to art than to life. A fine phrase of his may be cited as a testimonial to his modesty as well as to his conversational talent. When we met between Steinbach and Weissenbach for a walk, I hurried up to him to express my enthusiasm over his drama in verse, *Gestern*. "It no longer satisfies me," he replied. "It sounds to me as if a canary were trying to imitate a thunderstorm."

I feel like applying that striking poetic utterance to my vain endeavor to describe the inward and outward fulness of my life during those first years under the influence of Mahler. I had come in contact with creative greatness, felt that I was on the right road, and believed that there could be no doubt about what further steps I must take. I bade farewell to Mahler and his sisters in speechless gratitude and set out expectantly toward my new engagement in Breslau.

IV

AFTER Hamburg, Breslau was in the nature of a come-down. It wasn't a descent, though, like those of my mountain tours, where all the Saints helped — this was unhallowed ground. I did not fall, but neither could I boast of having overcome the treacherous obstacles in my path with a firm tread and a proudly raised head. I was in for trouble.

My first meeting at the Breslau Stadttheater showed me what I had happened into. I entered the office and asked to see the director. To this, Secretary S., a man with a long gray beard, said with a serious face: "I am sorry, Director Loewe has just died." When he noticed my look of horror, he added in a somber voice and in the Austrian dialect: "The funeral 'll be tomorrow from the animal hospital." I knew then that I was dealing with a wretched joke-smith who by a habitual joke wished to introduce the newcomer to the atmosphere of the theater. In fact, the gray-bearded man used to give the same answer to every inquiry about one of the theater's functionaries. He was a kind of mental starveling, able to subsist for years on the same meager jest. I learned to my dismay that such jokes and a certain low form of heartiness were customary among the heads of the institute and the artistic personnel.

At the Breslau Stadttheater joviality flowered. It was so rampant that it made art wither. Art could not flourish in the soil of that *Gemütlichkeit* which turned its back on seriousness and found pleasure in familiarities, pats on the back, and practical jokes. The Hamburg stage, with all its constitutional weaknesses, was an institute of art to the extent that a strong personality and his assiduous aides did their share in behalf of general accomplishments and the maintenance of art's unwritten and unwritable commandments. Here, in the busy atmosphere of the Breslau Stadttheater,

I felt as if I were in the abode of the godless. There was no reverence for art, and the "commandments" were not even known. How, then, should I, one of the young second conductors, have been able to enforce them? How could I have obtained from the members a higher degree of attention and concentration than that which was demanded by the theater's leading functionaries, the first conductor and the chief stage director?

Dr. Theodor Loewe, the director, was by no means an insignificant or uninteresting man. He had studied law and philosophy and had occupied himself with the doctrine of perception of Hume and Berkeley. How, with such a mental tendency, he had become a theatrical director, I do not know. His attention, by the way, was centered chiefly on the drama. That was probably the reason why the accomplishments in that department overshadowed those of the opera. We remained practically strangers to each other during my Breslau engagement, and I was rather astonished when, years later, I was told that he had spoken with pride of my activity under his direction, and when, at a chance meeting in a train, I saw the eyes of the then aged man sparkle with pleasure and heard him say words of praise of myself. The one thing worthy of praise in connection with my days in Breslau was my good intentions, but surely not my accomplishments. At any rate, I was gladdened by the man's belated warmth. My recollections of him — adversely critical, though by no means disinterested — were those of a clever man who had a superficial affinity with art and was constantly sidestepping serious artistic discussions and decisions. He was in the habit of using his caustic wit to avoid compliance with requests or heeding complaints. It was next to impossible to interest him even in questions of order and discipline, subjects of the utmost importance in an institute of art. An example of his masterly art of evasion, likely to drive a serious artist to despair, was said to have occurred a year before my engagement. A horn-player had been chided at a rehearsal by the chief conductor. The indignant man's retort had been that the conductor himself was not a man "to set the Thames afire." This impolite and disparaging figure of speech had caused the conductor to lodge a complaint with the director. Loewe could not avoid summoning the two men in an effort to have the matter straightened out. The trio's sequence of discords concluded with a coda pronounced in Loewe's guttural tenor voice: "Herr *Kapellmeister,* if you will consider the essential substance of the phrase, you must objectively concede that, in fact, you cannot set the Thames afire. And that will be all, gentlemen!" It may be imagined how discipline was harmed by such directorial methods. True, in that particular case, Loewe's personal dislike of the conductor may have been a contributing factor to his "decision," but, altogether, he was not the man to see to order in the theater, and I could not look for any assistance from him in any important matter of discipline.

Chief Conductor W., successor to the man who had been hit by Loewe's dart of derision, was a gifted and rather temperamental Hungarian musician. He conducted everything demanded of him with assurance and a certain élan, but he was not fond of rehearsing and depended on the skill of his hand whenever a performance had to be steered through the reefs of uncertainty and disorder. The chief stage director belonged in the category sufficiently described by me. What was more, it was his hobby to try to induce young singers to adopt beautiful well-rounded motions of their arms. His senseless aestheticism and constant failure to perceive dramatic essentialities drove me to despair at rehearsals. There were a few talented and vocally gifted singers at the theater, but the majority of them were *gemütlich* and without discipline, which meant that they were easy to get along with personally but difficult from an artistic standpoint. Discouraged by the spirits of indolence, levity, and even cynicism, I began to feel that I was not equal to the situation. Even my endeavors to enforce elementary demands of correctness were met by the singers with indifference, if not downright resistance, because of the prevalent spirit of "toleration." There were unpleasant altercations, quarrels, and enmities. In a letter to Mahler, I told him about my troubles. Counseling patience, he wrote:

> Have courage and keep your chin up. . . . Do not permit them to make you lose countenance — be cheerful and friendly to everybody. Remember that you are carrying your marshal's staff in your knapsack. Today or tomorrow, what does it matter?

So I decided to keep on struggling and suffering and refused by all means to become acclimated.

What is even worse than a pailful of slovenliness is the drop of talent in it, which gives it its flavor and to which indolence triumphantly refers. There were, as I said, artists of talent and voice at the Breslau Theater. My radically critical attitude was therefore at times as wrong as my colleagues' Philistine complacency. There was one artist, however, who did not know the meaning of slovenliness and who was endowed with an overflowing wealth of talent. He was an erratic block in the desert, a tower of strength and comfort in my distress. I am referring to the great Swedish bass, Johannes Elmblad, a giant in stature and personality, with

whose demonic character I was familiar through the descriptions
of Mahler, who had known him in Prague under Angelo Neumann. My first meeting with Elmblad reminded me with dramatic force of Mahler's vivid tales. One evening, I stepped from the
brightly lighted rehearsal hall into the gloomy corridor leading to
the stage. To my panic fright, I found myself confronted with a
supramundane figure. It was the gigantic grim Hagen from Wagner's *Götterdämmerung* in clanking armor, with a black beard and
disheveled hair. But even if he wore civilian clothes, every meeting
with the blond, blue-eyed Swedish giant somehow had a mythological effect. No matter how he was attired, the gigantic man with
his rough, powerful voice made the beholder's mind go back to
legendary times. He towered over the theater's entire personnel
not only physically, but also in talent, in artistic inclinations, and,
above all, in the uninhibited force of his personality. I was gratified to notice that the prehistoric stranger from the legendary cycle
of the Eddas gradually came to like me personally and to appreciate my talent. So his fierce presence made me at times forget
Breslau's prosiness and Philistinism. It was a pity that the climatic
condition of his Nordic home had endowed him also with a pen-
chant for drink. He was not a regular drinker but, unlike his com-
patriot, Candidate Molvig in Ibsen's *The Wild Duck,* he revealed
a truly demonic obsession in his sudden spells of drinking. To the
sorrow of his charming and gentle wife, many of our meetings
ended in an orgy induced by Swedish punch, which changed him
into a rather dangerous, and finally quite helpless person. At any
rate, however, his artistic qualities and his professional activity remained quite uninfluenced by his unfortunate propensity, and I
have never come in contact with a more eminent, conscientious,
and accurate representative of the parts upon which his fame was
founded. His Hunding, Fafner, Hagen, and Kaspar were noted
for the awe-inspiring grandeur of their conception. I recall with
special pleasure also his Falstaff in Nicolai's *Merry Wives* and
other comic parts in which he irradiated an elemental, vigorous
geniality. When I was at his home, he made me acquainted with
Swedish songs, among them Sjögren's virile compositions. He told
me much about Strindberg, whom he had known well. Altogether,
I found in his stormy atmosphere relief from the generally oppressive lowland air of Breslau. Elmblad had two young daughters bearing the beautiful Swedish names of Inga and Saga. The charm of
a little story he told of six-year-old Saga still lingers in my memory. One day he heard the child sing a song in which the words
"in a hundred years" occurred. He bade her stop, saying that in
a hundred years there would be nothing left of them all, neither

of their mother nor of the two girls themselves. To this the girl had replied: "Oh, no, there will be enough left of all to attach wings to it." I recall how we both were moved by the words and how I especially, who happened to be in a dark, doubting mood, was struck by the child's assurance. I heard later to my horror and grief that mental derangement had brought Elmblad's life to a tragic end. I never ceased to remember with admiration the man's great personality and was particularly pleased to be reminded of him when I conducted in Stockholm in the thirties and was greeted in the artists' room by two stately women who introduced themselves as Inga and Saga.

While the mighty Elmblad drank only occasionally, but on those occasions like a worthy rival of King Utgard Loki, who according to the Edda beat even the god Thor in a drinking contest, the theatrical circles of Breslau were addicted to habitual, though moderate drinking. At the Café Fahrig, in the immediate vicinity of the theater, and at other similar places, all and sundry could be found between morning rehearsals and the noonday meal, fortifying themselves by an early potation at specially reserved tables. I, too, was thus led astray on a few occasions, but I soon became convinced that the mixture of matutinal beer and theatrical gossip was not for me. However, I tried increasingly to find comfort and oblivion in drinking in the evenings, surrounded by a crowd of good-humored people, and I stilled my scruples with Mephisto's words:

> Cease toying with thy melancholy
> That like a vulture eats into thy heart.
> No company so poor, but plentifully
> 'Twill teach that man with man thou art.

A circumstance contributing to my discontent was the fact that the town of Breslau itself did not interest me. Every attempt to win from it balm to my eye or mind ended in disappointment. But for a few archaic buildings, its streets and squares were colorless, its aspect devoid of charm. The course of the Oder ran outside the town, and the only water to be found within the city limits was the insignificant Schweidnitzer Stadtgraben, wending its way through dully ornamental grounds. On my wintry walks, its lazy waters conjured up nothing but premonitions of vile summer odors and itching mosquito bites.

My sluggish life in Breslau was guided into more pleasant paths by a likable but rather queer colleague. He spoke a German dialect — I do not recall whether it was Palatine or Saxon — had literary interests, and was devoted to me both artistically and personally. I do not know how he managed to make me fall in with a strange plan of his. Inspired no doubt by a Dutch painting, he succeeded in gathering a drinking party, whose members, meeting regularly in the evening, were required to smoke long white Dutch clay pipes. These picturesque implements had a thin straight stem of about arm's length, and their fragility compelled the smoker to maintain a quiet and somewhat stiff "Dutch" attitude. The Knickerbocker Club, as we called ourselves for reasons unknown to me, smoked, drank, and indulged in nightly discussions in a backroom of an old Silesian tavern situated in a gloomy suburb. It usually happened in the course of an evening that the smokers' tranquillity gave way to a spirit of mischief, so that, after we had left the tavern, there was a good deal of skylarking and the playing of students' pranks, as befitted the exuberant vitality of twenty-year-olds. My mornings after were often made dismal by a headache and the aftertaste of Dutch pipe tobacco, and neither the furnished room I occupied nor my landlady was of the sort to banish feelings of displeasure. An attempt on my part to relieve the dreariness of the room by a handsome reproduction of a Murillo Madonna with the child Jesus at her breast was frustrated by the strict morality of the morose landlady who found fault with the bare maternal breast on her wall. Her puritanic severity interested me, for I had never come in contact with anything of the kind. I was to find out that the strange, gloomy conception of piety that had been offended by my gently devout Murillo was by no means the specific property of my landlady, but lived in the minds of rather wide circles of Silesia's population. I was reminded of my Breslau experience when Mahler told me some time later that women on the Woerthersee in Carinthia had one summer protested against his little three-year-old daughter's playing in his private garden without benefit of clothes. They had said: "Nudity is not pleasing in the sight of God." Music, too, was considered by my landlady to be displeasing to God's ear. When I played Bach's B-minor Mass in my room one holiday, singing to it lustily, as was my habit, she entered the room resolutely and demanded that I sanctify the holiday and cease desecrating it by music. To my modest retort that it was church music and that I had just been singing a *Gloria,* she replied in Silesian dialect: "Nay, nay! No *Gloria* either! You'll have to stop — music is music." The fact that I remained in that abode of wretched bigotry was attributable less to my inertia or stoic indifference to unpleasant occurrences than to my sense of humor, which, after my momentary irritation had vanished, supplied me with long-lasting amusement at incidents

GUSTAV MAHLER, 1907

(*photograph inscribed to Bruno Walter*)

GUSTAV MAHLER, OSSIP GABRILOWITSCH,
AND BRUNO WALTER

Prague, 1908.

of that kind, and which, like a waterproof coat, protected me against the inclemencies of the weather.

At the theater, I was at first idle and forgotten. It may be that the stonily critical face with which I received the influential Secretary S.'s daily news of sudden demises had something to do with that. But I managed at last, by substituting suddenly for a colleague, to score a success. Because nothing is appreciated so much at the theater as versatility and quick-wittedness, I found myself in favor all at once. Operas came pouring in on me. They were repertoire performances, operas that needed no rehearsing. What I thus gained in experience I lost in musical tidiness. The personnel's increased friendliness toward me was counterbalanced by my self-reproaches, but, being an assistant conductor, I could not refuse to comply with the director's orders. There was no contractual provision for the adequate preparation of a performance, and I began to yield, consoling myself with hopes for the future, when I would be far away from Breslau — and from myself, as I then was — and would be chief conductor in no matter what dog-hole.

When I had proved my intrepidity in navigating the reefs and shoals of insufficiently rehearsed German operas, I was entrusted with similar salvaging actions in the Italian repertoire. I must admit that I reached a moral nadir in my existence as a musician when I began to take a kind of sporting pleasure in holding together a centrifugally inclined cast and in interfering with lightning rapidity when a collapse threatened on stage. This frame of mind would surely have gained me honorary membership in the Breslau Theater, had it not been for the fact that I was always aware of the true character of my aberration and continued to feel like a stranger in spite of my woeful attempts at adjusting myself. "A stranger I came in, and a stranger I leave again!" This thought kept recurring to my mind, and the words with which I headed my Pressburg diary — "O Lord, let me keep my despair!" — were prompted by my Breslau experiences.

I was puzzled by my undeserved gradual success, but success it was nevertheless. I was agreeably surprised when I was commissioned to put on and conduct Donizetti's *Lucrezia Borgia* and was granted a sufficient number of rehearsals. My work met with approval, and so I was given the task of taking charge of a revival of Mozart's *The Magic Flute*. I can remember only the uplift of my heart and the burdened condition of my conscience, but not the result of my enthusiastic and thorough endeavors. I seem to recall, though, that Elmblad, who occasionally acted as assistant regisseur, was in charge of the stage direction and that we collaborated harmoniously. The result was probably a rather vivid performance that assumed solemn proportions in the priest scenes with Elmblad's noble Sarastro. It doubtlessly also bore the marks of a twenty-year-old conductor's immaturity.

When, in spite of *The Magic Flute,* I felt deeply oppressed and torn by doubts, a compassionate fate lightened my gloomy mood for a moment by means of a rather comical experience, the memory of which has frequently caused me to chuckle. A young bass was to sing Sarastro at a guest performance, pointing to a possible engagement. As he was greatly agitated, he implored me, for Heaven's sake, not to fail him in any of his musical cues and to make my gestures very plain, for, you see, he was so terribly excited. The unfortunate fellow was pulled on stage in a chariot. When getting out of it, he caught his foot in his cloak and measured his length on the boards. This misadventure, so wholly incompatible with Sarastro's dignity, was the last straw. Pamina knelt before him, asking his forgiveness for her flight, but he paid no attention to her. He had eyes only for me who was to give him his cue for singing "Arise, console thyself, Pamina!" The moment came, and, my arm upraised, I gave him the sign, only to be met with a gloomy look of dull uncertainty. In despair, I repeated my signal, but the young man merely raised his hand, pointed his forefinger at his chest, and asked mutely: "Do you mean me?" Only when I nodded vigorously did he finally decide to sing, and the performance, which had come to a stop during our pantomimic question-and-answer game, got going again.

After *The Magic Flute,* Director Loewe offered to extend my contract for a considerable period, but I had firmly made up my mind to remain idle rather than keep on suffering the fate of a second conductor at a mediocre municipal theater. Just then, I was greatly and agreeably surprised to be offered the post of chief conductor at the highly regarded Stadttheater of Riga, where Richard Wagner had been active from 1837 to 1839. I joyfully accepted the position. However, my activity was not to begin until 1898, when a new director would take over the theater, and I was faced with the question of how to spend the intervening year. This problem, too, was solved. The director of the Stadttheater of Pressburg, a small but skilfully managed stage, must have heard favorable reports about me, for he sent me a very cordially worded telegram, in which he offered me the position of chief conductor. That was exactly what I had desired: a leading position in unpretentious surroundings where I'd have the chance to test my strength. I wired my enthusiastic acceptance. Now, I decided, I would begin to be myself.

The series of favorable events had not reached its end yet. Mahler had been invited to make a guest appearance at the Vienna Court Opera, with the understanding that he was being considered as a possible successor to Jahn, who was then director of the Opera. This turn in Mahler's fortunes meant more to me than the mere satisfaction of seeing the great musician in an important position and at the goal of his desires. Vienna could be reached by a mere hour-and-a-half train ride from Pressburg, and so there was the alluring prospect that I might witness important performances led by the great man and use a Mahlerian diet to restore the normal functioning of my system, upset by Breslau fare. I was firmly resolved that Breslau was to remain the low point in my life.

All I recall of the summer of 1897 is that I brooded over my moral defeat in Breslau, found diversion and encouragement in coaching Ernst Kraus, the Berlin Opera's new heroic tenor, and longed for autumn, which would enable me to find the way back to myself and atonement for my sins. Before that could happen, though, I was to have an experience for which I had been waiting many years: Vienna.

From my early childhood, whenever I stood on the local platform of the Friedrichstrasse depot or the Zoological Garden station in Berlin, my yearning gaze had traveled toward the long-distance station with its towering signs pointing the way into the wide world and enumerating the cities which the trains would touch. Large letters told alluringly of Paris and St. Petersburg, of Amsterdam and Brussels, of Vienna and Budapest, and of many other enchanting places. But the names of no other cities aroused so strong a yearning in the boy's heart as those of Paris and Vienna. Later, it was only Vienna that attracted me. Vienna — where Mozart, Schubert, Beethoven, and Brahms had lived, where music flourished, and which was the home of the world's most magnificent Opera — was identified in my mind with music itself. And now, autumn having come, I boarded a train and rode toward music. Whatever of cheerful spirit, of radiant hope and joy of life had remained in my heart after a long period of gloom burst into flame, sang within me, and kept me in a state of blissful intoxication throughout the thirteen hours of my train ride on a wooden bench. Saxony was crossed, Bohemia, and Moravia. The days I spent in Vienna prior to my departure for Pressburg were days of ecstasy. To say that I came to know Vienna or tried to find my way through its strange streets would give but a faint idea of my roaming, or rather floating, in a dreamlike familiarity with the streets and squares and monuments and buildings. There was the Prater, its

main avenue lined with magnificent chestnut trees and alive with
the famous and much-sung rubber-tired *Fiakers,* swiftly drawn
by spanking teams of trotting horses. There were the Burgtheater,
whose proud history was so well known to me; St. Stephen's Cathedral, whose lofty outline was dear and familiar to me from many
an illustration; the venerable St. Charles' Church, in whose shadow
Brahms had spent a lifetime; the Schwarzspanierstrasse, where
Beethoven had died; the proud and noble Imperial Palace, in
which Emperor Franz Joseph ruled; the incomparably beautiful
Ringstrasse; the museums, and the Musikvereinsaal, the symphonic
hall whose walls had resounded with all the splendors of music.
There was, above all, the wonderful building of the Imperial and
Royal Court Opera, erected by Van der Nüll and Siccardsburg.
And its destinies were now in the hands of the greatest living musician. How could I help being overwhelmed by all this magnifi-
cence? How could I help being in that strange condition of
"where have I seen all this before?" I felt the emotion of Palestrina
in Pfitzner's noble work — Palestrina who, surrounded by the spirits of long-dead masters, happily whispers to himself: "My own
world!" In the daytime, I enjoyed the sights of the Ringstrasse and
of the baroque maze of the Inner City, which remained an unsolv-
able puzzle to me for decades. In the evening, I drank a glass or two
of wine in a Grinzing wine garden or visited the Second Coffeehouse in the Prater, where I ate a small portion of goulash with a
large portion of bread — sold me by a perambulating bread boy
with a wicker basket slung from his shoulders — while I sat listening to Vienna music played by a ladies' orchestra. The Vienna
dialect sounded harmoniously and pleasantly in my ear. I felt that
I belonged in Vienna; that I had not found it, but had re-found it.
Spiritually, I was a Viennese.

Mahler's sisters had secured a modest room for me. It was in
Auerspergstrasse, in the Eighth District of Vienna. The house was
of the Old-Vienna type, with a winding stone staircase, a roughly
paved gateway, and a massive double-leaved front-door, in one of
whose panels a smaller door was inserted. The front-door, open
during the day, was securely locked at ten in the evening. If I got
home after that hour, I had to ring a bell, and the small door was
opened by a drowsy janitor, to whom I had to give a small fee —
a *Sperrsechserl* — for his trouble.

It was a fine experience to have dinner with Mahler and his sisters in their handsome apartment in near-by Bartensteingasse, but
it took one's breath away to behold the nobly luxurious interior of
the Court Opera, Mahler's stately rooms, his director's office, and

the adjoining rehearsal hall — all of which were to be mine forty years later, from 1936 to 1938. I made the acquaintance of Mahler's friends, of whom I had heard so much, and who were to be my friends for decades, to the end of their lives. The hours I spent in their company, the conversations I had with them, their obvious sincerity, vitality, and goodness — all these things meant more to me than I can tell. They made the future look bright and promising. I left Vienna with the feeling of "having won a world's possession." I was made happy by the thought that I would be able to return again and again during the following four months, as often, at least, as my work in Pressburg would permit.

V

It was a brilliant autumn morning when, at the Weissgärber Bridge Station on the Danube Canal, I took a steamer for Pressburg. The handsome little town, a short distance across the border, belonged to Hungary, its Hungarian name being Poszony. After the First World War, it became part of Czechoslovakia and was given the Slovak name of Bratislava. According to my six-month contract I was to spend four of these months in Pressburg, and two in Temesvar. The latter, then a southern Hungarian town, was later ceded to Romania. I had no illusions about the artistic resources of the little Pressburg theater, about its singers, orchestra, chorus, sceneries, and costumes, but I was determined to get all my co-workers to do their very utmost, to compel them to do so, if need be. The spirit, at least, of my performances was to be thoroughly artistic. I was resolved to make up for the Breslau setback, which weighed heavily on my conscience. In those days, I lived in a state of perpetual wrath against myself and was yearning to regain the self-esteem necessary for my future activity.

"*L'esprit d'escalier!*" The clever French expression refers to the tendency to think of a suitable retort only after a conversation has been terminated and a person is already on his way downstairs. A dubiously intentioned fairy must have placed in my cradle a gift endowing me with an inclination toward a similar retarded reaction. We might call it "*la colère d'escalier,*" the stairway wrath. It seems that my nature is slow to get to the boiling point over a wrong done me or anyone else, that I first experience a general feeling of displeasure, but that later, usually considerably later, I feel compelled to live in a state of burning and long-lasting indignation. "Thus must thou be, thou canst not flee from thine own self," my friends may say regretfully or smilingly of this or some other of my oddities. I should like to point out to them my dreamlike attitude toward life — of which I shall speak later — as a possible explanation of the dream tempo of that reaction.

Breslau had left within me a state of dissatisfaction which, in the course of the summer, grew into a burning indignation at myself, subsiding at times, as during the days of my "honeymoon" in Vienna, only to flare up again all the more violently. I realized that if I were to make my plans for Pressburg come true I would first have to purify myself. I decided to keep a diary whose daily entries were to shed light upon my conduct, guide it, and keep me on the right path. A number of previous attempts at written self-investigation had petered out, but now I intended to keep a strict eye on myself. In all my career, no critic has ever been so relentlessly strict with me as I was at that time in my self-criticism. It finally drove me to the brink of despair — something which music critics, I might assure them, never succeeded in doing. My criticism was turned not only upon my musical activity, but upon my entire nature and attitude, and it was — as no criticism should be — adversely prejudiced from the beginning. The fact that my escutcheon began to shine again in Pressburg was of no avail against the self-accusations that summoned me before the bar of justice not only as an artist but also as a human being. Neither was it of any avail against the gloom that had been spreading within me for a long time and that had made my Breslau experience appear more calamitous than it actually was. In a word, I fell prey to a crisis that seriously threatened my spiritual health. Soon the torturing thoughts stirred up and hurled at me by my diary gave me no peace by day or night. Powerless and almost bereft of will, I felt myself drift toward a catastrophe like a swimmer succumbing to the force of a whirlpool. I destroyed my diary later, and the origin and course of that "children's complaint" is no longer clear in my mind, nor is its violence quite comprehensible. But because it decisively influenced my development and future attitude in life, I shall try to reconstruct my mental condition, as far as the intervening years permit.

I well remember that, as a result of my "spring cleaning," a deep resentment against myself began to set in and grow within me: resentment because of my constant yielding to everyday conflicts; resentment because of my lack of resistance to the impositions of coarse and tyrannical people; resentment because of my spiritually treasonable readiness to fraternize with trivial persons; in short, resentment because of my weakness toward my fellow-men and the assaults of the world. But my self-vivisection would not lead to an improvement. I kept finding new faults in me and became finally convinced that I was no match for life, that I was not strong enough to bear up against people and fate, and that I was not made to dare a fight against superior forces. I fell prey to a kind of malignant joy at my every new proof of "lack of character" and began to hate myself for being such a weakling in life in spite of all my musical abilities. I shut my eyes to the fact that my premature spiritual and artistic growth had adversely affected my firmness of will and that a young man of twenty-one could not be expected to have reached the maturity that might have justified so wholesale a condemnation of his character.

As mentioned before, the childhood years I had spent among grownups at the Conservatory had unfavorably affected the development of my self assurance and power of resistance. Later attempts at arousing within myself an effective fighting spirit were rendered difficult by an unfortunate propensity: I was inclined to think that, in fact, the other fellow was right. And even if he was most surely wrong objectively, it nevertheless seemed to me that according to his nature, his reason, or his circumstances he was subjectively right in his opinion and action. Where, then, was I to find the strength to fight one who was right? My own position was weakened, untenable, as long as I felt instinctively that I had to put myself in the other fellow's place. Only he is strong in life's struggle and efficient in the assertion of his will who is aware of but himself and his purposes, who never even sees or hears the others, does not want to hear or see them, and, endowed from birth with "blinders," is able to concentrate all his strength upon his goal. Artistically, I may have been gifted with some of that sound egocentric inclination found in many men of talent, but it had apparently been denied me as far as my mundane existence was concerned. But was I an artist only? Didn't I have to live too? And did not life and art so intersect that the boundaries became obliterated, and personal weakness extended its effect into the realm of the artistic? Wasn't that exactly what had happened in Breslau? Thus I felt unable either to accept myself as a character or have confidence in my ability to assert myself artistically.

I wallowed in self-abasement, unwilling to grant myself "extenuating circumstances" or to see any chance for improvement. In retrospect, I may say today that I have always fought bravely and unyieldingly for the truly important decisions in life, but that my frequently yielding attitude in less important questions has remained with me; not because of indolence and peaceableness, but because of a kind of seclusion from life in which reality seemed shrouded in veils. This inclination, which from early youth to advanced years gave a dreamlike appearance to the world, found nourishment in the teachings of Kant and Schopenhauer. I had been taught by Kant that we knew only how the world of things appeared to our imperfect senses, but by no means what the "thing in itself" was. And Schopenhauer had proved to me that the world was what my imagination showed it to be; that it was "will" in itself. This, however, seemed wholly incomprehensible and nebulous to me. I did not know what to make of it, and so, to my moral depression, I found myself also spiritually groping in a dreamlike uncertainty.

In the end, in the midst of an imaginary reality, there remained not even the firm anchorage of my own ego as something that was real and — sure of nothing but itself — gazed into a world of dreams. After all, was the ego so indubitable and indivisible? Wasn't there in man the "it," known to us but all too well? Who is there who has not at one time or another in his life experienced something like this: I want to go out; but "it" wants me to stay at home? Much later, Mahler once wrote me: "What is it that thinks in us? And what acts in us?" My self-destructive brooding went even beyond these ominous doubts; it found nourishment in a German philosophical theory categorically denying the "I" and even led me into the realm of mysticism.

Along the stream, below the upward-sloping Pressburg, stretched the far-flung Danube meadows, interspersed with clusters of handsome trees. Late of an afternoon, in the evenings, and at times also at night, I loved to walk meditatively along the undulating roads. But toward evening, fogs began to creep up from the river and over the meadows, and melancholy found its way into my mind, sucked in as if it were a longed-for gift from heaven. A heartfelt friendship with fog has remained with me from those days. It grows more profound whenever the ghostly friend envelops reality with his somber magic. In those long wanderings through the Danube meadows, the self-hatred which drove me on, and the uncertainty which confused me, was joined in the end by a supramundane influence, offering a wonderful solution for my disquiet: I felt powerfully attracted by death. As a musician, nothing seemed to be more natural than that the pain of life's dissonance would be resolved in the peace of the final consonance, once we entered the dark domain. I felt as if what I could cling to in life were vanishing and, lost in a fog, I could see but the one comforting way out.

Had everything really vanished? Could I no longer cling to anything? One day — it may have been after some musical impression — my diary answered with the counter-question: How is it that I do not recognize music as my reality? Music, at any rate, was clear, was real, was not a dream. Let all material things be unreal;

music's immaterial essence was surely not a deception of the senses. Here I had an unquestionable reality to which I could cling confidently. And, altogether, wasn't there the inspired creative man, the intermediary between me and the deity, and did not every one of his works possess an actuality beyond all problematical reality? Could anything be more real than Goethe's *Faust*? As the world became enshadowed, the reality of the spiritual grew comfortingly clear to me. A more judicious Fiesco, I should have said to the painter Romano: "You have painted what I but did!"

While thus I once more gained for myself a firm spiritual orientation, I finally also found solace for my moral perturbation in the wisdom and kindness of a sublime poet. A happy instinct led me to Jean Paul. I opened his *Titan* and kept on reading and reading with the abandonment and profound emotion symptomatic of convalescence. For years, I read nothing but Jean Paul. The stream of love pouring from that noblest of hearts, the man's firm and profound piety resting upon a philosophical foundation, his lofty humor, and the wealth of his imagination succored me and pointed me away from the hell of self-investigation, which Roquairol, in *Titan,* had undertaken to lead *ad absurdum*. It was the same Roquairol whose self-scourging scorn had inspired the Death March in Mahler's First Symphony.

But the poet's hand led me away not only from sterile self-contemplation. His thoughts, his words, and his example guided me back again to the faith, to Christendom, to which I had come close years before, from which I had strayed, and which I was never to lose again. Thus, very gradually, I found my way back to a harmony with myself and to life, to which, had everything else failed, the thought of my parents might after all have compelled me to cling. A decided change in my mental vision had been the lasting result of that crisis in my life. A veil had spread itself between the world and myself, a veil which has never really lifted since, comparable to the one used on the stage to lend to fabulous and fantastic scenes the illusion of distance and dreaminess. But I had learned to believe in the indubitable reality of life in the spirit and of its creative manifestations.

While the inner tragedy developed slowly and took approximately the described course until it reached the catharsis, the longed-for purification of my artistic conscience proceeded vigorously. Ever since the Breslau setback, so firm a determination and a desire to achieve great things had grown within me that the combined theaters of the *German Stage Almanac* could not have furnished a sufficiently large object of attack. Urged on by this overabundant fiery spirit, I hurled myself upon the little Pressburg theater. Not only did it fail to put any obstacles in my way, but all doors opened wide to me. There was no trace of the "resistance of the callous world," that I had experienced in Breslau. Even had it existed, my fervor would have made me unconscious of it. The majority of the members of the theater were talented beginners. They were trying to outdo one another in fulfilling the wishes of a conductor bursting with energy. My immediate colleague was the second *Kapellmeister* and conductor of operettas. He called himself Baldreich, but his real name was Brzobohaty. An excellent Czech musician, he stood by me stanchly from the beginning. His attitude never changed, and he was always eager to act according to my intentions in working with the orchestra and the singers. The *Konzertmeister* supported me with conviction and was therefore a valuable help to me. The small chorus sang as well as it could, which was far from well. It was at times almost unbearable even to my optimistic ear. I suppose the artistic results were as mediocre as the small theater's resources, but they seemed far to exceed what the audiences had been accustomed to. There was general praise, the performances were crowded, the audiences applauded and shouted their approval, the director was proud, and I might have considered myself the hero of the day, but my soul's barometer pointed to storm, and no outward manifestations of favor on the part of Fortune could alter that fact.

I drew added strength and vitality from my occasional visits to Vienna, where I was privileged to witness performances conducted by Mahler, to realize their fascinating effect on the cultured audiences of the Court Opera, and to learn from them with an understanding which exceeded in maturity that of my Hamburg days. I recall an indescribably fine performance of Bizet's *Djamileh* with the highly gifted Marie Renard in the title part. Director Raoul of the Pressburg Theater, who kept a watchful eye on the Vienna performances of operas and operettas, immediately put *Djamileh* into our repertory. The comparisons I was able to make were as instructive as they were depressing. Mahler and the Opera were not Vienna's only attractions, however. The city itself drew me powerfully, and I thoroughly enjoyed its many facets. I went to the Carl Theater and took delight in its excellent performances of operettas. I shall never forget Girardi, the most Viennese of Vienna's popular actors. I am glad that I was able to see him in his famous part of Valentin in Raimund's *Spendthrift* and to hear him sing the Vienna *Fiakerlied*.

My work in Pressburg was not easy. The orchestra was small. I had, for instance, but two horns, and I had accordingly to rearrange the orchestration of almost all of the "grand" operas. I was painfully affected by the change in sound caused by these limitations. My conscience was burdened because of having interfered with a masterpiece. I always kept in mind my motto: "O Lord, let me keep my despair!" I constantly reminded myself that I must under no circumstances permit myself to become accustomed to the disgraceful things which the narrowness of conditions were forcing on me. That they were actually forced on me was my only justification.

A new opera I was able to put on was Leoncavallo's *La Bohème*. The composer of *Pagliacci* had used the book by Murger that had furnished the libretto for Puccini's opera. The performance was quite successful. While I have not the slightest recollection of the music, I do recall an occurrence after the first performance. When I and a number of friends entered the dining room of the Hotel Palugyai — I think that was the name — the gyspy band stopped their dance music and played a number of themes from the opera. Having listened to the unknown new work shortly before had sufficed the leader of the band to impress upon his memory some of the melodies, and the others to support him with cleverly improvised accompaniments. When later one of the gypsies made the round of the tables, I expressed to him my admiration, which seemed to please him very much. But when I tried to put some money on his collection plate, he drew back with a start: he couldn't take anything from a colleague.

After four months of work in Pressburg, I went to Temesvar by way of Budapest. The artistic personnel — all but the orchestra — went along with me. In Temesvar, I began to direct my gaze again to outward things, to become interested in my strange surroundings, and to follow Goethe's advice to live resolutely. The orchestra was even smaller than that in Pressburg. Whenever the score called for divided celli, a furrow of despair would appear on the forehead of the one and only cellist at my disposal. A man of good will, he would have liked to give me the benefit of continuous double stops, had his technique and the instrument's potentialities permitted it. I tried to restrain his hopeless attempts by showing him that I had assigned the second cello part to the violas or, if it was too low, to a bassoon, but the well intentioned and badly executed double stops as well as the furrow of despair were in evidence to the end of the season. The theater was part of the hotel in which everybody was living. It resembled the place described by E. T. A. Hoffmann in his *Don Juan*, though there were no music-drunk poets driven out into the corridors by the haunting memories of operas. Instead, there were any number of young officers of the Temesvar garrison, exhilarated by the spirits of wine and looking for far-from-ghostly adventures.

While I was able to maintain discipline within the Opera, a spirit of licentiousness grew in matters not directly connected with art. It did not actually hamper me in my work, but it offended and humiliated me. I found refuge in the company of the amiable and refined Brzobohaty, and we spent many a nocturnal hour playing chess in a corner of the café — my fondness for the game far exceeded my ability — while the gypsies played fervently, wine-inspired people raged, shouted, and sang all about us, and an occasional love-lorn couple attracted our gaze if the leader of the band, having left his place on the platform, bent over them, fiddling his exciting melodies right into their ears and causing their heads, arms, and shoulders to sway ecstatically to the rhythm of his music. After such an evening, I would often walk out into the Puszta, the Hungarian steppe, which stretched into unbounded distances in the moonlight. I would enjoy the old eternal peace surrounding me and the young new peace I had won so arduously. I can never think back on those magnificent nights on the silent steppe without once more being conscious of Beethoven's *A Recovered Man's Sacred Song of Thanksgiving to the Deity*.

When the season was over — it must have been April — I felt the desire to become better acquainted with the strange country at the edge of the Balkans before returning to more familiar surroundings. So, instead of turning at once northward in the direction of Budapest, which I had but touched on my inward-bound trip, and acquaintance with which I therefore still owed myself, I traveled south, down the splendidly wide Danube as far as Bazias, a picturesque, hilly place washed by the black waters of the river. I have seen the Danube in any number of colors, but, as far as I know, it is blue only in Strauss's waltz. I stayed the night at Bazias and dreamed away the following day. I listened to the most enchanting gypsy music, wandered about at night climbing from rock to rock in a fog that no longer cast a gloom about me but made me feel in the company of friendly ghosts. I continued my Danube trip down to Orsova, to the Iron Gate, and to the Turkish island Adah Kaleh, lying dreamlessly slumbering in the middle of the stream. A rowboat took me across the dark waves to its shore and waited until I had tasted my first real Turkish coffee and taken an uneventful walk through the island's strange desolation. Then I returned by way of glamorous Budapest and beloved Vienna to Berlin, where I spent the summer dreaming of the glories awaiting the future chief conductor of the Riga Opera.

VI

THE RIGA STADTTHEATER was listed in the *German Stage Almanac* and was considered a German theater in spite of the fact that it was in Russian territory. The language in opera and drama was as German as the audience, the theater's administration, and the preponderant part of the cultured population of the Russian province of Latvia and its capital, Riga. The governor, the officials, and the military were Russian, while the autochthonous population was Latvian. It was remarkable that Czarist Russia tolerated the preponderance of the German language and of German culture in a country that had belonged to Russia for almost two hundred years. Latvia, won from the natives by German knights of religious orders and Hanseatic merchants in the early Middle Ages, and conquered subsequently in turn by the Poles, the Swedes, and the Russians, still showed plainly in its German social structure the dividing line between the nobility and the merchant community, predicated upon history. Although the Germans were compelled to live side by side with the Russians, who had remained strangers to them, and with the suppressed, and therefore hostile Letts, they had failed to form a closely knit community. Relations between the Baltic aristocracy and the merchants of the Big Guild and the Little Guild were practically non-existent. It was my impression that, while the Germans and Russians in Riga led a separate existence, though a side-by-side one, they had one thing in common: their disdain of the Letts, who were excluded from any important position or activity. I can still remember how surprised I was when one day an opera by a native composer was submitted to me. Unfortunately, it had little merit, but the accompanying letter, written in faulty German, revealed to me a striving for higher goals as well as the bitterness of the oppressed.

I shall never forget how the native cab drivers were treated. Only rarely were they told where to drive a fare. A person would get into the droshky or the sleigh and call out the Russian word *pascholl!* The small bristly-haired horse would run on at a good pace until the driver was hit on either the right or the left arm, to indicate which turn he was to take. If the vehicle was proceeding too slowly, the fare would hit the driver's back, and by no means lightly. If the driver was to stop, the passenger would roughly grasp the cape of his cloak with both hands and pull him backward. Linguistic difficulties may have contributed to the establishment of these horrible habits, which, by the way, were not minded by either the passengers or the drivers. Then again, they may have been an infectious relic from the days of Russian serfdom. At any rate, consciously or unconsciously, they expressed a disdain that was to have gruesome consequences. When the termination of the First World War gave to the Letts the rule of their country, horrible things were said to have happened. I learned that, when political quiet was restored, serious and successful cultural efforts on the part of the natives were made. Many years later, I received a number of invitations to appear as a guest conductor at the Stadt-theater, which in the meantime had become Lettish. Unfortunately, I was so pressed for time that I was unable to accept.

In my time, the Riga Theater had a singular constitution. It had been in successful operation for decades. An assembly of well-to-do and cultural-minded citizens undertook to guarantee the economic existence of the theater, every guarantor obligating himself to pay a proportionate share of a possible deficit. The guarantors chose from their midst a Theater Committee, which in turn appointed a director who had to submit a report and render an accounting at weekly sessions of the committee. Herr Ludwig Treutler was the director when I arrived. He came from the dramatic stage and even acted a part occasionally. I still have a rather unfavorable recollection of his King Lear. Although the men constituting the committee were highly regarded citizens, they were alien to art. To them, the significance of the theater lay in the fact that it represented a pillar of German culture. A director with artistic ambitions, like Richard Balder, the man who occupied the post during my second year in Riga, was hard put to it to make headway with them. When, at my suggestion, he put on Mozart's *The Magic Flute,* which did not turn out to be a box-office success, the old white-bearded chairman of the committee dignifiedly expressed to him his disapproval and suggested in an asthmatic hoarse voice that he ought to put on "better pieces."

A fine steamer trip of thirty-six hours across the Baltic took me from Stettin to Riga. The town was situated near the beautiful Gulf of Riga, at the mouth of the Duna River. I expected Riga to furnish the answer to the momentous question of whether or not I could be successful as the leading conductor of a serious theater noted for its fine tradition as well as for its contemporary importance. A vital personal question had been decided, however, before my arrival, in the course of my trip. The opening scene of *The Avowals,* a comedy by Eduard Bauernfeld, a friend of Schubert's and Schwind's, shows a man and a woman coming on stage from opposite sides and passing each other. The man looks after the woman and says with determination: "There goes my future wife!". The scene to be recorded here differed from that of the Bauernfeld comedy in locality, but essentially — as far as the dramatic tempo was concerned — it was quite similar to it. The action took place on the swaying deck of a steamer, and the woman was Elsa Korneck, the lyric-dramatic soprano of the Riga Opera, almost the entire artistic personnel of which was on board. She did not walk, but was sitting wanly in a sheltered corner, obviously forced by the ship's motion to maintain a recumbent position. But no matter, one look was enough to convince me that there sat my future wife. I stuck to my resolution and carried it out two-and-one-half years later.

The momentous professional question was decided in Riga with a brilliance unsurpassed in my life, which was surely not lacking in successes. I was a fiery youth of twenty-two. What I had long striven for, I had victoriously achieved during the previous year: to have power over my co-workers. Now I had at my command the abundant resources of a highly regarded opera house and was privileged to work in a town devoted to art. I would at last be able to prepare and produce beloved and familiar works without being inhibited either by my own inward difficulties or by deplorable material insufficiencies. I felt as if I were soaring in a dream. It seemed that people were willing to overlook even my youth, although I was probably the youngest Chief *Kapellmeister* to grace the conductor's desk of the Riga Stadttheater. The general attitude was probably due in no small degree to my beard. When I had last visited Vienna during the preceding spring, Mahler's "family council" had come to the conclusion that I looked entirely too young for a chief conductor. I was instructed to make up for my lack of years by the dignity of a beard, and it seemed that it came up to our expectations.

The growth of my strength kept pace with that of my work and my standing in the theater and in the town. I became more firmly conscious of my abilities, without being made immodest inwardly or outwardly. The public's enthusiasm was heightened by the fact that the press was exceedingly kind to me. So I was made to feel thoroughly happy in an atmosphere of work and recognition. I am unable to say whether my accomplishments actually merited the enthusiasm they evoked. I was benefited by the fact that the Riga Opera had not had a good conductor in years. I was furthermore aided and inspired to increased efforts by the cheerful co-operation of the artistic personnel and the devoted attitude of the orchestra and the chorus.

The following little story is characteristic of the energy with which I insisted that my artistic demands be heeded. Most of the members of the cast were well-intentioned, but there was one man who was refractory. He was the heroic tenor S., a middle-aged Hungarian with a robust voice and musical assurance, but without feeling, temperament, or artistic sense. His face was constantly somewhat distorted, as if he were tasting some sour dish. No effort on my part seemed to be able to give him alkaline balm. I was pained by his coldness and prosiness in the warmly vital atmosphere of my rehearsals and performances. The result was a mutual antipathy which, on his part, manifested itself in an attitude of passive resistance. When I proposed to restore the so-called "secret ensemble" in *Lohengrin*, Mr. S.'s passive resistance became active. With mulish obstinacy he refused to study his part in the ensemble. He seemed to care nothing for possible disciplinary consequences and to be determined to stick it out, come what might. I knew that I could count on but lukewarm support from Director Treutler, whose vanity and ambition were deeply hurt by my continued success. So I decided to take matters into my own hands. There was a tenor in our chorus who had repeatedly sent me long and beautifully written letters, asking for an audition. The fact that, after signing himself Alois Luka of Znaim in Moravia, he never omitted to add the words "*prima vista* and *a capella* singer" gave me the idea that he might be sufficiently musical to learn the part of Lohengrin in the "secret ensemble" in the short time available before the actual performance. I sent for him and found that, while doubtlessly a bit balmy, he was a middle-aged man of good appearance, a fine voice, and rare musicality. My request caused him transports of joy, and on the very next day he sang for me the ensemble part, showing that he knew it correctly and by heart. I asked him to confine himself to humming the part softly at rehearsals with the orchestra. My antagonist S. kept a sullen silence on those occasions, so that, to the consternation of the other singers, the important voice of Lohengrin was not heard in that number. At the performance, however, the *prima vista* and *a capella* singer from Znaim proved himself a veritable *deus ex machina*. At the "secret ensemble" he stepped forward from the ranks of the chorus and sang the part of Lohengrin. I suppose it was the first time that two Lohengrins were ever on stage at the same time, one in shiny armor and embarrassed silence, the other looking like a poor relation of the Knights of the Grail, but beaming with the joy of singing. So I got my "secret ensemble," S. had to bear his colleagues' ridicule, and the somewhat muddle-headed second Lohengrin had a happy experience. It's a pity I do not recall the consequences of my stratagem. But since it has left on my tongue no bad taste *à la* S., I feel justified in assuming that everything turned out as I had wished; that at subsequent performances either a Brabantine Lo-

BRUNO WALTER CONDUCTING

*(above) at the Mozarteum, Salzburg, 1934 and (below) Grosse Musikvereinssaal
(Vienna Philharmonic Orchestra), Vienna, 1936*

BRUNO WALTER'S DAUGHTERS, LOTTE AND GRETEL

Salzburg, 1936

hengrin stepped forth from the ranks of the knights, or that S. had penitently decided to learn his ensemble part. His enmity, at any rate, did not relent. A year later, at a *Meistersinger* performance, he sang the part of Stolzing to my fiancée's Eva. During the long scene in the second act, while these two were sitting in the arbor in front of Pogner's house, the audience and I were astonished to behold the world's most unloving pair of lovers. Eva, her first tender advances having been repulsed, had assumed a resigned attitude, while Stolzing showed his insuperable aversion by turning his back upon her. After the performance, Director Balder explained to our tenor that a tender attitude toward Eva was as much part of his professional duties as the singing of the correct notes. He also tried to make him understand that his demonstration had been directed to the wrong address. Mr. S. acquiesced, but I cannot say that his tenderness in the same scene of the next *Meistersinger* performance was more convincing. His attitude was one of disdainful aloofness.

My relations with the other singers were quite cordial. Some of them even became my friends. My occasional tyrannical demands were accepted and complied with. When, a week before a revival or a *première*, I told the members of the cast that they would have to refrain from attending evening parties or going on sprees, they all agreed and, as far as I know, acted accordingly. The attitude of the singers, chorus people, and members of the orchestra at my very exhaustive rehearsals was exemplary. We formed a happy, peaceful, and enthusiastic family. It would be going too far to give an account of individual performances. I should like to mention, though, that a romantic and heart-warming performance of Weber's *Der Freischütz,* with my fiancée as Agathe, and a dramatically impressive rendition of Marschner's *Hans Heiling* seemed to me particularly effective at the time. Among the other operas I prepared and conducted were Mozart's *Don Giovanni* (with D'Andrade), *Figaro,* and *Magic Flute,* Beethoven's *Fidelio,* Tchaikovsky's *Eugen Onegin,* and Wagner's *Die Walküre, Lohengrin, Tannhäuser,* and *Holländer.* There was a performance of *Carmen,* lent added luster by the brilliant singing and acting of Gemma Bellincioni. Spinelli's *A basso porto,* with which I had become acquainted in Cologne, had its first Riga performance under my baton.

The stage directing, though primitive, made me feel less unhappy than before. The regisseur was devoted to me and was glad to act in accordance with my wishes. What was more, I began to develop in Riga an irresistible inclination to encroach on the regisseur's domain, an inclination that frequently drove my collaborators at the director's desk to despair and plunged me into conflicts. Although I was always extremely polite in my first requests for this arrangement or that, I soon lost my self-control and gradually became so overcome by the pressure of what I considered imperative that I was apt to turn directly to the artists on stage, a procedure which naturally placed the stage director in an awkward predicament. But if I was faced with the alternative of hurting either the spirit of the work or the feelings of the regisseur, I invariably chose the latter, though I felt sorry afterwards and was always ready to hold out the olive branch. Fortunately, I was frequently privileged to have collaborators at the director's desk who submitted to my actions because they felt that I was moved by an inward compulsion or because they realized the justification of my wishes. True, there were cases of outright opposition, but whenever important dramatic questions were involved, or matters on the borderline between music and the drama, I always proved inflexible and fought my way to the bitter end. On the other hand, I finally came to know how to make it easy for the stage director to yield or to accede to my wishes by expressing my requests in a particularly courteous tone and manner. This was by no means premeditated, but I had instinctively come to recognize it as the most effective method for achieving my artistic ends.

Early in my first year in Riga, in October, 1898, Gustav Mahler offered me a conductor's job at the Vienna Court Opera, to begin in 1900, after the expiration of my two-years' contract with the Riga Opera. He said in his letter that by then I would have gained the maturity necessary for such a position, that he would not be able to manage in the long run without an understanding collaborator, and that he counted on me. My heart urged me to go to Vienna, but careful considerations counseled against such a move. I felt that it was necessary to become firmly rooted within myself before exposing myself again to the powerful influence of Mahler. And how was I to know at the beginning of my Riga activity if, by 1900, I would have gained the necessary self-assurance? So it seemed advisable to wait until my ego had firmly crystallized. My reply to Mahler's letter was frankly to that effect, but he would not admit the justification of my standpoint, felt disappointed in me and forsaken by one on whom he had relied. Thus came about the first and only discord in our relations. While it lay heavy on my heart, it could not move me from my decision.

I was made conscious of being in Russia in spite of the German character of the town and the German theater. On the numerous holidays, the Czarist Hymn was played and sung by the entire artistic personnel, and I had to conduct it. The beautiful piece of solemn music gave me pleasure. On a number of occasions, when the Governor gave a reception, I and several of the theater's artists were asked to the castle. I recall a "transgression" that might have turned out badly for me. The Governor had requested a singer to sing a few songs and asked me to accompany her. But the room would not become still, and I could not bring myself to begin while people were talking. I told the adjutant, when he prompted me, that there would have to be quiet. The Governor was fortunately a reasonable man and, with a gesture, required his guests to be silent. In other circumstances, my attitude might have been interpreted as disrespect toward the Czar's representative and caused me to be severely punished. As it was, I was never asked to the castle again, as far as I can recall.

Although work took up most of my time, my life in Riga was made attractive and warm by a number of personal relations with fine people. My future wife and myself were attached by ties of a warm friendship to a charming and sincere couple. The husband, Richard Immelmann, the theater's heroic baritone, had a splendid voice and a magnificent figure. I had known him at the Stern Conservatory. His genial good-humor was a foil to my high-spirited impromptus. Our four-cornered friendship lasted for years, even after we had been professionally separated. A wonderfully kind and musically minded couple by the name of Irschik had become greatly attached to my future wife and myself. Our engagement was announced at their home on Christmas Eve, 1898. That friendship, too, lasted for years. A new member was added to the high-spirited circle of friends in the person of the theater's third conductor, Friedrich Weigmann, a splendid musician of wide general knowledge, varied interests, and fine qualities. An apparently shy and introverted man of about thirty, he had been rather reserved in his attitude toward me for a considerable time, until an acquaintance told me of a trip he and Weigmann had made to the seaside. Riga does not lie directly on the open sea, but a number of attractive bathing resorts can be reached by means of a short train ride. Weigmann, the quiet musician, was said to have been made ecstatically happy by his first sight of the sea. He had extended both his arms wide, stood thus for quite some time, deeply moved, and then suddenly hurled his hat into the air with a jubilant exclamation. "I'll have to become better acquainted with that fellow," I said to myself. I came to know a singular man, firmly balanced and of great personal worth. His outward appearance suggested a scientist rather than a musician. A Nietzsche mustache adorned his pensive features. An emotional and serious composer, he yet lacked inspiration. Altogether, I felt more strongly attracted by his humanistic accomplishments and tendencies than by his musicianship. He was an apt conversationalist: he talked well and listened well, but was able also to enjoy a peaceful silence. So our walks, some of which lasted for hours, passed off pleasantly between looking about, thinking, and occasional spirited conversation. Our way usually led us to the Duna, whose mighty width was spanned by a railway bridge resting on powerful pillars. A tall iron superstructure towered above it. We were fond of walking along the footpath at the side of the tracks. It was glorious and inspiring there on a wintry night, when a storm would rage across the river and make the heavy bridge tremble. Weigmann was fond of releasing some of the enthusiasm caused by the storm and the river by making daring excursions into the upper regions of the iron structure, a feat made possible by his long legs and gymnastic agility. He would join me again later to take part in one of our frequent adventurous descents over a flight of stairs leading from the center of the bridge down to a small island in the Duna — called Hasenholm, if I remember correctly. It was an elongated sandy stretch of land with a few dark primitive huts on it. Standing on the island, we felt as if we were in the midst of the black stream itself. Only the occasional blinking of lights on the distant banks reminded us that brightness, people, and the world still existed. Our small circle of friends, stimulated by the difference of temperaments and made pleasant by a kindly disposition toward one another and the world in general, was firmly cemented and virtually remained intact even after fate had separated its members. Immelmann, when he left the stage, returned to his original calling, that of a veterinary. Weigmann, whose interests had from the beginning been divided between music and socialism, was finally most powerfully attracted by the latter. He settled in a workingmen's suburb of Hamburg, took charge of local choral associations, and gave music lessons to children.

While I had ample opportunity for developing as an operatic conductor in an atmosphere of work and success, I felt that my musical capacity was by no means exhausted. Essentially, I was dedicated not only to dramatic music but, at the very bottom of my being, to absolute music too. Having grown up in its atmos-phere, it was but natural for the absolute side of my musical nature to demand that it be not starved while its dramatic *alter ego* was feasting. Gradually, I found my way back to chamber music. In the *Konzertmeister* of my orchestra I found an efficient, musicianly, and serious violinist. So I decided to give public piano-and-violin sonata recitals with him. The Schwarzhäupterhaus, whose name and interestingly pure early Gothic style recalled the ecclesiastical origin of the town of Riga and which was now the property of the mercantile Big Guild, contained a hall that, by virtue of its character, acoustics, and dimensions, was ideally suited for chamber music. Occasionally, we called upon the services of the orchestra's first cellist for trio performances. No account of my activities in Riga would be complete without mention of these recitals in beautiful Schwarzhäupter Hall. They attained importance in the town's musical life.

During the summer following my first theatrical season in Riga I went to Danzig, to call upon my fiancée's family. I spent a few weeks in the attractive Baltic seaside resort of Zoppot, a suburb of Danzig. Then I returned for some time to Berlin, where I again coached Ernst Kraus. At his home, I made the acquaintance of Hans Pfitzner, the composer of the opera *Der arme Heinrich* that I had studied with so profound an interest in Hamburg. I shall have more to say later of that singular and contradictory great man. He was then at work on his *Die Rose vom Liebesgarten,* which he played for me at his rather modest home from pages he had just finished writing. I was from the first captivated by the inspired melodies and the dramatic force of the opera and felt enriched and uplifted by every further contact with Pfitzner's creative work. Stimulated by my personal association with him and his clever and charming wife, the daughter of the Cologne composer and conductor Ferdinand Hiller, I returned to Riga to start my second season there. I was looking forward with joyful anticipation to the time when I would be able to continue my promising relations with Pfitzner.

On the day following upon my arrival, Richard Balder, the new director of the Stadttheater, called on me, resplendent in a Prince Albert coat, silk hat, and light-colored kid gloves. Shy as I was, I was greatly taken aback by this formality. My youth was not as yet equal to so solemn a social occasion, and I was racking my brain for a conversational topic that would furnish common ground for my visitor's elegant worldliness and my social inexperience. Our groping attempts to keep things going were not particularly successful. Suddenly an outside influence added to the *lento* introduction of our conversation a refreshing *allegro,* in the style of the early form of overtures. My flat, which had the advantage of being quite near the theater, consisted of two small rooms and was on the third floor of an old house in a narrow street of the town's central section. Another advantage was the fact that the windows afforded a view of the sky. The sight of the roof of the opposite house had to be taken into the bargain. When it rained, this sub-astral part of my view was lent added charm by quite a number of tail-waggling rats sitting in the gutter at the edge of the roof and quenching their thirst. We were in the midst of a painful exchange of civilities when there was a sudden downpour of rain. I noticed that my visitor's face at once assumed a boyishly merry expression. "What a fine view you have!" he said. From that moment, the conversation flowed freely. The especially well attended meeting of rats that afternoon had put an end to conventionalities, turned our talk into natural channels, and brought about a close contact between us. Balder told me later that he had thought it expedient to establish amicable relations with the popular chief conductor by paying him a courtesy call; he had been embarrassed by the unexpected impression of my half-grown ingenuousness, but after the rat interlude had felt that our future harmonious collaboration was assured. He was right; we understood each other well. When he directed the stage, which happened frequently, he adapted himself to my wishes with inward conviction and an outward display of well-bred politeness. Not only was he a man of the world to his fingertips, but he was also endowed with a pronounced theatrical talent, and so we got along famously. A lively social intercourse with him and his wife set in, and many were the occasions when we would sit up until the wee small hours conversing gaily and drinking copiously, as was customary in those latitudes. I recall a rather extensive festivity following the revival of Tchaikovsky's *Eugen Onegin,* which lasted not only into the early hours of the morning but was continued by a sleighride into the country. We stopped at an inn, got the innkeeper out of bed, and induced him to give us some breakfast. When we got back to town, the shops — they were called booths in Riga — were just being opened.

Since my days in Pressburg, my reading had been confined almost exclusively to Jean Paul's writings. *Onegin,* however, pointed the way to Pushkin, Rubinstein's *Demon* to Lermontov. The writings of both poets went straight to my heart. They have remained dear to me ever since. Their life, their creative work, and their absurd end — they were both killed in duels — afforded me a new insight into the Russian character.

It may be of interest that among the young singers who sang for me to get the benefit of my judgment and advice were two future stars: Hermann Jadlowker, the excellent tenor, and Joseph Schwarz, the wonderful baritone. I was glad to be told later by both that I had praised and encouraged them warmly at the time.

During my second season in Riga, my theatrical activity became even more intensified, if that were possible, while my outside activities, too, assumed a larger scope. I had agreed to take over a piano class at the Gyzicki Music School. A performance of Mendelssohn's *Elijah,* with soloists from the Opera and an excellent choral society of the town, gave me a very welcome first opportunity to try my skill at the oratorio style. There were also a number of concerts with the theater's orchestra in the large hall of the Trade Association. They signified my first excursions into the realm of symphonic music. I do not recall how they turned out.

Thus the first months of my second season in Riga slipped by. Balder began to talk about a new contract, and I rather liked the idea of prolonging my activity at a theater that in so gratifying a sense had become my own, in a town of which I had grown fond and in whose good-will toward me I felt I had found a safe haven, and with an artistic personnel devoted to me. When my benefit performance came along, people stood in line for hours at night to secure tickets. The enthusiasm with which I was honored once more revealed to me the affection that had warmed my heart throughout my activity in Riga. But before 1899 ended, I received a communication from the Berlin Opera offering me a five-year contract as Royal Prussian Conductor. How could I have resisted? Think of it! The venerable house in whose top gallery I had received the decisive impressions of my boyhood years and where I heard my first *Tristan* was to be the scene of my own activity. I was to conduct the orchestra whose sound had impressed itself indelibly upon my ear. I was to appear before the public in one of Europe's leading operahouses. I would be able to afford my parents and my brother and sister the pleasure of enjoying the work of their son and brother. Finally, the contract would make it possible for me to marry. So I accepted, but not before having informed Mahler of my decision and having received from him a conciliatory and approving letter.

There came the last winter months of my stay in Riga, during which I took many a meditative walk along the beautiful boulevards of the town. There followed the white spring nights, light as day, eminently suited to the most wide-awake thinking and wholly unsuited to sleeping. I came to the conclusion that in Riga I had actually become acquainted with my better self. Every bit of my strength was now focussed upon nothing but the next goal. I kept from brooding and worrying and had gained a healthy outlook on life in unrestricted attention to the duties of the day. Once more I saw how right it was to live resolutely. I was naïve enough to believe that I had fully and forever mastered the style of resolute living. At any rate, I lived according to that principle at the time, aided by the consciousness that I had made good as an artist and was determinedly pursuing my way. My aim was to grasp and realize opera in its artistic entirety, just as I liked to imagine Handel had done in London, as Weber had passionately striven to do in Prague and Dresden, as Wagner had taught and done, and as Mahler had undertaken to do in Hamburg. Quite spontaneously and without conscious attention, I had attacked my operatic tasks in Riga in that universal sense. And so, full of proud hope, I was looking forward to a continuation of my endeavors in more splendid surroundings, with more ample means at my command, and at one of the centers of the musical world.

The time came to go home. After having made the previous two trips by railway, we again went by way of the Baltic. A strange experience en route is worth recording here as an example of the "human — all-too-human" element and a tragi-comical contribution to Alfonso's teachings in Mozart's *Così fan tutte*. A handsome and charming young woman, a member of the Riga cast, had formed a friendly attachment to my fiancée during the past season. She had confided to her that she was practically engaged to a baritone at some German Court Theater and intended to marry him that coming summer. Her confidante was therefore somewhat startled to notice that tender relations were being established between Miss K. and a young actor in Riga. Eros was brilliantly victorious. The faces and actions of his helpless victims plainly showed to all and sundry how matters stood. A tragedy seemed to be in the making. Romeo accompanied his Juliet to the boat, and the parting of the lovers caused everybody to shed tears of pity. Sobbing, the departing beauty waved to her lovelorn swain until his figure had faded from her vision. Then she collapsed brokenly in a deck chair in a secluded corner. None of those passing her dared to disturb her grief, which seemed but slowly to give way to quiet sadness and melancholy. Gradually Miss K. grew calmer. She even began to talk with reviving spirit to my fiancée, who reported to me with astonishment that she thought she could discern symptoms of a certain anticipatory joy in the young lady. I, too, was aware of the change of mood. When the ship docked in Stettin, we all were amazed to see the favorite of Eros wave enthusiastically to a good-looking young man, obviously her fiancé, who was waiting for her at the foot of the gangway. Soon the two were in each other's arms. The worthy disciple of Despina married the baritone that very summer, and that was the last we saw of her. But whenever I conduct *Così fan tutte,* Dorabella becomes identified in my mind with Miss K., and I feel amorally moved to compassion, tolerance, and sympathy.

Acting upon my parents-in-law's suggestion, my fiancée and I postponed our wedding until the following spring. True, I had a promising career ahead of me, but I was still so "exceedingly young"! I agreed that we would not marry until my economic existence was made secure by a successful Berlin season. So my fiancée accepted a one-year contract at the Stadttheater in Basle, while I took up bachelor quarters in Derfflingerstrasse in Berlin, only a few minutes' walk from the Falk Real-Gymnasium which, about nine years before, I had left with so much impatience. After a summer spent partly in Zoppot, partly in the Black Forest, composing, studying, and enjoying long walking tours, I reported to the General Management of the Royal Prussian Theater. I was ready to start upon my new activities.

VII

THE BERLIN OPERA was ruled by Prussian officials and the methods of Prussian officialdom. The supreme chief of both theaters, the opera and the drama, was His Excellency Count Hochberg, the Opera's director Privy Councillor Pierson, the head of the administrative department Privy Councillor Winter. All manner of other councillors served under them. If one of the artists had a request to make, he submitted a "petition" and "begged respectfully." The bureaucratic spirit affected even matters directly concerned with art, and the harsh voice of command mingled disharmoniously with the chorus of the Muses, to serve whom should have been the institute's only purpose. But another service was involved — the Royal Service. If the orders were not of a downright military character, they were at any rate "official instructions" to do so and so. In the last analysis it amounted to the same thing: there must be strict obedience. And so obedience was enjoined upon the artists. Artists could be made into subordinates and commanded by instructions, but not in connection with the exercise of art, which in the absence of freedom loses its essential character. In spite of all appearances, artistic results cannot be achieved, even in the case of an orchestra and its leader, if the relation of superior and subordinate prevails. No oboist obedient to a master's command is able to play a solo beautifully: his soul must lend charm to his playing, and the conductor, respecting its freedom, must influence it by methods more subtle than a superior's paralyzing command.

The artists were subjected to the commands issued by the bureaucratic administrative apparatus, but whenever these commands encroached upon the realm of art they resulted in nothing but inhibition and failure. Truly artistic accomplishments took place outside the sphere of command. It was not surprising or preventable that bureaucratic pressure occasionally led even to an abandonment of artistic discipline. Administrative activities and artistic efforts lived side by side, their different aims and outlooks causing constant friction, hampering art without being able to subordinate it and posing problems outside the administrators' sphere of comprehension.

As an institute of art, the Berlin Opera was an oligarchy administered by the heads of the artistic departments by various methods. The oligarchs, in turn, were subordinate to a bureaucratic absolutism. As, however, the methods of strict Prussian discipline were inapplicable to artistic work and an artistic spirit was unable to prevail under the pressure of administrative measures, the institute might have been compared to Pegasus harried by a Spanish riding-master and unable either to be ridden or to fly.

The inexpediency of the system was not improved by the fact that the complicated official apparatus, responsible to His Majesty for the "Department — Muses," was headed by Count Hochberg. The tall and somewhat effeminate man had written the amateurish opera *Der Werwolf* and felt that because of this abortive flirtation with art, or rather in spite of it, he was enough of a musician to act as an oligarchic adviser and a commanding chief in operatic matters. I clashed with him on several occasions during my year at the Berlin Opera, a fact that eventually made it easier for me to bring about the desired annullment of my contract. Hochberg's man Friday, Privy Councillor Pierson, was a rather kindly disposed and well-intentioned, but at the same time overburdened and confused operatic director. He was a kind of liaison officer between the administration and the artistic forces. The irreconcilability of officialdom and the cultivation of art gave birth to a wealth of daily conflicts both in the excited man's office and inside of him. What added to his misery was the fact that he was the husband of one of the principal singers. He did not lack appreciation of artistic questions, and his personal attitude toward them frequently clashed with the official attitude he was forced to assume. Harassment arising from his constant efforts to square the circle was plainly visible. I got along quite well with him. He had confidence in my artistic and personal qualities and would have succeeded in preventing my resignation by the great efforts he made and the persuasion he used, had not Count Hochberg's antipathy confirmed me in my attitude.

The Opera's conductors at that time were Richard Strauss, Karl Muck, and myself. Weingartner was no longer active at the Opera, but confined himself to conducting concerts given by the Royal Orchestra. My immediate predecessor had been Franz Schalk, whom Mahler had summoned to the Vienna Court Opera. My two colleagues, considerably older and much more famous than myself, were active only in a strictly musical sense, realizing perhaps that a more universal interpretation of their task would have been out of place in the narrow confines of a rigidly regulated workshop. A chief stage director and several assistants took care of the scenic department conscientiously, unimaginatively, and strictly according to tradition. No wonder, then, that I felt cramped and at a loss to realize my artistic ideas.

But because I had made up my mind to "live resolutely" I refused to be discouraged by the wide divergence between my ambitious goals and my unfavorable initial position — my mountain-climbing experiences had thoroughly broken me of such depressing contemplations — and told myself that when systems and personalities clashed the individual's chances for victory were by no means negligible, that there was no system so wrong that a strong and purposeful will could not make it yield favorable results, and that, on the other hand, even the most ideal system was bound to be sterile if handled weakly. So I waited for my chance to come — in vain, I might as well say right now — content to enjoy the Opera's fine artistic equipment: the excellent orchestra with its proudly upheld noble tradition, the splendid and vocally vigorous chorus, and a number of oustanding singers. I should like to mention the superbly gifted Emmy Destinn, who at times sang like a veritable angel. She was my first Berlin Carmen, Aïda, Agathe, and Elisabeth. I shall never forget the saintly sound of her voice in the *Tannhäuser* prayer or the *Freischütz* cavatina. There was my friend Ernst Kraus, a radiant Lohengrin, a mighty Siegfried, and a powerful Samson in Saint-Saëns' opera. Finally, there were the fine basso Paul Knüpfer and the versatile tenor Julius Lieban.

I was soon on a good footing with most of the singers and members of the chorus. The orchestra seemed to like my conducting and played well under me, but the personal contact was lacking. As a body, it remained strange to me, though I was able to form friendly relations with some of its members. The generally excellent musicians were infected by the spirit of bureaucracy and inclined rather to obey those in charge than to co-operate enthusiastically. I found this spirit in the orchestra unchanged when, in the days of the Republic more than twenty years later, I conducted a number of concerts and operas in Berlin. True, the artistic level, too, had been maintained.

My Berlin activity started with a performance of *Carmen*. It was a decided and widely recognized success. Any number of operas were entrusted to me by the management. I had plenty of opportunity for proving my efficiency, but little chance for a display of my higher qualifications. Then a miracle happened. Pfitzner's *Der arme Heinrich* was to be put on, and I was to conduct it. At last there was a task to enlist all of my strength. The troublesome question of stage directing would not likely bother me, for the composer himself was present and would see that his scenic intentions were carried out.

The days I spent upon the vivification of the profound work were happily agitated ones. They were made unforgettable, too, by my intimately personal association with Hans and Mimi Pfitzner. I came to know the composer of the ascetic *Heinrich* and the vitally fresh *Die Rose vom Liebesgarten* as the writer of a large number of songs and of important pieces of chamber music. We spent many an hour in a passionate exchange of opinions, warmed now by the consonance of enthusiastic approval or unhesitating rejection, agitated now by disputes and disagreements over questions close to our heart. Pfitzner was a powerful fighter, able to formulate his thoughts poignantly and discuss them imaginatively. To call him a brilliant conversationalist would be going too far, because he was given too little to listening and was too passionately ruled by his own views. What he lacked in breadth of views, though, he made up for by intensity. I doubt that anyone ever conversed with him who did not feel enriched by the experience. Not only was he ready to give of himself lavishly in serious discussions, but he was fond also of merry prattling in the circle of his family, of the congenial company of good friends — and of wine. Almost inexhaustible in conceiving witty ideas, he was, of all the musicians I knew, the one who came closest to being Hans von Bülow's equal as a punster.

A meetingplace for our circle of friends was the home of *Kommerzienrat* Willi Levin. A lover of art and artists, he proved helpful and devoted to Pfitzner throughout his life. He had also befriended Richard Strauss, whose *Elektra* was dedicated to him and his wife. The sculptor Lederer and the actor Max Reinhardt joined us on a number of occasions, and Engelbert Humperdinck showed up once in a while. There were many others in that circle of friends, men of a similar trend of mind, men of imagination, brains, and heart, but their names have faded from my memory.

That the performance of *Der arme Heinrich* was not a brilliant theatrical success was due mainly to the gloomy and painful atmosphere of the work. It made a profound impression, however, and furthered Pfitzner's cause. Paul Nikolaus Cossmann, Pfitzner's oldest friend, had come to Berlin to attend the final rehearsals and the first performance. This extraordinary man, of whom I shall have more to say in the record of my days in Munich, contributed to the friends' conviviality by his enthusiasm, his deep artistic understanding, and his exceptional mental power.

A little later, Pierson asked me to conduct the *Ring* Cycle. I felt strangely moved when I, a man of twenty-four, was privileged to conduct the stupendous work from the very place toward which, but eight years before, I had yearningly looked from the astronomic heights of the top gallery.

This miracle of fulfillment was followed by a vexatious experience. Karl Haliř, chief *Konzertmeister* of the Royal Orchestra and for many years a member of the Joachim Quartet as its second violinist, was not well disposed toward me. I was under the impression that the excellent musician's self-esteem was hurt by being required to play under a conductor who was so little known and was yet so exacting. He may have suffered also from the fact that the only means of manifesting his disapproval was the assumption of a stony facial expression and a similarly unmoved inward attitude whenever he had to sit at the first desk and play the violin. Nothing could have hit me harder than that very attitude. To see such a face before me and to have to drag along the leaden weight of an assistant musician's inward immobility — a fortunately rare experience in my life — had never failed to be an almost irresistible temptation to my anything but bloodthirsty nature to transgress the Sixth Commandment. I would readily have forgiven the stout man had he bodily stepped on my toes; that he did it figuratively was bound to evoke my fighting spirit. And there was a fight. Just as I had made up my mind to call my portly opponent to account, an ill-considered action of his brought the matter to a climax. The chorale fugue in *The Magic Flute* is followed by Tamino's words: "By fear of death I am not shaken," which Mozart intended to have sung in the same sustained tempo and with an expression of quiet manly determination. Although no change in tempo is indicated in the score, an evil tradition was responsible for the introduction of a *piu mosso* at that place, a distortion of Mozart's intentions bound to be offensive to all those of discerning taste and serious understanding. The part of Tamino was sung by Robert Philipp, a highly gifted but not particularly musical singer. In the course of the rehearsals I had, by dint of taking great pains, got him out of the *piu mosso* habit, but on the evening of the performance he had an unfortunate relapse. When I tried to keep my sustained tempo with the following eighth-notes in the strings and thus catch up with the runaway, Haliř thought that his moment had come. Disregarding my conducting, he reverted to the traditional *piu mosso* — very markedly, and *forte* instead of *piano* — dragging a number of the strings with him and threatening to bring about an upset that I could avert only with difficulty. Unable to control my sudden anger, I censured the rebel in terms of the utmost severity and in a voice plainly heard in the foremost rows of the orchestra floor. I had the satisfaction of seeing my enemy speechless and breathless with indignation. A highly interesting correspondence ensued. In a written complaint to the General Manager, Haliř pointed out the difference between his great prestige and my untried youth. In my reply, sent to the same address, I stated that if the first desk were occupied by even the most important violinist in the world he was in duty bound to follow the beat of the world's worst conductor, lest the performance end in catastrophe. Richard Strauss, asked for his opinion, wrote that, while he considered my attitude essentially well-founded, he thought my attitude was personally impugnable because of Haliř's standing as an artist. Finally, there was a letter from Muck, who stated emphatically that I was right. And there the case rested. I do not recall whether Haliř ever played under me again, or whether an intelligently arranged schedule of work relieved me of his presence, and him of mine.

I had a good deal of trouble with violinists that year. A new concert agency — whose name I have forgotten — wished to introduce itself into the musical life of Berlin. The head of the concern told me that he considered me the coming man. He wished to take charge of my affairs and proposed a concert with the Berlin Philharmonic Orchestra. It was to take place in a new hall which, if I am not mistaken, was near the New World. The man's flattering words and assurances fell pleasantly on my ear, and as he had proved reliable, I accepted. So it came about that toward the end of the year 1900, or at the beginning of 1901, I conducted my first symphony concert in Berlin. I believe that the principal piece in my program was Berlioz's *Symphonie fantastique*. The assisting soloist, who was to play Beethoven's Violin Concerto, was the widely known violinist B. During the orchestra rehearsal it became apparent that, while we got along fairly well in the first and second movements, we were most certainly at odds in the finale. When he had played the first measures of the third movement at an exaggeratedly fast tempo, I stopped the orchestra and told him in a low voice that I felt unable to share his conception and asked if he would not start again at a more moderate pace. He replied loudly and with a great deal of dignity of speech and attitude that it was he who was playing the concerto and that all I — young man! — had to do was to accompany him. That, however ran counter to my conviction, for in the *tutti* it was unquestionably I who was responsible for the tempo. Not for anything in the world would I have played

[126]

the theme at so headlong a pace. So, after the rehearsal, I told the man who was looking down at me from his cloudy heights that I recognized his responsibility for his tempi and would accompany him as fast or as slow as he wished, but that in the orchestral interludes I would choose a tempo to suit my own conviction. And that's exactly what happened on that strange evening. The tempo of the *rondo* changed abruptly from the breathless speed of the soloist to the vigorous and tranquil *allegro* which I had all my life considered the natural tempo of the piece, a point, by the way, on which the world's leading violinists have always readily agreed with me.

An interesting and even exciting experience was connected with the performance of Siegfried Wagner's *Der Bärenhäuter*. Herr Braunschweig, an assistant stage director regularly employed at the Bayreuth Festival Plays, informed me that "the Mistress" would attend the performance conducted by me that evening. On the following day, he handed to me an invitation requesting me to call on Cosima Wagner at the Hotel Windsor. I looked forward with awe to meeting the legendary woman. Although I was disappointed after our two-hours' conversation, the mere presence of the daughter of Franz Liszt, the wife of Hans von Bülow and Richard Wagner was an overwhelming event. I was received by her daughter Eva and shown into the Presence. Clad in black and carrying herself regally, Cosima came to meet me, saying that she wished to thank me for the beautiful performance of her son's opera: the fact that it had been so natural had given her a great deal of pleasure. Relieved, I took up the cue and said that I was impressed by the natural and folklore-like qualities of the work. That, however, was not enough for Cosima's motherly pride. She replied, and her words have remained unforgettable to me: "It is rather more than natural and folklore-like. My son has succeeded, in his *Bärenhäuter*, in writing the finest non-tragic opera since the *Meistersinger*." After that unbelievably daring, yes, blasphemous utterance of Richard Wagner's widow, there was nothing I could do but change the subject. Our conversation soon assumed the character of a lecture delivered by the regal woman. Only now and then did I manage to make a modest remark. She touched upon any number of topics, the nature of which I do not recall, until I blundered once more. This time I acted in total disregard of a strict Bayreuth rule by mentioning the name of Verdi. Frau Wagner's face became icily rigid, and when, in my unsuspecting guilelessness, I dared to speak of the astonishing change and development in Verdi's work, from *Ernani* to *Aïda* and finally to *Falstaff*, she merely remarked: "Development? I can see no difference between *Ernani* and *Falstaff*." I never saw Cosima Wagner again, and I am under the impression that my remark about Verdi had served thoroughly to dispel her initially favorable opinion of me. My feeling of reverence, too, had suffered from the meeting. While her personality had made a lasting impression on me, my disappointment caused by her views grew, and when, many years later, I had an opportunity to read her correspondence with her son-in-law Houston Stewart Chamberlain, author of *The Foundations of the Nineteenth Century*, it served to create a picture of the extraordinary woman that caused me definitely to turn away from her.

Strange to say, I am able to recall hardly any operas or concerts witnessed by me that year in Berlin. A *Tristan* under Strauss seemed to me subjectively fiery, but musically super-*rubato*, in contrast to a powerful performance under Mahler that I had heard in Vienna several weeks before. I was strongly impressed by a *Götterdämmerung* under Muck, though it lacked the spontaneous dramatic impetuosity for which I longed. I have no recollection of any concerts given by the Royal Orchestra under Strauss and Weingartner, but do recall a number of truly magnificent evenings at Philharmonic Hall when Nikisch conducted. I was warmed by his natural and fundamental musicianship and considered his conducting technique admirable. An overpowering rendition of Tchaikovsky's *Pathetic* and a perfect and romantically conceived performance of Weber's *Euryanthe* overture still sound in my ear. I also recall with pleasure a number of Ibsen performances at the Lessing Theater and of Schiller and Shakespeare performances at the Schauspielhaus, with Matkowski as the superlative portrayer of the heroic parts. Far less favorable were my impressions of the stage directing of the Meininger school, then in vogue on the German dramatic boards. Emphasis was put on pomp, authentic costuming, mass displays, and resounding pathos. This rather superficial tendency was called *Meiningerei*. Otto Brahm, and later Max Reinhardt, saw to it that its theatrical style, which had found its way into opera too, was replaced by naturalness, seriousness, and a spirit of reverence for the drama itself.

By spending two nights in trains, I managed to witness occasional Mahler performances in Vienna. I was present at the Vienna *première* of Smetana's *Dalibor* and was enchanted by the magnificent work and its presentation. After my groping and toiling in the shadowy domain presided over by Hochberg and Pierson, the Vienna Court Opera appeared to me like a world steeped in light — my world. Everything seemed perfect: the singing and acting, the playing of the orchestra, the appearance of the stage, and, finally, the conducting. Moved to my very depths, I listened to a performance of Mahler's youthful work *Das klagende Lied* at a Philharmonic Concert. I became firmly and unalterably convinced that here was the sphere of my activity.

A kind fate delivered me — not very gently, to be sure — from my Berlin bondage. Business reasons, presumably, prompted the General Management to supplement the regular evenings at the Opera by performances of works of a lighter genre at the Kroll Theater. As I had proved my "light touch" in connection with operas like Auber's *Fra Diavolo,* Lortzing's *Zar und Zimmermann,* and works by Mozart, I was told to conduct Gilbert and Sullivan's *The Mikado* at the Kroll house. The presentation of the charming work, which had the benefit of a particularly brilliant cast, was highly successful. This induced the General Management to try its luck with another light opera, and I was asked to put on Lecoq's *La Fille de Madame Angot.* I protested. As a boy, I had played a melody from that operetta on a child's instrument until I got sick of hearing it. I could hardly use that as an argument, though. But my very principles were strictly against the production of a work that, clever though it was, was so decidedly below the artistic level even of *The Mikado.* In the end, I yielded to Pierson's friendly urging that I take charge at least of rehearsing the work and that I conduct the initial performances. That was the beginning of an unpleasant time. It was bound ultimately to lead to my resignation.

Mahler had written me once more, offering me a five-year contract. I was unable to accept while my Berlin contract was still in force, but my way would be open if I were to succeed in terminating my Berlin obligations amicably. That was the end toward which I now strove, for the prospect of having to stay at the Berlin Opera another four years actually made me shudder. It soon became apparent that by arranging for simultaneous performances at the Opera Unter den Linden and at Kroll's the General Management had bitten off more than it could chew. The resulting chaotic condition might have been considered all right at the Breslau Theater, but, when mixed with strict Prussian bureaucratic methods, it represented a thoroughly indigestible hellish brew. One evening, when I was conducting *Das Rheingold* at the Opera and had started the first measures of the Nibelheim Scene, I had to stop, for there was no sign of either Alberich or Mime. A few minutes passed before I was able to start again, this time *prestissimo,* for the two dwarfs, confused and out of breath, sang their first measures at a precipitate tempo. Lieban-Mime had been singing the part of Alfred in the first act of *The Bat* at Kroll's. The act over, he had been driven to the Opera and had hurriedly put on his make-up and costume for *Das Rheingold,* intending to return to the Kroll

Theater for the final act of *The Bat*. Too bad that the time-table did not work properly. The last drop to make the bitter cup of such and similar experiences overflow was the casting of the basso Knüpfer for Larivaudière in *Angot* at Kroll's and at the same time for a part at the Opera. When the impracticability of such a combination became obvious, Pierson sent an old and well-tried theatrical attendant to the Linden Café, where singers at liberty were in the habit of spending their mornings. The man was to look in that strange "stock exchange" for a formerly well-known operetta singer. He managed to locate him and bring him to my office. To listen to the man and decline his services was a matter of but a moment. Knüpfer must be relieved of his duties at Kroll's and made available to me. I told Pierson that I considered such occurrences disgraceful and would have to tender my resignation. He assured me of his personal esteem and held out brilliant promises for the future, but I refused to listen. I addressed an energetically worded petition for my release to Count Hochberg, and it was finally granted. I hurried to the telegraph office. There I ran into Leo Slezak. We told each other radiantly that the same errand had taken us there — to telegraph our acceptance of Mahler's offer. Slezak, who was destined to achieve world fame, had had to content himself with modest parts in Berlin. Like myself, he had been thinking of nothing but his resignation and the moment when he'd be able to go to Vienna.

Whenever my Berlin activities permitted, I had made hurried trips to Basle, to see my fiancée on the stage, to find relief from my Berlin disappointments in her presence, and to talk over our plans for the future. We were married in Berlin early in May and moved into a pleasant flat in Brückenallee near the Tiergarten. No sooner had the summer vacation started than we went to Bayreuth as guests of Ernst Kraus. We shared his handsome villa in Donndorf with Anton van Rooy, Bayreuth's powerful Wotan, Flying Dutchman, and Sachs. The house resounded with music. Van Rooy proved himself an apt lieder singer, a fact that subsequently led to a number of joint Schubert recitals. We heard several fine and carefully prepared performances conducted by Mottl at the Festspielhaus, spent a few weeks in the Tyrolean Alps, and then proceded to Vienna.

It may seem strange to my readers that this part of my life's story, covering events from 1893 to 1901, contains no reference to the political happenings of that epoch. The fact is that my life, of which this book is a record, had remained untouched by political influences up to that point, not because — to quote Jacob Burckhardt — culture was still in the foreground of happenings during that period, but mainly because national and world events had as yet failed to arouse me to the partisanship that alone would have made me consider them "politics." My nature prompted me to view those events contemplatively. Whenever I did take sides, as in the Dreyfuss trial, it was because I was provoked humanly, and not politically. The very fact that, unless my feelings of humanity were aroused, I inclined toward a historical contemplation of events made me an unpolitical person and prevented my taking up a definite position. To me, Clio was actually a Muse. I read the historical writings of men like Mommsen, Ranke, Carlyle, Macaulay, and others as I would read literature. Instinctively, I viewed events like Kaiser Wilhelm's Kruger dispatch, his reference to the "mailed fist," the Spanish-American War, and the Fashoda incident from a historian's point of view. I was unable to see them in the light of actuality, and therefore did not feel impelled to take sides politically. What makes a politician is a feeling of *tua res agitur*. How, though, was I to regard as my affair what was happening behind that veil to which I referred in a previous chapter?

It was a different matter when political questions bordering upon the realm of humanity were concerned — the social questions. The growth of the Social Democratic movement as a protest against old injustice, the democratic principle of equal rights for all, the disparagement of privileges of birth, the recognition of the individual's dignity in his relation to the state — all these tendencies and endeavors were close to my heart and moved me deeply, though they did not induce me to take an active part in political life. My conviction that I was born to be a musician made me content to leave a struggle to which I felt unsuited in hands more competent than my own.

Besides, wasn't life pleasant in the Germany of those days, its quite undemocratic constitution notwithstanding? In spite of Bismarck and his like-minded successors, social thinking and social welfare were thriving, culture was flourishing, economic conditions seemed sound. The system was faulty, but the results were satisfactory. My windows were open, my door was unlocked, but no politics were wafted in. I could see no reason why I should look for them and invite them in.

But 1901 had come. I went to Austria, and there politics were waiting for me.

BOOK THREE

✿◈

I

WHEN the Viennese leave the Innere Stadt — the central part of
the city — at the Schottentor, pass the gracefully beautiful Votiv
Church, and enter Währingerstrasse, their gaze is met by the delightful silhouette of Kahlenberg, outlining the horizon above the
street. What a novel and never-aging charm, what an inspiration to
my daily life, lay in the fact that I was able to look beyond the
noisy street of the large imperial city toward the tranquil beauty
of that chain of hills! What a refreshing comfort, to have before
my eyes the silent friendly beckoning of the Vienna Woods whenever my way took me in that direction! And when I was able to
leave behind me the hum of that unique large city, overtopped by
gentle hills, and stroll through the charming suburbs at the foot
of the Kahlenberg, from Heiligenstadt, along the Pastorale Brook,
toward Nussdorf. . . . Can you imagine what the musician must
have felt who was following in the footsteps of Beethoven?

Let us not underestimate, either, the soothing effect upon my
ear and mind of the somewhat ceremonious Austrian social amenities, mitigating the grayness of humdrum everyday life by many
an "I kiss your hand," "I have the honor," "Your Grace," "Gra-
cious Sir," "Herr Doctor," or, at the very least, an ennobling "von"
as the prefix to one's name. True, the charming "I kiss your hand,"
used in greeting or taking leave of a person, was more at home in
Vienna than in Upper Austria and the mountain districts. It may
have come into existence as a metropolitan expression of Austrian
amiability and represent but the small change of everyday courtesy. But it points the way to the golden treasure of friendliness
that, according to my firm conviction and contrary to the by no
means friendly history of the Austrian monarchy, lies at the
bottom of the people's and the country's character.

History! Can we learn a people's character through its history,
a history formerly made by princes and statesmen with an utter disregard of, frequently even in opposition to, its interests? Is not its
nature disclosed rather by its poetry, by its general habits of life,

by its landscape, and by its idiom? Are we not able most deeply to penetrate into a nation's soul through its music, provided that it has actually grown on its soil? May a musician be pardoned for believing that, beyond his personal impressions of the country and its inhabitants, he came to know and understand the Czech people through Smetana's music? Is anyone entitled to speak with authority of the Russians who has not become familiar with Pushkin, Lermontov, Gogol, Dostoyevsky, Tolstoy, and Gorky, and has not listened to the music of Mussorgsky, Borodin, and Tchaikovsky? I realize that I am now treading the hallowed, but uncertain ground of intuition, of divination, of the irrational. But because I have dared to go so far, I shall make a more daring use of the privilege of that airy sphere by confessing that of Europe's many national profiles with which I have become familiar and every one of which has revealed to me dear, impressive, and interesting features, the Austrian face attracted me most strongly by its particular kind of friendliness. To me, there was laughter in the Austrian landscape of the Vienna Woods, of the Salzkammergut, and of the Tyrol; smiles in the dirndl dresses of the young women of those districts, in the dialect of the people, in the poetry of Raimund, and in the satire of Nestroy. And I have always considered most illuminating the war joke of 1918, according to which the Germans considered the situation "serious, but not hopeless," while the Austrians said it was "hopeless, but not serious." Herein is revealed the heart of the Austrian who, realizing the terror in the terrible, is yet able to smile. Such an inclination has its many gradations. It may deteriorate into downright criminal frivolity or be sublimated into a philosophical and religious tranquillity of the soul. At any rate, it is not a source of political strength, for Austria has perished. But her fall has been survived by the world-comforting Austrian friendliness, transfigured into music and given immortal form by Mozart, Haydn, Lanner, Johann Strauss, and above all, by Schubert. Are we not perhaps justified in assuming that it was Austria where the floating 3/4 measure was born, a rather ethereal addition to the family of the more earthbound 4/4 and 2/4 measures? Was it not perhaps in Austria that music first learned how to smile? But I never doubted, even after I stood again on more secure ground than during my excursion into the fanciful realm of such dreams, that the invasion of music by the 3/4 measure must be considered an event of spiritual and historical importance. Leaving aside these daring fantasies, musically supportable from neither a historical nor a scientific point of view, the fact nevertheless remains that the large number of foreign visitors to Vienna and Salzburg felt drawn to these places mainly by

[133]

the peculiar metaphysical friendliness so symptomatic of the Austrian people, of their culture, their landscape, and, more convincingly even, of their music.

The fact that Mozart, Haydn, Schubert, Lanner, Johann Strauss, Bruckner, and Mahler were Austrians and that both the soul and the work of Beethoven and Brahms became deeply rooted in Vienna shows in what important and particular sense Austria may be called the home of music. And another thing. How revealing of the Austrians' nature was their genuine love for music, their singing and playing! What could be more characteristic than their *Musi'*, so essential an ingredient of the atmosphere prevailing at the suburban drinking places where young and old, high and low, partook of the *Heuriger*, the young wine grown on the slopes around Vienna? No less characteristic were the passionate interest with which musical events and personalities were discussed and the great popularity of the Court Opera and the principal concert halls. Music was a power in Austria. Countless memories of my lifelong affiliation with Vienna have one thing in common: they have left an echo in my soul.

And does not many a specific sound of folklike music give us a deep insight into the Austrian character, deeper than that which painstaking psychological research is able to reveal? The Austrian march music is essentially *fesch*. The approximate meaning of the word is smart, dashing. But as it is a specifically Austrian word, hardly understood in the German Reich, to say nothing of other countries, and since its very untranslatability must make it as characteristic of the Austrians as other untranslatable words are of their respective nations, the best I can do is to fall back again on music: *fesch* is Johann Strauss's *Radetzky March*, the *Hoch-und-Deutschmeister March*, Schubert's Military March in D-major, and — although in a somewhat less subtle manner — even the *Double Eagle March*. A more exalted kind of "*fesch*-ness" is sounded in many a turn of Austrian classic music, in some of Mozart's and Haydn's compositions, for instance. *Fesch*, too, were Vienna's lightheartedly pert youths who, in former and better days, used to stroll along the Ringstrasse with so provoking an air of devil-may-care insouciance, the rubber-tired cabs — the *Fiakers* — dashing down the Prater's main avenue, the change of the guards — so easy and un-Prussian in its manner — in the courtyard of the Imperial Palace, and the cymbals' and bass-drum's introductory bar preceding the brilliant Austrian military music. And there was that other sound in Austrian popular music, that floating and beguiling sound of the waltz, whose effect upon the Vienna heart, when played or sung, was most aptly described by the saying: "Go sell my clothes, I'm off for Heaven!" its meaning being that in the ecstatic mood brought about by the music — and perhaps by the wine too — one no longer cared to be burdened with mundane encumbrances.

This saturation with music had revealed to me one characteristic side of the Austrian nature. Another side became known to me through the poetic writings of Raimund, Grillparzer, Stifter, Schnitzler, Hofmannsthal, and Wildgans. The experiences of everyday life tended to complete the picture. Without going into too many details, I should like to mention a characteristic nation-wide custom, at which, to be sure, my own Austrianism inclined to balk. I am referring to the custom of frequenting coffeehouses. How in the world could all those people from every conceivable walk of life afford to spend several hours a day in one of the in-numerable coffeehouses? When I first went to Vienna, in 1897, I several times visited the Café Imperial on the Opernring. Among a group of men who met there every afternoon, my attention was attracted by a youngish man with a clever face who seemed to be a keen debater. A casual introduction revealed the fact that the man's name was Doctor Eckstein. He later published an interesting book, entitled *Old Unnamable Days*, dealing with his experiences with Bruckner and Hugo Wolf. Whenever in the course of the following four decades I happened into the Café Imperial, the man was there, and we would bow politely to each other. In February, 1938, shortly before my last departure from Vienna, I saw the aged man sitting at the same table at which, every day of his life, he had been debating by the hour. He was a typical Austrian, a man to whom the daily stay at "his" coffeehouse was as natural as dress-ing and undressing. Let a man go to the same coffeehouse but a few times, and the waiter would know him well enough to serve him unasked with his favorite mixture of coffee — there were any num-ber of blends — and to place at his elbow the newspapers he had asked for the first time. A man could have letters or messages ad-dressed to him at the coffeehouse. Coffeehouses were the scenes of decisions and events of historical and cultural importance, of weighty political and scientific discussions, and were naturally also a hotbed of intrigue and endless gossip.

As for myself, I was by no means insensible to the attraction of the coffeehouse, and I spent many an hour there. The "principle," however, remained strange to me, and I don't know but what I was right in attributing some of my co-workers' tendency toward negligence and indolence as well as a good deal of intrigue and evil gossip to the "spirit of the coffeehouse." But no matter, good or evil, here was an integral feature of the Austrian character. How could we ever make a friend and hold him, gain a woman's love and keep it, if we did not meet their weaknesses and oddities with tolerance and, in the end, with sympathy? At any rate, there was one feature of the coffeehouse of which I fully approved: its atmosphere encouraged conversation. The epoch of remarkable correspondences, of spiritual and emotional epistolary confessions, was over, but conversation flourished. In my opinion, although a well-considered letter is unquestionably superior to improvising talk, this superiority is more than counterbalanced by the spontaneity of an oral exchange of personal opinions. The speaker's words kindle in the listener's mind new ideas, whose utterance — in contrast to the finality of the written word — and to use a splendid phrase coined by Hofmannsthal — has the "blessing of retractability." In our day of the telephone, the film, and the radio, I still insist that the mighty Goddess of Presence will not be dethroned and that in the playing of music, in dramatic presentations, in conversation — and in love too — only personal presence will be able to produce the soul-warming climate in which man is spurred on to his highest potentialities in giving and taking. I also believe that I am not mistaken in asserting that the epoch from the turn of the century to the outbreak of the First World War was distinguished in Austria by a particularly high cultural level of conversation. When I think of the interesting figure of the brilliant satirist Karl Kraus and his circle, prominent in which was the ingenious Alfred Polgar, and the strangely spectacular poet Peter Altenberg and his friends in the Café Central, I feel impelled to give the Vienna coffeehouse its just due in connection with its stimulating effect upon the genius of conversation.

During the eleven years I spent in Vienna — from the autumn of 1901 to the end of 1912 — Austria's spiritual and cultural life was flowering richly. The Court Opera glowed in the pure light shed by the genius of Mahler, the Burgtheater continued to maintain its glorious tradition, other Vienna theaters — the Volkstheater among them — gave excellent performances. Literature and formative art had the benefit of daringly new and highly gifted personages. Great scientific work was being done — think of the international reputation of the Vienna medical school represented by Billroth, Nothnagel, Wagner-Jauregg, Neusser, Pirquet, and Freud — and social life was invested with a splendor and charm hardly ever equaled in the old Monarchy. Yet, the Monarchy was old and ill, and its precarious political situation was eloquently reflected in the Cassandra calls of the *Neue Freie Presse,* the *Tagblatt,* and the *Zeit.*

True, the non-political sections of the newspapers seemed to indicate that the Periclean age, in which the arts flourished, was still with us. The brilliant Eduard Hanslick had been succeeded by the brainy and thoroughly musical Julius Korngold as chief musical critic of the *Neue Freie Presse*. Speidel had been followed by clever men like Wittmann and Auernheimer, Salten and Lothar, and occasional contributors like Widmann and Spitteler who knew how to keep up the tradition of attractive feuilletonism. The *Tagblatt*'s musical department was headed by Max Kalbeck, the biographer and friend of Johannes Brahms, an adroit writer but a man of reactionary tendencies. And while the country's rich spiritual life was brilliantly depicted in carefully chosen words, editorials and daily reports written with equal skill and mastery recorded the dangers inherent in the country's policies, both domestic and foreign. There was the *mene tekel*-warning of impending catastrophe.

Lueger, the mayor of Vienna, had made anti-Semitism a power in the public life of Vienna. From the Sudetenland, another and still more powerful anti-Semitism was spreading, represented by Iro, Schönerer, and Wolf, the precursors of Nazism, who were proposing to abolish the Christian calendar and to replace it by one beginning with the Battle in the Teutoburger Forest. Physical encounters occurred in Parliament, the relations between Germans and Czechs in Bohemia took a turn for the worse, and those between Hungary and Austria, between the various nationalities represented in the Austrian Empire, and between Christian Socialists and Social Democrats became ever more critical. In the Balkans, the Austro-Hungarian interests collided with those of Russia. When, in the morning, I read newspaper reports of the sessions of the Austrian and Hungarian Parliaments, of the disturbances in Prague, of the revolutionary mood in Russia, of the Morocco Crisis, and of the "panther's leap of Agadir," I had the feeling of having once more partaken of my daily cup of poison, without, unfortunately, having been rendered immune by it. There were two newspapers in Vienna at the time which were wholly in the service of anti-Semitism. While I never read them, I received plenty of reports from both well-meaning and evil-minded quarters concerning the lies and calumnies by which they made a living, and concerning their attacks on Mahler and myself.

It must be regretfully admitted that the home of music was at the same time the source of those hateful sentiments whose popularity helped National Socialism gain power. A psychologically oriented historical research may someday trace Austria's downfall to that national dualism, or a least to the irreconcilability of highly pointed cultural inclinations and deeply barbarous tendencies.

II

UNINFLUENCED by thoughts of impending calamities and insensible to attacks for political, artistic, or other reasons, Mahler conducted the destinies of the Vienna Court Opera, imparting to it the strength of his soul. When he left the institute, it stood dominant, the center of cultural endeavors. To this day, the memory of his ten years of activity has remained alive in the minds of his collaborators and of those who were privileged to be witnesses of the proud pioneer work of a great personality and a great institution.

The magnificent edifice on the Opernring was surpassed by the very similar Paris Opéra only in its site. There, the façade of the building dominates the grandiose sweep of the Place de l'Opéra, while the Vienna Opera stands soberly in the row of Ringstrasse houses, and even the opposite side of the wide avenue has no gap that would add to its effectiveness. A careful observer will be somewhat oppressed, too, by the vertical aspect of the building, encroaching upon the otherwise proud impression it makes. It is said that the architect Van der Nüll was promised a lowering of the street level and that he hurled himself from the balcony of the finished building when that promise was not kept and the noble proportions he had envisioned had been so irremediably harmed. The outside of the building nevertheless impresses the beholder by its beauty, and the interior — the grand stairway, the arrangement of the boxes, the offices, and the workrooms — has no equal among any of the opera houses I know. Aristocratic was the house, and courtly were its traditions. Among the latter, when I came to Vienna, was a court carriage service made available to the female artists, who were called for at their homes and driven back again after the performance. The ladies of the Burgtheater enjoyed the same privilege, which was abolished only in the days of the Republic.

The offices of the General Manager were in Bräunerstrasse, a ten-minute walk from the Opera. A vast amount of calculating, registering, and administering was done there, but none of the officials — for there, too, officialdom had its finger in the pie — would have dared interfere in the purely artistic affairs of the Opera. Mahler submitted his reports directly to the Emperor's Lord Steward of the Household, Prince Montenuovo, who was the chief of the Court Opera, the Burgtheater, and their joint administrative apparatus and who, in turn, gave Mahler whatever powers he required. The Prince's offices were in the Imperial Palace. I often accompanied Mahler to the entrance of the wing, atop which the double-headed eagle spread its wings. During the 1911–12 season, I frequently went there myself, endeavoring to get Prince Montenuovo to accept my resignation.

Emperor Franz Joseph's Lord Steward, a grandson of the Austrian Princess Marie Louise whose second husband, after Napoleon, had been Baron Neipperg — Italianized into Montenuovo — was an elegant silver-haired man of medium height, his face adorned by a gray mustache and beard. He was cold and self-assured, rather dryly bureaucratic, but thoroughly reliable, and unshakable in his convictions. He deserved high praise for having resisted for ten years the intrigues and hostilities against Mahler. Men and women of high society, some of them even in the entourage of archdukes, were trying to gain his ear in their efforts to dethrone Mahler. And Mahler did not make things easy for Montenuovo either, though his heart was gladdened by the Prince's sincere esteem, by the sympathy under his dry manner. One day the Prince told Mahler confidentially that a "distinguished personage" was interested in a certain songstress and had requested that she be engaged at the Court Opera. After an audition, Mahler declared that artistic reasons compelled him to veto the engagement. When, after a while, Montenuovo asked Mahler whether, in view of the exalted favor enjoyed by the lady and the further fact that the Emperor himself had given his consent, he would not reconsider his decision, he replied: "I realize, Your Highness, that His Majesty's and your wishes have to be complied with at the Opera, and so I am looking forward to His Majesty's command to engage the lady." Montenuovo told Mahler later that he had given the Emperor a verbatim report of Mahler's words, to which the old gentleman had replied: "Well, I'll surely not command such a thing." And so Mahler remained victorious in a matter to which he attached serious fundamental importance.

When Mahler's departure had been definitely decided upon, Montenuovo asked the great man's advice in connection with his possible successor. The conference over, Montenuovo shook Mahler's hand and said earnestly: "We are friends." I am able to testify to the fact that this scarcely amiable or warm-hearted man — the bitter enmity he bore the heir to the Austrian throne and his wife was harshly manifested even at the funeral ceremonies of the murdered couple — proved his sympathy for Mahler throughout the latter's tenure of office. It is doubtful that Mahler could have otherwise stayed at his post ten years. Although the Prince was surely not artistically inclined, he believed in the great artist and his integrity. After the wealth of human experiences he had accumulated at Court, Mahler's moral purity meant to him a refreshing change, to which he responded with an intrepid faithfulness. I also gratefully remember his later attitude toward me.

When Mahler entered upon his duties in Vienna, he found a roster that included a number of excellent artists. On the other hand, there were a few yawning gaps in the ensemble. Some of Vienna's favorite singers had reached an age that made it advisable to be on the lookout for younger representatives of their parts. The result of Mahler's endeavors was the engagement of such singers as Erik Schmedes, Slezak, Leopold Demuth, Weidemann, Wilhelm Hesch, and Richard Mayr among the men, and Anna von Mildenburg, Marie Gutheil-Schoder, Selma Kurz, and Förster-Lauterer among the women. They were splendid representatives of a younger generation, and their rise to popularity and fame was connected with the Mahler epoch in Vienna. It was a fact that Mahler's endeavors to attract new artists met with a good deal of opposition on the part of an evergrowing counter-clique in the artistic personnel, the public, official circles, and the newspapers. There were those whose genuine attachment to some of the older artists made them fearful lest their favorites' positions be endangered by the influx of youth. The indignation of others was directed against Mahler's general acts of aggressive daring. There was criticism of the spirit of unrest that had invaded the solemn tranquillity of the distinguished institute of art. Mahler himself furnished ample material to his opponents. With the optimism of a productive man, he permitted the guest appearances of singers who had at first impressed him favorably, but whose actual performances fell short of what their auditions had led him to expect. Thus he lent support to the legend of the senselessness of a program that presented to the expert Vienna public inexperienced beginners in important parts in place of the well-tried great artists to whom it had become accustomed. But Mahler kept steadily to his course. It did not matter to him if he had to pronounce an untalented amateur a singer whom but a few days before he had hailed as a rising vocal genius. Every disappointment only made him search harder. He continued to arrange for guest appearances and sent me on scouting trips to every conceivable German town. My judgments were frequently even more faulty than his own. We finally succeeded, however, in assembling a cast of artists whose vocal accomplishments and personalities ought in justice to have silenced every resentment caused by previous mistaken moves.

The vocal and histrionic qualities of an opera singer can be properly judged only at a public performance on the stage for which his services are intended. Neither auditions in a room or empty theater nor public performances on another stage enable us reliably to judge a singer's suitability to a certain organization. A singer whose work had delighted me on the stage of the brilliant Wiesbaden Opera was found decidedly wanting at a guest appearance in Vienna. Voices that had sounded magnificent in an empty house were hardly audible at the evening performance. Only after many mistakes have I succeeded in getting myself to adopt a more careful and discerning method of hearing and judging, but I am ready to admit that until quite lately I had to be on my guard against exaggeratedly optimistic judgments.

As far as I can remember, one of the most important powers in Vienna's operatic life never let Mahler down, though the most passionate debates for or against certain singers took place within its sphere. I am referring to the "Fourth Gallery." Its importance would entitle it to an appreciation *in extenso,* for I am by no means exaggerating when I claim that almost all Vienna musicians and singers as well as the general youth devoted to art received their decisive artistic impressions "up there," and that the contemporary frequenters of the top gallery dreamed of their future "down there." An agitatedly interested community populated the Olympic heights of the Vienna Court Opera. The behavior of its members was neither vulgar nor noisy, but they loved music, raved about their favorite artists, and vigorously expressed their sentiments with youthful impetuosity. In spite of that, the Vienna Fourth Gallery never, to my knowledge, indulged in orgies of hissing or the other coarse demonstrations of disapproval not uncommon in Italy and Spain. The gallery gods were emphatic but moderate in their disapproval, fiery and uninhibited in their enthusiasm. There were any number of amusing oddities connected with that lofty realm. The admirers of the wonderful baritone Theodor Reichmann, for instance, were as numerous as those of the powerful tenor Hermann Winkelmann, and the two hosts tried to outdo each other in applauding. Because the names of both favorites ended in the same syllable, the admirers of the tenor confined themselves to shouting "Winkel," to which the baritone's adherents responded with "Reich." The short "i," however, was less suited to a powerful vocal display than the broad "ei." Thus it happened that at the end of *Tannhäuser* or some other opera in which both singers had starred, a long-drawn-out choral duet occurred in the gallery. The "Winkel, Winkel" uttered in a fast rhythm and by high-pitched voices contrasted interestingly with the sustained and deeply stentorian "Reich, Reich." The duetists were surely not concerned with any comical effect produced by their demonstration. All they cared about was to express their enthusiasm in a most effective manner. How seriously the Fourth Gallery took its art may be gathered from its reactions to cuts in Wagner's musical dramas. By restoring all the cuts previously made in them, Mahler had earned the special gratitude of that part of the audience. When his successor reintroduced a cut in *Die Walküre,* the Fourth Gallerists, who both loved and knew their Wagner, protested so vigorously that he returned to the uncut version at subsequent performances.

Youth and the Fourth Gallery were not Mahler's only stanch supporters, though it was but natural that they should be particularly attracted by the fiery impetuosity of his character, by his courage, and even by his extravagances. There were the old aristocratic public, the patrician middle classes, and, generally, all those to whom Austria owed her fame as a land of music. Consciously or unconsciously, they all saw in Mahler the musician destined to continue and revitalize the exalted tradition of Viennese cultivation of music. They were his friends to the last. When Mahler suffered an attack of illness, hostile undercurrents within the autonomous Philharmonic Orchestra deprived him of its leadership and placed it in the hands of Joseph Hellmesberger, a gifted composer of ballets, but a not particularly prominent symphonic conductor. However, Mahler continued to appear frequently at the conductor's desk of the Opera, and all the attacks directed against his artistic policies in connection with engagements, repertory formation, casting, and other details proved powerless against the overwhelming force of his musicianship. No matter what performance was involved, whether it was Wagner or Mozart, *The Tales of Hoffmann* or *Les Huguenots, Eugen Onegin* or *La Juive, Zar und Zimmermann* or *La Dame Blanche,* his place in the hearts of the audience was never in danger.

Mahler the operatic conductor, whose musical power had an electrifying effect upon Vienna, developed in the course of years into the founder of a superior and purified style of operatic renditions. What he strove for was a harmonious blending of music and stage. The novelty of the solutions split the public and the press into two opposite camps, but the searching and experimenting prepared the law of today and tomorrow.

Alfred Roller had submitted his entirely novel designs for *Tristan* to Mahler. Mahler had at once grasped the musico-dramatic significance of such a use of forms and light and decided then and there to join hands with Roller. Their association was productive of a number of successful as well as of some rather questionable treatments of stylistic operatic problems, until it finally led to ideal solutions in Gluck's *Iphigenia in Aulis* and Beethoven's

Fidelio. That Roller's artistic tendencies inclined toward the monumental, the heroic, and the solemn was shown by his sets for Wagner's *Tristan* and *Ring,* by his treatment of the stage in *Fidelio* and *Iphigenia in Aulis,* and by the work he did for Reinhardt. His relation to Mozart, though, was uncertain and groping. There, he was lacking in congeniality. Mahler, whose superiority Roller was ready to admit and whose guidance he gladly followed, was unable to set him definite tasks because he himself felt that the dimensions of the house forced him into compromises which changed with every work. Only *The Magic Flute* fitted readily into the mighty frame. The creation of a "Mozart style" was not feasible for the simple reason that there can be no such thing. The deeply discerning will recognize that there is a distinct *Don Giovanni* style, a *Così fan tutte* style, and so on. While thus Mahler's Mozart performances bore traces of experimental work and were moreover handicapped dynamically and stylistically by the peculiarities of the Vienna Opera, they still had the effect of a vigorous and revealing originality. Fully to appreciate Mahler's imperishable service to the works of Mozart, one would have to be familiar with previous performances. Mahler saved Mozart from the lie of daintiness as well as from the boredom of academic dryness. He imparted to the performances the composer's dramatic seriousness, his sincerity, his vivacity. He thus managed to change the public's inanimate respect for Mozart operas into an enthusiasm that shook the house and enraptured even the sober heart of the box-office manager.

As I said before, I consider *Tristan* at the beginning of that epoch and *Iphigenia in Aulis* toward its end the culminating points of Mahler's activity as the head of the Opera. In the performance of *Tristan,* scenery and lighting were so expertly adapted to the music and the presentation, and the music was so filled with the spirit of the drama, that, in the resulting harmony, Mahler himself may be said to have established a standard for his future work. But because the music and dramatic style of the pre-Wagner works demanded a suitable difference in presentation and scenic style, the supreme postulate of unity changed its sense with every new task. The musico-dramatic synthesis in a performance of Mozart's *Così fan tutte* had to be accomplished in an entirely different spirit and by the use of entirely different means from those employed in Wagner's *Die Walküre.* Weber's *Der Freischütz,* again, presented a wholly different problem. One of the main difficulties of an ideal presentation of one of those older works was that its inherent and unexpressed laws had to be recognized before a harmonious blending of music and stage action could be accomplished. The works of Wagner had sprung from an original vision of the stage, and

he himself had stated explicitly the laws governing their performance. As for the older works, the absence of scenic remarks, and
perhaps also the composers' somewhat vague vision of the stage,
may have contributed to the negligence and arbitrariness of their
scenic presentation. The imperishable service rendered by Mahler
to the creation of an ideal style of presenting a work like Gluck's
Iphigenia in Aulis therefore seemed obvious. Nothing had been
said by Gluck in so many words. The work's inherent law had to
be discovered in the work itself, be transformed into music, presentation, and scenic effect, and made to govern the entire performance. And that was exactly what happened. Gluck's lofty understanding of the Hellenic spirit found a congenial interpretation,
hardly surpassable in the realm of musico-dramatic renditions.

In his daring ideas of a superior method of operatic production,
Mahler pursued his way, not by consciously following a certain
system, but by intuition and experimenting. The large community of his faithful adherents rallied round him more stanchly and
enthusiastically than ever, but his adversaries were at the same
time furnished with ample material for their attacks, launched
with Philistine indignation and scornful mockery. "Well, what
have the honorable chiefs to say?" Mahler was in the habit of asking on the morning after a first performance. He was of course referring to the critics, and the critics' remarks were frequently quite
uncomplimentary. This was pronouncedly the case after the performance of *Don Giovanni*. Roller had designed two stationary
towers, one on each side of the stage, between which the various
changes of scenery took place. The critics were unable to discern
that a principle had been created that — not in the manner of its
execution, but in its basic idea — would be a determining factor
in the future development of the scenic picture. It is hardly doubtful that all important operatic interpretations since then have been
inspired and influenced by the Mahler epoch in Vienna.

While the Opera's director made light of the attacks upon his
pioneer work, the composer suffered greatly from the public's and
the critics' initial lack of understanding. Bruckner had not as yet
been able to assert himself either. Vienna's rather reactionary concert public assumed a hostile attitude toward the daring new sound
in Mahler's symphonies. As for myself, I considered myself fortunate to be able to witness and co-operate in an activity concerning
whose historical importance I had never entertained the slightest
doubt.

III

THE TIES of friendship I formed in Vienna, friendship that filled my life there with warmth and beauty, contributed much toward a sense of ease and well-being and enabled me to weather a precarious period of enmity, not wholly unharmed, to be sure, but without lasting bitterness. It was then that I learned the true meaning of friendship and the invaluable comfort in feeling secure in the affection, faithfulness, and care of worthy people. And because these friends proved unchangeably true to me to the hour of their death, because they formed part of the life whose story is recorded in these pages, I must try to describe those to whom I owe the good fortune of warm-hearted personal intercourse, steady enrichment of my knowledge, and above all, an idea and standard of human values to which I was able to cling even in the darkest moments of my existence. The circle of which I am about to tell was formed by Mahler's oldest friends. Foremost, there were Nina Spiegler and Siegfried Lipiner. The ties that bound Mahler to Nina Spiegler were essentially musical ones; those existing between him and Siegfried Lipiner were literary and philosophical. His relations with both, however — and with Nina's husband Albert and Lipiner's wife Clementine — were those of an affectionate friendship going back to the days of his youth.

Siegfried Lipiner, a rather short man with Zeus-like curly blond hair, a full beard of the same color, and radiant blue eyes, was a poet endowed with vision, formative force, and eloquence. Carried away by a topic of conversation, by a memory, or by a picture, he was likely to be "seized with the spirit." On such occasions, a wealth of thoughts and wisdom, improvised, but perfect in form, would flow from his lips. As a lad of seventeen, he had written a piece of poetry entitled *Prometheus Unbound*, concerning which Nietzsche had this to say in a letter to Erwin Rohde, the author of *Psyche:* "Quite recently, a truly consecrated day was vouchsafed to me by 'Prometheus Unbound.' If the poet is not a veritable genius, I have forgotten the meaning of the word. Everything in it is wonderful, and I was made to feel as if I were face to face with an exalted and deified self. I bow low before one who was able to experience and produce such a thing." While I do not know whether or not the poet entered into personal relations with Nietzsche, I do know that Wagner took a lively interest in him and induced him to come to Bayreuth in the early eighties. But the close association planned by Wagner came to naught when the independent mental attitude of young Lipiner refused to adapt itself to certain ideologies of the Wahnfried circle.

Hofmannsthal's words referring to a poet's covered roots that were more widely developed than his spreading top, might aptly be applied to Lipiner. He did more living than writing, spent lavishly of himself, and hoarded few treasures in his mind. His printed works included *Prometheus Unbound, The New Don Juan,* the drama *Adam* — a prelude to a Christ trilogy, which occupied him throughout his life, which he wrote and rewrote and never completed — and the tragedy *Hippolytos,* in which he had grasped the original meaning of the Phaedra subject and had formed it into an exalted piece of dramatic poetic writing. I also recall an enlightened and enlightening essay from his pen concerning the figure of Homunculus in *Faust,* but I do not know whether or not it ever appeared in print. If Lipiner's own works have fallen victims to Nazi rage or the catastrophes of war, his poetic inspirations may be lost to posterity, but his supreme command of the language will at least be preserved through his masterly German translation of *The Forbears* and *Pan Tadeusz,* the works of Adam Mickiewicz, Poland's most eminent poet.

While he was still at school or at the University, Lipiner's teachers and fellow-students had been amazed at his mental power. Count Lanckoronski, considering him one of the coming men in Polish literature, had taken the destitute young man under his wing. With the co-operation of literary-minded Polish members of the Austrian parliament, he had secured for him the post of Parliamentary Librarian, which was to relieve him of everyday cares and give him ample time for writing and thinking. But Lipiner did not write much, for he was by nature an improviser and made to give of himself freely in speech and personal communication. Had he lived in the days of the Peripatetics, he would have been one of those who, walking about, taught his disciples by talking to them. In an epoch when a poet spoke to his contemporaries mainly through the printed word Lipiner was an incongruous figure. Besides, absorbed as he was by human relations, he needed the others, the listening, the comprehending, the eager to learn, the enthusiastically inclined, to be kindled by their questions and their understanding. There was no want of those. Neither was he lacking in women who were made happy by being permitted to live for a time in an atmosphere of spiritual brightness and warmheartedness. It was natural that Lipiner, a poet so passionately devoted to life, should again and again be taken captive by love. It seemed singular to me, though, that Eros and Caritas, who usually go their separate ways, had apparently formed an alliance in his soul. I do not know of a single instance when some female need of help — physical ailment, financial difficulty, or spiritual distress — was not at the bottom of his love affairs. It was strange, too, that the considerable number of women in his life were well disposed toward one another, that they knew, or at least had an inkling of one another, and that their brief happiness was mostly an unbegrudged happiness — presumably a result of his teachings. Like Hera, his wife was the only one to suffer from this Zeus-like man's thirst for life. Nevertheless, her love, her admiration, and her readiness to forgive remained unshaken to the day of his death.

I had the good fortune to enjoy Lipiner's communicativeness, his friendship, and his sympathy with my musical endowments. When I think of the good things presented to me by life, I feel I must count among them the hours I was privileged to spend in Siegfried Lipiner's company during more than ten years of friendly intercourse. Whether he took from one of his huge portfolios reproductions of antique art or of Renaissance paintings and placed them on an easel in his studio in order to get inspiration from them, whether he spoke of Sophocles or Euripides, of Plato or Aristotle, of Plotinus or Angelus Silesius, whether his deeply penetrating exegesis made us visualize the figures of Isaiah or of St. Paul — it was always the inspired who spoke, the poet, the lover. I never heard a didactic word from the lips of the man who was so rich in knowledge, nor a polemic one either, unless he felt like attacking the commentators on Goethe's *Faust,* which he considered his special domain. He felt a deep affinity for Dostoyevsky, to whom, by the way, he bore a striking resemblance when his hair began to turn gray.

Lipiner was not much past fifty when he died, in January, 1912, and so he did not long outlive Mahler, who died in May, 1911. The man who used to "speak with tongues" died from cancer of the tongue. He bore the intense pain with indescribable spiritual fortitude. His innate cheerfulness did not leave him until the very end.

One day I met Lipiner, a fearful sight, on a street car. Shocked by his appearance and alarmed at seeing him alone in his obviously precarious condition, I asked him where he was going and if I might accompany him. "By no means," he replied with difficulty, "and don't tell anybody that you saw me. I am going to the clinic for an operation and shall have them 'phone Clem about it in the afternoon." Clem was short for Clementine. He put his finger to his lips, enjoining me to keep silent. But after a few minutes he asked me what I was doing. I told him that Mahler's fiftieth birthday was approaching, that I was busy getting together a volume

containing the contributions of his friends, and that I was terribly
sorry that he, of all persons, would not be represented. He pressed
my hand silently, motioned me almost impatiently to stay when I
made to follow him, and got off. About five days later, I received
a poem from him, written in his own firm hand, and entitled *The
Musician Speaks*. It was his contribution to Mahler's birthday.
Written in free verse, it represented Lipiner's last answer to Mahler's fundamental problem, discussed by the two friends on many
an occasion: the question of immortality. They had not seen much
of each other during the preceding few years, partly because Mahler, with his American engagements, had not been in Vienna for
any length of time, and partly because a certain estrangement had
set in between them. I succeeded in having them meet again in
Lipiner's office in the Parliament building. On that occasion,
Mahler was as happy and insatiable in asking questions as Lipiner
was kind and prolific in asking counter-questions and answering.
When we had left, Mahler said to me, "How fine that was! One feels
like sitting at his feet — a boy, learning."

Lipiner's poem had an overwhelming effect on Mahler. "I think
it is the most beautiful poem that has ever been written," he said
with his childlike extravagance. He always carried the poem about
with him. Mahler, wavering all the time between conviction and
doubt, clung to Lipiner's pronouncement of a continuation of our
being after death as to the dogma of a man who knew. It is deeply
touching to think that the poet's last greeting to the musician was
those prophetic words, holding out to the searching the promise
of eternal life, that both men were already on its threshold at the
time, and that it will have reunited them soon thereafter. The
death of that fiery spirit, of that wonderful friend, meant an irre-
mediable loss to us.

All the more strongly did the bonds of friendship unite our little
group. Its members, in addition to ourselves, were Lipiner's widow,
her brother Albert Spiegler, and his wife Nina. Albert, who died
an octogenarian in 1938, was one of the most kindhearted men I
have ever met. By profession a research chemist in dietetics, he tried
to prove the value of certain of his theories by private work and
experimental studies. But his more urgent duties as the husband
of an ailing woman, as a friend to those who needed help and advice, and as a philanthropist, kept him from dedicating himself
entirely to his science. Living in comfortable circumstances as a
private scholar, free from everyday cares, he never had the heart
to place his professional work, to which he was greatly devoted,
above the innumerable demands made upon him by life. It was
wonderful to have him as a friend. Whether a severe spiritual up-

heaval was involved or merely an infant's slight ailment, one felt secure in the knowledge that Albert was there and would do everything in his power to help. What was more, he displayed a never-varying childlike cheerfulness — it reminded me of my Father's — gave a good deal of thought to scientific and artistic problems, and occupied himself in a highly personal manner with social questions. Some of the outstanding men in the prominent Social Democratic movement in Austria, men like Viktor Adler and Engelbert Pernerstorfer, were his and Nina's friends. I spent many an hour at the Spiegler home in animated and stimulating conversation with Pernerstorfer.

In spite of Albert's active kindness and universal humanity, and in spite of Lipiner's lavish genius, it was Nina whom we all considered the heart of our little circle and whom we regarded with love and devotion. The effect Nina had upon those around her cannot be more aptly described than by saying that a gentle radiance issued from her tranquil being and that she made us feel as if we were in the presence of one living on a somewhat higher plane. Everybody, whether a member of the inner circle or a less intimate friend, came to her with his cares and problems, not only because of her sympathizing kindness and penetrating understanding, but essentially because of the blissful atmosphere surrounding her — an atmosphere in which all felt elevated and the harassed found comfort and reassurance. A sufferer from physical ailments and ethereally delicate, she reminded me of one of the noblest women in Goethe's poetic works, of Makarie in *Wilhelm Meister*, and this all the more because of the devotion, bordering upon awe, of all those who came in contact with her. To point out the source from which her nature, brimming with life and thirsting for knowledge, drew its sustenance, I should like to add that she felt thoroughly at home in Siegfried Lipiner's spiritual sphere. Her exceptionally high conception of maternal comradeship was most aptly illustrated by the fact that, for the sake of her growing son, she studied Latin, and later Greek, and was not content until she could without difficulty read works like St. Augustine's *De civitate dei* or Sophocles' *Antigone*. Brilliantly faceted though her mind was, it was wholly embedded, as it were, in her love of music. To understand her nature, one had to realize that fact. So saturated was she with music that she might have been called a creature of the musical universe, just as Goethe's Makarie was a creature of the solar system. Her musical absorption led to her friendship with Mahler, and the same may be said of our friendship, which remained a vital force for forty years. Never in my life did I feel so thoroughly understood as a musician as by Nina Spiegler.

[149]

Theme and Variations

Friendship in its highest sense was disclosed to my wife and myself by these people. They joined in the life of their friends as if it were their own. Charitable though their inclinations were, ready though they were to help actively or by giving advice at every opportunity, their friendship also manifested itself in that other form of human sympathy: shared joys, a shared life.

It may be asked why I do not place Mahler's friendship, to which I owe so infinitely much, in the same category with that of those people. The reason is that his was the matter-of-fact egocentric inclination of the exalted creative man whose task makes him lose sight of his fellow-man, and whose absorption in music often blots out his feelings for humanity. Mahler was by no means alien to pity or unable to share joys. He could espouse a cause and be thoughtful of others, be ready to aid and feel sympathy. He knew the meaning of friendship; he was a friend in his own way. But there was not within him a steadily flowing source of warmth. It would gush forth or cease, and though he clung to his friends to the end of his days, I used even then to call his relation to them an "intermittent loyalty." We could rely on him, but the authentic meaning of friendship was revealed to us by those constant people. They proved as stanchly true to him as they did to us. The fact that Lipiner, who was also a creative spirit, was so constant in his manifestations of human friendship perhaps contributed to his inability to attain to the highest type of creativeness: he was lacking in that very egocentric disposition which is the characteristic foundation of all great productive work. It does happen, though rarely, that the interests of the genius of mankind are thwarted by such impractical combinations as those represented in Lipiner's nature. His contemporaries' gain is posterity's loss.

I do not recall where and when I made Arthur Schnitzler's acquaintance. The work of the author of *Liebelei,* the Anatol cycle, the masterly novelettes *Lieutenant Gustl, Dying,* and *The Wise Man's Wife* had long been dear to me. I almost made his *Call of Life* into an opera. He was extremely fond of music. It was his enjoyment of my musical activities at the Opera and in the concert hall that got us into personal touch with each other. I relished the presence of the warmhearted, clever poet, who in conversation liked to spend freely of his wealth of thoughts, knowledge of life, and extensive interests. I felt stimulated and warmed whenever I knew him in attendance at the Opera or spied his thoughtful, friendly face, with its reddish hair and beard, in one of the front rows of the concert hall. I knew that here was a man who really enjoyed music and shared my feelings. One day he and his young wife came to see me. He wished to consult me about her voice, which stood in need of technical improvement. From my days at the Conservatory, I had retained a lively interest in questions pertaining to singing technique. In the course of many years of daily contact with singers, my ear had become attuned to the advantages of a well-placed voice and the disadvantages of a constricted one. I thought I could be of help to Olga Schnitzler, and I think I succeeded. At any rate, this gave us a welcome opportunity for meeting frequently. There is the memory of an unforgettable afternoon at Arthur Schnitzler's home. Hugo von Hofmannsthal was among those present. I still recall the exalted mood and the animated conversation so characteristic of that entire circle of intimately associated poets. Among them were Jakob Wassermann and Richard Beer-Hofmann. I think I made the latter's acquaintance only later, but Wassermann and Hofmannsthal were close to me even then. Wassermann, the author of *Laurin and His People, The Goose Man,* and *Caspar Hauser,* lived on the Kaasgraben in Grinzing with his wife Julie, to whom, in the figure of Ganna, he had raised so horrible a monument in his *Doctor Kerkhoven,* one of the most harrowing matrimonial tales ever written, transcending any hell ever devised by Strindberg. He was an eminently gifted story-teller. The construction of his big works, as for instance *The Maurizius Case* was masterly. But he was heavily and visibly burdened by a sense of responsibility imposed by his struggle toward high goals. My memories of him are fraught with admiration for his powerful endeavors and great accomplishments and, at the same time, with profound sympathy for the sufferings of his dark nature. How diametrically opposed to him was Hofmannsthal's floating, relishing, and humorously inclined nature. He was universally loved and admired by his friends. The author of *Death and the Fool* and the adapter of *Everyman* and *Electra* was able to reach incomparable heights in his conversation, a quality that distinguished his slowly and thoughtfully pronounced judgments as well as his lightest kind of small talk. A splendid evening at my home, spent with him and the singular poet and Dante translator Rudolf Borchardt, has been retained in my memory because of the frequent abrupt change from exuberance of spirits to thoughtful contemplation. I also recall with much pleasure Hofmannsthal's charming house in Rodaun, where I visited him on a number of occasions. I remember that his study faced a well-tended garden. On his desk he kept a small box filled with colored glass balls that the play of his imagination caused him to let slide through his fingers, a rather pleasant contrast — as I told him — to Schiller's poetic dependence on the smell of rotting apples.

While enjoying the spiritual atmosphere of my intercourse with literary people, I was made happy, too, by the warmhearted association with others who were devoted to us. There were Arnold Rosé and his wife Justine, Gustav Mahler's sister. She was a charming and high-spirited woman, passionately devoted to her brother, but always mindful of her old friendship with me, and greatly attached to my wife throughout her life. There was the uniquely original Czech bass Wilhelm Hesch, whom I knew from my days in Hamburg. He lived with his wife and children far out in Ober St. Veit, at the western edge of the Vienna Woods, in Kezal Castle, a large garden-enclosed house he had named after his famous role in Smetana's *The Bartered Bride*. A peasant, he would stalk about his garden in enormous high boots. The place was alive with all kinds of animals. We were fond of dropping in for a pleasant call after a long walk. Berta Förster-Lauterer and her husband, the composer Josef Bohuslav Förster, were warm-hearted loyal people, whose company we frequented. My association with the brilliant Marie Gutheil-Schoder was at first based on a fine mutual artistic understanding. It developed into a beautiful heartfelt friendship, shared by my wife, and terminated only by the singer's death in the thirties. Her most enthusiastic admirer was Countess Misa Wydenbruck-Esterházy, who had been attached also to Mahler from the first, and soon became my loyal friend. The charm of this graceful, vivaciously cheerful, slender, and elegant woman was pronouncedly Austrian and typical of her class. She was bubbling with enthusiasm for art and artists and spoke an aristocratic dialect that frequently disregarded grammatic rules. Her omnipresence at social events was proverbial. But in her slender breast, under the strings of precious pearls, beat an extremely kind and loyal heart. From the first day of our acquaintance to the very end — she must have died in the twenties — she was a stanch adherent of mine. On several occasions at her home, I met her friend, Princess Pauline Metternich, who was quite an old lady at the time. I felt greatly interested in the eccentric woman, with her resolute manner and her energetic bass voice. When the young wife of the Austrian Ambassador to France, she had attended the first Paris performance of *Tannhäuser*. Enraged by the scandalous anti-Wagnerian behavior of the gentlemen of the Jockey Club, she had demonstratively crushed her fan. This impetuous action, unusual for a lady attached to the *corps diplomatique,* gained her a lasting place in Wagnerian literature. A daughter-in-law of the legendary Prince Clemens Metternich, she was a popular figure in Vienna. The spirit of Austrian history came alive in her presence and in her speech.

Vienna "society" as a whole saw but little of me. But I should not like to omit mention of the Wittgenstein Palace in Alleegasse. The Wittgensteins continued the noble tradition of those leading Vienna groups who considered it incumbent upon them to further art and the artists. But they were impelled not so much by a sense of duty imposed on them by their prominent social position as by their genuine enthusiasm for art. Brahms had been on friendly terms with the Wittgensteins, and Joachim and his quartet had frequently played at their house. Unless I am mistaken, Brahms's Clarinet Quintet had its first Viennese performance there, the magnificent clarinetist, Mühlfeld being the assistant artist. The Wittgenstein house was frequented by musicians as well as by prominent painters and sculptors, and by the leading men from the world of science. Karl Wittgenstein was greatly interested in contemporary art. Klinger's *Beethoven* had found its way to his home from the Sezession Exhibition. Gustav Klimt, among other modern painters, was prominently represented in one of the rooms. I was made happy by the fact that the Wittgenstein family had set their affection on me. There was Ludwig Wittgenstein, a brother, with whose extremely musical and charming wife I played music on a number of occasions. There was Clara, a sister, who had undertaken to further the destinies of the Soldat-Roeger Quartet. Whether I dropped in for a friendly visit, or we played some chamber music in the *salon* hallowed by tradition, I always enjoyed with gratification the all-pervading atmosphere of humanity and culture. Paul, Karl Wittgenstein's son, had lost an arm in the First World War. Nothing daunted, he had by means of assiduous study and energy trained himself until he became an exceptionally accomplished and highly regarded one-arm pianist.

A place in my recollections is due the composer and poet Julius Bittner. He was a highly gifted man dramatically and musically, but his superlative creative facility prevented the production of works of art of permanent value. Mahler had been quite interested in Bittner, and first introduced him to me. I was responsible for the first performance of some of his works. After Mahler's departure from the Vienna Opera, I had put on Bittner's *Die rote Gret*, with Gutheil-Schoder unforgettably portraying the leading part. This was followed by *Der Musikant* and *Das höllische Gold*. In Munich, before I became director there, I produced his *Der Bergsee* and, at the Berlin Municipal Opera, about 1926, his *Mondnacht*. In all these and other operas there was unmistakable evidence of dramatic and musical talent. In spite of any number of striking details, however, he seemed never able to accomplish a perfectly rounded whole or to reach maturity. Bittner's best work perhaps was his play *Der liebe Augustin*. I was quite fascinated by some of his *feuilletons* in the *Neue Freie Presse,* written with a charmingly light touch. His personality could not fail to move one deeply. He was a typical Viennese, a tall, ponderous, blond man with a reddish face, loud voice, and roaring laugh. He was clever and full of good humor too. His profound religiousness helped him overcome a terribly painful physical ailment and the amputation of both legs. He remained cheerful and patient to the very end. His energetic noble wife stood by him lovingly and devotedly. Neither her husband's illness nor frequent financial difficulties were able to break down her vital energy. Much could be learned from these two people. They were typical of the aforementioned Austrian ability not to take the hopeless seriously. Typical, too, was their Viennese dialect, which they spoke in its most unadulterated form.

Shortly before Mahler's departure from Vienna, I became indebted to him for an exceedingly interesting acquaintance, which gradually developed into a friendship. Ethel Smyth had called on him, carrying under her arm the score of her opera *The Wreckers.* He referred her to me. Before me stood a gaunt Englishwoman of about forty-eight, clad in a nondescript baggy dress. She told me she had formerly studied in Leipzig. Brahms had been interested in her chamber music, her opera *Der Wald* had had its world *première* in Dresden, and now she was here in Vienna to make us acquainted with her latest opera, based upon Henry Brewster's *Les Naufrageurs*. I sighed inwardly at what I presumed was in store for me, but she had hardly played ten minutes, singing the vocal parts in an unattractive voice, when I made her stop, rushed over to Mahler's office, and implored him to come with me: the Englishwoman was a true composer. Mahler was unfortunately unable to spare the time, and so I had to go back alone. We spent the whole morning on her opera, and when we parted I was wholly captivated by her work and her personality. I asked her to my home, and we saw as much as possible of each other while she was in Vienna. Ethel Smyth, who died quite recently at a ripe old age, was remarkable for the consuming fire of her soul. It burned ceaselessly when she composed, when she wrote — among the many products of her pen were the highly attractive *Impressions That Remained* and *A Three-Legged Journey in Greece* — when she was active as a militant suffragette, when she conducted an orchestra clad in a kind of kimono, and when she conversed. Unfavorable circumstances prevented me from producing her opera either in Vienna or in Munich. But I did present the prelude to the second act, with its suggestive ocean atmosphere, at a number of concerts and was able to conduct the whole work in London in 1909.

Theme and Variations

Among my Vienna friends in a wider sense, I must count the chorus of the *Singakademie* and, later, the Philharmonic Chorus. Our relations were of a most cordial nature. As for Vienna's musical public, so warm a personal relationship developed in the course of many years between it and myself, the joyful demonstrations when I appeared at the desk and the marks of approval at the end of a performance bore the character of so deep an affection, that I feel justified in giving my relations with musical Vienna, too, the name of friendship.

I think it is highly significant of that city and of the importance it attributed to music that so marked a feeling of friendship could be established with the seemingly amorphous and anonymous crowd called the public. But, after all, it was not so wholly amorphous a crowd in Vienna. Musical Vienna was a body of a very special kind. All the Austrian levity, all wanton indifference, dulness, and Philistinism, all the scornfulness and fault-finding under which Schubert, Mozart, Beethoven, Grillparzer, Stifter, and other noble spirits had suffered, could not detract from the significance of that phenomenon.

The artistic atmosphere of Vienna had a magic power of attraction for the Germans, while those Austrians who disdained the easy-going attitude of their countrymen, felt drawn toward the more hardy and sober air of Berlin. Delusion was at work on both sides, and disillusionment was often the result. Huge Berlin's objective surroundings did not influence or lend color to the mighty and ever-growing wealth of the city's artistic life. After the turn of the century, Berlin grew to be a kind of international market of the world's cultural happenings. The drama under Max Reinhardt reached great heights, and symphonic music was splendidly represented by Arthur Nikisch. Opera only, under the general management of Hülsen, failed to play a leading part. Vienna was not an international market, nor could anyone say that Vienna formed the objective surroundings for artistic events. Vienna did influence and lend color to its culture. There was in its institutes of art and its practice of art a certain element of subjectivity, just as there is in the musical renditions of a strongly subjective conductor whose personality makes itself felt at his every appearance. The performances at the Burgtheater, at the Court Opera, and of the Philharmonic Orchestra — in fact, every cultural event in Vienna — tasted of Vienna, and it was a taste that even the most fastidious palate found pleasing at all times.

IV

WE moved to Vienna in the autumn of 1901 and took up temporary quarters in Neustiftgasse, behind the Deutsches Volkstheater. From there, we proposed to attend at our leisure to the establishment of a home of our own. We ate our noonday meals at one of the attractive restaurants on the Getreidemarkt. I mention this because I still think with a nostalgic smile of the bills we paid in gulden and kreutzer, the old Austrian currency. They were soon to be replaced by kronen and heller. My wife was cordially received by Mahler and his sisters as well as by the families of our friends. Mahler himself introduced me to the various officials and heads of departments at the Opera. When I had conducted my first rehearsal with soloists, chorus, and orchestra — I started my activity with a performance of *Aïda* — and was congratulated on it by Mahler, I looked forward tranquilly and confidently to a richly varied activity in an exalted atmosphere of art.

It was of great interest to me that among the conductors at the Vienna Opera was Hans Richter, still surrounded by the glory of Bayreuth and his many years of friendship with Wagner. I witnessed a performance of Meyerbeer's *L'Africaine,* which he conducted with obvious distaste, and one of *Die Meistersinger,* at which he displayed the full mastery of his leadership. I also recall that Mahler was anxious to show Richter every mark of respect to which he was entitled as a master in his art and a musician of world fame. I happened to be in Mahler's office when he opened the gigantic repertory book, resting on a standing desk at the window, and asked Richter to choose the operas he wished to conduct. But all of Mahler's efforts to retain the services of the famous colleague proved unsuccessful. Richter left Vienna very soon. His departure was probably hastened by his resentment at seeing his established fame obscured by the new brilliance of Mahler's activity. He went to England and took charge of the Hallé Orchestra in Manchester. He also conducted a number of regular concerts in London. I recall with pleasure a highly stimulating evening I spent there with him and his daughter.

My other colleagues were Robert Fuchs, a man of about sixty, who soon retired on pension, and Franz Schalk, thirty-eight at the time, who had been my predecessor in Berlin and whose personal acquaintance I now made. I was to collaborate with him for eleven years in Vienna and, later, in Salzburg. One of the offices at the Opera was the "abode of routine," personified by Chief Stage Director August Stoll, a former tenor, and of the Artistic Secretary

Karl Wondra, a former chorus master. These men had been sitting at their desks facing each other for decades. There, or wherever their duties took them, they represented the persevering and untouchable spirit of a former epoch, until the only power superior to them, Time, put an end to their activities.

My hopeful mood was soon to vanish under the influence of a severe shock. I did a good deal of conducting. Mahler assigned to me some of the operas he had prepared, confident that I would maintain the artistic level and spirit of his performances. In addition, a considerable number of other works were entrusted to me. Among them was *Tannhäuser*. I felt that the performance, not counting one role that was woefully miscast, was not lacking in dramatic and musical vitality. How surprised, nay shocked I was when I read on the following morning a furious attack on me in one of Vienna's leading papers, the *Neues Wiener Tagblatt*. It was more than adverse criticism, more even than a personal insult. What I read was a loud protest against my activity in so prominent a place, a summons to fight against my very existence. It was the first time in my life that I had been so violently abused. The expressions used were so extravagantly uncomplimentary — one of them was that "I would not do as the leader even of a riflemen's band" — that the obvious malice should have weakened the general effect. I was nevertheless deeply dismayed, and my bewilderment increased when a number of similar voices were raised against me in quick succession. Mahler told me at once — and I found out later how right he had been — that these attacks were nothing but the first bugle call of a campaign directed against him, and that the strategic plan was as clever as it was malicious. At that time, the fourth year of Mahler directorial activity, his relentless opponents had closed their ranks firmly. It must be admitted that Mahler's violent actions, his peremptory manner in questions of art, his engagements and dismissals, and his fight against tradition and time-honored customs had helped to swell the ranks of his enemies among the artistic personnel, especially among the members of the orchestra, but also among the theater's officials, the public, and the newspapermen. But even if he had been innocent of any tangible offense, the very fact of his positive creative existence would have been an insult to the Philistines and a challenge to the *internationale* of the negatively inclined, abundantly represented in Austria. The rich flowering of culture had its counterpart in a violent oppositional current. Among the people who hated Mahler and tried to undermine his activity there were some who were actuated by matters of principle; some were of a fundamentally negative disposition; some were Philistines; and others, specially numerous in Vienna, were "scoffers" in the sense of the Psalmist. They all hated Mahler and campaigned against him as Cato had done against Carthage. But an attack directed against him personally would no doubt have mobilized his many adherents. It was hoped, on the other hand, that the appointment of a young and inexperienced conductor to so prominent a place in Vienna's musical life would furnish a particularly glaring proof of the director's lack of responsibility in making engagements. At the same time, a counteraction on the part of his supporters was unlikely, as he himself had not been attacked.

That was how Mahler and his friends explained the attacks to me, and so I tried to make the best of things. But the acts of hostility increased and spread until I noticed opposition to me even among the ranks of the artists. A number of small, but widely read newspapers joined in the fight. Mahler and I — he because he had engaged me — were attacked in their critical columns. Nobody seemed to take my part, and there was nothing Mahler could do to help me. To make matters worse, he was personally preoccupied. He had become acquainted with Alma Schindler, "the most beautiful girl in Vienna," and had fallen in love with her. As might have been expected, the spiritual storm unleashed rather late in his life — he was then forty-one years old — eclipsed everything else. He seemed to be unaware of my position, or at least of its dangers, and felt disinclined to take my worries quite seriously. As for myself, the more clearly I recognized the perilous aspect of my situation, the less I felt inclined to bother my friends or those who were well disposed toward me with my affairs. I was astonished beyond expression and wholly perplexed.

My work surely did not merit reckless insults, but my nature made me wonder if it did not deserve serious censure. It would have been unlike me not to have tried to become conscious of my every possible weakness and mistake. It seemed to me that I was wanting in critical watchfulness while at work; I found that my modifications of tempi was immoderate; I discovered unreliability and even awkwardness in my technique of conducting; and so, hardly had a few weeks passed, when I was actually unable to conduct and became convinced that there was more than a drop of truth in the flood of malicious criticisms.

The foundation of my professional existence had been shaken. I began to be doubtful, if not of my musicianship, of my mission as a conductor. All my previous successes did not seem to count. Here in Vienna, the city of music and the home of my choice, I had been weighed and found wanting. It happened that at that very time the Cologne Opera offered me the post of chief conductor under exceptionally favorable conditions. Great was the temptation to forsake the unbearable Vienna atmosphere at the end of the season and to regain my self-assurance in more sympathetic surroundings.

My wife and I had almost made up our minds to accept the Cologne offer, when she decided to hear Mahler's opinion first. I suggested to her that she save him the embarrassment of having to take sides. Were he to counsel against Cologne, he would add to his responsibility for my fate in Vienna, while in the other case it would seem as if he wished to offer me as a sacrifice to his enemies. My wife disapproved of what she considered my exaggerated considerateness and decided to consult Mahler without my knowledge. Then she confessed having called on him and reported to my surprise that in his opinion I had, through no fault or weakness of mine, "lost the game" in Vienna: he who had once lost in Vienna could never again be victorious. Mahler would, of course, be willing to abide by the terms of my contract, but in my own interest he would advise accepting the Cologne offer. This report had a rather unexpected effect on me. I suddenly felt strong, was conscious of my responsibilities to myself, and quite certain of my decision: I had been done a wrong, and it would be cowardly to take it lying down. "Let me be victorious here first, and then I'll go," I said to my wife. She bravely consented, we stayed, and I was victorious.

But my road was a long and arduous one. It was most arduous at the beginning, when, as I said before, I had come to the conclusion that I did not know how to conduct. With what evil forebodings did I look forward to every *pizzicato* chord of the strings and to every freely entering upbeat in any orchestral group. No matter how I beat, both the chord and the upbeat would lack precision. How terrible that slow 6/8 measures became inexact when I beat them in two and stiff when I beat in six. And not only did I, in these and similar instances, feel insidiously inhibited in my conducting technique, but I also began to droop musically. My excessive watchfulness of details interfered when I had to anticipate a longer phrase or tried to satisfy the demands of synthetic interpretation. I felt as if I had happened into a bog and was sinking lower and lower. And there was no one in sight to come to my aid.

There was nothing for me to do but help myself. Like the fantastic Baron Münchhausen, I pulled myself out of the bog by my own bootstraps. I increased my watchfulness, self-criticism, and technical experimenting at rehearsals. On the other hand, I vetoed every bit of self-observation during performances, forcing myself to concentrate exclusively upon the music as a whole and to subordinate details. Above all, however, I tried to become conscious again of my own strength of mind and to re-establish contact with my former firm ego. The method proved successful. My technical studies at orchestra rehearsals bore fruit, and my reproachful appeal to my own strength of mind produced a reinvigoration of my musical work. Gradually I felt at my performances that I could afford to make conscious use of my growing technical accomplishments, that I was able to insert a certain amount of critical listening and observation without jeopardizing the flow and continuity of the music. I knew then that the most important part of my fight, that against my own uncertainty, had been won.

I had never again spoken to Mahler about myself. I was under the impression that he was too thoroughly absorbed in his personal affairs to be greatly interested in my musical activities. What was my surprise, therefore, when, after a performance of Gluck's *Orfeo*, Hassinger, Mahler's factotum, handed me a folded piece of paper on which were words to this effect: "Bravo! Very fine. Noble in expression, moderate in the tempi. Greatly pleased. M." These were the first encouraging words from him during that critical period. They had upon me almost the effect of a draft from that fairy-tale bottle of medicine that causes every wound to heal.

It had in the meantime become clear to me that the sham insurrection against me would have to subside before I could think of bringing about my rehabilitation in the sphere in which I had almost been wrecked. I therefore decided first to prove my musicianship in another field. It was a fortunate coincidence that Arnold Rosé, with whom I had had many a private musical session, invited me to be the assisting pianist at one of his chamber music recitals at Bösendorfer Hall. The distinguished audience that frequented the Rosé recitals, and the press received me with a most gratifying warmth. It was both significant and fortunate that the praise bestowed on me on that occasion as well as on following ones came from what might have been called Vienna's musical conscience. From that time, my connection with Arnold Rosé became ever closer, and we joined later in giving classic sonata recitals, beyond his regular evenings of chamber music. Our recitals were continued regularly through fifteen years and became a fixed institution in Vienna's musical life.

From his seventeenth year, Arnold Rosé had been the leading first violinist of the famous orchestra of the Vienna Court Opera and the Philharmonic Concerts. I shall never forget the sublime beauty of his violin solo in the third act of *Tristan*. It made me realize for the first time how inspiring an individual sound could be detaching itself impressively and eloquently from the warm *tutti* of the violins. The magic of Rosé's orchestra solos lost none of its enchanting effect on me in the course of a great many years. My gratefulness to that man for his magnificent work as *Konzertmeister* will remain alive forever. He seemed to be able to divine the conductor's every wish. Never for a moment did the high tension of his playing relax, whether at rehearsals or performances. He used his unique authority in the orchestra solely in support of the conductor. Thus, in the more than fifty years of his activity, he set a classic example of the "idea" of a *Konzertmeister*. His quartet, succeeding that of Joachim, became fully its equal in accomplishment and European reputation. The instances when Rosé appeared as concert soloist were rare, but he was successful on those occasions too. Arnold Rosé's musicianship was innate and intuitive. His intonation and sense of rhythm were infallible, and he was also gifted with a perfect ear. He was ardently devoted to Mahler from the first day of his activity at the Vienna Opera, and also displayed a deeply gratifying, unshakable loyalty to me both at the Opera and on the concert platform. We have remained personal friends to this day. His musical eloquence contrasted strikingly with his personal taciturnity, which, by the way, contributed to his authority over the members of the orchestra and the members of his quartet. It was hard to believe that the robust, bearded man with the characteristic head of a professor had been a typical Viennese man about town in his younger days, that he had even driven his own horse and carriage, and that he had lived a gay life in the avenues and restaurants of the Prater and the fashionable gathering places of the Inner City, in the company of youths of similar inclinations. He married Mahler's sister Justine in 1902, and turned out to be an exemplary husband and head of his family. When, at the age of seventy-five, Rosé had to leave Austria, England received him hospitably, a fact that did great honor to that country's sincere appreciation of the services the artist had rendered to music.

At last, in 1902, I was able to score the operatic success I had longed for and that was to make up for the many disappointments I had suffered. Mahler entrusted to me the revival of Verdi's *Un Ballo in Maschera,* to which the Opera assigned its finest young voices. On that evening I made a conquest of the Opera, and even my enemies succumbed to an attack of nervous aphonia. Although they recovered later, their voices never regained their original metallic resonance. My critical adversaries finally confined themselves to the part of the professional faultfinder, less effective, but greatly in vogue in Vienna. When, soon thereafter, Angelo Neumann, the head of the Prague Theater, invited us all to come to Prague, so that his audiences, too, might enjoy the much-praised

Vienna production, I understood that a new and more pleasant epoch had set in for me. I spent many a stimulating hour in the company of the majestic Neumann. His long theatrical career had supplied him with a wealth of anecdotes and tales. He regretted that "because of a blunder in theatrical history" — as he expressed it — I had not continued his series of conductors. He had much to tell about Anton Seidl, the conductor of his *Ring* tour, and about Nikisch, Mahler, and Muck.

It was an honor, indeed, to conduct at the famous old Prague Theater on the Obstmarkt, where Mozart himself had directed the world's first performance of *Don Giovanni* in 1787. I made a little pilgrimage to Bertramka, Josepha Duschek's charming little house in which the immortal work had come into being. Walking along the interesting old streets, past the baroque façades, through the Powder Tower, up to the Hradschin, and across the Moldau bridges, I became deeply attached to the strangely imposing, gloomily romantic, and characteristically colorful town — an attachment which was intensified in the course of my numerous visits to Prague and my frequent concerts there and which has lasted to this day. I shall always remember Prague in connection with the fact that Mozart had been permitted to score his greatest successes there and that the enthusiasm of the Prague audiences had shed a ray of sunshine upon his sorrowful life.

Not long after that performance of *Un Ballo in Maschera,* Rosé and I were asked to give a sonata recital in Prague, in the beautiful hall of the Rudolphinum, which was later taken over by the Bohemian Diet and ceased to be a scene of music. Thereafter, musical Prague unfortunately no longer had a hall compatible with its artistic achievements and the important part music played in its public life. Yet I like to think back with gratitude on the splendid evenings with the Czech Philharmonic Orchestra in the Luzerna or in Smetana Hall. In the course of years, these concerts served to form a charming and lasting relation between musical Prague and myself.

Mahler married Alma Schindler in March 1902. She was the beautiful and diversely gifted daughter of the painter Jakob Emil Schindler, whose attractive marble figure is one of the pleasing sights of Vienna's Stadtpark. It was Alma who aroused Mahler's interest in the visible arts, which thus far had been rather alien to him. Alma's mother's second husband, Carl Moll, was an excellent painter. While his colorful and poetic Vienna scenes and landscapes could hardly be called modernistic, he yet used his considerable propagandist ability in furthering the cause of progressive artists. An enthusiastic admirer of Oskar Kokoschka and Gustav

Klimt, he had been instrumental in calling into being the Vienna Sezession Exhibition, grouped around Max Klinger's half-nude *Beethoven* and surrounded by Klimt's daringly bizarre murals. Kolo Moser, co-creator of the Wiener Werkstätten, another member of that circle, was one of those who extended a hearty welcome to the brilliant musician and director of the Court Opera. It was through this association that Mahler made the acquaintance of Alfred Roller.

That Mahler's friendly social contact with the circle of Vienna's painters was followed also by an inward turning toward creative art was mainly due to Alma's influence, though his association with Roller was no doubt a contributing factor. Alma had studied counterpoint with the blind theorist and organist Josef Labor and composition with Alexander von Zemlinsky. But, awestruck before Mahler's gaze, she locked away in her desk the songs she had written to poems by Goethe, Heine, Novalis, Dehmel, and others, and only during her husband's last year on earth could she be induced to let him select a few of these songs for publication. In addition to her lively interest in music, literature, and painting, the young woman was a rather gifted sculptress. I recall that one day Mahler and I wandered out to the Prater to call for her at the studio of her teacher Edmund Hellmer. I can still see her before me, daubs of clay on her hands and her sculptor's smock, her face flushed with the tension of her work — and very beautiful. I shall have more to say later of this singular personality.

The winds of disaster having calmed down, we gave thought to the establishment of a permanent home of our own. We spent hours on end in a furniture store on the Mariahilferstrasse, lost in yearning contemplation of the most beautiful and expensive household articles. Needless to say, this was always quickly followed by the purchase of rather inexpensive pieces of furniture. But it was wonderful, at any rate, to move into the handsome flat in Köstlergasse and to be the proud owners of all it contained. The occasion was rendered especially festive by the sudden and unannounced appearance of two friends of ours: Julius Bittner and Gustav Brecher. The latter, at that time a humble assistant conductor at the Opera, was later to become the director, successively, of the Frankfurt and Leipzig Operas. Wearing full-dress suits, silk hats, and white gloves — in broad daylight — and carrying armfuls of wine and delicatessen, they had come to help us celebrate the event.

We had been careless enough, when renting the apartment, not to take into consideration the possibility of an increase in our family, and so, when it became apparent that we had to make provision for it, we moved into larger quarters at No. 7 Theobaldgasse. There, at an interval of three years, our two daughters, Lotte and Gretel, were born.

Those were the only years in my life during which I discovered within myself a wholly un-Faustian tendency to enjoy a comfortable middle-class existence. Matrimonial happiness, the births of our children, our joyfully interested observation of their development, thoughts concerning their bringing up (aided by advice from Jean Paul's *Levana*), an economically untroubled existence, the beautiful Phaeacian city with its charming surroundings, the splendor of the old Empire, cultured sociability, friends — I began to enjoy my comfort and become a consciously contented bourgeois. On a fine Sunday afternoon in spring we would indulge in a *Gummiradler,* a rubber-tired cab, for a drive in the Prater. To my inquiry: "How much?" the jaunty jehu would invariably reply: "Aw, Your Grace'll know what's right." Of course, I knew. I knew that I'd have to give him five gulden, plus a handsome tip. But it was worth it. When we drove along the Prater's main avenue, with its double rows of blossoming chestnut trees, to the *Krieau* or the *Lusthaus* for some excellent coffee, and when we watched cab upon cab discharge new groups of gay and smartly dressed people, I myself felt gay and contented. Somehow, the feeling of being urged on, which from the days of my childhood had dominated my restless existence, seemed to have vanished. After the *allegro con fuoco,* my life apparently had slipped into an *andantino*. It was but a brief intermezzo. The renewed upsurge of inward and outward agitation was never again to be interrupted by the recurrence of a similar feeling of contentment.

To prevent my being too thoroughly coddled by a friendly fate, the guardian angel to whom my education and chastisement were entrusted had felt it proper to insert into that period of peaceful contemplation an illness that caused me a great deal of anxiety during the year after the birth of our first child. I was attacked by an arm ailment. Medical science called it a professional cramp, but it looked deucedly like incipient paralysis. The rheumatic-neuralgic pain became so violent that I could no longer use my right arm for conducting or piano playing. I went from one prominent doctor to another. Each one confirmed the presence of psychogenic elements in my malady. I submitted to any number of treatments, from mudbaths to magnetism, and finally decided to call on Professor Sigmund Freud, resigned to submit to months of soul searching. The consultation took a course I had not foreseen. Instead of questioning me about sexual aberrations in infancy, as my layman's ignorance had led me to expect, Freud examined my arm briefly. I told him my story, feeling certain that he would be professionally interested in a possible connection between my actual physical affliction and a wrong I had suffered more than a year before. Instead, he asked me if I had ever been to Sicily. When I replied that I had not, he said that it was very beautiful and interesting, and more Greek than Greece itself. In short, I was to leave that very evening, forget all about my arm and the Opera, and do nothing for a few weeks but use my eyes. I did as I was told. Fortified with all the available literature about Sicily, I took an evening train for Genoa, strolled through the interesting streets of the picturesque town, gazed with awe at the mighty stairways of the ancient palaces, and, after having procured a steamer ticket at the office of the Navigazione Generale, sailed out into the Ligurian Sea and toward Naples on the following morning, not without casting a look of admiration back upon Genoa.

Milan and Venice were the only Italian beauty spots thus far known to me. I had purposely chosen the sea route, because I would have considered it unbearable, if not sinful, to rush in a train through cities like Florence and Rome just to get to Sicily quickly enough and be able to use for the intended purpose what little time my finances permitted me. I arrived in Naples toward noon. When my eyes took in Mount Vesuvius, the town, and its environs, I did not die, but neither did I quite feel of this world. It took all the importunity and cheating tactics of the cabbies, all the smells from the street kitchens, all the noise made by street vendors, all the naïvely immoral propositions in the Galleria Umberto, and all the other rather worldly peculiarities of that paradisiac place, to get me back to earth again. I was deeply sorry that I had to forgo Capri, but I was anxious to get to Sicily, and I took the regular steamer to Palermo the following evening. The boat was small, the seas were high, and I was disgracefully seasick, but I felt richly compensated by the splendid entrance into the port of Palermo and the sight of Monte Pellegrino in the morning air.

Mindful of Freud's instructions, I endeavored not to think of my affliction. In this I was aided by the powerful and exciting effect of my first meeting with Hellenism, which burst upon my eye and soul from every side. I was deeply impressed by the Greek theater in Taormina, the boatride on the Anapò beneath the papyrus shrubs, and the temples of Girgenti. But all these individual sights were outshone by the magnificent landscape with its grandiosely shaped mountains, the sublime solitude surrounding Syracuse, the rivers, the fields, and the nobly shaped bays. This, indeed, seemed an ideal scenery for Goethe's *Walpurgisnacht*. Thoughts of a tempestuous past, of the monuments commemorating it, and of nature that seemed to bear its imprint agitated me for weeks and made me forget the present and my troubles. In the end, my soul and mind were greatly benefited by the additional knowledge I had gained of Hellenism, but not my arm. Besides, it was cold, and I felt I needed warmth. So I decided to use what little was left of my money and my time on the French Riviera, whose fine sunshine was extolled in newspaper reports.

I had to pass through an uncomfortable hour, which made me wonder if I'd ever be privileged again to bask in the rays of the sun. I had planned to go to Naples by way of the Strait separating Sicily from the mainland. Night found me in a hotel in Messina. I was awakened by a feeling of dizziness, my room seemed to rise and settle down again, and my bed, which had suddenly come alive, hurled me to the floor like a bucking bronco getting rid of its irksome rider. This comparison was of course suggested by screen impressions gained at a much later date, but even if I had been acquainted with western habits at that time, I doubt if there would have been room in my mind for anything beyond the thought: an earthquake! When I tried to get up after a few minutes of quiet, a new rising, trembling, and falling of my room and the tumbling of pictures from the walls — what was a paltry steamer trip to Palermo compared with that? — made me think better of it. It seemed wiser patiently to await the end of the terrestrial spasm before entrusting myself again to my bed. How disappointed was I on the following morning when I saw no faces pale with fright, heard no excited tales, but was reminded of my fearsome experience merely by my waiter's polite phrase: *"Un piccolo terramoto, Signor."* Obviously it took shocks of an entirely different caliber to draw the attention of the blasé inhabitants of Messina. I told myself that their indifference was due probably to the frequency of quakes in that vicinity and that I need not be ashamed of having been so violently frightened by my first experience of the kind. It is really terrifying to feel the foundation of our animal existence, the firm ground under our feet, rock and sway. Man's sound instinct probably responds to no elemental events with the abysmal terror caused by an earthquake. When I read, in 1908, that a monstrous seismic catastrophe had brought death and destruction to the beautifully situated flourishing Messina, I was reminded of the *piccolo terramoto* and could imagine the waiter's polite smile freeze into a Medusa-like grimace, while the walls came tumbling down upon him.

A regular ferry service was maintained between Messina and Reggio di Calabria, but after the night's experience I balked at so prosaic a combination as that of Scylla and Charybdis with a sea-going bus. Heedless of what dangers might be lurking in the passage through the whirlpool, I hired a man and a boat to row it. To my question in Italian whether he and his boat were strong enough for the trip he answered with many a flourish of his arms and a flood of proud assurances uttered in a wholly unintelligible Sicilian idiom. I heard nothing on our trip of the Charybdis roar described in Schiller's *Der Taucher,* but the whirlpool was fierce enough to toss our little boat about violently for quite some time, until my boatman finally succeeded by means of a small red sail, a wealth of imprecations, and calls upon the Madonna and his patron saint in reaching smooth water and, finally, Reggio di Calabria. A night ride by train took me to Paestum, where the sight of the world's most wonderful Greek temple in the light of the full moon impressed itself indelibly on my mind. From there I went back to Naples. I attended an evening performance of *Rigoletto* at the Teatro San Carlo, and though I was not interested in the performance itself, I admired the magnificent house, enjoyed the noisy enthusiasm of the audience, and was particularly amused by a little incident that, at that time, could hardly have occurred anywhere but in southern Italy. When I got up to leave my seat during the intermission, my neighbors begged me to wait a bit. A few seats away from me a young mother was nursing her infant, and the Neapolitans, so noisy and unrestrained at other times, waited patiently and with sympathetic awe until the baby had drunk its fill. Then, to be sure, they crowded their way out with Neapolitan impetuosity.

Boarding a boat train again, I sailed back to Genoa, where I was met by my wife. Together we proceeded to Monaco. Every day I climbed a rock in order to expose my ailing arm to the sun, but in vain. When I got back to Vienna, I poured out my troubles to Freud. His advice was — to conduct. "But I can't move my arm." "Try it, at any rate." "And what if I should have to stop?" "You won't have to stop." "Can I take upon myself the responsibility of possibly upsetting a performance?" "I'll take the responsibility." And so I did a little conducting with my right arm, then with my left, and occasionally with my head. There were times when I forgot my arm over the music. I noticed at my next session with Freud that he attached particular importance to my forgetting. I tried once more to conduct, but with the same discouraging result. It was at that time that I discovered Feuchtersleben's *Contributions to the Dietetics of the Soul.* I read and studied, trying assiduously to find my way into the lines of thought expressed in the brilliant book, in which a physician, who at the same time was a poet, wisely tried to point out to suffering humanity a way that has since been made practicable. I also tried to familiarize myself with Freud's ideas and to learn from him. I endeavored to adapt my conducting technique to the weakness of my arm without impairing the musical effect. So, by dint of much effort and confidence, by learning and forgetting, I finally succeeded in finding my way back to my profession. Only then did I become aware that in my thoughts I had already abandoned it during the preceding weeks.

V

I AM not a composer. Yet I think I ought to mention my early compositions and my experiences as a creative musician at a time when I still entertained the illusion of being one.

I had played for Richard Strauss, the chairman of the *Allgemeiner Deutscher Musikverein,* a Symphonic Fantasy I had written. This, I believe, occurred while he was in Vienna, attending the final rehearsals and the first performance of his *Feuersnot.* Strauss seemed to be genuinely interested in my work. It was performed at the next Music Festival in Frankfurt-am-Main, in 1904, under my direction. I had tried to reproduce symphonically the fantastic atmosphere of Ibsen's *Peer Gynt,* and had chosen for the ending the mood of the lullaby in which Solvejg brings forgiveness and peace to the dying. Opinions about the work were divided, but the fact that it was received with interest was at least encouraging. At another concert of the same Music Festival, Strauss's *Sinfonia Domestica* had an overwhelming success. I should like to remark in retrospect that the choice of contemporary works of the most divergent trends and styles spoke well for the open-minded attitude of the Commission. Altogether, I recall with a great deal of respect the brisk and progressive spirit and the sense of responsibility of the *Allgemeiner Deutscher Musikverein* and the valuable service it rendered in connection with the stimulation of musical life. At a previous Music Festival in Krefeld, in 1902, Mahler's dionysiac Third Symphony had scored a prodigious success. This marked an epoch in his life. It stamped him as a great composer and assured him of his proper place in the foreground of contemporary interest. His Fourth Symphony, by the way, did not have its first performance at a Music Festival, but at one of the Munich Kaim Concerts.

A piano quintet of mine was performed at the Music Festival in Essen, in 1906, on the occasion when Mahler's tragic Sixth Symphony had its first performance. As far as I can remember, my quintet was able to arouse the interest and sympathy of the audience. My First Symphony was performed in Vienna in 1908 under my own direction, and I also conducted it later, I think it was in

1909, at one of the Strasbourg orchestral concerts arranged there by Pfitzner. There were a Second Symphony and a Ballad for chorus and orchestra based upon Schiller's *The Victory Feast,* but I no longer tried to have them performed. My doubts concerning my creative ability had become certainty. Only a piano-and-violin sonata, dedicated to Arnold Rosé, managed to outlive my renunciation by several years, probably because of its *andante,* for which I still have a certain fondness.

We had founded in Vienna an Association of Creative Musicians. Among its members were Alexander von Zemlinsky, Arnold Schönberg, Gerhard von Keussler, and myself. Mahler had been made Honorary President. Schönberg unquestionably outranked us all as a composer, and he was also able to create more of a stir in Vienna's musical life than anybody else. He had just written his string sextet *Verklärte Nacht,* and Rosé was preparing to perform it. Mahler, who had attended one of the rehearsals, spoke to me about it with a great deal of warmth. As for myself, I was overwhelmed by a splendid performance of the work in Bösendorfer Hall. In spite of its Wagnerian atmosphere and its infection with sequences, I found it highly original, full of ecstasy and convincing force in its moods, and at the same time rich in musical substance. From the first low D, I felt profoundly moved, spellbound in a magic circle. There were many who felt as I did, Mahler among them. But while we applauded enthusiastically, there were others who hissed furiously and shouted derisively. Mahler told me later about a man who had been hissing right in his face and to whom he had suggested that he had better restrain himself when he saw him, Mahler, applaud. To this the man had replied: "Why, I hissed at your symphony too." Mahler had given the man a keen look and then turned away with the words: "I might have guessed it." As a matter of fact, the Fourth, the idyl among Mahler's symphonic dramas, had caused so much excitement at its first Vienna performance but a short time before that the enthusiasts and their opponents had almost come to blows. Such warlike scenes in the concert hall were usually followed by weeks of heated debate among musicians and the public, proof of the widespread and passionate interest in musical events. No less of a furor was later caused by Schönberg's symphonic poem *Pelleas und Melisande,* and possibly even a greater one by his string quartets, especially the second one, the soprano solo of which was sung with expressive force by Gutheil-Schoder. All these works had served gradually to create a picture of Schönberg's firmly knit personality that, undaunted by the turmoil it caused, courageously pursued its way. Much as I admired Schönberg's courage and unwavering attitude, profoundly though I was impressed by his exquisite musicianship, and attracted though I was by much of his later chamber music and vocal compositions, I felt increasingly unable to follow him on his way, because I considered it a devious way. To this day, I have been unable to reconcile my moral approval of his imposing existence with my rejection of a musical language that seems to me abstract and experimental. The heroic romanticism, the lofty lyricism, and the bizarre boldness of his *Gurrelieder* have become dear to my heart. I performed the powerful work on a number of occasions. It gave me a great deal of pleasure, too, to make *Verklärte Nacht,* in its setting for string orchestra, sound forth in New York, as late as 1943. But I must admit that my musical constitution is no match for the works he produced after his quartets. Arnold Schönberg is undoubtedly not only a pure and incorruptible idealist but also a powerfully and uniquely intuitive musician. I am quite serious when I say that I should be happy if in a future existence, in which I shall have the benefit of superior organs of musical perception, I were to be able to ask his forgiveness for my primitive mundane lack of understanding.

The world *première* of Mahler's Fifth Symphony in Cologne, in 1904, was connected with an occurrence I should like to record because it impressed me deeply and was quite characteristic of Mahler. After his Krefeld success, he had found a publisher. Such was now Mahler's reputation that the man offered him a large honorarium for his Fifth, upon which he was then at work. Gratified by this symptom of his growing importance as a composer, Mahler accepted the offer. When he had finished the orchestra score, he received the sum of, I believe, fifteen thousand marks, an unusually high fee in those days. The Fifth Symphony marked the beginning of Mahler's use of a more highly developed polyphonic style, which confronted his technique of orchestration with new problems. The Cologne performance revealed that these problems had not been solved. Somehow, the web of the voices did not sound with the intended clarity, and I could not help confirming Mahler's unfavorable impression. He decided at once upon his course: he would reorchestrate the whole symphony. He returned to the publisher the money, which was needed partly for reprinting the material, partly for correcting it, and spent months of arduous work in rearranging almost the entire score. Thus a considerable part of his worldly reward was sacrificed to the demands of spiritual purity.

As long as Mahler was active at the Opera, my position and that of my colleague Franz Schalk were overshadowed by his. This seemed a matter of course to me in view of his artistry and mastery and his standing as the institute's director. My position had nevertheless changed decisively even during Mahler's incumbency, and my activity had gained in importance and authority. The Fourth Gallery never missed an opportunity to tender me an ovation, and, altogether, I sensed the audience's warmly sympathetic attitude at my performances. Musical Vienna had clasped me to its heart. This gratifying fact became apparent to me also outside the Opera, at the increasingly frequent concerts I conducted and my occasional appearances as assisting pianist at chamber-music recitals. There were also a number of invitations to conduct in Budapest, and my relations with Prague, too, were continued. Carl Goldmark, the composer of *The Queen of Sheba* and of *The Cricket on the Hearth,* both of which I had conducted in Vienna, asked Mahler to entrust to me the production of his *A Winter's Tale.* Although the opera revealed a decline of the composer's creative power, the very fact that the preparatory work had brought me in frequent contact with the clever, distinguished, and still fiery old master made me enjoy it. I should like to mention also my revival of Auber's *Masaniello.* I had acted upon Alfred Roller's suggestion, and had experimentally assigned the mimically very exacting part of Fenella, the mute girl, to Grete Wiesenthal, a young member of the *corps de ballet.* It turned out that I had not only acquired a touchingly effective Fenella, but had unknowingly opened a way that was to lead to a thorough appreciation of this highly gifted dancer's novel style, and to fame.

More important to me, however, than my own work, was the chance I had of witnessing Mahler's constantly more sublimated activity during his last years in Vienna. After the brilliant performances of former days, such as Charpentier's *Louise,* Hugo Wolf's *Der Corregidor,* and Offenbach's *The Tales of Hoffmann,* his association with Alfred Roller had now started him on the creation of that higher musico-dramatic style which I mentioned before. Much of this work, as I said, was of an experimental nature, and not everything could be expected to be successful. After the splendors of Mozart had been revealed to me by Mahler, my understanding of the master grew ever more profound and I drew knowledge even from an occasional weakness or a daring innovation in the reproduction of his works. I was disturbed, for instance, by the luxurious red of the rosebeds in *Don Giovanni.* Roller had probably meant them to express colorfully the exuberantly vital spirit in the champagne aria. But, for the first time, I realized that Mozart's temperate orchestral coloring was ill suited to so rich a hue and that, generally speaking, the scenic picture of a Mozart opera ought to keep at a respectful distance from the work itself. A certain reserve and modesty seemed indicated by Mozart's dramatic-musical style. While I should never have been able to prove my contention, I was so certain of the correctness of my intuitive perception that I decided to speak to Mahler about it. After some hesitation, he admitted that I was right. I was quick to realize the importance of the basic principle underlying those scenic arrangements — the fixed frame within which stage settings could be changed quickly — though I considered the famous *Don Giovanni* turrets a bit too artificial, and much that happened between them un-Mozartian. While I felt irritated by everything tending toward a drastic treatment or overemphasis in a Mozart work, I was wholly gratified by the seriousness of expression in Mahler's interpretations. The playful manner of operatic and concert performances of Mozart had become unbearable to me. I even preferred the occasional alternatives: an academic dryness. Gradually, I had begun to realize Mozart's strength and greatness behind his moderate forms, expressions, and means, and I sensed with all due reverence and modesty that I had gained access to his soul.

I felt greatly enlightened, too, by some of Mahler's casting experiments. I recall, for instance, his assignment of the bass part of Kaspar in *Der Freischütz* to the baritone Josef Ritter. All of the Opera's basses were good-natured fellows, whom nobody would ever have considered capable of satanic villainy. While the eminently gifted bass Wilhelm Hesch was fully able to portray demonic characters, he was also, unfortunately, the possessor of a pronounced Czech accent, which, in the *Freischütz* dialogues, would have sounded rather comical to the Viennese. Ritter, on the other hand, had a decided talent for the portrayal of fierce and evil characters, and Mahler was inclined to place the dramatic demands of the part above the vocal ones. The experiment was only partly successful. Ritter felt handicapped by the low pitch of the part, his strong personality was unable fully to unfold itself, and his demonic expression, instead of covering up his vocal insufficiency, was prevented from displaying its full dramatic force by the musical demands of the role. In a word, the artist did not show up well even in the dialogues. But even in this unsuccessful experiment the unfailing accuracy of Mahler's vision was revealed. It was this very vision which imparted to his whole activity the character of the exceptional, the festive, the artistic. Humdrum and routine work had no place in his domain. There was all the more danger, though, that the dusty powers of humdrum and routine work affect the Opera's other performances, but I believe I proved equal to the task of banishing these dark spirits from the sphere of my activity.

[172]

Theme and Variations

In 1905, Mahler produced Pfitzner's *Die Rose vom Liebesgarten*. His initial aversion to the book and, to a certain extent, perhaps also to the musical style of the work had finally yielded to the realization that the opera was entitled to a hearing in Vienna. Alma, an enthusiastic admirer and personal friend of Pfitzner, had done her share by placing the opened piano score of the *Rose* on Mahler's piano every morning. Mahler, who did not even notice the persistence of that "accident," had at first confined himself to thumbing the music absentmindedly and with surprise. But this unavoidably led to a growing interest and to serious study. Whenever he got home, he would hear Alma revel in the melodic beauties of the *Rose*. I used to play and sing whole acts both to the more intimate and the wider circle of my friends, and I particularly recall an afternoon at the home of Gustav Schönaich, a clever and high-spirited man of the Falstaff type, a friend of Felix Mottl and a champion of Bayreuth, when I succeeded in thoroughly convincing a rather unfavorably disposed group of musicians, music lovers, and literary lights of the beauties of the *Rose*. Whenever in my life I used the persuasive power of my music in an attempt to arouse in the hearts of my audience enthusiasm for the works I loved, I followed one of the most profound impulses of my nature. I confess that this "apostolic" side of my being, of which I have become increasingly conscious, has given sense and an impetus to my whole artistic activity.

The day of the first performance drew near. Pfitzner had arrived in Vienna for the great event. He stayed at our home, a dear and stimulating guest, spending much of his time as "Uncle Hans," playing with our two-year-old daughter and being generally as cheerful, sociable, and communicative as only he could be when the sun was in a favorable position to his star. But it seemed that the position was getting worse, and Pfitzner's spirits sank. The woman who was to have sung the leading part in the opera fell ill a few days before the *première*, and where were we to hunt up another Minneleide? Friends of Pfitzner's from abroad had arrived in Vienna to attend the performance, Willy Levin from Berlin and Paul Cossmann from Munich among them. Between us tottered Pfitzner, gloomy and inconsolable, considering himself the victim of a hostile fate. Before long, there was a slight improvement in the firmament. We learned that there was a singer in Graz, five hours by rail from Vienna, who had sung the part of Minneleide before. But at the same time we found out that the lady was scheduled to appear at the Graz Opera on the evening of our *première*. Thereupon Mahler decided to send a representative to Graz to induce the director to change his repertory and grant the singer a leave of absence. Would the director be willing to make such a sacrifice? That fateful question caused us a good deal of anxiety and filled Pfitzner with a mixture of hopelessness and tension of which only he was capable. I was worried also by another aspect of the matter: how were we to get Pfitzner over the period of uncertainty, how could we relieve his agony of waiting? As Mahler's delegate could not be expected back in Vienna before noon of the following day, I suggested that we all meet in Levin's room at the Hotel Bristol at nine in the morning and keep Pfitzner company. I would read to them aloud and thus try to make him forget the slow passage of time. My suggestion was accepted in spite of Pfitzner's listless attitude. We sat in the hotel room, gathered about the dejected man, and I began to read Lipiner's *Hippolytos*. Pfitzner's attitude was at first one of inattentiveness and indifference. Soon, however, he began to listen. His tension and interest grew, until he was hanging on my words. The hours slipped by unnoticed. Suddenly, there was a knock at the door, and an official from the Opera came rushing into the room: "Gentlemen, we've just heard from Graz . . ." Pfitzner interrupted him impatiently: "Be quiet, please! Don't disturb us." Then he turned to me and begged me to continue.

I have recorded this occurrence because it is so characteristic of Hans Pfitzner and, in a general way, of the nature of a romantic artist. It shows the thorough concentration upon the impression that happens to enthrall his mind, making him oblivious of everything else. This tense concentration was one of Pfitzner's lifelong characteristics. In it lay the source of his strength and of his suffering. The message, by the way, had been favorable. Minneleide arrived, Mahler conducted a splendid performance of *Die Rose vom Liebesgarten,* and from that day there was a Pfitzner community in Vienna.

A somewhat later event is worth recording here because of the deep impression it made and its importance in connection with theatrical history. Max Reinhardt brought his production of Shakespeare's *A Midsummer Night's Dream* to Vienna. The daring style of the rendition, the naturalistic representation of the forest with its ample opportunity for enchanting airiness in the elves' scenes, the spicily blunt comedy of the craftsmen's scenes, and the spirited romanticism of the whole play made a profound and long-lasting impression and helped spread Reinhardt's fame. Pfitzner's conducting of Mendelssohn's music contributed much to the buoyant mood of the performance. I had not seen Reinhardt since his gay Berlin enterprise of *Sound and Smoke,* which by an exuberantly clever parody of Schiller's *Don Carlos* had taken Berlin by storm. He had in the meantime become the director of the Deutsches Theater and was now surrounded by the young glory of an activity to be recorded indelibly in the annals of theatrical history. Mahler, too, thoroughly enjoyed the performance of *A Midsummer Night's Dream,* and I recall a meeting between him and Reinhardt, of which both men spoke to me later with a great deal of warmth. Reinhardt's success in Vienna was all the more remarkable because the Viennese were jealously guarding the prestige of the Burgtheater. Although the great actors of the "Old" Burgtheater had gone, the famous playhouse could still boast of an excellent ensemble directed by Paul Schlenther. Among the prominent actors of that time were Josef Kainz, Bernhard Baumeister, Lotte Medelsky, and Hedwig Bleibtreu. Fine performances and a worthy repertory served to maintain the institute's legendary reputation.

Unless I am mistaken, the sensational first Vienna appearance of Enrico Caruso occurred in the last year of Mahler's incumbency. I much enjoyed conducting the majority of the performances in which he sang. I well remember how disappointed the audience was by his *"Questa o quella"* in the first act of *Rigoletto,* Caruso having sung it with a tone volume unsuited to the Vienna house; how the people's enthusiasm gradually rose; and how the fourth act would not come to an end because of the thunderous applause and the *da capo* shouts. I loved Caruso's voice, his vocal talent, the sense of beauty expressed in his tone coloring, his *portamento* and his *rubato,* his noble musicianship, and his naturalness. I may say that there was a perfect understanding between us. I also conducted a number of Vienna performances with Mattia Battistini, and learned a great deal from the artist's tone production and breath control.

The Mahler epoch drew to a close. Mahler felt that his hour had struck. Although his adherents stood by him stanchly, his enemies were able to work against him all the more effectively because he refused to heed their attacks and intrigues. The only large newspaper to stand by him was the *Neue Freie Presse.* Its leading musical critic, Dr. Julius Korngold, the impassioned fighter against atonality, supported him with the force of his eloquence and conviction. In addition to Korngold, there was really only Richard Specht on Mahler's side, while the rest of the press opposed him with various degrees of violence.

Once more, as if it were irradiated by the setting sun, the brilliant picture of Mahler's working and striving was revealed. Cyclically arranged, the Opera's repertory offered at brief intervals a series of those model performances which represented the culminating points of his and his co-workers efforts. That was Mahler's parting message to Vienna. He was made happy by the visit of a number of French friends of his, who had expressly come to Vienna to enjoy his performances. Among them was Colonel Picquart, the hero of the Dreyfuss trial, the mathematician Painlevé, and Paul Clemenceau, the Tiger's brother. Thirty years later, I was to renew my acquaintance with Painlevé, when he presided at a Paris banquet in my honor. Paul Clemenceau, too, was present. Picquart had died in the meantime. He had most strongly impressed me on the occasion of that visit in Vienna, probably because of his heroic attitude in the *affaire*.

Mahler's first-born, a handsome grave-faced girl of four, died in 1907. Soon thereafter, a medical examination revealed that Mahler was suffering from a severe defect of the heart. So, in addition to sorrowing over his child's death, he had to worry about how to reconcile his physician's advice to take care of himself with his professional duties and his habits of life and work. The thought of leaving Vienna gained in convincing force. He had an offer from Heinrich Conried to join the Metropolitan Opera in New York. To accept meant that he would have to work less while earning considerably more. Thus he would be able within a few years to make the provisions for his family necessitated by his heart disease.

One morning, when I was rehearsing, Hassinger, Mahler's factotum, asked me to call for Mahler at his office when I was through. Our morning work done, we would frequently go for a walk. Making a detour through the beautiful Stadtpark, I usually saw him to his home in the Auenbruggerstrasse. We followed our usual route that day. But as we walked along he told me that the die was cast and that he would leave. When I spoke of the Opera's terrible loss and of the void the renunciation of his work would leave within him, he answered me with the words: "In the ten years at the Opera I have completed my circle." I was deeply moved and walked silently at his side as far as his house. In the evening, I wrote to him concerning the significance of his decision and the historical importance of his work. I expressed to him my gratitude. He wrote me in reply: "We don't either of us have to waste any words about what we mean to each other. I feel that nobody I know has understood me as you have, and I believe that I, too, have penetrated the depths of your soul . . ."

There followed his beautiful farewell letter to the members of the Opera, in the course of which he said: ". . . instead of the whole, the consummated, of which I dreamed, I leave patchwork, the incomplete, as man is fated to do. . . . It is not for me to pass judgment on what my work has come to mean to those to whom it was dedicated. But at a moment like this I may say of myself: I meant well and aimed at high goals. Not always could my efforts be crowned with success. Nobody is so much at the mercy of the resistance of matter, of the 'malignity of the object,' as the performing artist. But I have always given my all, have subordinated my person to the cause, my inclinations to my duty. I did not spare myself and was therefore justified in demanding that others, too, exert their strength to the utmost.

"In the crush of the struggle, in the heat of the moment, wounds were sustained, errors committed, by you as well as by me. But when a work had turned out right, a problem had been solved, we forgot all our care and trouble and felt richly rewarded — even without any outward sign of success. We have all progressed on our way — and with us the institute which was the object of our endeavors."

There was a final performance of *Fidelio* under Mahler's guidance. His Second Symphony was played at a farewell concert in Musikverein Hall, and soon thereafter I and a number of friends were at the Western Railway Station, bidding Mahler and Alma *bon voyage* to America. An important chapter in Europe's cultural history had come to an end. A brilliance that had shone forth from Vienna had faded, had vanished, and the lamp of life that had shed it was flickering alarmingly.

VI

THE CHOICE of Felix Weingartner as Mahler's successor was by no means surprising. He was a conductor of international reputation, an exceedingly well read and well-bred man, and the member of an old Austrian family. He was actually one of the few persons to be considered for the position, especially as the principle of conductor-director was to be maintained.

I had heard Weingartner only on the concert platform and had come to appreciate his fiery temperament, his naturalness and simplicity, and his thorough command of the orchestra. His advent was a piece of good luck as far as the Philharmonic Orchestra was concerned. A famous concert conductor was once more at its head, and because he was at the same time the director of the Opera, a smooth co-ordination of work schedules could be expected. Respectful though I was of Weingartner's musicianship and the services he had rendered to symphonic music, I could not consider him a dramatic nature and foresaw that he would be found wanting as an operatic director and conductor.

His performances were distinguished by their neatness and

smoothness, they had the élan and brilliance symptomatic of his concert work, but the dramatic element in the playing of music, so essential in operatic reproductions, was not sufficiently in evidence. In matters pertaining to stage directing he relied entirely on Wilhelm von Wymetal, whom he had engaged and who was actually an exceptionally capable regisseur. Wymetal had a vivid theatrical imagination and was a gifted teacher of histrionics, but even so, he needed the musician's guiding and helping suggestions. In that respect, there was a lack of co-operation between Weingartner and him, and in their performances music and scenic representation pursued separate ways. I am further reminded of a rehearsal, in the course of which the absence of dramatic feeling in Weingartner's nature became strikingly apparent. He had undertaken to put on *Fidelio* and, as Mahler had done frequently, wished to take charge of the business rehearsals. It may be that Wymetal had not yet arrived or that other reasons induced Weingartner to put himself in charge. The orchestral prelude to the canon, those deeply stirring soft harmonies in the violas and celli, with the serious *pizzicato* of the basses, had been expressed by Mahler with noble restraint and great dramatic impressiveness. After Rocco's words: "Hush, do you think I cannot look into your heart?" the four persons on the stage were expected to express in a quiet attitude their anxious and expectant mood. Weingartner, surprised at the lack of outward movement on the stage, which he considered undramatic, wished to introduce some action. He therefore requested Fritz Schrödter, the Jacquino, to pick up during the prelude the laundry basket containing the linen Marcelline had ironed and to carry it off stage. Schrödter, though resisting inwardly, did as he had been told, but his instinctive awe of those sacred harmonies made him leave the scene on tiptoes.

Weingartner's position in Vienna developed in a direction conformable to his nature. Particular stress was laid upon his concert activity, while at the Opera he was accorded the respect due an artist of his standing, without being able to gain the enthusiastic acclaim of those who could be roused only by a dramatically gifted man.

His attitude toward me was friendly from the start. Throughout the three years of his incumbency, and also later, our relations were altogether pleasant. We did not, however, get close to each other personally, due probably to the fundamental difference of our natures.

I was thirty-one years old then, had been active at the Vienna Opera for more than six years, and the mere matter of my years had long since ceased to make necessary the masking of my face by a beard. So I had the hirsute adornment removed after the final performance of a season, with the effect that my three-year-old daughter, frightened to tears by my beardlessness on the following morning, was moved to a long and awed contemplation of my face during our railway journey and to the question: "Has the father with the beard stayed in Vienna?" The affectionate child had over-estimated her father even then. I had not left behind me in Vienna the young man who would so dearly have loved to act with more authority than was given him. He was sitting there within me, beard or no beard, and though I had acquired a measure of artistic stature and had made for myself an attractive position, I still con-sidered myself quite young in my surroundings and in the face of the world at large. There were good reasons for that, and silly ones. Among the former was my respect of people or, to express it politically, my innate democratic inclination, which made me see in every fellowman a being enjoying equal rights. This rendered difficult the acquisition of a tone of authority, so essentially impor-tant in my vocation. I made believe as well as I could, but it sounded false from my lips, and it took a long time until the actual superi-ority gained by experience led to a natural expression and to the necessary weightiness. What was more, I felt so uncertain and at a disadvantage in the face of the resoluteness of my fellowmen be-cause my process of gaining maturity was very slow. In a nature resting on a broad foundation there is more that has to be devel-oped, and the process of maturing lasts longer than in one pointing only in one direction. But I considered silly the shyness I had to overcome before every rehearsal, almost before every meeting with persons unknown to me, even at my being in the presence of others. I clearly recall how, when I had to wait several hours in Brussels on my first journey to England, I felt so great a dread of the im-pending orchestra rehearsal at Queen's Hall that I was tempted to telegraph a cancellation of the London concert. I was comforted by Toscanini's assurance, when many years later I casually told him of my shyness and of my Brussels attack, that he himself had had the same inclination and had been in a similar condition before his first orchestra rehearsal at the Metropolitan Opera in New York. Fortunately, my dread disappeared as soon as the rehearsal had begun, because, as I said before, I was dominated by an in-ward compulsion. Besides, I never suffered from such inhibitions before or during a performance.

Although I had long ceased to be considered a disciple of Mah-ler in Vienna, and though a body of personal adherents had gradu-ally come into being, I was unable to feel contented either with my activity or my position at the Opera. The artistic prerogatives of the director, who at the same time was my colleague, were bound to limit the field of endeavor to which I thought I could lay claim because of the state of maturity I had attained. I was prompted not by mere ambition, but by a natural craving for larger responsibilities and tasks, for a wider field of activity than the one connected with my position, because I had become more urgently aware of my calling and my abilities. But I had learned to be patient. I thought of my comparative youth and of my activity at the Opera which, to all outward appearances, must have seemed abundant, and I realized that I had to carry on and wait until one of the few director-conductor positions in the realm of German opera would become vacant.

In the meantime, a long-desired field had been made available to me sooner than I had dared hope. It was in 1908, I believe, that my activities started to arouse the sympathetic interest on the part of foreign musical institutes and friends of music. First came the Royal Philharmonic Society in London, which invited me to conduct one of their concerts. This marked the beginning of my connection with English musical life. Soon thereafter, Thomas Beecham requested me to conduct Wagner's *Tristan* and Ethel Smyth's *The Wreckers* in the course of the operatic season managed by him at Covent Garden in 1909. I do not recall what impression my appearance with the Royal Philharmonic Society or at Covent Garden made, but it must have been favorable, for invitations from London were repeated and increased in number. What I do recall, though, is the impression London made on me. It was overpowering, indeed.

I would not say that I went to London well prepared. I was not any more familiar with English ways than a zelaous reader of English novels could hope to be. My ideas of the history of the British Isles were general and vague, with some atmospheric admixture gathered from Shakespeare's historic dramas and Scott's novels. Yet, during my visit, which was wholly devoted to current affairs, I did not see London merely with the eye of the curious tourist. My sentiments were divided between a tense interest in contemporary events and the peculiarities of this center of world happenings and a stirring awareness of being in the country of Sterne, Dickens, Thackeray, and other "friends." It was singular that this London, with its mighty world-power presence, did not at all affect me in a present-day sense. My "tourist" observations, some of which are mentioned below, afforded me an emotional approach to the grandiose conservatism of the English character. Later and more thorough observations confirmed my first impressions. I suppose that this conservatism is one of the great nation's sources of strength, and I am convinced that, in some form or other, it will continue to live also in the renewed and rejuvenated England of today.

London's street life was dominated by the hansoms, those picturesque one-horse cabs whose drivers sit enthroned way up in the rear of their vehicles and, through a flap in the top of their cab, convey bits of friendly cockney information to their passengers. I felt myself magically transported into the past, an impression strengthened by the wigs I saw at public ceremonials and the silently immovable horse guards in Whitehall Court. That a pitcher of hot water was automatically placed at my door in the afternoon before dinner seemed as characteristic to me as the heating machine in the old Langham Hotel opposite Queen's Hall. My room, which was as cold as ice, was guaranteed a half hour's warmth by the insertion of a shilling. The open fire, at which one could toast one's back while one's front was freezing, the strict separation of the sexes immediately after dinner, the meals at the London restaurants with their excellent roasts of mutton or beef and their squarely cut and wholly inanimate vegetable side-dishes — all these and a large number of similar peculiarities were a bit troublesome to the foreigner but, in an imposing way, they were rather attractive too. From the very first, I had a feeling of being safely at rest in what had long proved true. Together with the perfect civility and friendliness in public life, this gave me a sense of well-being and security such as I have not experienced in any other large city. I shall have more to say about Queen's Hall and Covent Garden later. But let me mention here that the performance of my friend Ethel Smyth's opera *The Wreckers* was a great success and that, in the course of the same season, Strauss's *Elektra,* conducted by Beecham, made a profound impression.

Soon thereafter, I accepted an invitation from the Accademia di Santa Cecilia in Rome to conduct a number of concerts with the orchestra of that society in the rotunda of the Augusteo. I have a vivid recollection of that first visit to Rome and of the concerts that marked the beginning of a happy association with the Accademia, extending over a number of years. I seem to recall that I conducted the first performance of Strauss's *Don Quixote,* promoted by that society, and that I was highly gratified by the surprisingly warm reception accorded by the Roman audience to that brilliant, but by no means easily accessible, work. Two occurrences from that time have remained in my memory. They seemed to me characteristic of the frequenters of the Augusteo's gallery and, generally speaking, of a certain type represented in the Italian musical audiences. I had put on my program Mussorgsky's *Night on Bald Mountain,* a work that in addition to brilliant passages contains a distressing chain of sequences. When the same phrase occurred for the fourth time, a man who had obviously followed the development of the composition carefully shouted *"Basta, basta!"* and I must say I rather understood his reaction. At an all-Wagner program, the audience vociferously demanded a repetition of Siegfried's Rhine Journey. But the hornist felt tired and signaled to me his request to spare him the repetition. I, in turn, tried to make the audience understand pantomimically that there could be no *bis*. When, after several minutes of this noisy demonstration, things finally quieted down, I started with the next number, only to be interrupted by a renewed outburst. The hornist finally decided to save the situation and informed me by a sign that I might repeat. Quiet reigned again, and when I started the Rhine Journey, a man in the gallery rewarded me for my *docilità* by a rather melodious shout of *"Bravo, Bruno!"*

But my great experience of the days of my first concerts at the Accademia was naturally Rome herself. There I succumbed utterly to the power of the past. The connection of the Eternal City with the present seemed to me as inorganic and discordant as the intrusion of the Victor Emmanuel Monument, viewed from the fountain in front of the French Academy, into the city's classic silhouette. I had come by no means unprepared. But far more vivid in my mind than anything I had read or learned about Rome and Roman history, far more vivid than the descriptions of Mommsen, Gregorovius, Burckhardt, and others, were the tales Lipiner had told me and the memory of Goethe's profound emotion. As a matter of fact, my youthful longing for Italy, nourished by reading and by reproductions of Italian art, should have sufficed to open wide my receptivity. Mine was surely more than the usual inclination of the North European toward the Italian landscape and Italian culture. I remember that even during my boyhood visits to the museum I had felt mysteriously attracted by Italian landscapes, that Mignon's *" Kennst du das Land"* had filled me with a sympathetic melancholy and yearning, and that, later, the blue of the Italian sky and sea, the shapes of the pines and cypresses, the narrow streets of the towns, even the washing hung from balconies or strung high above the street and the atmosphere of the smallest osterias never failed to cast a spell upon me. It has frequently occurred to me that the sense of fascination that really never left me while in Italy and the charm the Italian language has for my ear may be indicative of a Mediterranean strain in my nature, expressed also in my relation to Italian music.

In those days, the trains in Italy were always late; the streets

and squares were alive with beggars; the children were as picturesque as they were dirty; and one could enter no church and enjoy
none of the magnificent sights without being bothered by importu-
nate street vendors. It was no easy matter to guard against such
interruptions of one's enjoyment of beauty, but my Italian friends
taught me a number of appropriate methods. The most effective of
them seemed to be a slow wig-wagging of the up-stretched forefinger of the closed and quietly held right hand.

Rehearsals at the Augusteo took place from twelve-thirty to
three-thirty in the afternoon and from eight-thirty to eleven-thirty
at night. This served my purpose well. It left me the whole morning and, after I had fortified myself at the Café Aragno, the whole
afternoon — for seeing. For it was in Rome that I really began to
learn how to see. All of my mornings were devoted to the contemplations of works of art at the Museo delle Terme or the Vati-
can, while I spent the afternoons in refreshing myself with antique
Rome or in enjoying the Roman landscape on the Pincio or from
the Passegiata Margarita. Unforgotten are the evenings at the
Forum, moonlit nights in the Colosseum, the carriage drives in the
Campagna. And when there was no evening rehearsal and I had
eaten well at the Osteria Fedelinaro and partaken freely of the
wonderful Tuscan wine, I used to stand for a long time at the
most beautiful fountain in the world, the Fontana di Trevi, and
listen to the music of the water. Never once did I omit to toss in
a copper coin so that, according to an old superstition, my return
might be assured. It held good in my case, for I did return. Again
and again I walked through the old Via dei Pontefici to the entrance of the Augusteo, and even after it had been torn down,
I kept returning as the guest of the Accademia, to conduct at the
Teatro Adriano.

London in the west and Rome in the south were not the only
foreign cities to call me. I was summoned to the east, too, and became acquainted in Moscow with a world that was strange, peculiar, and excitingly interesting. There were concerts at the Imperial
Russian Musical Society. I was carried away by the orchestra's
genuine musicianship, by its temperament and technical brilliance,
and by the audiences' passionate love of music. I appeared also
as guest conductor at the Imperial Opera. I do not know whether
it was on that occasion or on one of my following visits that I conducted Tchaikovsky's *Pique-Dame* and, at the Simin Opera, Mozart's *Don Giovanni*. I well remember the latter performance for
two reasons. Sergey Taneyev, a legendary figure in Moscow's musical life of those days, did me the honor of showing me his special
interest by daily visiting my rehearsals. Besides, the *Don Giovanni*

performance was followed by a night such as I never knew existed except in Russian novels. Taneyev, a friend of Tolstoy's and Tchaikovsky's, was held in great esteem in Russia. I was made happy by the fact that this truly important musician seemed to be pleased with my way of producing Mozart. My wife and I gladly accepted his invitation to tea at his home. We found that he lived in a small house standing in the center of the paved courtyard of a sprawling old tenement house. There he lived, taken care of by an ancient woman who had once been his nurse and who treated the gray-haired and somewhat feeble old man with rough severity. That he was actually afraid of her was quite in keeping with his naïvely childlike nature, so rarely found in a man of so comprehensive a learning and so clear a philosophical mind. From a samovar on the table tea was poured for us again and again. There were Russian pastries of all kinds, baked apparently by the hard, but skilled hand of the female tyrant. Taneyev only needed to switch around his chair in order to reach a score he wanted to show me, which was lying on his music-covered desk at the window. I was under the impression that the only physical exercise he ever indulged in consisted in turning around between the dining-table and the desk. He spoke a little German, and I enjoyed his tales of Tchaikovsky, his opinions on music, and, generally, the atmosphere of kindness, simplicity, and deep earnestness surrounding him. He did not like to speak of Tolstoy. It seemed that the recollection of the conflict in the poet's house before his death made him suffer. He grew silent also when I praised Brahms and abandoned a subject obviously painful to him with the words: "Certainly, was verrry respectful composer."

Following Director Simin's invitation we went to the Restaurant Slava after the *Don Giovanni* performance. The carousing which followed was possible only in pre-war Russia. A fantastic amount and variety of *hors d'oeuvres,* called *sakuski,* and a bewildering array of schnapps were served by men in high boots and white blouses and made one abandon all hope of ever surviving that first course. But the charms of the Russian cuisine seemed to produce miracles of digestive faculties. This was made possible, too, by the length of such feasts. They usually lasted into the early hours of the morning and were followed by other adventures. It was about three in the morning when Simin assured me that he had been made very happy and grateful by the performance, and wasn't there any wish he might grant me and thereby prove the sincerity of his sentiments? It occurred to me how often in Russian literature I had found mention of the vehicle of past days, the troika, and how I had wished to see one of those sleighs drawn by three horses driven abreast. I asked our host if such things still existed. Half an hour later, three troikas were at the door. Simin, my wife, and myself got into the first one, and the other guests crowded into the two vehicles following ours. A moment later, the horses, bells tinkling, rushed over the hard-frozen snow, through the icy air and the deeply snow-covered forest. After an hour's drive, we got to Strelna, a place frequently used to give the finishing touch to a gaily spent night in Moscow. A chorus of Russian gypsies, summoned by Simin, soon appeared in our private room. They delighted us with their magnificent voices and their singing of beautiful Russian folksongs. The morning was dawning when we drove back through the forest. When our sleighs rushed through the streets of the city, shouts of glad surprise from the pedestrians greeted the rare sight of the historical vehicles.

I was in Moscow several times before the outbreak of the First World War, always as the guest of the Imperial Russian Musical Society. On one of my visits I made the acquaintance of the young conductor Serge Koussevitzky, who was at the head of an excellent orchestra of his own. I heard him play Brahms's Third Symphony. It was an excellent performance. My wife and I had dinner at his sumptuous home. I recall with pleasure our cordial, cozy, and stimulating companionship and can still see before my eyes the fine rooms of the palace-like building and its yellow façade. I even remember our host's exceptionally intelligent dog, whose affectionate disposition and cleverness were a delight to a dog-lover's heart.

Guest tours like these, during the years from 1908 to 1912, meant a welcome interruption of my activity at the Vienna Opera. I was especially pleased with my aforementioned invitation to Strasbourg, which at that time still belonged to Germany and whose Opera was conducted by Pfitzner. The town, the Minster, and the attractive surroundings were of great interest to me and served again and again to turn my thoughts back to Goethe and his *Dichtung und Wahrheit*. It was splendid to be in Pfitzner's company and to become acquainted with the select circle that had formed around him. It gave me joy, too, to perform my symphony with a fairly competent orchestra. A young musician, who was one of Pfitzner's assistant conductors, impressed me as being a gifted and singular personality. He was Wilhelm Furtwängler, then twenty-three years old.

As for Vienna itself in 1911 a field of activity had finally become available to me that offered opportunities for highly inspiring work and for a better acquaintance with myself. There were at the time in Vienna two large choral associations dedicated to the cultivation of secular and sacred oratorios. They were the Vienna

Singverein, a branch of the famous Society of Friends of Music, and the Vienna Singakademie. Both of them had been led by Johannes Brahms for several years. The Singakademie now offered me the leadership of its concerts. For two years, until I went to Munich, I conducted the performances of that old and noble institute. I started my new activity by a production of Handel's *Messiah*. This was followed by Beethoven's *Missa Solemnis,* which had been my *sanctissimum* from the days of my boyhood and whose performance now became an overwhelming experience.

Occasionally, I conducted Philharmonic Concerts, the regular leadership of which was entrusted to Weingartner. The Konzertverein Orchestra, too, invited me on a number of occasions to be guest conductor. As Mahler's opponents remained quiet after his departure and his adherents were yearning for him, I was able to begin including his works in my programs without encountering much resistance. The symphonies that in his presence had been vilified and mocked were now demanded and extolled, and it was not long before the announcement of a Mahler symphony sufficed to sell out the hall.

Adolf Busch was the first concertmaster of the Konzertverein Orchestra. He had been engaged for the position when he was a young man of twenty-two. I shall never forget the glorious beauty of his violin solo in the *Benedictus* of Beethoven's *Missa Solemnis.* I may say that, then and there, the deeply concentrated musician had fiddled his way into my heart. His congeniality and lofty musicianship brought joy to my soul in my rehearsals and performances with the Konzertverein. I deeply regretted that because of numerous invitations to give concerts abroad he was seen but rarely at the first desk. A few years later, he left the position to devote himself entirely to solo work and to his quartet. The future brought about many a meeting between us. On a number of occasions, he played the Beethoven or the Brahms Concerto or one of the Mozart Concertos with an orchestra conducted by me. The purity of his style, the weightiness of his musicianship, the nobility of his expression, and especially the profundity of his feeling stamped him in my mind as Joachim's worthy successor.

I had occasional letters from Mahler. They revealed a spiritual condition most aptly described by Rückert's beautiful words: "lost to the world." I saw him and Alma whenever they returned from America and spent some time in Vienna. I also met him in Prague on the occasion of the first performance of his Seventh Symphony. In the meantime, however, his soul had experienced a new upsurge, inspired by Hrabanus Maurus's hymn *Veni Creator Spiritus.* Thus he had written the first movement of his Eighth and completed the

symphony by a musical interpretation of the final scene of *Faust*.
I hoped that this tremendous excess of vitality had relieved him of
the farewell mood that seemed to have taken possession of him.
He told me of a puzzling inspirational experience vouchsafed to
him while the first movement was coming into being. When he
had composed the first verses of the hymn in a burst of enthusiasm,
he noticed that he did not have the rest of the verses. He sent a
telegram to Vienna, but through some unfortunate circumstance
did not receive a reply for a long time. Impatient and unable to
restrain the flow of the musical inspiration caused by the first part,
he continued to compose and had almost finished the symphonic
form of the entire movement when the complete Latin text finally
arrived. He was ready to start all over again, but found that it
was not necessary. The words easily and faithfully conformed to
the music, which a miraculous sense of visualization had enabled
him to write.

Emil Gutmann, the concert impresario, had the courage to back
the gigantic enterprise, which Mahler with a shudder called a
"Barnum and Bailey show." About one thousand participants had
to be gathered for the first performance at the Munich Exhibition
Hall. One of the choruses, the Vienna Singverein, was trained in
Vienna, while another one and the children's chorus were coached
in Munich. I had undertaken to select the soloists and to study their
parts with them. I believe that the evening in September 1910
marked a culminating point in Mahler's life and that none of the
participants or listeners will ever forget the occasion. *"Accende
lumen sensibus, infunde amorem cordibus"* ["Inflame the senses
with light, instill love into the hearts."] That he was permitted to
call out to the world with the voices of a mighty host of singers this
leitmotif of his greatly agitated soul, that he was able to pronounce
the message of life and faith while the seeds of death were already
in his heart was a thrill beyond anything he had ever experienced.
When the performance was over and the enthusiastic applause of
the audience filled the hall, Mahler hurried up the steps of the
platform to the children's chorus. He passed down their lines and
pressed ecstatically every one of the little hands extended to him.
It was a symbolical greeting to youth.

At our next meeting in Vienna he handed me the orchestral
score of his *Das Lied von der Erde* so that I might study it. It was
the first time that he did not play a new work to me. He was probably afraid of the excitement it might cause him. I studied the
work and lived through days of a most violent mental upheaval.
I was profoundly moved by that uniquely passionate, bitter, resigned, and blessing sound of farewell and departure, that last

confession of one upon whom rested the finger of death. The late and affectionate friendship between the Austrian musician and the Chinese poet was productive of another musical inspiration, his Ninth Symphony, filled with a sainted feeling of departure and enveloped in the shadow of death. It was not until after Mahler's death that I saw the orchestral score of the work. At Alma's request I had it published together with *Das Lied von der Erde*. He was not permitted by fate to hear either of the two works.

In February 1911 Mahler fell ill in America with an inflammation of the heart. Upon his return, he had to be taken to a Paris sanatorium. The bad news reached me in Vienna while I was preparing Débussy's *Pelléas et Mélisande* for production. I took a leave of absence and went to Paris with Mahler's sister, Justine Rosé. I found Mahler in a hopeless condition in a sanatorium in Neuilly. I spoke to him of his works, but he replied with bitterness, and I thought it best just to entertain him, which I partly succeeded in doing. When it appeared that, in spite of all disappointments, he was yearning for Vienna, Alma took him there. On the evening of May 18, I was informed that the end was at hand. I hurried to the Loew Sanatorium. Mahler died soon after my arrival. It was a violently stormy night when Moll, Rosé, and I followed his coffin to the chapel of the Grinzing cemetery. When he was lowered into the ground on the following morning, an immense crowd stood in reverential silence. I was reminded of Jean Paul's lofty words at the death of Schoppe in *Titan*, because they so well suited Mahler's death:

> Thou soughtest behind, beneath, and beyond life something higher than life; not thy self, thy I — no mortal, not an immortal, but the All-First, God! . . . Now thou art reposing in real being. Death has swept away from the dark heart the whole sultry cloud of life, and the eternal light stands uncovered which thou didst so long seek; and thou, its beam, dwellest again in the fire.

VII

WEINGARTNER left the Opera in 1911, and Hans Gregor, who had been in charge of the Berlin Komische Oper, was appointed his successor. Weingartner did not leave Vienna, however, and continued to conduct the concerts of the Philharmonic Orchestra. Before going out of office, Weingartner had renewed my contract for several years. I heeded a suggestion from authoritative quarters and acquired Austrian citizenship, after having been active as the Opera's conductor over a period of ten years. The engagement of Gregor meant a change of system, for instead of a conductor — as Jahn, Mahler, and Weingartner had been — a so-called theatrical expert was taking charge of the house on the Opernring. Gregor had a good deal of stage experience and practice in the administration of a theater. Because he had also acquired in Berlin the reputation of being a modern operatic stage director, Montenuovo thought he was justified in taking a chance with a new kind of management at the Opera. Although Weingartner's leaving meant an enlargement of my and my colleague Schalk's activity, this apparent improvement was more than counterbalanced by the fact that a new style and spirit were introduced into the Opera. Gregor was certainly not lacking in a knowledge of the theater and in talent, but neither his personality nor his views of art were compatible with the singular atmosphere of the house. Even his accent — he was a native of Dresden — sounded strange in the quiet distinction of the directorial rooms. What was infinitely more important, however, was the fact that his background and nature made him view operatic reproductions from a position so diametrically opposite to Schalk's and mine that even with the best of intentions artistic solidarity was out of the question. The new director impressed me as being a kindly disposed man. In our conferences, he yielded with a good grace and with real modesty to my opinion and decision in musical matters. All the more unshakably was he convinced of his worth as a regisseur. There are still in my mind a number of his utterances whose ludicrousness proved that his strangeness to art was bound decisively to lower the artistic level of the Court Opera in spite of his vigorous theatrical instinct. When, for instance, we were planning a new scenic production of *Das Rheingold,* he came up with the question if a progressively minded stage direction ought not to put on stage more than three Rhinemaidens. When I objected that Wagner had provided for only three voices, he replied: "Well, why shouldn't there be three to sing, and another four to swim?" It was no easy matter to convince him that his arrangement would make the stage look like an aquarium. On another occasion, he found fault with me because of some scenic action in a Wagner performance. I explained to him that it was in accordance with Wagner's instructions, but he said: "Wagner did not know much about the theater. If he had submitted his *Flying Dutchman* to me, I should have told him: 'What, two ships on the stage? Go home and change that, and then you may come back again.' " I tried to make clear to him that I was at all times ready to bow reverently before the creative artist, but he protested: "Let me be frank. You have entirely too much respect for the work of art. As for me, I have the composers turn in their scores at the porter's desk." In spite of all that, Gregor was a genuinely gifted stage director in a certain genre. *Pelléas et Mélisande,* for instance, the only opera that brought us into close contact with each other, was put on by him with a distinct sense of "atmosphere."

One of the many differences of opinion between Gregor and myself gave me great and lasting pleasure. There were to be auditions on the stage. That was at the time when my resignation had already been accepted and I was busily on the lookout for gifted young artists for Munich. A pupil of the well-known singing teacher Amalie Schlemmer-Ambros appeared on the stage. She looked quite young and small and delicate. When she had sung a coloratura aria and, unless I am mistaken, Mimi's tale from *La Bohème* I knew that I had been listening to a future star. At the same time I realized that "this flower was not blooming for me," and that within the hour she would be leaving Gregor's office with a contract for the Vienna Opera. My premature sorrow was turned into joy when, after the young woman had finished singing, Gregor turned to me and expressed his judgment in the radical words: "Not a chance!" I hurried backstage and had quite a long conversation with the shy girl. A few days later, Maria Ivogün, who was to be one of the most brilliant singers on the operatic stage, was a member of the Munich Opera. She was one of the artists to whom that epoch was indebted for its splendor.

But I must not anticipate. Let me go back to the days when, under the prevailing circumstances, I longed to be gone from the Opera, to have weighty responsibilities of my own and the authority they would entail, and to be at the head of an institute of art as its independent leader whose ideas would be decisive. Felix Mottl died in July 1911. He had been General Musical Director of Bavaria and the artistic head of the Munich Court Opera. Although I had met him but casually, the manner of his death affected me deeply. He had been conducting *Tristan* and had collapsed while Isolde was pronouncing the words: "Death-doomed head, death-doomed heart." He died a few days later. Mottl had been one of the important Bayreuth figures. His international fame had been still further enhanced by the splendid services he had rendered the annual Mozart and Wagner Festival Plays in Munich. How could I, a man twenty years his junior, hope to be taken into consideration as his successor in so important a position in Europe's artistic life? But the miracle happened. I received a confidential inquiry from Munich, asking whether I was at liberty and willing to accept the position. I had to reply that, while I was willing, I was not at liberty, but that I would do my utmost to bring about an amicable termination of my Vienna contract. Thereupon, at a *Götterdämmerung* conducted by me, Anton Fuchs, Munich's chief stage director, bobbed up in a box of the Vienna Court Opera. The General Musical Director of Bavaria, and Mottl's successor, must above all be a Wagner conductor. The confidential representative of the Munich Court Theaters' General Management had been delegated to inform himself on that point and to report to his superiors. About a week later, after a telegram had announced his coming, Zollner, the administrative director of the Munich Court Theaters, called on me in Vienna as the delegate of General Manager Baron Speidel. We reached an agreement according to which the contract we entered into would become operative as soon as I had succeeded in obtaining my release from Vienna.

And now there started a seemingly endless chain of endeavors on my part and refusals on the other, for neither Gregor nor Montenuovo was willing to accept my resignation. The matter dragged along interminably, and I began to fear that Munich would not be able to manage so long without a musical leader and that I would thus lose an opportunity that came but once in a lifetime. But the Munich General Management proved steadfast and waited for me more than a year. On January 1, 1913, I entered upon my position as "Royal Bavarian General Musical Director," which I was to occupy for ten years.

My agreement with Zollner also provided for my appearance in Munich as a guest director. We chose Julius Bittner's *Der Bergsee* for the occasion. It was a new opera and would enable me to present myself to Munich with a production I had thoroughly prepared. I do not recall whether I made this presentation coincide with the world *première* of Mahler's *Das Lied von der Erde.* The two events could not have been far apart, for the briefness of my leave of absence from Vienna would seem to have made the joining of the two performances advisable.

All I remember in connection with the *Bergsee* event is that everybody at the Munich Court Theater, artists as well as administrative authorities, met me in a spirit of confidence, and that the success fulfilled our expectations. I have a clear recollection, however, and for a number of reasons, of the first performance of *Das Lied von der Erde,* in which Madame Charles Cahier and William Miller, both American singers, sang the solo parts. For one thing, I was deeply conscious of my responsibility in first presenting to the world the dearly beloved posthumous work of Mahler. For another, I felt as if I were from now on taking the master's place.

And finally, the first stirring sounds made me more painfully aware than ever of what the departed man had meant to me.

There is another reason why I remember those first weeks of my musical activity in Munich. I gained a new friend. As in Vienna, my life was once more enriched by a friendship that only death could terminate. I had made Ossip Gabrilowitsch's acquaintance in 1906, on the ococasion of the first performance of Mahler's Sixth Symphony, and met him again in Prague and Munich when the Seventh and Eighth, respectively, were performed. I had been touched by his enthusiasm for the works and his personal admiration of Mahler, but I don't think we came in close touch with each other on those occasions. Now, in Munich, I received a letter from him, alive with his unique spirit of kindness and unselfishness, and from that moment our ways never lay in different directions. Ossip was at the time in a process of transformation. The wonderful pianist and warmhearted musician was no longer content to play the piano, though that activity had brought the comparatively young man considerable fame. Drawn toward symphonic music and the orchestra, he had made his home in Munich, intending to engage the Kaim Orchestra for rehearsals and concerts by means of which he meant to test his conducting ability and gain experience in a conductor's tasks. Emil Gutmann, the impresario, was in charge of the preparations for *Das Lied von der Erde,* but he unfortunately proved less efficient than he had been in connection with Mahler's Eighth. It appeared that he had not assured himself of the services of the orchestra for a sufficient number of rehearsals. Gutmann's perplexity and my own were changed into surprise and emotion by a letter from Ossip Gabrilowitsch. "I have learned," he wrote, "that you are having difficulties with the rehearsals of *Das Lied von der Erde.* A glance at the orchestra's work schedule shows me that the time available to you must be insufficient. Luckily, I am entitled to a number of orchestra rehearsals for my forthcoming concert. Please help yourself to as many of them as you need for *Das Lied von der Erde.* I shall know how to manage." I paid Ossip a visit to express my gratitude. He lived in a handsome villa in Aiblingerstrasse, near Nymphenburg Park. Little Nina was swinging ecstatically in the garden. I shook hands with Ossip and his wife Clara, the daughter of Mark Twain. When we parted, we were friends.

Gabrilowitsch was deeply concerned with his fellowmen. His sympathetic attitude made him at all times ready to act, to fight. He might have been willing to put up with an injustice inflicted upon himself, but he was up in arms if somebody else was the victim. He happened to be in America at the time when H. E. Krehbiel, the *Tribune's* highly respected and influential musical critic attacked Mahler in a manner that he considered malicious, disrespectful, and unjust. The rising young pianist, whose American career meant infinitely much to him, did not hesitate a moment to launch a militant pro-Mahler pamphlet in which he wrathfully took Krehbiel to task. Ossip Gabrilowitsch's noble figure will appear again in these pages. I merely wished to mention here his self-sacrificing help in connection with my performance of *Das Lied von der Erde,* and to recall the joyful anticipation with which I looked forward to our further intercourse.

Back in Vienna, I plunged into the preparatory work for my performance of Mahler's Eighth with the Vienna Singakademie, joined by another large chorus, a number of male choruses, and the Peterlini boys' chorus. The choral rehearsals, in which almost nine hundred singers participated, took place in Weigl's mammoth Katharine Hall in Meidling. The masses had turned into waves of sound. Standing on a rickety table, I spent blissful hours of enthusiastic work. I feel sure that the memory of those hours is as lasting in the hearts of those who are still alive as it is in mine.

There was a Music Festival in Vienna in the spring of 1912. I availed myself of that opportunity to produce for the first time Mahler's Ninth. At another concert of the same Music Festival I made Vienna acquainted with *Das Lied von der Erde,* for which — or was that at the following performance of the work? — I had chosen a baritone in place of an alto. Mahler himself had been of two minds about this. His instructions permitted the alternative, and so I thought I owed him the experiment. Friedrich Weidemann of the Court Opera, a serious man of high artistic standards, had always been loyally devoted to Mahler. I studied the part with him, and he sang it in his usual heartfelt manner, but I have never repeated the experiment because I had become convinced that an alto was better able to fulfill the vocal demands made by the part, and that in the six songs the contrast between the sound of an alto and a tenor voice was more welcome to the ear than that between two male voices.

The summer of 1912 came and, following the Munich General Management's invitation, I conducted for the first time the Mozart and Wagner Festival Plays at the Residenz Theater and the Prince Regent Theater. At last! I feel unable to describe the sense of satisfaction that filled my whole being. I do recall, though, that on the day before my rehearsals were to begin I made a pilgrimage to the Residenz Theater, in which Mozart had conducted his *La Finta Giardiniera,* in 1775. From there I walked past the Court

Theater, across the Isar, and slowly up to the Prince Regent Theater, a worthy realization of a Wagnerian idea. To have at my
disposal these three theaters, each one of which was almost ideally
suited to the works presented in them! To be able to prepare and
produce in them operas and musical dramas in accordance with
my own ideas! Here, indeed, was the life-task for which I had
waited, for which I felt I was cut out, and which — if I obtained
my release from Vienna, and I did not doubt that I would — had
come my way at just the right time between youthful vigor and
manly maturity. Floating in a dream that was reality and moved by
wishes that were about to be fulfilled, I wandered through the
grounds at the bank of the Isar on that beautiful summer evening.
So intoxicated was I with happiness that, in retrospect, I must count
those moments among the culminating points of my life. Vital energy foamed and gushed within me, as did the stream down below
whose home mountains had imparted to it their wild force. I, too,
felt strength within me, a will, and a goal. My time had come!
I am a bit ashamed to admit my Napoleonic intoxication, but I
was determined to conquer Munich, and from Munich the whole
musical world. The upsurging power of the thirty-six-year-old
man's ego and the rushing to the surface of long suppressed forces
demanding to be put to work, were really but the intensification
of a condition with which I had been familiar from my childhood
days and from which my power to perform has throughout my life
received its dynamic impulse. The practice of any art, no matter
how much humility and devotion are at the bottom of it, is an
excess of the ego. No wonder, then, that, in that presentiment of
fulfillment, the thought of future great tasks set my heart and my
imagination aflame.

I was therefore made all the more impatient by the resistance
with which my request for release was met in Vienna. When all my
efforts directed through the usual channels had proved unsuccessful, I decided to try my luck in a roundabout way. Katharina
Schratt, Emperor Franz Joseph's friend and confidante, was an
influential personage. A former Burgtheater actress, she would
know what professional satisfaction means to an artist, and so I
made up my mind to appeal to her. True, I had been told that
she made it a principle to turn down the innumerable requests to
influence the Emperor in any personal matter, but rumor had it
that there were exceptions. One of these exceptions is recorded here
because it reveals a rarely referred-to lovable side of the Emperor's
nature and because I based my hopes on that very tale — for whose
authenticity, to be sure, I am unable to vouch. Frau Schratt had
been asked to interest the Emperor in a painter's exhibition. After

she had several times declined, she finally yielded, moved by the artist's distressing circumstances. She suggested to the Emperor that he visit the exhibition and buy one of the paintings. A few weeks later, a large van stopped at Frau Schratt's villa in Hietzing, and a huge object was carried into the house. A number of servants from the adjoining Schönbrunn Palace appeared "by order of His Majesty" and helped carry the object into the *salon*. In the afternoon, the Emperor called as usual to have tea with Frau Schratt. He took her by the hand and led her to the *salon,* one of whose walls was entirely covered by a repulsive, poisonously green picture. The Emperor smilingly pointed at it and said: "You asked for it."

Although I should have assumed that after such an experience Frau Schratt would be disinclined once more to use her influence in behalf of an artist, I appealed to her understanding mind and asked for her help. At the same time, I sent a petition to the Emperor himself, motivating my wish to resign. I also tried to interest Count Paar, the Emperor's adjutant general, in my case. More weeks passed, and Munich asked me again and again to do my utmost to hasten the decision. One day, when I was rehearsing, one of Prince Montenuovo's servants appeared with the request that I call at the Lord Steward's office. On entering, I saw my petition to the Emperor on the Prince's desk. He received me with a show of irritation and said that he regretted my attempt to obtain a decision directly from the Emperor and over his head. "Here's your petition," he said. "His Majesty is very correct and will make no disposition in a department under my jurisdiction unless I approve of it. And Frau Schratt, to whom you have also appealed, can't do anything about that either." He was obviously quite annoyed. "You got an exceptionally favorable contract from us only last year. What more can you want?" I replied that the Munich post was far superior to that in Vienna both in function and in distinction. There I would be director, while here in Vienna my sphere of activity was overshadowed by that of the director. I urgently requested that in this decisive moment in my career no obstacles be placed in my way. He asked me about the duration of my Munich contract, and when I told him that I would have to bind myself for six years his mood suddenly changed and he said rather warmly: "I have confidence in you and will speak quite frankly. Mahler was my friend, and he recommended you to me as the future director of the Court Opera. That's the reason why I wanted to keep you here until the end of our present commitments. You are wrecking my plans with your requests to be released, but, after all, I can't keep an artist who wants by all means

[195]

to get away. I shall approve your resignation, but under one condition. You'll have to sign a secret agreement obligating yourself to accept the post of Director of the Vienna Court Opera at the expiration of your Munich contract. And we'll shake hands on this being treated confidentially." So it happened that, when my Vienna contract was rescinded, as of December 1912, and I was able to enter upon my position at the Munich Court Opera, I had in my pocket a secret contract binding me to the Vienna Court Opera as its director, beginning January 1, 1919. I naturally kept the matter to myself, but not without a certain feeling of awkwardness toward the Munich authorities. But by January 1919 Montenuovo was no longer in office, there was no Court and no Court Opera — it had become a State Institute — my contract had lost its validity, and I stayed in Munich.

It was unavoidable that, in the course of my eleven years' activity at the Vienna Opera, I had become increasingly political-minded. But, as a matter of fact, for a long time I had felt like an interested spectator in the political arena. A change came over me when Bosnia and Herzegovina were annexed in 1908. From that moment, I felt the threatening seriousness of European contrasts. How could I have failed to foresee the coming disaster when I gradually learned through the newspapers and my friends' conversations of the irreconcilability of political tendencies within Austria-Hungary and within Europe? At that, peace was maintained again and again; there were even occasions when prospects did not look quite so gloomy. When I went to Munich, my mind was so overwhelmingly occupied with artistic tasks and plans that my ear was once more struck with its old deafness to political cacophonies. Only the dull rolling of the general march beaten in front of the Prince Regent Theater on July 31, 1914, awakened me to the terrible reality of a burning and smoking world, for a contact with which I was so insufficiently equipped, but in which fate had decreed I must from now on live, and to which I must accommodate myself.

BOOK FOUR

I

AN eminent institute of art was now entrusted to my guidance and care, an Opera whose glorious past and important present imposed great responsibilities on me.

The oldest of the three houses in which operatic performances were given was the Residenz Theater. As it was built in 1750, its charming rococo style bore witness to the Bavarian electors' artistic taste and reminded one of the interesting epoch in Munich's theatrical history during which Mozart appeared at the conductor's desk. Nothing in its magnificent interior had been changed. It was still ideally suited to the eighteenth-century operas and other stage works depending upon intimate effects. The Great House, the Court Theater, which had existed in its present form since 1823 and in which operas were presented six times a week, had received its supreme consecration when, at the command of Ludwig II, the first performances of Wagner's musical dramas took place there, including the famous presentation of *Tristan und Isolde* under Hans von Bülow's guidance in 1865.

It must not be assumed that the Munich Opera lived merely upon its old glory. The most recent past was still strongly influenced by the activity of Ernst von Possart, a brilliant actor of pronounced individuality, who, as General Manager of the Royal Bavarian Court Theaters, had inaugurated the Mozart and Wagner Festival Plays, thereby powerfully enhancing Munich's attractive power both in the country itself and abroad. The creation of the Munich Festival Playhouse, the Prince Regent Theater, was also mainly due to his initiative. Munich's operatic presentations bore the imprint of Possart's vivid theatrical gift for stage direction. If the performances were not filled with the spirit of musical dramatics, they were at least benefitted by the methods of a thinking, frequently ingenious, and serious intentioned director and were thereby lifted above the conventional level in vogue on most operatic stages at that time. After Wagner and Bülow, the conductor's desk had been occupied by men like Hermann Levi, Hermann

Zumpe, and finally Felix Mottl, men who had added to the theater's old glory. True, since Mottl's death, eighteen months prior to my coming to Munich, they had been without a leader. It was now my task to keep alive or reanimate my precious inheritance, to fight harmful influences, to fill gaps, and to use the artistic current of my own life to keep the wheels moving.

What I had to do first was study the theater's present condition and its accomplishments in the most recent past. I fully realized how greatly Munich was indebted to Possart and Mottl for the creation of the Mozart and Wagner Festival Plays and for the cultivation of the two masters' works during the ten months of the regular season, and I was naturally made very happy by being privileged to enter upon so glorious a heritage. At the same time, I became aware that other operatic realms and contemporary music had been treated with considerably less care, and that I would therefore have to make provisions for enlarging, elaborating, and modernizing the repertory. Besides, I had had an opportunity during the Summer Festival Plays of 1912 to acquaint myself with the virtues and weaknesses of the available casts. As might have been expected, they included excellent artists at the height of their ability as well as aging singers and others of mediocre talent. A number of gaps had to be filled. What was more, my direction of the Mozart and Wagner Festival Plays had made it clear to me that the artists and especially the whole atmosphere of the theater were suited to Wagner rather than to Mozart. This was natural because Wagner's own activity, the influence of Bayreuth represented by Levi, Zumpe, and Mottl, and the work of Anton Fuchs, the chief stage director, favored the creation of an authentic Wagner style, while the dramatic renditions of Mozart's operas had received their inspiration from Da Ponte and Beaumarchais rather than from the music of Mozart.

Mottl had by no means been merely an interpreter of Wagner's works. He conducted Mozart with the warmheartedness and sound instinct of the born musician at home in every branch of true music, and imbued the performances with the dramatic vitality of his genuine theatrical talent. If, nevertheless, he was most convincing in his renditions of Wagner's musical dramas, it was because he was more richly gifted with electrifying spontaneity and improvising force than with the ability carefully to consider minute details and with the inclination to do educational work with the singers. My task during the coming years was clearly defined: the cultivation of Wagner had to be continued and the general repertory had to be carefully expanded and made more varied. As for Mozart, there was much to be done. Here my responsibilities were grave indeed, but fraught with promise.

It seemed to me of the utmost importance that rehearsing work be increased and intensified, especially with individual artists. As I had done in Vienna and before, I attached much value to coaching singers vocally and dramatically in their parts, to making their talents systematically yield the utmost of their potentialities by making them understand their tasks thoroughly. I had always considered that kind of an educational activity — though it must not appear educational — the foundation of every constructive work in the theater, and have been able to appreciate the improvising élan and dramatic fire of musical performances only when they had been preceded by the most loving and faithful elaboration of details. These two elements — order in details and a seemingly improvised freedom in the flow of a presentation — comprise the task of reproductive art, and no performance can fulfill the demands made by a musical or a musical-dramatic work if it lacks in either.

While I was thus plentifully provided with rehearsing work, I felt refreshed by the daily reward it yielded and by the vitality of the constant association with "the other." The cast of well-tried and popular artists was complemented during my incumbency by the engagement of youthful singers. It was my aim to surround myself with strong artistic personalities. No matter how ardently I strove for a proper synthesis in my performances and for the individual's faithfulness to the work, I never lost sight of the fact that the theater's fascination had its source in the eminent personalities on the boards and in the forcefulness of their ego. Frequently, my choice of revivals or new productions was influenced by my interest in strong artistic personalities. I never planned a revival or the production of a new work unless I felt sure that I had at my disposal eminent artists for at least the principal parts.

In my work with the orchestra, I was made happy by the musicians' artistic seriousness, their individual aptitude, and their general zeal in complying with my wishes. I recall with gratitude, and even with deep emotion, the artistic and human harmony that characterized the ten years of our association. I met with the musicians' understanding and support even in my endeavors to rejuvenate the orchestra, to pension off aged and ailing members, and to engage valuable young players. However, the War and the subsequent economic depression made it difficult for me to act with the necessary energy. I also paid a great deal of attention to the artistic development of the chorus. Gratefully do I remember the enthusiastic and expert co-operation of the excellent chorus master Konrad Neuger. I was highly pleased to meet him again in the same capacity at the Metropolitan Opera in New York twenty years later.

In Munich, too, the question of stage direction turned out to be one of my principal problems, though Anton Fuchs, the chief stage director, was quite devoted to me. Wagnerian performances were almost the only occasions when we worked together, and there he was on the right road, religiously observing Wagner's stage directions. I did not get along so easily with the stage director Willi Wirk, but I managed to carry my point. Josef Geis, the incomparable Beckmesser, who occasionally directed the stage, was an exceptionally capable man with whom I got on well despite his hardheaded stubbornness. I enjoyed the deeply understanding co-operation of the brilliantly gifted ballet master Heinrich Kröller, who died an untimely death. In the incidental pantomimes and dances in Gluck's *Orfeo,* he was able so perfectly to co-ordinate the ballet style of the eighteenth century and the mytho-poetical sense of the solemn choreography that I did not hesitate to entrust to him the entire staging of Walter Braunfels's charming opera *Die Vögel,* based on Aristophanes. He was splendidly successful in accomplishing that difficult and entirely novel task, calling for dramatic expression in conjunction with a birdlike style of attitude and gesturing.

Ludwig Kirschner was stage designer when I came to Munich. We complemented each other excellently in the revival of Weber's *Euryanthe,* whose romantic spirit he depicted brilliantly and poetically in scenic effects and costumes. He left the theater for reasons I do not recall, and I turned to the highly gifted and delicately attuned Russian Leo Pasetti, whose imaginative work often gave me a great deal of pleasure. When I was about to produce Gluck's *Iphigenia in Aulis,* I wrote to the sculptor Adolf Hildebrand, an expert in Hellenic art, inquiring if he would not take charge of the staging. He declined. A man of over seventy, he probably shrank from the unusual nature of such a theatrical job. His works of art had thus far been monumental and static, and he obviously did not care to become involved in a world of moving persons and changing lights. I regretted his refusal, for I had visualized entirely new scenic ideas for *Iphigenia* from a sculptor of such heroic visions. I now turned to Emil Preetorius, a sprightly, short man with sharply cut, spiritual features. He had made a name for himself as a graphic artist and illustrator. My knowledge of him was actually confined to his unique illustrations of Eichendorff's novel *The Good-For-Nothing*. They were as romantic as the book itself. I realized that it was a far cry from poetic illustrations to a heroic Greek stage picture, but I had confidence in the man's versatility and adaptability. I had become personally acquainted with this highly gifted artist. Spiritually related to the Stefan George circle, he had taken a fancy to Eastern Asiatic culture and become deeply engrossed in it. At the same time, he was devoted to classic art, and I thought that he possessed at least the spiritual qualifications for the unusual task. His work entirely justified my expectations. It marked the start of his successful theatrical activity which, after I had withdrawn from the German theater, took him as far as Bayreuth, where he designed new settings for the *Ring*. He did quite a number of jobs for me after *Iphigenia*. The best of them and the most suitable to his talents was *Così fan tutte* at the Berlin Municipal Opera. Emil Preetorius was a friend of Grand Duke Ernst Ludwig of Hesse, and played an important part in Munich's intellectual life. I derived much pleasure from his conversation and his strangely romantic sense of humor.

When I put on a Munich revival of the *Ring* with new stage settings, Pasetti, I believe, was in charge of the scenery and the costuming. I have no clear recollection of the event, but plainly recall that Anna von Mildenburg directed the stage — Anton Fuchs was probably dead by that time — and that her powerful personality and Bayreuth schooling made a great impression on the artists.

My assistant conductors were Franz Fischer and Hugo Röhr. Their attitude toward a colleague both younger than they and their superior was friendly and obliging. Röhr was the *routinier* who was supposed to know and be able to do everything. Always available, he was a man of moderate pretensions. I greatly appreciated the fact that I could rely on him at all times, and though his performances were tinged somewhat with the drabness of routine, they were distinguished by orderliness and care. Franz Fischer, a simple, straightforward old musician, confined himself at that time exclusively to conducting Wagner. The dyed-in-the-wool Wagnerites in the public — there were gradations — would whisper to one another that "Fischerfranzl" was really much greater than Mottl. A similar heresy was confided to me by Administrative Director Zollner, but I was under the impression that his judgment was somewhat parochial and influenced by Fischer's unadulterated Bavarian nature. A rumor, which assured him of the heartfelt sympathies of every beer-loving inhabitant of Munich, had it that ever present under the conductor's chair in the Prince Regent Theater's submerged orchestra pit was a stein of beer from which he would refresh himself at quiet moments. I am all the more disinclined to believe that his Bavarianism went to this extreme because our few conversations had shown me how sacred to him were the works of Wagner. I don't suppose that I witnessed more than a few of his performances, but I, too, sensed the greatness of his musicianship. I was pleased to be told not only by himself but, later, by his daughter, that he was devoted to me as a musician.

Long before my coming to Munich, the General Management had practically decided who would be Fischer's successor. Their choice was Otto Hess, leading conductor of the Aachen Opera. I had been told that he was quite successful there. A native son, he had the right to be considered. An appearance as guest conductor gave me the opportunity to appraise his qualifications. He conducted a Wagner opera and generally made a highly favorable impression. He fulfilled Hans von Bülow's well-known demand that a conductor must not have his head in the score but the score in his head. So, with my consent, he was appointed Franz Fischer's successor. His work and his professional zeal fully justified his engagement, though his growing dynamic excesses were as opposed to my striving for orchestral culture as his morbid ambition was to my endeavor to have peace reign in the house. Hess was a difficult and unfortunate man. At the slightest difference of opinion in a harmless conversation, two fiery spots would appear on his cheeks, and his heavy breathing would make it advisable to stop the talk. I did my best to give him a sphere of activity that ought to have satisfied any conductor. But so inordinate was his ambition that he would have considered my suicide but the first instalment payment on the immense debt fate owed to his justified demands. I decided to keep on living, to do what I thought was right and just, and to bear with equanimity the man's undeserved enmity. During my Munich incumbency Otto Hess died of a tubercular ailment that explained the red spots on his cheeks and his abnormal irritability. His place was taken by Robert Heger. He was not his predecessor's equal in temperament and dynamics, but was his superior in musical and personal culture. His urbanity gave me a chance during my last years in Munich to recover from the senseless and unnecessary interferences with my endeavors, which were directed solely toward the institute's best interests.

Baron Speidel, the Bavarian General Manager, who had conducted the negotiations with me and had waited so patiently until Vienna would set me free, was a former general of cavalry. He died soon after my coming to Munich. He had been a simple and sincere man, concerning whose naïveté in matters of art any number of anecdotes were afloat. I told him of a magnificent chorus alto, to whom I had granted an audition. When I mentioned the lady's

talent and fine appearance and urged that she be engaged as a soloist, he said to me in unadulterated Bavarian dialect: "Go on, isn't
it a fine thing to have such a good voice in the chorus?" I had quite
some trouble explaining to him that the chorus voices needn't be
better than those of the soloists. The name of the singer was Louise
Willer, the subsequent leading alto of the Munich Opera. She sang
most of the prominent contralto parts under my direction. I shall
never forget her deeply moving performance in *Das Lied von der
Erde.*

Speidel's place was taken by Clemens von Franckenstein, a
brother of Georg von Franckenstein, for many years Austria's ambassador in London. I had made the former's acquaintance in a twofold manner. First, through Arthur Schnitzler's novel *Der Weg ins
Freie,* which portrayed the two brothers — under different names,
needless to say. I remember Clemens von Franckenstein's com-
plaining to me about the portrayal's want of resemblance. Second,
through an actual meeting in Wiesbaden where I had gone at
Mahler's behest to listen to a singer. Franckenstein had been the
Wiesbaden Court Theater's second conductor at the time. He had
heard of me and invited me to have lunch at his home. I spent
an exceptionally stimulating hour with him and his young wife, a
handsome reddish-blond Irishwoman. It was not surprising that I
enjoyed the occasion, for Franckenstein had been a member of the
circle around Hofmannsthal, Schnitzler, and Andrian, and was
greatly devoted to Mahler. So there were enough musical and literary points of contact between us to make the time fly. A kind fate
had now decreed that this representative of an old aristocratic family, partly Austrian and partly Bavarian, a man who was acceptable
to the Court personally and to the public as a musician, was made
my official superior, as chief of the general management. During
the approximately six years of our co-operation, terminated by the
revolution in November 1918, the artistic sense, tactful modesty,
and firm energy of this irreproachable and extremely cultured man
gave me nothing but pleasure and satisfaction.

The two brothers did not resemble each other at all. Georg von
Franckenstein's tall slender figure, his prematurely gray and naturally wavy hair overtopping a finely cut longish face; his dignified
demeanor, and his quiet elegance made him the typical Austrian
aristocrat. Clemens von Franckenstein, on the other hand, called
Cle by his friends, was a broad-shouldered man of rather ponderous
figure and walk. His Caesar's head was characterized by firm features, a prominent nose, a serious mouth, and a slightly protruding
forehead. He was an excellent musician, and aroused my interest
even as a composer. His songs, his ingenious variations on the

night watchman's call in Meyerbeer's *Huguenots,* and his opera *Li-tai-pe* showed individuality, ability, and — especially in the variations — a highly developed technique of orchestration.

I have already referred to the Munich Court Orchestra and the ties of mutual sympathy that united us during the ten years of my activity. In addition to questions of engagements, advancements, pensionings, and disciplinary matters, I concerned myself also with the social and economic affairs of the orchestra. The effects of the war and the post-Revolutionary changes gave rise to new problems and caused me to take an active interest in the musicians' efforts toward social betterment. While no details have remained in my memory, I should like to mention that the final statute which we had worked out at committee meetings and whose acceptance by the financial administration Franckenstein had obtained was recognized as a model by other German orchestras. A general feeling of good will had enabled us to reach a result that individual musicians might have considered slightly prejudicial to their own interests but whose general advantages could not be denied. Once more I had to admit to myself on that occasion that, as a matter of fact, each of the contending groups was right in its arguments and that I was heartily in accord with the sailor in Ludwig Thoma's *Altaich,* who, when asked for his view, always replied: "I have two opinions." I concluded that there was but one way to deal with all mundane contentions — tolerance — and that it was inapplicable to but one frame of mind — intolerance.

My duties included the leadership of the Odeon Symphony Concerts. I could have as many rehearsals as I thought necessary, and it was up to me to see that they did not conflict with the Opera's orchestral rehearsals. According to an old Court tradition, a blue carriage drawn by two horses and with a liveried coachman and attendant on the box, took me from my home to the concert and back again. We usually took along Thomas Mann and his wife, who were our friends and neighbors. This convenience was rather acceptable to them, especially during the war.

Shortly before a concert at the Odeon, members of the Royal family would appear in the artists' room. They were among my most regular and most musically inclined devotees. There was Prince Ludwig Ferdinand, the King's cousin, of whom I shall have more to say later, and his wife Maria, *née* de la Paz, related to the Spanish royal family. They were usually accompanied by their daughter Princess Pilar, with whom we became more closely associated later. There was the extremely sympathetic Princess Klara and, finally Princess Gisela, daughter of Emperor Franz Joseph of Austria and wife of Prince Leopold of Bavaria, the King's brother. All these

Theme and Variations

"Royal Highnesses" betook themselves to their respective seats in the front rows shortly before the concert was to begin, listened with perfect attention, applauded enthusiastically, and thanked me personally at the end. Princess Gisela was the only one to make me feel uneasy. A few minutes after the music had started, she would fall asleep. Her head, adorned by a tall feather, would droop to one side, and she was awakened only by the applause, in which she joined with a friendly smile.

In spite of the love of art displayed by the members of the House of Wittelsbach, who honored my operatic and concert performances with their presence and their joyful approval, any comparison with the past was bound to be unfavorable to them. Nowhere in German lands had the arts been so magnificently supported by princely devotees as in the old Munich. There had been the somewhat nebulous Dukes of Wittelsbach, responsible for the erection of the splendid Residenz Theater and for its fine work. One of them, Duke Albrecht, had founded the State Library and the Art Chamber in the sixteenth century and had drawn Orlando di Lasso to his court. After them had come King Ludwig I, the admirer of Goethe, and his son Maximilian, builders of important streets and edifices. Their names shone in Munich's cultural history because of their creation of institutes devoted to arts and science and the summoning of eminent men to "Isar Athens," as Munich was frequently called in recognition of the services to art that these two princes had rendered. The House of Wittelsbach had reached the height of its glory in the fascinating figure of Ludwig II, whose lofty decision had swept care from Wagner's brow and smoothed the way of his art. The tragic end of that noble spirit is sufficiently well known. Ludwig III, whose coronation I witnessed, and by whose grace the theaters at which I worked were maintained, fulfilled the duties of a Maecenas only from a sense of loyalty to the traditions of his house. The unpretentious and simple man was rather sober-minded, and unless some special occasion demanded his presence, he kept away from the theater and from music. When, in 1913, thirty years after Wagner's death, we performed *Parsifal* at the Prince Regent Theater, an opera which up to that time had been the prerogative of Bayreuth, the King was obliged to be present at so momentous an event. After the long first act, Franckenstein and I called at his box to inquire how he had been impressed. The King replied with fine sincerity: "Gentlemen, I thank you, but wild horses could not drag me here again." After having thus voiced his impatience, he became quite affable and explained apologetically that he was quite fond of pictures but, he just couldn't help it, he didn't care for music.

Theme and Variations

Those ten years in Munich, with their wealth and intensity of artistic happenings, when I was permitted to live my life as the conductor of operas and concerts untrammeled by any laws but those dictated by my own conscience, seem to me today the most prolific period of my life. And the wealth and intensity of giving found a joyful response in the warmth of taking. So far does that time lie behind me, so different was the young man of thirty-six to forty-six from him who, near the Biblical age, is filling these pages with his memories and telling of his former self as of another person, that I may be allowed to refer to the uninterrupted high tension of my activity and to the enthusiastic reception it was accorded without being accused of vanity. My recollection of Munich, beyond all details, is a climatic one, as it were. I can still feel the splendidly stirring warmth of those days wafted toward me from every figure and from every experience conjured up by my retrospective thoughts.

Those were the days of thorough self-devotion, yes, of self-squandering, of enthusiastic appeals to the lovers of art, of their jubilant understanding and gratitude, of the enthusiastic co-operation of one's coworkers, and of the trustful exchange of thoughts between friends. No wonder that they appear to me today so flourishing, beautiful, and happy when I think that in spite of war and revolution and political reconstruction I still lived in a world in which literature and music, science and humanity, maintained their ordained place, a world in which the Ten Commandments and human conscience still exercised their age-old sovereign authority, in short, a world in which people, though they lied, hated, and killed, did so with a consciousness of wrong, and in which they were permitted to respect, love, and help with the consciousness of right. That was the world in which our music and the great creations of the human mind had come into existence. Its foundation became noticeably endangered at about the time when I left Munich. Then, toward the end of 1922, those dark powers of hell had already begun their work; but beyond the blood-red placards on the walls of Munich, displaying the sinister swastika and announcing that Adolf Hitler would speak, I knew little of them. Gradually, the struggle began to gain in threatening importance. It started as a fight against the Decalogue, against human conscience, against the principles of respect, helpfulness, and love, against the spirit, and against the works of the spirit. It grew into a war against humanity itself, whose elemental essence was to be most foully disgraced.

DURING the Festival Play time of 1912, my wife and I had come to like Herzogpark, the fine suburb on the other side of the Isar, and we had hopefully inspected some of the villas of the district. No sooner had I obtained my release from Vienna than my wife went to Munich to rent the most suitable of them. We were made happy by the prospect of living in a house by ourselves. On the raised ground floor there was a handsome entrance hall, from which a curved stairway mounted to the two bedrooms and two spacious nurseries on the first floor, while a rear stairway, hidden by a door, led to the kitchen and accessory rooms below, to the servant and guest rooms on the second floor, and to the attic. Along the wall of the front stairway we had hung a number of pictures, which, when we would take the children upstairs in the evening, were the subjects of endless questions, conveniently delaying the moment of their going to bed. Doors in the entrance hall opened upon the study, the music room, and the spacious dining room. The latter gave access to a large terrace overlooking a garden, which surrounded the whole house. Taking in the adjoining gardens, my gaze could roam over a wide, tree-studded, park-like quiet. There was a high gate, though it was not too high for the jumping technique of Torleif, our German shepherd dog, whose gymnastic exercises nearly caused a passing lady to swoon and me to be involved in a lawsuit. Stepping through that gate, I got into the quiet Mauer-kircherstrasse, gradually wending its way through grassland and bushes until it reached the charming meadows along the quickly flowing Isar. The grounds, which Thomas Mann, too, loved to roam with his dog, have been lovingly and vividly described by him in his idyl *A Man and his Dog*. Such walks through the meadows were rare, indeed, in my work-filled life. I usually went into town from my house, heeding my wife's injunction to cover the way to the theater on foot, a heroic task in view of the wealth of my professional duties. After half an hour of quiet walking through the beautiful English Garden, I would sit in my high and spacious office, conferring about pertinent institutional questions with my next-room neighbor, Artistic Secretary Malyot. Passing through his room and the adjoining waiting room, I got to the office of the General Manager, with whom I discussed the more important matters. I started rehearsing at ten. My afternoons were taken up by the study of new operatic or concert works, conferences with heads of departments, administrative affairs, and correspondence. Frequently there were rehearsals, too, unless I was to conduct in the evening. Throughout my life, with but rare exceptions, I have kept clear the afternoons preceding my conducting.

No amount of conjugal love could induce me to walk to the theater again in the afternoon. Half-way down the Mauerkircherstrasse, a flight of stone steps led to a higher-leveled street and the terminal of the "Number Thirty Electric," the *Dreissiger*. So, in the afternoon, or when the weather was bad, I used this means of communication. I soon got to know the faces of all the conductors and the regular passengers. They formed a large circle of unacquainted acquaintances. It happened quite frequently that a man would give me a friendly nod in a restaurant. To my question where I had had the pleasure, he would say: "Aw, I'm a *Dreissiger*, y' know."

In the summer of 1912, and I believe in 1913, too, we had chosen charming Feldafing on the Starnbergersee for our sojourn. From there, convenient railway traffic made it possible for me to reach the city by day or night. Quite near us was Castle Possenhofen, where the Bavarian Princess Elisabeth, the subsequent Empress of Austria, had been born and spent the years of her youth. Almost opposite, on the other shore of the lake, stood Castle Berg, the last abode of Ludwig II, who from there had gone to his death in the waters of the lake. From 1914, I rented the wood-encircled Jägerhaus between Dorf Kreuth and Bad Kreuth for our summer home. It was a rather imposing and solidly built villa, the property of the ducal House of Wittelsbach. A large fenced-in, tree-bordered meadow gave the children ample opportunity for romping. This seemed to include the frequent mischievous removal of a primitive field gate, unavoidably followed by an invasion of our neighbor's cows. Of course, we had to drive them out again. This was attended by a great deal of unwonted trouble and excitement on our part, but the proceedings were hugely enjoyed by the children and the dog. It took some time before we discovered the cause of these "wild-west scenes" in our civilized domain, and could, by improving the field gate, insure the peaceful quiet of our idyllic retreat. A bumpy rustic driveway ran along the fence and through the woods, and beyond it rushed the Weissach, a foaming cold mountain brook, in which the children bathed on hot days. The highroad from Tegernsee was only a few steps away from our house. To the left, it led to quiet Bad Kreuth, whose one-story spa building reminded me of Jean Paul's Bad Maulbronn in *Katzenbergers Badereise*. To the right, it led to the wonderful Achensee in the Tyrol. From a large balcony on the first floor of our house we could enjoy the fine view and the strong aroma of the forest. Often we would mount our bicycles and ride up to the Achensee or down — by way of Egern, where the tenor Leo Slezak

AUDITORIUM OF THE VIENNA OPERA HOUSE

showing its iron curtain

ARTUR SCHNABEL, BRUNO WALTER, ARTUR
BODANZKY, AND ELSA WALTER

St. Moritz, 1937

held forth jovially at his handsome country seat, to Tegernsee, an hour and a half by rail from Munich. Between Dorf Kreuth and our Jägerhaus stood the large Schloessl Dreyfuss, a nobly but simply proportioned building with wooded slopes at its rear. It had been rented by Gabrilowitsch and his wife. There, or at our house, we spent a good deal of our summer leisure in pleasant intercourse, playing music, discussing things, or taking walks.

Gabrilowitsch's town home and mine were separated by the whole width of Munich. Yet, during the eighteen months from my coming to Munich to the outbreak of the war we managed to see much of each other even in winter time. Besides, Ossip attended almost every one of my operatic performances and concerts. I highly appreciated his presence, and it gave me the utmost pleasure to discuss the events with him afterward. But our conversations were by no means restricted to music. Ossip was a man of varied interests. His pugnacious nature led to many a heated discussion, which would be continued at our next meeting. We had particular difficulty in seeing eye to eye with regard to Tolstoy and Dostoyevsky. A fundamental trait of his nature caused many of our friendly fights. The affectionate and romantically agitated man, the poet of the keyboard, was a pessimist who viewed the world critically and frequently disdainfully. I proved to him again and again that, while he was thinking pessimistically, he was feeling and acting optimistically, but he would not be convinced and tried to point out to me that he was consistent, and I mistaken. We played duets on one or two pianos. He was the soloist at some of my Odeon concerts, and I often asked him privately to play for me Impromptus by Brahms, *Moments Musicaux* by Schubert, or Préludes by Chopin. Laughter, too, had its place at our meetings, for Ossip had a strongly marked sense of humor. I recall our discussion of the unhappy function of the male ballet dancer in a *pas de deux*, where the man had nothing to do but give physical support to the *prima ballerina*'s onrushes, pirouettes, and other daring terpsichorean evolutions. To demonstrate to our wives the strange subject of our conversation, Ossip assumed the part of the *ballerina*, rushing toward me and performing the most astonishing gyrations, while I had to be content with the stabilizing part of the vacuously smiling stationary dancer. We scored a great hit and had to do a number of encores. I also recall our week's walking tour through the Tyrol with rucksack and alpenstock. Most clearly, however, do I remember the concerts he conducted with the Munich Kaim Orchestra. I attended them with a great deal of sympathetic interest. It was an epoch of heartwarming friendship, suddenly and threateningly, though but temporarily, terminated by the outbreak of the War. It goes without saying that our friendship outlasted it and was even closer after it.

Friendly relations existed between me and another Russian musician. On our side of the Isar, near the Prince Regent Theater, and in a house similar to ours, lived the violinist Alexander Petschnikoff, then one of the most brilliant European concert soloists, with his beautiful German-American wife and their three children. Lili was also a violinist, and we heard the couple give an excellent rendition of Bach's Double Concerto on a number of occasions. Their musical and human association was not to last long, however. Their married life went on the rocks, but we remained on a friendly footing with both. I even played chamber music in public with Petschnikoff several times. Lili and the children left Munich and Germany before America entered the war. After many adventures and dangers, which put her rare energy and her irresistible power over people to a hard test, she reached her home country, where we met her frequently later.

Near our house in the Mauerkircherstrasse, a short street branched off. At its end, close to the bank of the Isar, and shielded by an extensive front garden, stood the stately and dignified villa of Thomas Mann. Around a corner, one came upon a white garden gate. Visitors were frightened at first by Bauschan's barking, but quickly reassured by the overwhelming affection displayed by the dog whom the poet had immortalized. Soon the wide terrace of Mann's house was reached. We spent many an unforgettable hour on that terrace during the warm season and in the comfortable sitting room adjoining the author's fine library and study during the winter.

I do not recall where I first met Thomas Mann. It may have been at the home of Dr. Hallgarten, the art-lover, or at that of his father-in-law, the well-known mathematician Professor Alfred Pringsheim, a collector of exquisite Italian ceramics. He was quite a character and had formerly been associated with Hermann Levi. A musical enthusiast, he had gone so far in his passionate Wagnerism as to make piano arrangements of some fragments of Wagner's operas. His wife, Hedwig Pringsheim, *née* Dohm, retained her beauty until far into old age. Her father was the publisher of the Berlin *Kladderadatsch,* her mother the well-known feminist Hedwig Dohm. On gala evenings all Munich met at the hospitable house in the Arcistrasse, but we naturally preferred quiet meetings in a more intimate circle.

Having read Thomas Mann's *Buddenbrooks* and *Royal Highness* and the novelettes *Tonio Kröger* and *Tristan* before making his acquaintance, I was naturally looking forward eagerly to meeting the author. Katja Mann was not in Munich in 1913. Not until the early summer of 1914 did she return from Arosa, where ill health had compelled her to go, but a young girl's enchanting portrait by Kaulbach in the Pringsheim home had shown me her features. That, and the figure of Imma in *Royal Highness,* a poetic paraphrase of her being, had to some extent prepared me for the acquaintance with the theme of the two variations.

A friendly intercourse soon developed, encouraged by the proximity of our houses and enlivened by our daughters' comradeship with Klaus and Erika Mann. The children's wild pranks and their mutual instigation to imaginative mischief kept furnishing us with material for excited telephone calls and personal consultations. But the misdeeds of the children were not the only cause of discussions among the grownups. More amiable pursuits of the young generation frequently served to entertain us and to provide a topic of general conversation. I particularly recall a juvenile performance of Lessing's *Minna von Barnhelm,* in which our daughters played the parts of Minna and Francisca, Erika the part of Sergeant-Major Werner, Klaus that of Just, a young Hallgarten that of Tellheim, and — an irresistibly funny episode — Mann's youngest son, the eight-year-old Golo, that of the Lady in Mourning. He was quite little and spoke with a lisp. His earnest endeavors to portray a ladylike sadness contrasted most strikingly with the rakish hint at the cleft of a woman's bosom by means of a self-devised charcoal line on his extremely *décolleté* childish breast. The young actors attended to their tasks with a fiery zeal. Not only did they have the benefit of two grown-up stage directors, but — a strange artistic whim! — they had even asked for criticisms, for which Thomas Mann and I had volunteered. I suppose that on the occasion of a subsequent performance of Wilde's *The Importance of Being Earnest* I sinned against the supreme moral law of criticism, that of strict impartiality, by unjustly giving the evening's chief honors to seven-year-old Monika Mann, whose cherubic sweetness had quite overwhelmed me.

Our amicable relations, so charmingly stimulated by incidents connected with family life, were still further benefited by a proximity more beautiful and inward than that of our homes. I felt instinctively captivated by the singularity of Mann's creative work — I had been profoundly moved by his masterly novelette *Tristan,* while his essentially musical nature seemed in turn to be attracted by my musicianship. Soon it came about that I played for Thomas and Katja Mann from the works I happened to be rehearsing and with which I was therefore overflowing, works like Weber's *Euryanthe* and Mozart's *Don Giovanni,* symphonies by Beethoven or

Mozart, Schubert or Mahler. I also made them acquainted with Pfitzner's *Palestrina*. Mann's essay on the subject sounded the very depths of this work. I also recall my playing for him the second act of *Tristan* and my amazement at his unbelievingly thorough knowledge of the work when he subsequently pointed out that I had omitted the soft E-flat of the trumpet at the words *"Das bietet dir Tristan."*

I cannot undertake to speak of the poet Thomas Mann within the framework of this book. I can merely try to say a few words about my relation to his work. It seemed to be the young poet's gravest problem — a problem to which he gave the most thoughtfully clear expression in *Tonio Kröger* — that his nature was so wholly governed by art; that, in other words, he felt so irresistibly driven to formulate artistically his every experience. There was the danger that this urge to contemplate life and to mirror it poetically would cause him to become lost to life itself. The mastery of his instrument, language, might indeed have tempted him to see in man and fate nothing but the material for brilliant writing. He had to beware of the artist's "ivory tower," of egoistic self-enjoyment. He was saved from its allurement by the warmth, the moral strength, and the humanity of his deeper self. The gentle irony and toleration characteristic of the tone and mood of his earlier works never induced me to conclude that he was cool, stood aloof from life, or looked down upon man with condescension. They were to me rather symptoms of his artistic style, bashfully cloaking a wealth of heartfelt sympathy, all-understanding, and pity. Had there still been any doubters, works like *A Man and his Dog, Lied vom Kindchen,* and *Disorder and Early Sorrow* would have utterly convinced them of the poet's love of the creature and of nature, and of his devoutly tender involvement in elemental human relations. Larger works like *The Magic Mountain,* tend to put the author himself in the shade. The way leading from *Buddenbrooks* to the *Joseph* story seemed to me symptomatic of the development from the "growing" to the "being" Thomas Mann, to his "idea"; the way from the poetical representation of temporal happenings to that of eternal man and his fate; and I am tempted to say: from the word to music. Anyway, Thomas Mann and music! Does it not dominate him more than he himself suspects? How enlightening that at the climactic moment of the Joseph story the poet bids music to lead the son, believed to be dead, into his father's arms, that the supreme pathos of an incomparable human event is dissolved in the lovely song of the child Serach!

And does not the poet's path of life run parallel with his creative work — if such an apposition be at all permissible? The man who belonged to the bourgeoisie grew out of it as soon as political events sharpened his gaze and took hold of his heart. He turned toward the people. The man who by his language, his culture, and his soul was a German became a European, and the European became a citizen of the world.

It was my good fortune to make Thomas Mann's acquaintance at an early stage of his interesting and admirable wandering through life, before the revolutions that steeled his forces and raised him to the twofold apostolate as a poet and a citizen of the world. Many a thoughtful Munich conversation during the War and the years immediately following it revealed to me his endeavor to grasp the sense of world events, his emotional affection, but also his effort to preserve the poet's inward quiet as a thing apart from the onrush of wildly agitated reality. It was this tendency that, in 1926, made him hasten into the world of his Joseph, into whose distant domain he returned again and again, throughout seventeen years, from his campaigns against the dragon world of the present.

Although I had left the Munich Opera at the end of 1922, there were occasional later meetings with Mann and his family. His indignation at rising Nazism had in the meantime been expressed with increasing vehemence. I vividly recall his Berlin lecture at Beethoven Hall in 1930, which the Nazis, scattered among the audience, disturbed so threateningly through outcries and interruptions. Mann was forced to bring his drowned-out remarks to an *accelerando* close and to leave the hall, much to the relief of the wife of his publisher, S. Fischer, who had sat in the front row and had kept whispering to him tremblingly: "Stop as soon as possible!" The demonstrations were directed by the "poet" Arnolt Bronnen, rendered partly unrecognizable by monstrous black spectacles. No sooner had Mann left the platform than my wife and I hastened to his side to save him from coming in contact with the rabble. Using a number of familiar connecting corridors, we led him and his family from the artists' room to neighboring Philharmonic Hall, groping our way through the darkness to the Köthenerstrasse exit. A gloomy foreboding had made me park my car there. It finally carried us to safety.

The tender vulnerability of this poet's existence, endangered in spite of his philosophical armor, had been entrusted by a kind fate to his wife Katja's thoughtful protection, without which Thomas Mann's creative power would hardly have been able to remain undisturbed by world events. Back of the charming mockery and pliable agility of mind of his model for Imma stood the reliable straightforwardness of a vigorous and brave nature, dedicated as much to the sixfold obligations as a mother as to the thousandfold ones of a wife, a helpmate, a guardian, a fighter, a congenial companion, and an efficient intercessor with the world. My gratitude for the enrichment of my life goes out to the poet and friend as well as to Katja Mann. Although I have not at my command the verses in which her rare combination of mental strength and worldly efficiency ought to be sung, I hope that her tenderly attuned ear will discern with satisfaction the latent enthusiasm in the prose of my paean of praise.

One of the most singular characters with whom life brought me into both spiritual and friendly contact was Paul Nikolaus Cossman, philosopher, musical devotee, and publisher of *Süddeutsche Monatshefte,* a distinguished monthly of literary, scientific, and artistic tendencies. When the war began, Cossman became wholly absorbed in politics. He left *Süddeutsche Monatshefte* and assumed a leading position with *Münchener Neueste Nachrichten,* the most influential Bavarian newspaper. But the center of his spiritual existence still remained his love of Pfitzner's work. Around this central point were grouped such strangely assorted impulses as his militant political sentiments, his growing affiliation with Catholicism, a wealth of charitable inclinations, and his genuine reverence for classic music. We had many points of contact and were especially united by our devotion to Pfitzner. Our meetings were as frequent as they were welcome to us, and though I never quite succeeded in fathoming the nature of this singular and excellent man, I was at all times conscious of the powerful attraction of his mentality, his moral purity, and his highly individual sense of humor. It is understandable that Cossman was made very happy by my espousal of Pfitzner's cause, by my revivals of *Der arme Heinrich* and *Die Rose vom Liebesgarten* and the first performance of his *Palestrina. Christelflein,* too, had its first performance under my direction at the Munich Opera, as had *Das dunkle Reich* and *Von Deutscher Seele* at the Odeon. On a number of occasions, in Cossman's company, I met the learned Josef Hofmiller and the witty political economist Paul Busching. Pfitzner's coming to Munich from his country house in Schondorf on the Ammersee was always the occasion for a remarkably spirited and heart-warming symposium.

An interesting personality, steeped in Europe's bellicose past, entered my field of vision when I made the acquaintance of ex-Queen Maria of Naples. She was the daughter of the eccentric Duke Max of Bavaria and the sister of Empress Elisabeth of Austria, with whom she had grown up in Castle Possenhofen on the Starnbergersee. At the age of twenty she had induced her husband, King Francis II of the two Sicilies, to decline Cavour's invitation

to join in the war against Austria. When Garibaldi besieged Gaeta
in 1861, the Queen rather than the unenergetic King, became the
soul of the defense. Placing herself personally at the head of the
loyal troops, she led them against the besiegers. Gaeta was eventually forced to capitulate. Opinions of the cause for which Maria
fought may differ, but she was at any rate surrounded by the glory
of a daring deed. A quiet radiance, spreading a lofty atmosphere
round her, went out from the still beautiful woman of more than
seventy. She always wore black, and her abundant gray hair,
wound round her head like a crown, added to the dignity of her
appearance. She was very fond of music and faithfully attended
my operatic and concert performances. Nothing gave her more
pleasure than to be invited to tea at my house and to enjoy an
afternoon of music participated in by some singers from the Munich Opera. She lived at the Hotel Regina, if my memory serves
me. Whenever we were asked to have luncheon with her, we were
waited on by her factotum Luigi, obviously one of the loyal fol-
lowers from her Neapolitan past. He looked like a relic of the old
Italian feudal epoch. One day, a young man entered the room,
addressing her as *"chère tante Marie."* He was King Manuel II of
Portugal, another enthusiastic devotee of music. He had lost his
throne in 1910, and was now looking for a place of permanent domicile. He thought for a time that he had found it in Munich. Public opinion was then interested in him chiefly because of his generally known association with the beautiful dancer Gaby de Lys,
but, contrary to newspaper reports, his seriousness, modesty, and
frank heartiness revealed him as anything but a playboy and
man of the world. Later, in London, when we came in closer
contact with each other, I found my first favorable impression
confirmed.

Although my personal life in Munich was thus not poor in human relationships of the most varied kind, neither they, nor the
increasingly prosperous conditions at my home, nor the enjoyment of the magnificent lake and mountain districts could fill me
with the sense of well-being I had felt during certain years of my
activity in Vienna. I was too heavily burdened by the consciousness of my responsibilities. Then, in August, 1914, came the War,
which was bound to change into pangs of conscience any feeling
of contentment I might have harbored. The revolution of 1918
added to my duties and fatefully changed the picture of the world.
Irrespective of all outward occurrences, however, and in spite of
my natural evenly cheerful attitude and my frequently high-spirited intercourse with my children, an increasingly dark fundamental mood had taken possession of me. Flowing from inward

sources, it barred the way to an unencumbered enjoyment of life's amenities.

III

My first new production as Bavarian General Musical Director was, I believe, Richard Strauss's original version of *Ariadne auf Naxos,* with its framework of Molière's *Le Bourgeois-gentilhomme.* Strauss himself had played the opera for me at his home in Garmisch. I am still conscious of the pleasure the composer's cool and perfect piano rendition of the rather artificial but masterly opus gave me. His playing was as lucid and objective as his written music on the desk before us, but in spite of its uniform coolness it still left the impression of latent agitation. True, the storm and heat of the dramatically moving scenes impressed me as being ordained by the enthroned power of a weather god rather than by the upsurging of a human emotion. I was strangely affected when I found at the end of the neatly written manuscript the words in his handwriting: "Finished on Bubi's birthday." My chilled soul thawed slightly at this indication of a friendly family feeling.

Of my many new productions, my memory retains in addition to Strauss's *Ariadne* his *Die Frau ohne Schatten,* Schreker's *Der ferne Klang* and *Die Gezeichneten,* Braunfels's *Die Vögel,* Korngold's *The Ring of Polycrates* and *Violanta,* Klenau's *Sulamith,* Pfitzner's *Palestrina* and *Christelflein,* Courvoisier's *Lancelot and Elaine,* and Graener's *Don Juan's Last Adventure* — a surely rather incomplete list. My endeavors were also directed toward the reanimation of German romanticism. Revivals of such operas as Weber's *Der Freischütz, Euryanthe,* and *Oberon,* of Marschner's *Hans Heiling,* of Lortzing's *Undine,* of Goetz's *The Taming of the Shrew,* of Hugo Wolf's *Der Corregidor,* of Pfitzner's *Heinrich* and *Die Rose vom Liebesgarten* were to make it flourish anew, not only musically but also scenically and dramatically. My ever-growing admiration of Gluck induced me to make increased efforts on behalf of his *Orfeo* and *Iphigenia in Aulis.* I also spent happy hours in the preparation of Verdi's *Falstaff* and Cornelius's *Der Barbier von Bagdad.* Other conductors were entrusted with the production of works like Klose's *Ilsebill,* Donizetti's *Don Pasquale,* Handel's *Giulio Cesare,* and of a great many other operas.

The thought governing my entire activity in Munich was that of bringing about between music and scene that unity whose introduction through Mahler I had witnessed in Vienna and whose further systematic intensification and development I considered my object in life. I was gratified to notice that the Munich Opera's successful saturation of the drama with the spirit of the music was appreciated by the fair-minded not only locally but, to an increasing extent, also abroad. I tried to further international recognition by enlarging the scope of the Summer Festival Plays. In addition to Wagner and Mozart, works by Gluck, Weber, Hugo Wolf, Pfitzner, and others were put on the program. During the years of the war there was of course no international public, nor did it return very fast thereafter.

My greatest artistic gain in Munich was the increased depth of my relation to Mozart. It had taken quite some time until I had wholly and definitely done with the "musician of the eighteenth century," "the graceful and smiling rococo composer," in short, the blithe Mozart of Tilgner's monument in Vienna. The "dry classicist," had never been a danger to me. I finally discovered behind a seemingly graceful playfulness the dramatist's inexorable seriousness and wealth of characterization: I recognized in Mozart the Shakespeare of the opera. At the same time, I understood the unique creative miracle vouchsafed us in Mozart's work. With him, everything was dramatically true: nobility as well as baseness, kindness as well as malice, wisdom as well as stupidity, and he turned all truth into beauty. My task in Mozart performances had become clear to me: every characteristic and truthful detail must be given vigorous dramatic expression without impairment of the vocal and orchestral beauty. This beauty permitted no exaggeration in dynamics and tempos, in gesturing and action, in forms and colors on the stage. The problem therefore consisted in achieving all fulness of expression within the limits prescribed by beauty and in resolutely filling that beauty with musical and dramatic power without putting too great an earthly burden upon its unearthly lightness. In addition to this general problem, Mozart set his interpreters the special one of doing justice to the stylistic differences in his creations. For, as I said before, every work is only *sui generis*. Just as the manner of presenting Shakespeare's *Othello* is inapplicable to *Troilus and Cressida*, so the style of *Don Giovanni* is by no means adaptable to that of *The Magic Flute*. My Munich activity enabled me to plunge deeply into all these questions and to try my strength at their solution. It is not for me to say to what extent I succeeded. But I thought I could feel in Munich and, later, Salzburg that I was on the right road. There and in other places, I occupied myself again and again with that illimitable task.

I felt fascinated by the Prince Regent Theater from the very beginning of my Munich activity. It stood detached, above the level of the city, in an outlying district of quiet streets and fine approaches by way of bridges spanning the Isar. A few steps farther, and one was in open fields. About four in the afternoon on Festival-Play days, from the portal of the house would sound brass fanfares composed of motifs from the work to be heard, summoning those who were still tarrying outside. The tall doors of the auditorium closed, and while the fanfares sounded once more, this time from outside, the lights dimmed. When perfect quiet and darkness reigned, the strains from the invisible orchestra began to rise. This ceremonial, devised by Wagner for Bayreuth, and adopted by the Prince Regent Theater of Munich, never failed to exert its effect on me, for in the magic realm of musical dramatic art I was one of the magicians as well as one of the bewitched. To me, nothing was comparable to my entering the gigantic lowered orchestra pit — ah, the incredible and inspiring sight of the six harps back there behind the horns and tubas! — where my musicians, unfestively arrayed but in festive readiness, were awaiting my coming. And when I had taken my place and could see by the mighty curtain shutting off the stage that the lights were going down, when the silence in the invisible space behind us had increased our tension to a state of ultimate composure, when the mystic moment had arrived in which reality, time, and space faded away and we began magically to fill the ideal void with our light and sound, with myth and drama, I felt as wondrously powerful as Faust, holding in his hand the key that would open "the phantoms' unbound realms far distant."

Munich, the "gay center of art," was revealed to me in the frolicsome spirit of the fantastic carnival festivals of 1913 and 1914, arranged by the city's colony of painters. Little though I was inclined toward so calendarily ordered a prankishness, I yet felt — and differently than twenty years before in Cologne — that such an outburst of merriment, traditional of the Munich carnival and influenced by an Italian sense of the festive, was not without its characteristic charm. And so I moved through the masses of people in the streets and through the imaginatively and tastefully decorated halls, bewildered but interested. Amusing, too, was the popular October Festival on the meadow at the *Bavaria,* with its tents, its roasting spits turning over open fires, its steins of beer carried by buxom waitresses to the long wooden tables with an incredible combination of skill and strength, and its merry burghers, eating, drinking, and chatting. And yet, the difference between that kind of festive mood and the one prevalent at the Vienna *Heuriger* seemed to me about that between beer and wine. The Munich Hofbräu on the Platzl furnished a miniature picture of a permanent October Festival. There, too, were the primitive long tables and benches, the robust waitresses with their surprising stein technique, and the *Radi,* the large sharp radishes, which an ingeniously devised screwing implement changed into a kind of accordion and whose spiral turns were generously sprinkled with salt. This made the radishes "weep" and deprived them of much of their bite. Class distinctions and differences of opinion disappeared before the beer and the *Radi.* A pleasant equality and sociability were in evidence. Everyone, be he a minister of state or a porter, was "Neighbor!" to the other. Occasional visitors from Northern Germany or from abroad were amazed by this manifestation of Munich's democratic spirit, a tendency, by the way, that was in the Bavarians' very blood and, when sprinkled with the dew of beer, flourished richly at the Hofbräu and other similar drinking places.

My experiences in the sphere of popular entertainments were further amplified by the peasant summer dances at Tegernsee and Kreuth, where I saw my first genuine *Schuhplattler,* a kind of clog dance. These entertainments took place even during the early months of the war. Finally, I had the unique opportunity of witnessing a royal coronation. Unfortunately, I can only mention, but not describe it. Nothing of it has remained in my memory beyond a general picture of a festive assembly in brilliant surroundings, of magnificent clerical robes, and of resplendent court uniforms. Prince Ludwig, who had been Regent, since the death of his father Luitpold, ascended the Bavarian throne as Ludwig III in November 1913. As I was a Court Official, I had to be present at the solemn state function in the throne room of the royal residence. What I do recall distinctly is the very personal side of the affair. I had to don my court uniform, complete with sword and two-cornered hat, much to the admiration — and amusement — of my family, and go to the scene of the festivity with the uncomfortable feeling of being wholly unsuited to such a disguise. I took my place at the side of Franckenstein in a group of other officials and was given the opportunity to reply to a few embarrassed words of the good King with equal embarrassment. I have an even more vivid recollection of a court concert I had to conduct soon thereafter, again in uniform, and at which a case of downright insubordination on my part put my friend and superior Baron Franckenstein in an awkward position. The court guests had taken their places, the King and Queen slightly in front of the first row center, my orchestra was ready to begin, but no tapping of my baton would induce the assembly to stop their loud talking or even to lower their voices. Franckenstein motioned to me again and again with his ceremonial staff to begin, but I did not care to play a symphony by Haydn or Mozart as an accompaniment to court conversation. I waited. Franckenstein, in despair, dispatched one of his officials, who whispered to me with a most amiable face that I would cause serious unpleasantness to the General Manager unless I started at once. So I struck in with the *forte* indicated in the score, but at once directed the orchestra by word and gesture to continue *pianissimo*. It turned out that I had calculated correctly. The visible but inaudible concert caused surprise and amazement. The quieter the audience grew the more I permitted the orchestra to increase its sound. Everything turned out well in the end. Franckenstein had enough sense of humor not to take offense at my attitude.

There came June 28, 1914, and the Sarajevo assassination of the heir to the Austrian throne and his wife. Exciting weeks followed. The threat of hostilities grew. Then came the declarations of war. When, on July 31, I stepped from the stage entrance of the Prince Regent Theater out into the warm summer afternoon during the first intermission of an opera I was conducting, the sinister roll of drums, already referred to, crashed against my ear, announcing the outbreak of war.

Wild rumors were current in Munich. Dynamite was said to have been found near the railway bridges. A tall woman with a market basket had been exposed in a train as a Russian spy, and there had been a bomb in the basket. Serb agents were living in Munich hotels under assumed names. One evening, when I was walking with my wife and an acquaintance through the crowded Kaufingerstrasse, a thin man of hysterical appearance suddenly pointed at me, shouting: "A Serbian! A Serbian!" I replied at once: "I am not from Serbia, but you" — here I pointed at my head — "are surely from Eglfing." Eglfing was the seat of the state insane asylum, and my hint had a magic effect. A good-natured grin appeared on the face of the hysterical man. That kind of talk was a sure means of identification. "No offense, neighbor!" he said with a laugh, and went on his way.

Another more serious case of suspected espionage was to cause me a good deal of worry. My family were still in Kreuth, and Gabrilowitsch, too, was in his country house there. One morning at the theater I was called to the telephone and heard Clara Gabrilowitsch's voice say: "A terrible thing has happened. Ossip . . ." Here the conversation was interrupted. I realized at once that the general fear of spies had led to the arrest of Gabrilowitsch, who was a Russian. I learned that he had been at a meal with his family when he suddenly became aware of his house being surrounded. He was not permitted to change from his rustic clothes and was taken to the prison at Tegernsee, and from there to Munich. I hurried to Police Headquarters. The whereabouts of the prisoner were ascertained, but I was regretfully informed that nothing could be done: the authorities had to proceed very rigorously against spies. I was prepared for the worst when I understood the implication of the ominous words, but the Chief of Police, whom I had finally managed to interview, proved a compassionate man. "Personally," he said, "I can't do a thing. These matters are handled by the military authorities, and you won't have any luck there either. If you are really convinced of Herr Gabrilowitsch's innocence and are ready to vouch for him, try your luck with the clerics." This reminded me that the Catholic Church was still the supreme power in Bavaria. I asked Franckenstein, who greatly admired Gabrilowitsch as an artist and a man, to help me, and we called on Nuncio Pacelli, of whose noble personality and love of music I had heard a good deal. The Nuncio listened to us with sympathy and promised us his help. Ossip was a free man the next day. He was permitted to take lodgings at the Hotel Vier Jahreszeiten. There he was reunited with his wife and child. He utilized the days before his departure not only to settle his own affairs but to offer through his lawyer confidential help to a number of friends whom he thought the outbreak of the war might have put in an awkward predicament. Gabrilowitsch and his family went to Zurich and later to America. The sympathetic and helpful Nuncio Eugenio Pacelli was made Pope in March, 1939, taking the name of Pius XII.

IV

THE WAR posed many problems at the theater. As the responsible head of the Opera, I was declared "indispensable." The uninterrupted functioning of the important institutes of art all over Germany was considered essential. But the induction of a number of the theater's staff made things difficult. The French and Italian repertories had to be curtailed to prevent nationalist demonstrations. I also had to abandon works requiring an enlarged orchestra. Strauss was very much against that and reproached me for not putting on his *Elektra*. When I pointed out to him that the score called for eight clarinets, and that I did not have that number, nor seven, six, or even five, he replied: "Four will do!" He would not listen to my objection that that would mean the elimination of some important voices. I was greatly surprised to see that he was less affected by the corruption of his most important work than by its absence from the Munich repertory. There were unpleasantnesses of a different kind. The newspapers, for instance, fulminated against the retention of my first solo cellist Disclez, because he was a Belgian, an enemy alien. The man was both an excellent musician and a fine fellow generally. I succeeded in keeping him at his desk throughout the war, a fact that proved that, all counter-currents notwithstanding, it was then still possible to appeal to reason and tolerance.

In spite of these and other effects of the war, the Munich Opera flourished, and if I had required an incentive to do my very utmost it would have been supplied by the wish to make people more than ever conscious of the serious importance of art and to demonstrate as far as lay in my power the genuineness of cultural values as opposed to the delusion I considered the leitmotif of the world's history. The six harps, to be sure, which had presented themselves to my unbelieving gaze during the Festival Plays of 1912 and 1913, had shrunk to the usual pitiful two, which, counter to Wagner's instructions, had been resignedly accepted the world over by conductors of the *Ring*. I had to be content also with a reduction in the strings, but I insisted upon the maintenance of the full number of wind instruments required by Wagner.

There was one first violinist I could count on for the Festival Plays at the Prince Regent Theater throughout the war — a volunteer who was not a regular member of the orchestra. He was the highly popular Prince Ludwig Ferdinand, a zealous physician and enthusiastic violinist. The rather corpulent man with the brownish-blond beard and friendly blue eyes actually radiated democracy. He was as popular with the stagehands as with the members of the orchestra. He never failed to place on the table of my room in the Prince Regent Theater a bottle of French champagne — when such things were still obtainable — and insisted on taking me and my family home in his car after the performance. His place in the orchestra changed between the second and the third desks. If there were solos provided for the second desk, as for instance in *Lohengrin,* I would say to him: "Your Royal Highness will have to play at the third desk today," to which he would reply with a somewhat resigned: "All right, maestro! All right!" There were times when he would add reproachfully in his broad Bavarian dialect: "And to think that I've brought my Bergonzi along today." He was very proud of this Italian violin, and even when he had been shunted to the fifth desk, as for instance in *Palestrina,* he never omitted to ask me on the way home, flatteringly overestimating the acuteness of my ear: "Maestro, how did my violin sound today?" My hypocritical words of praise gave him much joy. He usually sat bent forward while playing, his shortsighted eyes behind large spectacles anxiously focused on the notes. At difficult passages, such as occur in the third act of *Siegfried,* he would entirely disappear behind the desk and emerge only when smooth water had been reached again. When I performed Pfitzner's *Die Rose vom Liebesgarten,* which begins with an F-sharp that is taken up and repeated for some time by all kinds of instruments, he enthusisatically shook the composer's hand and uttered the classic words: "A single tone! But it's fine!" Prince Ludwig Ferdinand was a simple, modest, friendly man, a "jolly good fellow." The popularity he enjoyed in Munich was quite genuine. When I met him at the theater during the disturbances of November 1918 and said to him: "Your Royal Highness ought not to go in the street, it is dangerous," he replied: "My people won't do anything to me." And he was right.

I was responsible for the first performance of Erich Wolfgang Korngold's two one-act operas, *The Ring of Polycrates* and *Violanta,* in March, 1916. These works revealed the young man's remarkable musical and dramatic talent. He was the son of the musical critic Dr. Julius Korngold, and I naturally knew him from Vienna, where I had become acquainted with other compositions of his and had even performed some of them. It was Mahler who had first told me of the six- or seven-year-old boy whom his father had brought to see him and by whose musicianship and precocity he had been strongly impressed. The pantomime *The Snowman,* which Korngold had written at the age of eleven, was performed at the Vienna Court Opera, and I still recall the charming melodies and the strange sense of form of that juvenile composition. Rosé, Buxbaum, and I had given a very interesting and harmoniously daring piano trio of his its first performance. When the eighteen-year-old composer played for me his two operas, giving them a rousing performance on the piano, I thought they were so full of music and at the same time so genuine in their fiery dramatics that I immediately accepted them for Munich. They were a great success, and I was overjoyed at having been able to champion so pronouncedly talented a composer. I knew all the members of the Korngold family. We had even lived in the same house for some years in Vienna, but the natural reserve between artist and critic prevented a close contact. Only in America, long after Julius Korngold had given up his critical activity, did I become more intimately acquainted with the learned, passionate musician and mentally alert man. I liked to read his critical or scientific musical *feuilletons* in the *Neue Freie Presse* of Vienna, enjoying the masterly treatment of his themes and the force of his formulation, and watching with satisfaction his clever and high-spirited attack upon atonality and atonal composers and his struggle against those symptoms of a musical disease.

Pfitzner had completed his *Palestrina* in 1917 and entrusted to me the first performance of his masterpiece. I was made happy by the eminent task, but, at the same time, could not help feeling apprehensive lest certain daring features in the second act prove a stumbling block. What worried me was that the representation of the Tridentine Council might cause a last-minute objection on the part of the Church, perhaps even after the dress rehearsal, and that the performance might be prohibited. Franckenstein and I forestalled this by paying a visit to a high Church dignitary in Munich and by telling him just enough of the second act to arouse his interest. We even hinted at certain poetic and dramatic licenses, without, however, mentioning any of the striking details that might displease him. He seemed to be favorably disposed and promised to attend the *première*. As it turned out later, the seriousness and depth of the work proved so irresistible that neither in Munich nor in Vienna nor in any other prominently Catholic city did the daring details of the Council scene give any offense. Personally, I count the performance of *Palestrina*, which I consider the mightiest musical dramatic work of our time, among the great events of my life. Unforgettable are the weeks spent in preparing and rehearsing the masterpiece. So extraordinary was the effect produced by the performance and so outstanding an accomplishment of the Munich Opera was it considered that the thought was conceived to send us on a propaganda tour to Switzerland to demonstrate to the world the high level of German operatic art in the third winter of the war.

And so, one fine day, a special train carried the entire *Palestrina* apparatus — soloists, orchestra, chorus, technical personnel, and scenery — to Zurich, where the noble new work was to be shown to the outside world by one of the great German operatic institutes. The heavy military traffic caused a great many delays. Once, we were unexpectedly delayed beyond the Swiss border. Almost everybody availed himself of the opportunity to take a first short walk in neutral air. I can still see one of our female chorus singers stop with amazement in front of a delicatessen store of the small Swiss town and, with tears in her eyes, gaze at the hams and white bread in the window. Such things had been unobtainable in Munich for a long time. Others rushed to a boot shop to provide themselves hurriedly with some decent Swiss footwear. We got to Zurich one hour and a half late. Pfitzner was waiting for us at the station. While en route, I had pictured to myself the composer's satisfac-

ARTURO TOSCANINI, BRUNO WALTER,
AND STEFAN ZWEIG, 1937

LOTTE LEHMANN, BRUNO WALTER, AND ERIKA MANN
(*standing*) AND THOMAS MANN (*seated*), 1943

tion at having the whole Munich Opera start on a pilgrimage for the sake of his work. But he disappointed me. When I alighted from the train and hurried toward him, he pulled his watch from his pocket and said reproachfully: "I've been waiting here for an hour and a half."

The performance took place on the following evening. Again Pfitzner disappointed me. The first act had been more beautiful than ever, and the deeply stirred audience gave enthusiastic expression to its emotion and approval. I had difficulty, though, in dragging Pfitzner before the curtain to acknowledge the applause. He was depressed because Schipper, the Borromeo, at his wrathful exit, had merely snatched up his red cardinal's cloak from the chair on which he had deposited it at his entrance and thrown it over his arm instead of draping it round his shoulders. "Can you imagine a cardinal in the streets of Rome with his cloak over his arm? I can't." These were Pfitzner's words, and his depression continued. Next evening, in Basle, I threatened Schipper with all the punishments of hell if he were again to forget to put the cloak round his shoulders. He heeded my warning, and after the first act Pfitzner fell on my neck and said that now he was happy. The third performance took place in Berne, and on the following day our train carried us back to Munich and to the deprivations that in 1917 had become oppressively noticeable.

In my own family, too, malnutrition had made itself painfully felt. In order to cope with the difficulties of provisioning our home, we had engaged a housekeeper whose efficiency, vouched for by splendid references, was to bring about an adjustment between hunger and the food laws. Fräulein Lahr, a woman of steely character, whose whole appearance, too, somehow suggested steel, was as rigid in her attitude as her body was bereft of any of the usual feminine curves. Merciless, she kept us on short rations. In those days, while the cities were starving, the villages still had enough food. To be on good terms with a farmer was worth more than to know a black marketeer. But Fräulein Lahr was against taking advantage of the well-stocked condition of the rural districts. She luxuriated, as it were, in our deprivations. Although some sacrificially minded adherents secretly helped us along from time to time, we made the evil discovery one day that our younger daughter was suffering from malnutrition. We had just arrived at the place chosen for our summer sojourn and, on the following day, had to take the feverish child back to the Pfaundler Children's Clinic in Munich. The sickroom became a favorite meetingplace for doctors and nurses who felt attracted by the sparkling wit and the high-spirited notions of the little patient and were loath to tear themselves away. But the child continued to ail, and even a stay of several weeks in a sanatorium in Oberstdorf failed to return her to complete health. Fräulein Lahr had left us before the child fell ill. My two daughters, so amiable as a rule, had secretly conspired to drive out the domestic tyrant by means of mischievous excesses. The dark plan was successful. After a metallically clanking short notice she left our house without stating the true reason of her precipitate flight. It was only much later that it was divulged by the triumphant miscreants.

In the meantime, my work and my responsibilities in Munich had grown and become more onerous. Besides, I could not decline all the invitations for guest appearances. Some of them came from Vienna, and I felt morally impelled to accept them.

During the early months of 1913 I had had to go back to Vienna several times to conduct the rehearsals and the performance of Verdi's Requiem with the Vienna Singakademie, whose leadership I subsequently relinquished. But many were the times when I had to make the eight-hour rail trip because the musical life of Vienna would not loosen its hold on me. There was not a year of the ten I spent in Munich during which I was not called back to Vienna to conduct concerts of the Philharmonic, the Konzertverein, and the Tonkünstler Orchestras or, later, to take charge of choral concerts of the Philharmonic Chorus. It was not easy for me, the General Musical Director of Bavaria, to grant a leave of absence to the Vienna guest conductor. Besides, the inconveniences grew as the war progressed and conditions became more difficult. I recall icy-cold night trips in the winter of 1917 in unheated cars with broken or wood-covered windows. Yet, Vienna remained the powerful magnet in my life, and I was less able to resist its attraction as conditions there grew sadder.

Occasionally, I had to conduct in Berlin, Frankfurt-am-Main, Cologne, Mannheim, and other cities. I recall with special pleasure a trip to Speyer, in whose magnificent ancient cathedral I conducted Beethoven's *Missa Solemnis* after I had performed it with the Teachers' Singing Society and my orchestra in Munich. I recall that occasion all the more vividly because it marked the first time that I introduced a musical rendition with a lecture. The concert itself was to have taken place several days later. The particular problematics of the dearly beloved work, in which musical, spiritual, personal, and visionary prophetic elements combine to form a mighty monument of inspired human creativeness, induced me to give utterance to my views, supporting them by musical examples on the piano. Because I received the impression that I had been helpful to my audience in preparing them spiritually and emotionally for the coming event, I returned to the lecture desk on a number of future occasions, but only in rare cases of a similar nature, when I hoped that words would clarify artistic problems. Generally, however, I adhered to the principle of playing music and keeping quiet.

My unusual extramusical effort in behalf of Beethoven's work had also a moral reason for which I was able to account to myself only later: it seems that I wanted to make up to Beethoven for my sins against Bach. For I hereby confess that I transgressed in Munich against the *St. Matthew Passion*. For ten years, with the splendid soloists, chorus, and instrumentalists at my disposal there, I performed Bach's work with cuts. This was unjustifiable, and weighed heavily on my conscience. And yet, I seemed unable, partly because of the overwhelming amount of my operatic and concert work, fully to recognize the extent of my transgression, nor had I the strength to insist upon an unmutilated performance, which alone could have done justice to Bach. I sinned in permitting myself to be kept from penetrating to the ultimate depths of the work and in accepting the cuts former performances of the *Passion* had made traditional. Fortunately, I cannot recall similar transgressions in the course of my career. As far as that one is concerned, my confession is made somewhat easier by the fact that I gave a New York performance of the *Passion* in 1943 in its entirety and after a most painstaking preparation. The work is an organic whole, and he who meddles with it violates it as well as a fundamental law of art.

A sense of sincerity seems to require me to define my attitude toward the First World War. Although I was fully convinced of the outrageous conduct of Baron Berchtold, the Austrian Secretary of Foreign Affairs, and of the grave mistakes made by the German Kaiser and other personages in the governments of the Central Powers, and though I had been horrified by Germany's violation of Belgium's neutrality and by Bethmann-Hollweg's reference to a "scrap of paper," my heart was still partial to Germany and Austria. I wished to see preserved undamaged the cultural life in which I had my roots. So closely was I in contact with noble spiritual currents and high moral tendencies in both countries; so wholly was I cut off from contacts with the outside world; and so constantly was I under the influence of spoken and printed pro-German propaganda that I wished with all my heart a termination of the war that would assure their world position to the Germany and Austria I loved — not to the Germany of the Kaiser and the Junkers, but to that of Goethe, Hölderlin, Beethoven, and Bach, and to the Austria of Mozart, Schubert, and Grillparzer. I was not a chauvinist by any means, nor did I take part in the so-called "Professors' Declaration" against England. It goes without saying that I never entertained any feeling of hatred either. Wilson's Fourteen Points and especially the demand for the peoples' right of self-determination made me feel hopeful. Yet, I considered the outcome of the war a misfortune and looked forward to Europe's future with fearful presentiments.

V

ON November 9th, 1918, the *Münchener Neueste Nachrichten* carried the news that the King and the Queen had been deposed, that Bavaria was a Republic, and that Kurt Eisner and other members of the Left had taken over the government. The past few days had witnessed angry street scenes between soldiers and officers. Rumors concerning mutinies in the fleet and the formation of Workingmen's and Soldiers' Councils were current. As bad luck would have it, Pfitzner happened to give a concert on the evening of November 8. So perturbed were the few courageous people in the audience by successive horror reports and by the sound of distant shooting that, one by one, they left the concert. Pfitzner thought that nobody but he could have been singled out for so revolutionary an inconvenience. If my memory serves me, he came to my house afterward, and we anxiously discussed the situation without foreseeing the decision the newspapers were to convey to us on the following morning.

Franckenstein telephoned me at seven in the morning, and we made an appointment to meet in Kaufingerstrasse. While we were walking back and forth, he explained to me that the elimination of the Court meant that his hour, too, had struck and that he would have to leave. I replied that, after almost six years of collaboration, I felt so closely bound up with him that I did not feel like staying on without him. He would not listen to that, but implored me to preserve what we two had built up. I should stay and protect from possible revolutionary destruction what in its deepest sense was more important than the political events in store for us. Thus we walked about for hours, and in spite of the weightiness of Franckenstein's arguments I was unable to reach a decision. At the theater, there was a revolutionary meeting at which it was decided to depose not only Franckenstein, but also Zollner and other administrative officials. The actor Viktor Schwanneke was made the supreme representative of all the operatic and dramatic members of the house. He came to see me and asked me in the name of the artists to take over the entire direction of the Opera, which meant merely a continuation of my work without the benefit of Franckenstein's co-operation. He told me that the direction of the drama had been offered to and accepted by Albert Steinrück. I replied that I would have to have time to consider before making a decision. I wanted to see my way clearly. Realizing that a system of councils in the theater might hamper me artistically, I decided to wait and see which way the movement was swinging — to disorder or order, to obstruction or the support of an energetic artistic leadership.

After careful deliberation I recognized that all my personal feelings and moods counted as nothing against the thought that Franckenstein, too, had emphasized: what had been accomplished at the theater had to be preserved; the work had to go on. My way was clearly defined. The political changes must not be allowed to interfere with either the working methods or the artistic discipline of the house. I must vigorously use what reputation I had gained to protect the theater against interference from outside and infringement from inside.

The new Prime Minister requested Steinrück and me to call for a discussion of the situation. At the government building I met excited crowds of soldiers brandishing rifles. Young civilians with red brassards and hoarse voices were milling about. Our conference with Kurt Eisner was continually disturbed by undisciplined comings and goings. The chief of government, a former dramatic critic, showed himself more interested in Steinrück's task than in mine, but I could not help feeling on our way back that in spite of, or perhaps because of, Eisner's interest in the drama Steinrück rather shared my misgivings concerning any direct relations of the theater with the new men. It was clear to me that a purely political government department, irrespective of its tendency, was unsuited to the administration of institutes of art. The heads of such a department could not be expected to be artistically interested, while they would moreover be likely to infuse politics into the theater. I also realized that, since there was no longer a Court and the theaters had therefore to depend upon the state for the necessary subsidies, the Ministry of Education was the only logical government department to take care of the cultural interests of the country. Quick action on my part was needed if I wanted to protect art against interference from the excited political center of the new government. I took the necessary steps that very day. Ministers changed, I knew, but the lower officials usually remained in office. So I applied to the highest of the lower officials in the Ministry of Education, Dr. Korn. The man seemed delighted to see me and declared himself ready to do all in his power to have the National Theater included in his administrative sphere. There was a meeting in which Steinrück, myself, Ministerialrat Dr. Korn, and the chosen trustees of all the members of the theater took part. The representatives of the theater realized that the well-trained and still stable apparatus of the Ministry of Education held out the promise of a steadier method of administration than that of any other government department. An agreement was reached. It proved entirely expedient and practicable. I worked in cordial agreement with Dr. Korn to the end of my Munich activity. Safely anchored, the theater was able to weather the storms of the following revolutionary changes.

I expected that the days after the overthrow would decide whether my activity could be continued in an atmosphere of indispensable order and discipline or whether the artistic personnel would try to subject my directorial measures to a control for whose results I would not be willing to take the responsibility. The decision was favorable. I was to have no complaints about any encroachments on my rights. I heard that unruly elements were making work difficult in the drama, but in my own domain there was a gratifying continuation of the good old relationship between myself and the soloists, choristers, and members of the orchestra. From the first, when I had entered upon my duties in Munich, I had favored the system of "trustees" in the orchestra. They were to submit to me every wish or complaint. Soon they were convinced of my sincere sympathy with the economic and social problems of the musicians. The system was now continued. It was adopted also by the soloists, who chose Karl Erb and Paul Bender as their representatives. They, too, discussed with me peaceably the affairs of their group. Neither at my rehearsals nor in connection with my administrative activities did I meet anything but a spirit of unaltered confidence. Under these circumstances, the Opera continued its vigorous life, and the transfer of the theater from the Crown to the state — or, if you will, from the King to the people — would have been effected quietly if the state or the people had settled down peacefully after the November revolution.

But the opposite was the case. Revolution and counter-revolution, pressure from abroad and a passionate reaction from the interior created an atmospheric condition that kept the political barometer continuously at a low point. I foresaw from newspaper reports, and I felt wherever I was — on a streetcar, in a restaurant, at the homes of friends, in the street — that the excitement was bound to lead to explosions. When, late in February, Kurt Eisner was shot by Count Arco, I held my breath. Disaster was in the air. It broke like a thunderstorm. Machine guns were posted in the squares, at corners, and on the bridges; riotous crowds assembled; on the walls appeared placards with ordinances, nullified by other placards with other ordinances; houses were searched. Acquaintances came, warning us of impending measures against the "propertied classes" and of attacks on the districts in which they lived.

Certain occurrences rise up in my memory. It is evening, and ghostlike figures are seen digging in an adjoining garden: they are burying silver and other valuable objects. Whispered words across a garden fence: no trains are leaving Munich, and wall placards are summoning every owner of a safe-deposit box to appear with his key at the bank at eleven on the following morning. But don't go! Nobody must go, in spite of the fact that non-appearance calls for dire punishment. All arms must be surrendered on pain of death. Barbed wires shut off the passage from the Court Garden to Maximilianstrasse, but I get a typewritten slip of paper, saying: "Bearer of this, Operndirektor Bruno Walter, may pass through the barbed wire from the Court Garden to Maximilianstrasse." I hurry home from the theater. My wife, wringing her hands in despair, informs me that the children and their governess have gone into town. I hurry back. There is shooting at the Isar Bridge. After an hour, things quiet down. I find the children and their governess in Widenmayrstrasse, chatting animatedly about the many interesting events. I take them home. One day, the younger one falls ill. Measles, the doctor says. In the evening, the shadows are whispering again at the garden fences. Soldiers on trucks are rushing through the city, looting, arresting. It is eleven at night. A truck stops at a neighbor's house. Through the blinds of my unlighted room I watch soldiers run into the house. Fifteen minutes later, they come out again noisily. I learn later that they had been treated to wine. Now they are at the other neighbor's. Our turn next. My wife and I are discussing what we had better tell them. Blows at our gate. I open, and am confronted in my entrance hall by eight or ten armed men, no longer quite sober, demanding to search my house. I say something about a sick child. It makes no impression. I produce my slip of paper, permitting me to pass through the barbed wire. The paper has a miraculous effect: "Why didn't you say so right away? Let's go!" Out tumble the would-be marauders, climb onto the truck, and rush off.

Things grew worse, and I had to admit to myself that I was not made to "live dangerously," at least not in the sense indicated by the prevailing circumstances. I do not remember whether there were any performances at the theater, but our decision to leave Munich makes me assume that it was closed at least temporarily. When we met trustworthy people in the street, we exchanged whispered news. That was how I learned that on a certain evening a train for Tegernsee would be leaving from Holzkirchner Station. Since our child had in the meantime got over her attack of measles, we assembled the most necessary luggage, managed to hunt up a cab, and went to the station. A number of soldiers with red brassards brusquely sent us back again because we had no official documents. It was then that I remembered the German awe of official stamps. I hurried to the office of the theater, took out the rather worn barbed-wire slip, and covered it with every stamp I could lay my hands on: "Approved . . . The General Management . . . Complimentary ticket . . . The Box Office . . . Property of the Munich State Theaters . . . Settled." We put on our oldest clothes, strapped rucksacks to our backs, and returned to the station. Approaching the guard in an assumed attitude of utter indifference and greeting him with a Bavarian *Grüss Gott!* I casually held out to him my stamp-covered slip. The man saluted. We passed him leisurely and got to the ticket office, and to the train. After a ride that took four hours instead of the usual hour and a half we were at quieter Tegernsee, where we decided to wait until conditions had become more bearable.

The "Republic of Councils," proclaimed on April 7, 1919, came to an end when the Prussian and Bavarian Free Corps marched in early in May. Munich became quiet again, and I immediately returned from my several days' stay in Tegernsee and plunged into work. A great deal of evil had been done by both sides. For a long time, the air was pregnant with bitterness and excitement, feelings that probably never quite subsided. Work was taken up again. The message of art sent forth from the theaters and the Odeon was bound to act like a warming Gulf Stream, moderating the rough climate of political dissension. It was left to Nazism to insinuate politics even into art, to poison it, and to paralyze its salutary effect.

Although the war had been over six months, the food problem was still acute. Everything was *ersatz*. The "genuine" turnips that graced our table almost daily became a horror to parents as well as children. What a day of joy when we received the first American "food box" from Gabrilowitsch, containing the most incredible luxuries: oranges, chocolate, canned goods of all kinds, and white flour. A pancake was made at once and devoured by the children, who had tears of joy in their eyes. But how much worse off in food was Austria! The bread I got in Vienna at that time could hardly be called food any longer. It caused even robust constitutions intestinal and stomach trouble.

Because conditions were improving only very gradually, I decided to spend the summer holidays with my family in Switzerland. We went to the Engadine, which I had never seen before and which at once became dear to my heart. Until 1939, we spent not only our summer weeks of leisure there, but also some time each winter. Although I was opposed to Nietzsche's anti-Christianity, his anti-Wagnerianism, his superman ideology, and even his aphoristic way of writing, I enthusiastically walked along the mountain paths used by the high-minded ecstatic man, visited the house in Sils Maria where *Zarathustra* had come into existence, gazed upon the sublime mountains, breathed the pure air that had inspired such lofty thoughts, and tarried on the Chasté peninsula, where he had written *O Man, Beware!* Nowhere have I met a nobler beauty than that of the Engadine's mountain world, and every walk meant happiness — until a horrible event caused the beloved sites around St. Moritz, Pontresina, and Sils Maria to become inescapably associated in my mind with the spirit of disaster.

Louise Wolff, head of the Berlin concert management, invited me to conduct a yearly cycle of symphony concerts with the Berlin Philharmonic Orchestra. That was how the "Bruno Walter Concerts" came into being. They grew into a regular feature of Berlin's concert life, until the year 1933 put a forcible end to them. My programs, made up of classic and contemporary music, proved attractive to the Berlin audiences, and I am fond of recalling that young Dmitri Shostakovitch's First Symphony, which he had played for me in Leningrad in 1926, had its first performance outside Russia at those concerts. They were responsible also for the first appearance in Berlin of the then eleven-year-old Yehudi Menuhin, whose serious precocity made a profound impression. I remember that Albert Einstein's gaze from his seat in the front row conveyed to me his surprise and enthusiasm. On another evening, I introduced Vladimir Horowitz to Berlin. Rachmaninoff, too, made his first appearance — or perhaps it was the first one after the war — with me. He captivated me by his original, sovereign personality as well as by his playing.

My Berlin concerts also led to the establishment of cordial relations and a friendly intercourse with Peter Landeker, the owner of Berlin's Philharmonic Hall, and his wife Mariechen. I had met them both at the Kreuth home of their friend Gabrilowitsch several years before. Now they opened to me their heart and their home. In those days, the homes of Landeker and Louise Wolff were among the most distinguished musical *salons* of the Reich capital. All the prominent musicians living in or visiting Berlin frequented the stimulating evenings at "Louise's" or "Peter's." From the Landeker home on Hafenplatzs, whose brisk traffic was familiar to me from childhood days, an inside passage led to Philharmonic Hall. After every one of my concerts, we walked through that secret passage to the festive board spread in the beautiful old-Berlin home, where animated conversation and the presence of interesting people usually kept us until a late hour. A festive spirit also reigned there after the Nikisch concerts, and I was privileged to spend some splendid evenings in the company of that superlative conductor and warmhearted and noble man. Unfortunately, these evenings were all too few, for my own concerts and rehearsals in Munich permitted me only rarely to visit Berlin. When we again took up our domicile there, Nikisch was dead.

I recall that the cause of one of those rare Berlin visits was a charity performance of Johann Strauss's *Die Fledermaus,* which I had been asked to conduct. It has remained in my memory because it gave me the opportunity to meet Fritzi Massary, the darling of the Berliners and light opera's most powerful magnet. I had expected to meet a *diva* type, spoiled by popularity, and feared that to come to an understanding concerning the airy and exuberantly Viennese style of the Strauss masterpiece would be connected with all kinds of difficulties. Instead, I found a great artist who disdained popular routine and centered all of her highly-tensed nature upon the essentialities of her task. The rapport between us did not have to be established, it existed from the first moment. Fritzi Massary combined in her person the talents of a *diseuse à la Yvette Guilbert,* the fabulous instinct for accentuating or dropping a point, the brilliant faculty for spreading a congenial mood, and the charm of piquant femininity and genuine musicality. It was bewitching to see her relax her intensity and assume the laughing sprightliness and charming frivolity of Adele. Those who have seen her jump on a table in the second act of *Die Fledermaus,* listened to her jubilant singing with the champagne glass in her hand, and watched her whirling dance following it, will not likely ever forget that inimitable picture of radiant *joie de vivre.* Fritzi Massary sang Adele when I conducted the Zurich Festival Plays, and, in 1926, I invited her to take the part at a performance at the Salzburg Festival Plays. From our first artistic co-operation, I regretted that so charming a personality should waste her exceptional theatrical and musical talent on the largely inferior productions of musical entertainment literature, with their long runs of performances. I asked myself if I had not in her found the Carmen for whom I had been searching so long a time. When I took over the Berlin Municipal Opera, I suggested that she undertake the part of Carmen. She considered my proposition very seriously, but, with the conscientiousness and self-discipline characteristic of her, declared that she did not feel equal to the vocal demands of the part. Thus, my attempts to gain for the German stage a real Carmen failed because of the artistic seriousness of a brilliant representative of the "light Muse."

In the spring of 1920, I accepted an invitation from the Teatro Liceo in Barcelona to present to the Spanish public a number of the performances which had been especially acclaimed in Munich. My journey to Spain made me pass through Paris. When I had last seen it, a long time before, Mahler's illness had made me feel disinclined to become acquainted with the incomparable city. Now again I had but little time at my disposal. Soon my train carried me toward the Pyrenees and across the gloomily threatening Cerbère — which did full justice to its name — to the then very gay and lively Barcelona. I liked the beautiful town and its magnificent surroundings. I enjoyed the fine view from Monte Tibidabo: the white expanse, the blue sea, and far-distant Montserrat with its legend of the Grail. I also liked the gorgeous Teatro Liceo and its enthusiastic audiences, and was interested in the baroque arrangement of the two proscenium boxes looking down upon either side of the stage. I can't say, though, that I was pleased, for when, at a *Tristan* performance, a slight commotion attracted my gaze to the left box I noticed that its lady occupant was trying to express by eloquent Spanish gestures her admiration of the tiara worn by her vis-à-vis — while in the space between the boxes Night and Death were being sung. During the following intermission, the eloquent lady came hurrying to the stage to pay me some compliments in the gloomy French spoken by the Spaniards. In reply, I told her how thoroughly I disapproved of her conduct and left her as ungraciously as Knight Delorges had left Fräulein Kunigund in Schiller's *The Glove*.

When I had conducted the spring season in Barcelona for a number of years, I felt it my duty to witness one of Spain's *corridas*. The bull fight fascinated me — up to the point when it actually began. The conflux of gaily clad people on foot, in carriages, in buses, in rustic vehicles, and in painted, high-wheeled, donkey-drawn carts; the spacious arena and the anticipatory excitement of the crowd, the skill of the sweets vendors who, when yelled at from far up, would hurl their merchandise and catch the flung coin with unfailing accuracy; the colorful entry of the *picadores, banderilleros,* and others; and finally the impressive dignity of the *espada*, striding all by himself — all these details had the effect on me of a historical and festive event. Grandiose was the moment of tension and quiet preceding the bull's sudden rush into the arena, his faltering, and the lowering of his head. But from the moment when the *banderilleros* began to torment the animal I took sides against the crowd, which seemed to be madly delighted with the danger to the magnificent beast and its daring tormentors. I also took sides against the skilled, elegant fighters, and my feelings finally rose to the wholly unsportsmanlike conviction that the bull was the noblest creature in all that wide space. When the horses had been wounded severely, the *espada* had at last gracefully killed the bull and been madly applauded for it, I left the arena, went back to my hotel and to bed, to recover from the depressing effect of a popular festival that was thoroughly foreign and repulsive to me.

I returned to Munich. A general strike had caused the failure of the Kapp *Putsch,* in March 1920. While the increasing feeling of unrest that followed did not affect my operatic and concert activities, it greatly influenced my thoughts. I tried to fathom the meaning of Bavaria's decided turn to the Right, of the medieval, secret *Vehme* proceedings, of the strange acts of violence in the streets, and of the movement which, under the artificially and discordantly sounding name of *Nationalsozialistische Deutsche Arbeiterpartei* — National Socialist German Workingmen's Party — invited people to attend its meetings. The old magic forms of the swastikas and the blood-red color of the placards aroused within me a dull feeling of horror and disgust.

VI

THE MOST interesting production of my Munich period took place in the year 1920. It was Walter Braunfels's *Die Vögel.* Those who were privileged to hear Karl Erb's song of man's yearning and Maria Ivogün's comforting voice of the nightingale from the treetop, and those who were cheered by the grotesque scenes and moved by the romantic ones, will surely remember with gratitude the poetic and ingenious transformation of Aristophanes' comedy into an opera. The composer was the son of the translator of Spanish dramas, Ludwig Braunfels, and the son-in-law of the sculptor Adolf Hildebrand. He was guided in his artistic creations by two fundamental impulses: a dramatic repletion and an intense religiosity, both of which were expressed interestingly and occasionally strikingly in his music. In addition to the Munich performance of *Die Vögel,* I produced the same composer's exceptionally fine and heartfelt *Te Deum* at the Odeon with the Teachers' Singing Society of Munich and, on a later occasion, with the Vienna Philharmonic Chorus in the Konzerthaus of that city, his clever orchestral variations on a theme by Berlioz in Berlin, Leipzig, and New York. Braunfels, the director of the Cologne College of Music, was an excellent pianist as well as a thorough connoisseur of church music. When the Nazis forced him to relinquish his Cologne position in 1933, he retired with his family to a small village on Lake Constance. There, in the quiet imposed on him by fate, he wrote an opera based on Grillparzer's *The Dream — A Life,* which I accepted for performance when I was at the head of the Vienna Opera but was no longer able to produce. Thereafter, I met Braunfels several times at the Winterthur home of Werner Reinhart, a Swiss lover of the arts. The composer, yearning for human companionship, frequently made the two-hour trip from his quiet village for the sake of a friendly interchange of thoughts. He became immersed more and more in Catholic thinking and feeling. At our last meeting, he played for me parts of an opera based upon a religious play by the poet Paul Claudel.

In the spring of 1920, Karl Muck appeared at my office in the Munich State Opera. After his highly successful activity in Boston, the United States government had considered him politically suspicious and interned him for a considerable period in Fort Oglethorpe. He had now returned to Germany and indicated his wish to take part again in the musical life of Germany. I had not seen him in almost twenty years and was moved by the contrast between the energetic, firm, and caustically sarcastic man in his forties whom I remembered and the serious and obviously tired man of more than sixty now facing me. I suggested that he take over part of the Wagner Summer Festival Plays at the Prince Regent Theater and also some of my symphony concerts at the Odeon. He fell in with my suggestion and proved that he had lost none of his mastery. His clear interpretative style revealed simplicity, greatness, and strength. These Munich guest appearances led to extremely amicable personal relations between us. Whenever I happened to be in Hamburg, the leadership of whose Philharmonic Concerts he had undertaken and where he was greatly revered, I never failed to meet him. I always enjoyed his company, for he was an accomplished conversationalist. Our new and closer relations made it clear to me that the Mephistophelian features and the sardonic expression of the thin, dark-haired man of less than medium height were a veneer. He was at heart a soft, serious, and unmocking man who barricaded his vulnerability behind sharp words and cutting remarks. I appeared as guest conductor of his orchestra the last time I saw him. He was seventy-one, aged beyond his years, and looked almost decayed. At that time, in 1932, the disease of Nazism was already virulent in the body of the German people. It was the year before Hitler came to power. Muck greeted me in the artists' room with a smile of joy which irradiated and rejuvenated his already senile features. He sat in his box, where he could be seen by everybody in the hall, and took part in the applause ostentatiously and to the very last. We had never discussed political questions, but it was quite like him thus to show his frame of mind. And, by the way, never, up to 1933, did I have to contend with hostile political demonstrations at any of my concerts or operatic performances.

During Festival-Play time and also during the winter season, musically inclined foreigners gradually found their way back to Munich. A young English conductor, Dr. Adrian Boult, visited me in the summer of 1921. I was as interested in being informed by him about musical life in England as he was eager to have news of musical conditions in Germany. We have never lost contact with each other since that first meeting. His exceptional artistic seriousness, his optimistic views of life, and his lofty aspirations made a deep impression on me and were revealed more convincingly at every new meeting. When the facilities of the British Broadcasting Corporation's musical department were enlarged, Boult was given a leading position, and there is no praise high enough for what he did on behalf of creating and developing its Orchestra, forming its programs, and endeavoring to vitalize English musical life. He did it in a manner as sincere as it was unpretentious and disdainful of outward splendor. He grew to be my friend in the course of years and has remained my friend to this day.

Mention must here be made of the conductor of the Boston Symphony Concerts of earlier days, Wilhelm Gericke, and his family. The heartwarming association with these friends contributed toward lifting the gloom of the post-war years in Munich and making my later visits to Vienna more beautiful. I had made Gericke's acquaintance years before in Vienna when, after having definitely left Boston in 1906, he contemplated settling there. In the summer of 1918, Max Kalbeck brought us together again in Munich, where Gericke and his family lived until the autumn of 1919. Because they seemed to derive pleasure from my performances and because, in addition to the general consonance of our minds, we had many interests in common, there were any number of animated meetings and discussions. I was fond of having him tell of his relations with Brahms, his many years of activity as the leader of the Vienna Gesellschaftskonzerte, and his close connection with Vienna's musical life in the days of Jahn and Richter. I was also interested in what Wilhelm and Paula Gericke had to tell me about Boston, where, during two periods of altogether thirteen years, he had done memorable pioneer work in America's musical life and rendered invaluable services in forming and developing the magnificent orchestra. Later the Gerickes left Munich again and went back to Vienna, where we met whenever my path led me there. When he died in Vienna, in 1925, an octogenarian, our friendship with the warmhearted and profoundly musical Paula Gericke and her artistically inclined daughter Käthi lost none of its intensity. After Austria's *Anschluss,* mother and daughter went back to Boston, where we visited them on a number of occasions.

The summer of 1921 was made memorable by a renewed meeting with Ossip and Clara Gabrilowitsch at St. Moritz, in the Engadine. We spent a few beautiful weeks in one another's company, and before returning to America, they looked us up in Munich. Ossip's remarkable energy, tenacity, and sacrificial spirit had made it possible for his brothers to leave Russia, where they had lived in constant danger during and after the Revolution. Their meeting in Munich was a joyful reunion. I happened to be a witness of the deeply moving moment when, after years of grievous separation, the brothers suddenly appeared at the hotel and speechlessly faced their savior.

An interesting visitor at that summer's Festival Plays was King Ferdinand of Bulgaria. Countless caricatures had made everybody familiar with his features, characterized by a prominent nose. I therefore immediately recognized the tall white-bearded man when he called at my room in the Prince Regent Theater after the first act of *Die Walküre* to give expression to his enthusiasm. The King's reputation gave him credit for exceptional political shrewdness and for superior skill in the subtle game of diplomacy. But the face of the man I saw standing before me with a friendly look in his eyes was eloquent of nothing but his deep emotion. The contrast between those political characteristics and the lofty spiritual condition now unmistakably revealed to me made me recognize for the first time the moral power of music, calling forth the best there is in man — a thought that, many years later, I tried to develop and formulate in words. The King frequently attended our Festival Plays. At a dinner tendered me by English friends at the Park Hotel, he showed that, even in an extremely democratic circle, he was a pleasant and communicative man.

It was natural that, during my last years in Munich, I should learn of agitations directed against my person. The National Socialist *Völkischer Beobachter* indulged, I was told, in orgies of insults, but I refused to read the paper and steadfastly ignored hostile sentiments, whose political weight I was unable to foretell at the time. The Opera's accomplishments and the public's attitude toward me were on the up-grade to the very day of my leaving in November 1922. The Ministry of Education, too, was co-operative to the last. Only later did I learn details of what forces had been at work against me before my departure. The choice of the new General Manager Karl Zeiss, appointed by the authorities as Schwanneke's successor, by no means indicated that the Ministry was yielding to the growing Rightist radicalism. Zeiss came from Frankfurt-am-Main, where he had gained a reputation as a literary man and efficient leader of the drama. The choice of a dramatic expert for the post of General Manager plainly showed the Minister's intentions not to disturb my circles at the Opera.

But while politics arrested my attention, and the chain of events made me feel uneasy without preventing me from attending to my artistic work, the growing inflation greatly affected the management of the theater. The gradual decline of the mark made necessary certain financial adjustments, developing into daily problems of a business as well as a moral nature. The members of the theater and the public were worried and depressed, and both my working faculty and my patience were put to hard tests. The country seemed to be seized with a general horror at this inconceivable and apparently incurable progressive economic plague. The mathematical principle of every quantity being equal to itself proved fallacious. This matter-of-course axiom no longer held true. A mark no longer was equal to a mark. Suddenly it was worth only twenty pfennigs, a few weeks later but one pfennig. The time came when one had to pay six thousand marks for a loaf of bread, and I remember that my wife told me that our cook had to pay five thousand marks for a quart of milk. After the occupation of the Ruhr, billions were spent for daily necessities. In November of that year, one thousand billion marks had the purchasing power of a single peace-time mark. On that basis, the new "sound" mark was being established. No system of orientation would do in connection with such astronomical figures, changing every day. Economic life became incalculable. Debtors were laughing, and creditors were crying, for even if a debt was adjusted to the Tuesday value of the mark, payment on Wednesday represented but a ridiculous fraction of what was actually due the creditor. Things grew worse. Besides, the infectious monetary depreciation brought in its wake a certain inflation of strength; the same result had to be accomplished by means of a multiplied effort. What was more, the murders of Erzberger in 1921 and Rathenau in 1922 glaringly illuminated the menacing effect of the Right's revolutionary fanaticism, determined to go to any length. It was natural that the knowledge of the agitations against me, though they did not as yet make themselves professionally noticeable, should contribute to a decline of my excessively exerted strength.

I had given of myself lavishly during the ten years of my work in a responsible position, and I became conscious that under such difficult artistic conditions and in view of the growing economic distress and the darkening of the political horizon I had reached the limit of my endurance. Besides, I realized ever more plainly that I had given Munich all there was in me to give and that my staying would mean no progress or growth but merely a continuation of my activity. I was reminded of Mahler's words, also after ten years of work, that he had "completed his circle." A strangely intangible, but none the less imperative dictate of an inward "sense of form" kept urging me to be off, though the idea of renouncing the wealth of duties and responsibilities that for ten years had filled my life with care and effort, but also with enthusiasm and meaning, was painful. I was grateful for the great tasks with which that period had confronted me, but I was also grateful to be able to shed the burden and renew acquaintance with myself.

Because I am trying to be quite truthful and frank in this book and to suppress nothing that influenced my more important decisions, I feel that I must at least hint at a personal motive that contributed considerably to my decision to leave Munich. Those were for me days of great and passionate involvement, bearing the seeds of tragic development. The thought of leaving Munich, generated by artistic considerations, offered a way out of a tormenting human situation. It was generally assumed that Nazi persecutions were driving me out of Munich. I repeat that to the day of my departure I was actually not made to suffer from political hostility, and that my leaving was partly caused by a feeling that I had completed my task and partly by personal considerations.

I now acquainted the Ministry of Education and General Manager Zeiss with my decision to leave my position, stating as the reason the overexertion caused not only by the many years of my work but also by the steadily growing difficulties caused by the war and the revolution. Dr. Korn and General Manager Zeiss, greatly startled, offered any relief that would make me willing to continue my work, but I declared that the general situation could lead only to an increase of my work, and surely not to a reduction. A letter from Zeiss urging me to remain in my position drew a friendly and regretful answer, but one of determined refusal. In my reply, I considered it appropriate to point out that the "currents" at work against me, though they had not caused my decision, "had contributed to my feeling of fatigue." In view of so firm an attitude the authorities could do nothing but accept the facts and look for a successor. To show its gratitude, the Ministry bestowed upon me the title of Professor and sent me a very cordially worded and gratifying written appreciation of the services I had rendered.

A letter was circulated in the city, requesting that I stay. It was signed by Munich's intellectual élite. Among the names were those of Franz Stuck, Adolf Hildebrand, Max Halbe, Ricarda Huch, Olav Gulbrannson, Thomas Theodor Heine, and, of course, Thomas Mann, Hans Pfitzner, and Paul Nikolaus Cossman. I was made happy by this show of devotion and by other manifestations of a similar kind, as well as by the public's spontaneous demonstrations at my performances. But my conviction that I must leave was unshakable.

While thus the feeling of farewell, that strange mixture of oppressiveness and relief, gradually began to take possession of my soul, my thoughts were busy with the realization of an artistic plan I had harbored for a long time. It was a question of faithfully and vividly reproducing past operatic styles, a task for which the Residenz Theater seemed to offer an ideal frame. I searched for an *opera seria,* an *opera buffa,* and a Singspiel, a playlet with interpolated music. They had to be works of art that, beyond their historical interest, would be able to hold an audience's attention musically and dramatically. I chose Handel's *Acis and Galatea,* Pergolesi's *La Serva Padrona,* and Schenk's *Der Dorfbarbier.* Preetorius was the man who would know how to impart to the Handel work its baroque atmosphere, while at the same time he could be depended on to do justice to the timeless loftiness of the final scenes. *La Serva Padrona* and *Der Dorfbarbier* offered no special problems, but rather a welcome opportunity for Preetorius's gift of adapting himself to varied styles and senses of humor. I recall with a feeling of deep gratification Delia Reinhardt's poetic representation of Galatea, Paul Bender's grotesque humor in the part of Polyphemus, Maria Ivogün's masterly Serpina in Pergolesi's work, Josef Geis's irresistibly funny barber's apprentice Adam, and the whole group of my artists in *Der Dorfbarbier.* If any detail were worthy of special mention it was that of Galatea's lament at Acis' death and her prayer to Zeus for his return. It was granted by the cleaving of the rock that had slain Acis and the gushing forth of a spring into which the god had changed the beloved youth. We thought we were justified in requiring the baroque stage to show real water and its rippling across the moss. While the chorus was singing softly, the curtain closed slowly over the transfigured reunion of the nymph and her transformed lover.

The performance afforded me the opportunity for making Walter Damrosch's personal acquaintance. His name and his activity in the musical life of America on behalf of German symphonies and Wagner's musical dramas had long been known to me. I was sincerely glad to salute the enthusiastic and youthful man of sixty and to learn to my surprise that, about thirty years before, Damrosch had been responsible for a New York scenic production of *Acis and Galatea*. We were of one mind in our enthusiasm for Handel's work. Our pleasant first meeting led to a wholly unexpected result. Damrosch invited me to go to New York as a guest conductor and take charge of his orchestra for several weeks, early in 1923. As Ossip had sent me a similar invitation from Detroit and as, moreover, Boston and Minneapolis also made me offers, I gladly accepted. So it came about that, in January of the following year, I made my first public appearance in America.

I chose *Fidelio* for my farewell performance at the Munich Opera. I recall with deep emotion the manifestations of affection with which the loyal public showered me in the theater and, after the performance, in front of the restaurant to which some friends and I had repaired. The demonstration did not stop until I had appeared on the restaurant's balcony and spoken a few words.

This probably happened in October 1922, and I remember that thereafter I began to train my gaze upon the future and upon America. There were still some concerts to be given in Vienna, and I had also accepted an invitation to appear in Bucharest. So I left Munich and did not return until it was about time to start for New York.

The political situation had become more menacing. Germany was torn by dissension. France was preparing to occupy the Ruhr. With a heavy heart I went to Hamburg, from which port, in gloomy weather, I started upon my first crossing of the stormy Atlantic Ocean.

BOOK FIVE

✿❖✿

I

THE BAROMETER was low when I boarded the *Minnetonka,* the rather unattractive medium-sized steamer that was to take me to New York. Typical Hamburg weather — that mixture of fog, rain, and wind so familiar to me — had greeted me upon my arrival at the seaport after my final concert at Berlin's Philharmonic Hall. I was filled with a strange, gnawing feeling of farewell, hardly justified by my impending absence of three months. Only much later did I fully understand it. I was reminded of it when I finally turned my back on Germany in 1933 and when, five years after that, the gates of Austria closed behind me. Even that first departure from Europe was in the nature of an uprooting, inasmuch as it signified the abandonment of a task to which my nature seemed to have predestined me: to be the guardian and keeper of a cultural institute and to make its blood circulate by the force of my heart. I had the dull feeling that, as far as Europe was concerned, a close affiliation of that kind was over for me once and for all. It seemed at least doubtful that America would offer me the chance to concentrate once more upon an important center of art. Thus the oppressive sense of leave-taking was subsequently revealed to me as a farewell to a settled artistic activity and the beginning of travels on which I would no longer be able to make full use of my powers, which were meant primarily for the cultivation of "my own soil." In fact, I have, from that time, been but a guest and wanderer. Even at the Berlin Municipal Opera, the Leipzig Gewandhaus, the Vienna State Opera, and the Salzburg Festival Plays conditions precluded the settled feeling of Munich. I still had a fixed place of work, but my walking staff was always within my reach at my side, never out of sight. With the striking of every hour came the hum of the question: how much longer? For though I continued to dedicate myself to every artistic task as if it were a sowing and my very life depended on its reaping, the knowledge never left me that the hope of a reaping could have only a transcendental meaning to me and by no means the immediate artistic one that had heretofore warmed me.

Theme and Variations

But I have never been a wanderer in the sense of Schubert's song — "a stranger everywhere" — or an exiled man or a refugee. True, I was no longer bound to the home soil, but I had surely not lost my home, for I carried it within me. And I have proved to my satisfaction that that home-feeling is not merely an illusion or an empty word. I have never felt a stranger, for I have always been enveloped in music, invigorated by the knowledge of great thoughts. More than that: how could I have lost my home when all mankind represented my fellow-citizens and I had the good fortune to speak the supernatural language of music?

Filled with that oppressive and ominous farewell feeling, I had restlessly wandered through the dark, wet streets of Hamburg and gone to the pier of the steamship line at the appointed hour. Louise Wolff, faithful and devoted, had come from Berlin to say good-by and, I presume, to enjoy the sight of a magnificent ocean liner and its stylish first-cabin crowd. The gray unattractiveness of the ship and its passengers must have fallen visibly short of her pre-war expectations, but it failed to put a damper on her glowingly optimistic descriptions of America's "bliss and splendor," toward which she saw me sailing out of the misery and the dangers of Europe. I carried a number of requests across the ocean. There was the Red Cross Hospital in Munich, whose heating facilities needed attention: its excellent head, Professor Albrecht, must have the aid of American dollars. There was the Holzen Children's Home in the Isar Valley near Munich, in which a friend of ours was greatly interested and whose maintenance I was to make possible. And there were many similar requests. In the eyes of the victims of inflation I was one of those highly privileged beings who had access to that wonder of the world: the stable American dollar. The "music of the future," produced by the jingling of the fabulous money in my pockets, filled the imagination of the reverently marveling and the fervently imploring who had made me the messenger of their entreaties.

So, an envied favorite of Fortuna, I steamed down the Elbe on the unpretentious *Minnetonka*. No sooner had we left Cuxhaven behind us than I had to forgo the sight of the disappearing coastline and submit to the discordant sounds of my stateroom's wooden groaning and creaking. I tried in vain to assuage my rebellious queasiness by lying down. It could not be done; the violent pitching and rolling of the steamer made it quite impossible.

A picture rises before me. I believe I saw it on that first one of my voyages to America: the Isle of Wight in the light of the moon reflected in turbulent waters, hurrying clouds now obscuring the disk, now letting it shine forth again, and I, the only wakeful soul, circling the night-covered deck, enjoying the quiet, pondering the old, and thinking forward to the new. We sailed away toward morning. After another stop at Belfast and a last look upon wide hilly pastures with herds of cows and flocks of sheep, we steamed out into the green desert of the ocean. The foam-crested mountains of water cast up and hurled menacingly at our ship soon forced me back again into solitary confinement.

The *Minnetonka* was no floating palace. Irrespective of the fact that "floating" was too euphemistic a term to be applied to her pitching, plunging, rearing, trembling, and groaning, the conception of a palace could not very well have been more modestly represented than by that unassuming and austere steamer. The staterooms were small and frugally equipped, the social rooms were not particularly comfortable, and the ship's regulations reminded one somewhat of barrack rules. At eight in the morning, a slow and badly sounded trumpet signal called the passengers out of their slumber and to the first breakfast. Those who did not care to get up promptly or failed to appear in the dining hall within a certain time had to go hungry. The friendly custom of serving meals in the staterooms had not as yet been reintroduced into the working arrangements of the line, owing probably to a shortage of help. The other meals, too, were uninvitingly announced by the cacophonous fanfare. Those with night-owl tendencies were forced to keep decent hours because the lights in the social rooms went out early. Among the many virtues denied me by fate that of being a good sailor stands in first place, and the wretched weather made me miss a great many meals. There were a number of calmer days, however, when I was able to occupy my place at the long common table and to convince myself that I had not missed much by having been absent so frequently.

I became acquainted with some of the peculiarities of an ocean voyage. During my subsequent frequent trips to America they became condensed into a fixed experience. There was, for instance, the monotony of the existence between one's stateroom, one's deck chair, and a circling deck promenade, interspersed with any number of attempts to interrupt the enforced idleness by some kind of occupation, indiscreetly frustrated by the motions of the ship and the ghostlike noises in the floors and walls of the rooms. When the weather was calm, I did spend a number of beautiful hours on the boat deck, permitting my gaze to travel into the limitless radiance or, at night, into the vast surging darkness surrounding us. One of my experiences has never lost its humorous aspect: it was the walk around the promenade deck whenever the ocean's mood made such an excursion endurable. The ship's bow would rise slowly and dip down quickly so that, after having climbed up laboriously, one was forced to run downhill quickly. When the ship rolled, it would seem as if those coming in the opposite direction were unaffected by the law of gravitation and, looking like men from Mars, were able to pursue their way at an acute angle to their base.

Bad weather caused our crossing to last longer than we had been promised. Moreover, the *Minnetonka* made an unexpected stop at Halifax. An uplifting memory is connected with my first comforting sight of the coast, after, I believe, ten days at sea. In the radiance of a sunny, windy winter day, I once more saw hills, houses, and people. There were harbor structures and railway tracks with freight cars bearing the name of the Canadian Pacific. My imagination followed these tracks across the mighty continent to the Pacific Ocean, and flew still farther and farther on. While thus the distance opened up to me and was, at the same time, lost alluringly in the haze, a sense of the world as a whole impressed itself for the first time on my mind. The phantom inheritance of the European who fancies himself bound within narrow limits was changed at that moment into a feeling of a wonderful affiliation with the wide world. I had to think of the magnificent ending of Adalbert von Chamisso's *Peter Schlemihl,* whom fate, to make up for the loss of mundane happiness, had presented with seven-league boots and thus vouchsafed a new and exalted existence.

We steamed on our way. I finally sighted the imposing and significant figure of the Statue of Liberty, sailed past the mountain chains of the skyscrapers, and was finally able to step ashore from the *Minnetonka*. It took me quite a time to find my land legs. My old friend the fog had presented itself for my reception. In the falling dusk, the upper stories of the gigantic buildings were lost in the haze. They seemed to stretch into the very skies. When I had checked in at the Great Northern Hotel and escaped again into the street from the excessive heat of my room, my senses, confused and fatigued by the wretched crossing, made me imagine with a shudder of horror that I was walking at the bottom of immensely deep rocky canyons. That cannot possibly be New York, I said to myself. Down here I see a light in a window, up there another one is gleaming faintly through the fog, and way up in the drifting clouds still another one shines forth fitfully. I had witnessed such things in my evening wanderings through the valleys of the Tyrol, when the lights of a lonely farmhouse high up on the mountain sent down their rays. Gradually the streets grew lighter, the advertising signs began to shine; and when my weary eye saw on the roof of a building the flash of the words "U. S. Tires," I thought to myself that my first impressions of the United States had actually tired me and I only wondered why this effect should be advertised from the rooftops.

Back at my hotel, I had the pleasure of an unexpected meeting. Maria Ivogün and Lili Petschnikoff, who accompanied the former as a friend and a kind of personal representative, happened to be staying at the same hotel, and so my first evening on American soil had a pleasant conclusion.

I shall not and cannot try to record the wealth, the power, and the novelty of the impressions assailing me on my first American visit. I can only say comprehensively that the healthy surging life of New York affected me powerfully after the wretchedness, impared health, and morbidity in Europe. It was not surprising that at the sight of the motley crowds on Broadway, of the well-regulated mighty traffic on stylish Fifth Avenue, of the demonic anthill gorges of downtown, of splendid Riverside Drive with its view of the majestic Hudson I had a recurrence of my childhood feeling on a railway station platform when a train would come thundering in and the hellishly steaming locomotive would seem to hiss at me angrily: "Get back! Out of my way!"

The same vital force spoke to me from the architectural aspect of New York. A new city-type, never seen on the other side, had developed here. It was a city dominated by the vertical line instead of Europe's horizontal one. The European city lay, this one stood. Peaceful Washington Square and similar islands in the city served to accentuate the predominance of verticality, expressed most forcibly in the sky-high, closely built Wall Street district.

Where was it that I had once before stood in front of an upward-striving, upward-pointing structure, impressed with its unapproachability? It had happened three decades before, when the Cologne Cathedral had been my untutored soul's first overwhelming experience in the language of stone forms. Now the well-ordered walls of the American city forcefully called up the memory of that youthful impression, and I thought I could recognize in those towering houses and streets the spirit of a modern Gothic style. True, it seemed to be expressive of a workaday rather than a holiday mood. It was civilized and made worldly by the gigantic buildings crowded close to each other in unbroken rows, while their spiritual forbears towered up singly from snugly horizontal surroundings. But in spite of the daring of the variation, there was an affinity with that Gothic feeling of life which, in Europe, had been sublimated into skyward-pointing pious poems in stone.

Thus what at first had been inaccessible gradually became accessible to my searching mind. My admiration and understanding of the great city and my aesthetic interest in it grew rapidly. It took me longer to adjust myself to the assaults of vitality in the daily contacts of personal life. But the very fact that in the face of the unquestioning and untrammeled spirit surging round me I felt so strongly bound by romantic ties and so burdened down by experience taught me finally to recognize in my seeming inhibitions the sources of my strength.

My stay in America during that year and the following ones was too brief to enable me to give a picture of the musical life of those days. I well remember the impression of virtuosity and brilliance made upon me by the American orchestras and their conductors and by the many instrumentalists of world fame. It was but natural that in this realm closest to my heart I should also feel the effects of the mighty vital force whose vibrations seemed to make the very ground tremble. But it was deeply gratifying that in the continuous musical Olympiad, with its contests of superlative performances, I also heard a wealth of noble and introspective music. Only in the thirties, when my stay in New York was of considerable duration, did I gain a more profound knowledge of the country's musical conditions. This knowledge grew in proportion to the intensity of my own activities.

After my concerts in New York with Damrosch's orchestra, I conducted in Boston, where Pierre Monteux was the regular leader of the symphony concerts. Artur Schnabel was my soloist. He had often played for me in Europe, and the longer I knew him the more I came to appreciate his profound musicality, his respect for the work, and the genuineness of his feeling. It is one of the encouraging symptoms of contemporary musical life that a pianist of so serious a bent, of so progressive an engrossment in his work, and of so strict an artistic morality can continue to be eminently successful throughout a long career. His human distinction and his highly active mentality had always attracted me, and I consider it a gain that I was privileged in the course of years increasingly to enjoy these qualities.

In Detroit I had at my disposal the orchestra created and trained by Ossip Gabrilowitsch. I remember how, at the beginning of my first rehearsal, I recognized in the beautiful rendition of the second theme of Weber's *Euryanthe* overture Ossip's poetic personality and its wonderful effect on his musicians. We enjoyed many hours spent at Gabrilowitsch's stately home on Boston Boulevard, where old agreements and disagreements were attractively revived. To my surprise, I grew to know Ossip as the driver of an old electromobile and to admire his skill, although not without some uneasiness.

Ossip Gabrilowitsch rendered an imperishable service to Detroit's cultural life and to American cultural life in general by the creation of this orchestra, by the unreserved devotion to his mission as his city's leading musician, by the formation of his fine and interesting programs, and, above all, by his enthusiastic and inspired musicianship. Don't let us forget either what it means that a man of so exalted a humanity was able to be active for decades in so exposed a position. Blessings have gone out from him as a musician and as a man. When, in 1940, four years after his death, I once more appeared in Detroit as a guest conductor, I found that his memory had been touchingly enshrined in the hearts of musicians and others, and that his spirit was still alive in the very playing of the orchestra, in its personal conduct, and even in the attitude of the audience.

A particularly enjoyable period of my first stay in America was spent in Minneapolis. I conducted for three or four weeks there. So cordial a relation between me and the orchestra and so personal a contact with the audience was established during that time that in that icy part of the United States I was made happy by the surprising, the exciting warmth of the musical atmosphere. On my walks along the Mississippi, which separates the twin cities of Minneapolis and St. Paul, and in the vicinity of the Hiawatha Statue inspired by Longfellow's poem, I was struck by the full force of the cold. Yet, I was drawn there again and again by the fascination of the legendary stream.

My first stay in America lasted about two months. I left after having entered into agreements that called for my return the following year. It is beyond my power of expression to say what the mighty country and its atmosphere of freedom did for me in those days in reviving my vital energy. I was deeply affected, too, by the historical fact that from the melting pot of the most varied peoples had emerged an American nationality of unexampled vitality and of distinct national characteristics, expressed even in idiomatic and physiognomic singularities. Every new experience confirmed my expectant belief in the future of the country, and I am grateful to a kind fate which, in my later years, has permitted me gradually to take part in its musical life.

II

Upon my return to Hamburg, in March, 1923, I had no sooner stepped upon the pier than excited porters told me their tales of woe. What I read in the newspapers was confirmed on the following day by my family in Munich: the country was headed for catastrophe. While I had been on my way to New York, France had occupied the Ruhr. At the Reich government's behest, all work in the district's industry had thereupon been stopped. This form of passive resistance, imposing upon the government the duty of providing for the unemployed, had brought about a total disruption of the country's financial condition. The mark had sunk to bottomless depths, and the distress and disunity of the people furnished fertile soil for the growth of radical tendencies.

A strange notice in the windows of Munich shops attracted my attention. A "multiplier" had come into existence. It was the figure by which the normal price of merchandise had to be multiplied, in accordance with the progress of the inflation. If the figure had been 150,000 in the morning, enabling people to buy a pair of gloves, normally worth two marks, for 300,000, it might be 160,000 in the evening of the same day. The gloves cost 20,000 marks more, although the buyer's earnings had in the meantime not increased proportionately.

A striking illustration of the fantastic speed of currency depreciation was furnished me on the occasion of a concert which the Berlin Staatskapelle had invited me to conduct in the spring of 1923. Max von Schillings was the General Manager of the State Opera. When we had exchanged greetings he begged me to be considerate of the orchestra's anxious mood. The first rehearsal took a thoroughly normal course up to a certain point. During the intermission, the representatives of the orchestra informed me that the musicians were just then being paid their salaries and they urgently asked me to understand that they would at once have to make some kind of purchase: if they attended to it two hours later, the purchasing power of their money would in the meantime have shrunk. Naturally, I yielded and contented myself with the rehearsals which were to follow. I no longer know in what queer merchandise the money was invested, though I believe a musician told me he had bought bags of salt. The experience in the orchestra furnished a particularly striking example of the currency's galloping consumption.

I recall the oppressed mood of the people and the irritation displayed on markets and in shops, in public conveyances, and in restaurants. At the same time, it was remarkable that professionally, at rehearsals or concerts conducted by me in Germany during that inflationary period, I never had cause to complain about a slackening of attention or an inferiority of performance. Vienna, which I visited in the same year, was also a sufferer from inflation. But the "multiplier" was smaller. Austrians were figuring in thousands when the Germans had already become accustomed to millions. There were no hysterical daily jumps in prices to frighten the more unstable mind of the Viennese. But while the Germans, after the restoration, returned with a sense of relief from thinking in millions to the former small figures, Austria kept luxuriating in her thousands even after the introduction of the stable schilling. As late as the thirties, some of my friends could apparently not resist the magic of an obstinate inward multiplier.

I had been able, during my first stay in America, to fulfill the hopes for assistance, and was entrusted with new requests to be attended to the next time. But while I was made happy by many expressions of sympathy and gratitude, I also learned of manifestations of a different sort. I had been attacked in the radical press of Munich after my departure. A picture of myself in a photographer's window had been defaced, and there had been similar expressions of hostile feeling. These reports did not greatly affect me. But I was disturbed and dismayed by news of the growth of that radical party, claiming as its goal the overthrow of existing conditions. For the first time, I heard of turbulent public demonstrations in popular restaurants and of disturbances in the streets, which caused a growing general uneasiness.

The Concertgebouw had invited me to conduct in Amsterdam, and I looked forward to the occasion with much joy. Mahler had been full of praise of the excellent orchestra, the Dutch public's genuine love of music, and the spirit of the noble institute that played and loved his works and whose yearly honored guest he had been since 1903. Holland's music lovers had to thank Willem Mengelberg for having made them acquainted with Mahler's works and for the opportunity to hear his symphonies regularly. Mengelberg's endeavors had culminated in a Mahler Festival in 1920. It had attracted a great many foreign admirers of the composer. Alma Mahler, too, had been present. Unfortunately, important work in Munich had prevented my joining in the pilgrimage of Mahler's faithful.

At any rate, I knew enough of the Concertgebouw and its spirit to make me go to Amsterdam with the feeling with which we meet the friend of a friend. My expectations were fulfilled: we, too, became friends. The "we" includes the management of the Concertgebouw, its wonderful orchestra, and the Dutch concert audiences of Amsterdam as well as of such towns as The Hague, Rotterdam, Arnhem, Utrecht, Haarlem, Eindhoven, and others, where I played frequently with the orchestra. I must also include the Toonkunst-Chor and the Wagner-Vereenigung, whose operatic performances I often conducted at the Stadsschouwburg, and a number of individuals from musical and other circles with whom I came in contact.

My feeling of a growing attachment was by no means restricted

to musical circles and institutions. I came to love the Dutch landscape, the colorful brilliance of the tulip-fields in the spring, the
tranquillity of the canals with their slowly propelled boats — they
called them *Schuiten* — the old windmills in the wide plains, the
picturesque small towns in which water played so prominent a
part, the light that had inspired the magnificent Dutch painters,
and the rustic costumes, the bright dresses and hoods of the girls,
the wide trousers of the men, and the wooden shoes. I thought of
the country's history of violent suppression and victorious insurrection and listened with interest to the characteristic tale of the
town of Leyden, which, after a nine-month siege by the Spaniards,
had been relieved by Prince William of Orange and, when given
the choice of ten years of tax exemption or the founding of a university, had decided in favor of the latter. I also enjoyed the Dutch
language and its antique forcefulness. My awakened sense of politics felt profoundly attracted by the country's democratic constitution, so eminently suited to the prevalent character of the people, the descendants of those old champions of freedom of whom
Charles de Coster has given us so deeply moving an account.

The distinguished, crowded hall of the Concertgebouw presented a magnificent sight. I liked to look down for a little while
from the raised, darkened box on the right before swinging open
the half-door in its front and setting foot on the top step of the
platform, thereby exposing myself to the public gaze. There followed the long descent down the steps between the orchestra and
the part of the audience seated along the side of the platform, until
I finally reached the conductor's desk. The audiences were in the
habit of honoring an esteemed artist or an especially artistic performance by rising from their seats. They could be relied upon to
listen raptly and with genuine devotion to the music. The memory
of an atmosphere of seriousness and cordiality at those concerts will
always be one of my cherished possessions.

My wife and I derived a great deal of pleasure from wandering
through the Amsterdam streets on a fine afternoon. I was particularly attracted by the interesting and characteristically antique
Grachten, though when getting out of the way of an automobile
in the narrow paved roadway I had the unpleasant feeling that I
might be plunged the next moment into the water, from which,
curiously, no railing protected me. There was also an imposing
new part of the city, with excellently constructed and highly
modern dwellings. And how we loved the richly stocked flower
market and the maze of the old streets in the inner part of the
city, which, to be sure, was impassable at certain hours because
of the locust-like swarms of cyclists. The occupants of groundfloor

flats rarely let down their shades. When, of an evening, we would stroll through the streets in our part of the city — they bore the names of musicians — we were charmed by scenes of cozy family life revealed by window after window. And how could my feeble words give the faintest idea of the wealth of the art collections — the Rijksmuseum, the Mauritshuis, the Franz Hals Museum, and others — to which we returned again and again to admire, enjoy, and marvel at the incomparable treasures this "small" people and country had given to mankind?

With the feeling that my life had been greatly enriched, we left Holland for Vienna where, since the summer of 1923, we again had our permanent home. I looked forward to my impending journeys to Rome and Moscow expectantly, but also with a certain uneasiness, for they would be my first visits to former enemy countries. I believe that I was the first "enemy" conductor to be invited there and to London in the following year. The thought of appearing before people who were possibly still influenced by sentiments caused by the war was not particularly pleasant.

Fortunately, my misgivings proved unfounded. Rome's Accademia, its orchestra, and its audience received me with their old cordiality. I saw and felt but little of the new Fascist régime, and Rome seemed to me as wonderful as ever. All the same, this first reappearance in Rome's concert life is listed among my unpleasant experiences, and it took me quite some time to get over the painful impression. Complying with the Accademia's request for a new work, I had put on my final program Schönberg's *Verklärte Nacht*. The daring work seemed to be more than the Augusteo's gallery were able to digest. After the first five minutes, the people up there became restless. Soon there were calls and other manifestations of displeasure. The request of other listeners for quiet and the counter-demonstrations only added to the noise. I decided not to be disconcerted and to play the piece, whose performance took almost half an hour, to its end in spite of constant disturbances. There followed the intermission, and when I returned to the platform to continue the concert I was received with general applause, which apparently was to tell me that the demonstrations had been directed against Schönberg's work and not against myself. Among those taking part ostentatiously in the applause I noticed in one of the front rows the former German Chancellor Prince Bülow and his wife, who had returned to their Villa Malta after the war. Highly indignant at a disturbance such as I had never experienced before, I made but a curt bow and continued at once with the next number. The concert finished, I left the Augusteo as quickly as possible, determined never to return there again. The management seemed unable to understand my sensitiveness. They were at a loss to see why a conductor should take the gallery's traditional forms of disapproval as a personal affront. I was long unable to get over my indignation, and declined subsequent invitations. It must have been all of nine or ten years before I returned to the Accademia.

Distressing in a different but rather serious sense were the impressions I received in Moscow, with whose musical life I renewed my old acquaintance in the same winter of 1923. Russia, which had passed through the Revolution after the war, was still in the process of reconstruction. I had been told that the theater and music were greatly furthered by the new régime, but that the destruction caused by the violent revolution was still felt everywhere and that the population lived in rather deplorable circumstances.

These reports proved true. What was more, tales of past horrors still dominated the conversations, and many people were worried about their and their next-of-kin's personal safety. The excitement over the monstrous things that had happened still trembled in the air, and anti-revolutionary activities were guarded against with a watchful eye. My wife had accompanied me. We stayed at the Hotel Metropole, the only one permitted to accommodate foreigners. The rooms were bearable, the food was not bad, but many of the restaurant's waiters and other employees of the hotel were said to be in the service of the secret police. Friends of former days, whom we invited for a meal, did not dare to come lest they arouse suspicion by appearing at a place of luxury, such as the dining room of the Hotel Metropole.

The worst feature of Russian life besides this feeling of uncertainty seemed to be the housing shortage. An acquaintance who wished to see us at his home had to do more than merely give us his address. He had to wait for us in the street in front of his house, take us upstairs and through crowded rooms, until we got to the combination sleeping and living room occupied by himself, his wife, and his children — and at times by other people too. I recall our visit to a musician who wished to play his symphony for me. His room was under the eaves, and while we were listening to the four-hand rendition of the interesting composition, water from melting snow kept dripping audibly through a hole in the ceiling and into a tin receptacle which had been placed at the side of the piano for that purpose. The people crowding the room seemed to be oblivious of the leakage, the tin basin, and the cramped condition. To have a roof over one's head was a stroke of good fortune. The Revolution had made Moscow's population mount tremendously, and those who worked in the city but were unable to find a place to live had to be content with suburban accommodations and to endure all the discomforts of a daily hike in the terrible winter cold. There were even those who could find no shelter whatever and were exposed to unspeakable suffering. I personally knew of such a case.

To play music in Moscow, however, was more than a joy. The orchestra and the public were as enthusiastic and full of vital energy as before, and the excellent musicians' devotion to their work at rehearsals and performances was exemplary. The Russian ballet, too, had maintained its great tradition, and I heard praise of its work on all sides. One of these excellent ballet performances was responsible for a profound impression. During the intermission, the director told us of a foyer that had formerly been part of the Czar's box and been changed into a chamber-music hall. He added that a string quartet was performing there at the moment. When I expressed the wish to hear it, we were led along the Opera's corridors and into an unlighted room. Through an open door in its opposite side light and music from the adjoining concert hall penetrated. I shall never forget the picture revealed to my sight: a hall-like, high-ceilinged side-room, from whose walls and ceiling the old splendor of Czarist days was here and there revealed in the semi-darkness; human figures leaning against the walls, squatting on the floor, or standing in deep absorption, plainly and stirringly showing how spellbound by music their souls were. I have never seen music become as visible as in the attitudes of those students, young men and women, enthralled by the adagio of a Beethoven quartet. My experiences before and after the Russian Revolution taught me that the souls of the Russians were truly and passionately yearning for music.

The year 1923, so rich in artistic yield, is alive in my memory chiefly because of its dramatic political repercussions and the growing importance of Gustav Stresemann's momentous personality in European events.

The chart of Germany's development after the war shows a decline until about the autumn of that year, marked by the economic collapse of the German Republic and the renewed gloomy aspect of the foreign political situation. Then the change set in, leading eventually to the discussions of Locarno in 1925. There began an epoch of hope, the hope for a new Europe. This hope, spurred on by a series of favorable events, mounted until 1929. In my own domain, I was able gratefully to enjoy the brightening aspect of the period between 1925 and 1929. As the General Musical Director of the Berlin Municipal Opera during those four years, I could witness the new flowering of Berlin's and Germany's cultural life. From 1929 on, the atmosphere became gloomy again; the evil grew until it came to power with Hitler in 1933.

The dates mentioned in this casual sketch have been entered in the book of history by Gustav Stresemann's strong hand. In 1923, when he was Chancellor, he had had the unparalleled courage to capitulate in the Ruhr struggle, an action that unleashed a hurricane of hatred against him in Germany. The discussions at Locarno took place in the autumn of 1925. The way to them was prepared by his wise policy and made practicable by Briand's lofty ideas. An end was put to the war-caused grouping of the powers, and Germany was set on the road toward equality. But Gustav Stresemann died in October 1929, and with him vanished the hope for the coalition of the European states, so strongly and convincingly advocated by him.

What an interesting historical figure! We see the twenty-year-old student who wished to place a wreath on the grave of the March victims of 1848; the nationalist optimist of the war, taught new wisdom by the defeat; the forty-five-year-old Chancellor, self-sacrificingly taking upon himself the disgrace of yielding so that Germany might be saved. How super-political and noble was the humanitarian attitude of the former politician, of the Goethe devotee, in the spiritual solitude bound to be his fate in a Germany dominated by party intrigues and nationalist orgies of hate! Misunderstood in his own country, misunderstood also in influential circles abroad, he strove clearsightedly for the establishment of a unified and flourishing Europe, in which a sound Germany was to have played an important part. Together with Briand, he pursued that goal. It seemed attainable when he died. "The enemy is at the Right," Chancellor Wirth had said, and it was upon that enmity that the strength of the outwardly robust, inwardly delicate, man was finally broken. The coalition between the Right and the Nazis sounded the death knell of the European thought.

Unfortunately, I knew the great statesman only casually. But I was aware of his artistic interests, of his literary talents, and of his frankly and impetuously expressed humanity. I had once been asked by him to have lunch at the Foreign Ministry in Friedrich Ebertstrasse. In addition to his family and a number of other guests, the famous baritone Mattia Battistini was present on that occasion. Stresemann's personal attitude toward me was shown in the spring of 1929, when I wanted to leave the Municipal Opera. At a meeting of his party, he requested its representative in the institute's managing commission to endeavor to keep me at my post. More gratifying still, he accepted the chairmanship of the board of the "Bruno Walter Foundation," which a group of my adherents had established and placed at my disposal when I left the Municipal Opera. I decided that its proceeds were to be used for the support of gifted needy young musicians.

Politics began to influence the course of my life after the First World War. But I still felt unharmed. During the period that, because of Stresemann's activity, held out prospects of peace and international conciliation, I was even vouchsafed a new optimistic and fruitful time of work in Germany. It is that fact which has impelled me to speak of the man who, with the aid of the equally great Frenchman, almost succeeded in saving Europe. An eminent but tragic figure, he will live in the memory of all internationally minded people.

III

EARLY in 1924, I went to America once more — this time on a comfortable steamer — and was again the guest conductor of Damrosch's New York Symphony Orchestra. I recall a number of animated evenings in the always stimulating company of Walter Damrosch who, a pioneer of dramatic and symphonic music in the early days of his country's musical life, himself represented a piece of America's musical history. I also enjoyed the cordial companionship of his brother Frank Damrosch, whose life was idealistically and effectively dedicated to musical education, and the warmhearted hospitality of Frederic and Julia Steinway. I remember Steinway with deep gratitude. An artistically inclined Pogner nature, he had shown a heartfelt understanding of me as a musician at a time when the American atmosphere still was bound to be strange to me.

Harry Harkness Flagler was president of the New York Symphony Orchestra. It was he who was subsequently instrumental in bringing about its fusion with the New York Philharmonic Society. I had naturally come in contact with this exceptional man at the very beginning of my guest activity, and had at once recognized in him a true friend of music and humanity. Our acquaintance has ripened into a friendship that has proved true in bright days as well as gloomy ones and that is treasured among the unchangeable and imperishable possessions of my life.

A pleasant recollection connected with my second stay in America refers to another visit to Minneapolis. The orchestra's conductor, Henri Verbruggen, originally an excellent violinist, had agreed to join me in a piano-and-violin sonata recital for the benefit of needy German children. I was made happy by the eminent Belgian musician's handsome readiness to open his heart to the need of the former enemy. My stay in Minneapolis was also made the occasion for a so-called "starvation dinner," a meal at which, though it cost a lot, one got very little to eat, so that the lion's share of the receipts might be available for charitable purposes. Among the speakers, in addition to myself, was Count Harry Kessler, a well-known friend of art and artists, an intimate of the circles round Hofmannsthal and Stefan George, and the author of the book of Richard Strauss's *Eine Joseph-Legende*. The son of an English mother and German father, educated first at Eton and later at Hamburg's Johanneum, he had entered the diplomatic service and been sent to the newly formed Poland as German ambassador immediately after the war. After three years spent there, he returned with a sense of relief to art and literature, to his own self. I met him again on the ship carrying me back to Europe. His spirited and interesting companionship most agreeably whiled away some of the unpleasantly idle hours of the voyage.

A politically rather important artistic event occurred in the spring of 1924. London had decided to restore the German season, which had been a yearly Covent Garden fixture before the war, and I was invited to take charge of its musical direction. The invitation made me very happy. Irrespective of the personal satisfaction derived from a summons to so important an activity in international musical life, I saw in it a promising step toward a return to the inter-cultural relations interrupted by the war.

Hopefully, and yet not without some misgivings, I went to London in May 1924. So violent had been the waves of hatred surging between England and Germany that there was justification for a feeling of apprehension lest the first sound of the German language on an English stage give rise to a spontaneous expression of antipathy. What was more, the *Ring* was to be performed, and the introductory *Rheingold* seemed less suited than any other of Wagner's works for drowning any possible feelings of aversion in the waves of passionate musical emotions. But it turned out that we need not have been apprehensive at all. We were received with fairness and friendliness before the performance, and were thanked by an overwhelming outburst of enthusiasm at the end. Thus, on the very first evening, was sealed the new pact of friendship into which the London public had entered with us.

Colonel Eustace Blois was in charge of the German and Italian seasons, which followed each other during the first years and were later combined. They were, unless I am mistaken, managed in the beginning by an Australian committee. Subsequently, they were sponsored by Lil Courtauld, the wife of the well-known industrialist. Mrs. Courtauld was an enthusiastic lover of music who very tactfully knew how to exert a beneficial influence upon the conduct of the Opera without putting herself in the foreground in any way. A number of exhaustive discussions between us revealed to me her deep understanding and sincere good will. I deeply regretted that, for reasons unknown to me, she withdrew from the Opera after several years. Sam Courtauld, whose beautiful Adamstyle home on Portman Square in London contained a wonderful collection of works by French impressionists, had the inclinations of both a Maecenas and a sociologist. He was a man of few words but great inward animation, an independent thinker, and an energetic doer. When his wife left the Opera, he founded with her and the conductor Malcolm Sargent the Courtauld-Sargent Concerts, an enterprise whose purpose was seriously artistic as well as philanthropic. He continued them after his wife's untimely death. I was a frequent visitor at the Courtauld home and even lived there occasionally when concerts took me to London. I recall with pleasure the valuable hours I spent in that highly cultured circle.

I think it was our third or fourth season that was opened with a particularly successful performance of *Der Rosenkavalier*. It no doubt contributed materially to the world success of that opera. Richard Mayr was the incomparable Baron Ochs, thoroughly enjoyable in his jovial humor, his mastery of the Austrian dialect, and his vocal and musical perfection. His first steps on the stage had been taken under my guidance in 1901, when he started his career at the Vienna Court Opera as Silva in Verdi's *Ernani*. I had been in constant artistic contact with him during my eleven years in that city, had later engaged him several times as soloist of my choral concerts, and was now glad to be once more associated with the sympathetic man, so typical of his native Salzburg. The part of Oktavian was taken by Delia Reinhardt, my poetic lyric soprano from Munich, who had studied and sung the part with me there and who, vocally, histrionically, and in appearance, was a uniquely charming representative of the boyishly fiery Austrian aristocrat. While the singers of the parts of the Marschallin and Sophie were then still unknown to me, I had heard so many fine reports about them that I had gladly assented to their engagement. They were Lotte Lehmann and Elisabeth Schumann. I can still see the two young singers, then on the threshold of their world careers, meeting me trustfully and modestly in the office of the theater. Vocally and histrionically, Elisabeth Schumann was the ideal Sophie; and as for Lotte Lehmann's work as the Marschallin, it was even then surrounded by the brilliance which has made her portrayal of that part one of the outstanding achievements on the contemporary operatic stage. Here, indeed, was that rare phenomenon of an artist's personality becoming wholly merged with a poetic figure, and of a transitory theatrical event being turned into an unforgettable experience. The smaller parts, too, had been cast with a great deal of care. If the German Covent Garden season had been in need of increased favor with the public, the *Rosenkavalier* performances, repeated, I believe, during all of the London seasons conducted by me, would surely have been a means to that end. There still sounds in my ear the final trio of the three beautiful young voices, seemingly created for each other, putting the stamp of nobility upon a piece that is by no means the most valuable of an otherwise frequently brilliant score.

True, one weakness marred the impressiveness of our performances, and neither stage director Moore nor his assistants were able to cope with it: the technical equipment of the theater was primitive and antiquated — the stage was modernized only later — its magic was somewhat shoddy. The column of fog supposed to hide Alberich when he changes into the dragon or the toad often materialized too late, issuing suddenly and explosively in front of the helplessly waiting, embarrassed singer, while a hairy arm was seen to hold the fog-producing tin-tube. The three mysterious Norns, whom Mr. Moore had instructed to disappear stoopingly in the darkness, became glaringly illumined and deeply bowed-down ladies sneaking off with a rope. The edge of the filed, melted, and reforged Nothung was hardly ever keen enough to cleave the anvil at one blow, the latter usually collapsing only after a considerable time, as if from inward debility. But our audiences patiently bore these and similar disillusionments. They were even tactful enough not to laugh. Only once, when the waiters in the third act of *Der Rosenkavalier* touched the wall candles at the left with their lighters, while those at the right flamed up, there was not only a burst of laughter but also applause. Generally, however, the audiences were noted for their seriousness, devotion, and genuine enthusiasm, and the emotional storm on the stage struck the hearts of the listeners with its full force.

Among the enthusiastic attendants of almost all our performances was my old acquaintance from Munich, King Manuel of Portugal. Accompanied by his delicate wife, a former Princess of Hohenzollern-Sigmaringen, he occupied his first-tier box, listening to our performances with deep absorption and never failing to come down to see me during the intermissions, to express his sincere emotion. The intermissions being long in London, they gave us the opportunity for conversations either in my room or in his box. I learned to know him as a socially inclined, thoughtful, and quite peacefully resigned man, and his wife for a serious and modest woman. My wife and I called on them several times at their attractive country house at Twickenham, beyond Richmond, where, so Manuel said, he lived for his books, his flowers, and his organ. His organ-playing revealed the shortcomings as well as the blissfulness of the amateur. I recall a luncheon, attended also by Lotte Lehmann, after which we took a long walk in his spacious garden in the rear of his house, listening to his loving and detailed remarks concerning his flowers. He became the victim of an accident. A piece of cotton, left in his throat by a doctor whom he had consulted, was said to have brought about his death by suffocation. I still think with affection and emotion of this enthusiastic, singular young man who met so absurd a death.

Mention must be made of my meeting with the composer Sir Edward Elgar, whose Second Symphony I performed at one of my Queen's Hall concerts and whom I got to know more intimately on that occasion. Although I was not very strongly attracted by his works, I did admire his mastery, especially in that symphony, in the *Enigma Variations,* and in his Violin Concerto. I was more deeply affected by his *Dream of Gerontius,* and no less so by his serious and sincere personality, revealed to me at a luncheon to which he had invited me.

I naturally met my old friend Ethel Smyth as often as possible. She had in the meantime become Dame Ethel, but had lost none of her exceedingly unconventional manner and original sense of humor. Although she was approaching the Biblical age, she was still the timelessly young and flaming soul I had come to know in Vienna. She composed, wrote, and took a passionate interest in contemporary history, expressed occasionally in brilliantly written and strikingly effective newspaper articles. It was through her that I met her intimate friend Virginia Woolf, the singularly gifted writer. We spent an afternoon at the home of the eminent and wholly introspective novelist. I carried away from my visit an almost painful impression of the unusual delicacy of the woman's soul, but neither Ethel Smyth nor I could have foreseen that Virginia Woolf, even then a middle-aged woman, would later seek relief in suicide from the *Weltschmerz* which had become unbearable to her.

It was natural that the vital warmth generated by the Covent Garden atmosphere should spread. It even flowed across the Channel, finding expression in the beautiful 1928 Mozart Cycle in Paris which I had been invited to direct while in London the previous year. Events of such a nature had of course been made possible only by an improvement in the political situation, by a policy of *rapprochement* entertained by Germany, France, and England. We saw at the time how valuable an aid to a policy of pacification could be rendered by culture, a fact gladly confirmed to me by the German ambassadors to London and Paris, Dr. Heinrich Sthamer and Dr. Leopold von Hösch, respectively. Symptomatic of this were the musical evenings arranged in the rooms of the German Embassy in London. English society had thus far kept rather aloof, but Dr. Sthamer's invitations to these concerts, at which I played the piano accompaniments for our most successful artists, induced ever larger numbers of English personages to attend events of so unpolitical a nature, until finally "all London" was again to be met at the Ambassador's house as in the days of old. I believe that in the course of each season we gave one or two of these musical soirées at the German Embassy. I recall with pleasure the half hour that followed the departure of the last guest, when the ambassador, a former Hamburg senator, would sit with us for a little while to thank us and assure us again and again how effectively our work at Covent Garden and our concerts at his house supported his endeavors to bring about a *rapprochement* with England.

To avoid a possible misunderstanding, I should like to mention here that I consider a similar conciliatory attitude after the present war both improbable and undesirable for a considerable time to come. The Nazi poison may long continue to be effective. The ravages it wrought in the realm of German culture — in religion, morals, science, literature, and art — would seem to counsel an attitude of restraint until a radical change of mind has taken place in Germany. Offended humanity has the right to impose a period of watchful quarantine, to assure the "export" of only that German culture which has remained pure or been demonstrably purified. It is true that art, and especially music, is least susceptible to those pestilential bacteria, but it is a fact nevertheless that the Nazification of the Muses was carried on with particular energy and that the people submitted more or less readily to those efforts. I am one of those who believe that the first *rapprochement* will be effected by art, but I am hoping for the use of precautionary measures that, though they were unnecessary after the last war because culture had remained pure, seem now highly advisable in spite of the apparent harmlessness of the realm to which they are to be applied.

I found musical life in London exceedingly brisk and varied. Almost every day, one of the foremost instrumentalists, singers, or chamber-music associations would appear before a music-loving audience. The numerous symphonic concerts played to crowded houses. Yet, orchestral conditions seemed to me problematical because the famous old London orchestras had not then at their disposal a full roster of permanent members, but were forced to engage for every concert a number of additional musicians. Thus, in spite of the high quality of individual instrumentalists, the ensemble effect had to be worked for anew at every concert. On the other hand, the English orchestral player is noted for his remarkable sight-reading ability, without which the habitually small number of rehearsals would have made the production of new symphonic works impossible. All these circumstances, however, made increasingly clear the necessity of permanent orchestral organizations. Efforts in that direction were gradually intensified, and I was made very happy — after cities like Manchester and Glasgow had been superior to London as far as permanent orchestras were concerned — by being able to witness the birth and development of permanent London orchestras of excellent qualities.

From childhood days, I had felt emotionally drawn toward English musical life. My feeling originated at the time when I used to pore over the biographies of composers and was made to suffer by the contrast between the inward wealth and the material wretchedness of the creative musicians. I rejoiced in much I read in those days about Handel's powerful prestige in London, and about the high esteem in which Haydn, Mendelssohn, and Weber had been held there; but nothing could equal the ineradicably deep impression made upon me by the tale of the Royal Philharmonic's gift to the dying Beethoven, and by all its touching details. Moscheles had submitted to the Society the request of the deathly ill Beethoven to consider his desperate condition and put into practice their former offer of arranging an "academy" for his benefit. The Philharmonic Society thereupon convoked a general meeting and unanimously decided at once to send Beethoven the sum of one hundred pounds sterling. Indescribable was the joy of the needy and greatly suffering man, and deeply moving the expression of his heartfelt gratitude. Even in the very shadow of death, after the last sacraments had been administered to him, Beethoven spoke or whispered words of gratitude, in which he included the English nation: "May God bless it!" I was by no means so sentimental as to draw general conclusions from that event and to see all of England's musical life irradiated by its brilliance. But there it was, to the lasting honor of an English musical society that did not intend it as a philanthropic action but as an expression of its admiration for a musical genius. Even in my youth, whenever it was asserted that music did not mean much to the English, I used to point to that striking proof of a genuine love of music in wide circles — for, joined to the Philharmonic Society was its public — and my subsequent personal experiences, both as an executive artist and a listener, as well as remarks made by esteemed English colleagues have proved English audiences' enthusiasm for music and their spiritual need of it.

It gave me a great deal of pleasure once more to wander about London after an absence of eleven years and to notice the changes wrought by those portentous times. The season kept me in London five or six weeks, in contrast to the three or four days which had sufficed for my pre-war concerts. So it was really only now that I came to know the magnificent city. The hansoms had almost entirely disappeared from the streets, and the strangely high-built taxis, with their lack of romantic charm, seemed to me a rather inadequate *ersatz*. The hotels and many private homes were now equipped with central heating and running hot water, but the Horse Guards in Whitehall Court still sat their horses with immovable rigidity; wigs were still in evidence at public ceremonials, and the flames in the open fireplaces still roasted a person's rear while his front was freezing. Culinary culture had advanced considerably, but the strict division of the sexes after meals was still observed. I was touched by the patient waiting of long lines of people at the theaters. Their time was whiled away occasionally by street musicians, by dancers, and even by acrobats. I was again struck by the general friendliness in public life, revealed, for instance, by the readiness with which the place of one of the waiting, who had brought along a portable camp chair to make things easier for himself, was reserved when he left the line for a cup of tea, and by the general compliance with the silent request expressed by a slip of paper attached to the seat and bearing the rightful owner's name. Again I rambled through London with an eye for sights or types with which the novels of Dickens and other literature had made me familiar. I never went from Dover to London without imagining on the road running parallel to the railway poor David Copperfield and his painful journey on foot to Aunt Betsey. In the evil eastern districts near the Thames I fancied I could see the sinister figures of Bill Sikes and Fagin; I expected grim Ralph Nickleby to step forth from one of the old houses of the dark and narrow streets of the City; and I looked for Marley's ghostly features on a door-knocker. The fenced-in squares, accessible to the occupants of the surrounding houses by means of private keys, smiled at me pleasantly. The Drury Lane Theatre, which I had to pass from my way from the Waldorf Hotel to Covent Garden, impressed my retrospective imagination as a magnificent memento out of old English theatrical history. Gradually, I began to feel at home in London. I was thoroughly in sympathy with the free use of the lawns in the public parks and gratified by the people's obvious enjoyment of floral displays. Countless evidences of their love for gardens impressed themselves on my mind in town and country. I was greatly interested in the general strike of 1926. A feeling of solidarity manifested itself in a general and spontaneous readiness to be of help, while a vigorous sense of humor tended to mitigate annoying inconveniences. With but a few exceptions, a spirit of moderation and self-discipline prevented outbursts of violence. A similar experience, under more harmless circumstances, was due to one of those unpleasant London fogs which turn day into night and the streets into a spirit world. The boat-train that was to take me to Dover was unable to start, and there were hundreds, and gradually perhaps even thousands, who, like myself, had to wait for their trains. The large hall of the Liverpool Street Station looked like an encampment. People were sitting on their luggage, were standing or lying about; and in all the hours of waiting — my train left at three in the morning instead of five hours earlier — I did not see a single sign of impatience or fretfulness. Everybody put up with the unpleasant situation quietly and good-humoredly and was considerate of his neighbors. Unforgettable, too, are the exuberantly gay scenes on Coronation Day, when men and women in full evening dress were dancing in the streets to any kind of improvised music, and all London seemed joyfully to participate in the festive event.

I could now count myself among the older generation. If the season 1918–19 had not been a time of defeat and revolution, I could have celebrated in Munich the twenty-fifth anniversary of my activity as a conductor. Needless to say, I did nothing of the sort. Four years later, I had left Munich and had succeeded in organizing my future artistic existence as a kind of ordered migratory life. My new independence was an agreeable sensation. Moreover, I considered it appropriate to the unsettled conditions in Europe. From the wealth of invitations to act as guest conductor I accepted only what my conscience would permit, in other words, what I knew I could accomplish by means of my usual method of working. There was no impresario, no agency, to represent me in Europe, for I did not care to have anybody dispose of my time or arrange my work schedule. Nor would I have permitted anybody to offer my services. I wished to appear only where I was wanted. The concerts I conducted in Berlin were enterprises of Louise Wolff and her office, while the Vienna concerts were arranged by the concert manager Hugo Heller or the Philharmonic Orchestra. The Philharmonic Chorus or the Konzerthaus would invite me, and the invitations from other parts of Europe came directly to me. My activity took me all over the Continent, from Scandinavia to Italy and

Spain, and from France to Russia. There were invitations from the concert associations of musical cities and from the managements of operatic festival plays. I had made up my mind to avoid permanent ties and to limit my appearances to artistically attractive occasions. Thus I would gradually gain more time for my constantly growing spiritual interests and inclinations. Since, for reasons explained before, my staying in Munich seemed inadvisable, it was a question of either Vienna or Berlin for my family and me. I mentioned before that we had decided to stay the winter of 1923–4 in Vienna, but it appeared that Berlin was more favorably located for my travels. In the autumn of 1924, we therefore took up tentative quarters in a furnished apartment on Lützowplatz in Berlin. In contrast to Munich, there was hardly any trace of Nazism in Berlin, and, bad though the political situation was, things looked rather hopeful. It was the epoch following upon the miraculous establishment of a sound currency, when Stresemann had spoken of a silver lining on the horizon, a period during which artistic forces boldly bestirred themselves anew.

I was on my way to America for the third time, in January 1925, when a telegram from the board of directors of the Berlin Municipal Opera reached me in Southampton, requesting me to assume the duties of General Musical Director in the autumn of that year. Once more a field of activity suitable to my nature was offered to me. I was again to devote myself to an institute of art, plan and execute a program systematically, create and form an operatic ensemble, bear responsibilities, and perhaps also have a share in a new flourishing of cultural life. After three years of agreeable independence, I naturally hesitated to reassume permanent ties, especially as I had to reckon with the possibility of political disturbances and their effect upon a public institution. But was I justified in disregarding a summons once more to place my strength at the disposal of a great task? I wired my request to defer the whole matter until my return, when I would have an opportunity thoroughly to investigate the task I was to undertake. The delay was agreed to. When I was in Berlin once more, I was called upon by Heinz Tietjen, head of the Breslau Opera, who had been chosen General Manager of the newly to be organized Municipal Opera of Berlin. He assured me of his unlimited readiness to comply with every one of my artistic wishes. Because these first discussions, and a later one during a railway journey, had impressed me with the man's artistic understanding, and because all my contractual demands had been complied with, I finally accepted, and found myself once again in a responsible position at an Opera, where, as a matter of fact, I belonged. We took an apartment on

Kaiserdamm in Charlottenburg and thus definitely moved to Berlin
— or at least so it seemed to us.

IV

In his memoirs, the English ambassador to Berlin, Viscount
d'Abernon, speaks of the time after 1925 as of an epoch of splendor
in the Reich capital's cultural life. Alfred Kerr calls it a new Periclean age. It was indeed as if all the eminent artistic forces were
shining forth once more, imparting to the last festive symposium of
the minds a many-hued brilliance before the night of barbarism
closed in. What the Berlin theaters accomplished in those days
could hardly be surpassed in talent, vitality, loftiness of intention,
and variety. There was the Deutsches Theater and the Kammer-
spiele, in which Reinhardt held sway, imparting to tragedies, plays,
and comedies the character of festival plays — from Shakespeare to
Hauptmann and Werfel, from Molière to Shaw and Galsworthy,
from Schiller to Unruh and Hofmannsthal. The Tribüne, under
Eugen Robert, was devoted to the careful and vivacious rendition
of French, English, and Hungarian comedies. In the State Theater,
Leopold Jessner's dramatic experiments caused heated discussions.
Karlheinz Martin conducted the destinies of the Volksbühne with
a genuine understanding of the artistic popularization of plays and
the theater. Other stages vied with those mentioned in their endeavors to raise dramatic interpretative art to new levels. Actors
and stage directors alike were able to display the full scope of their
talents. Contemporary native and international creations as well
as those of the past had their day on the boards. There was a great
deal of experimenting. There were oddities, and occasionally even
absurdities, but the common denominator, the characteristic sign
of those days, was an unparalleled mental alertness. And the alertness of the giving corresponded to the alertness of the receiving.
A passionate general concentration upon cultural life prevailed,
eloquently expressed by the large space devoted to art by the daily
newspapers in spite of the political excitement of the times. Musical events naturally aroused public interest to no less an extent.
The Philharmonic Concerts led by Wilhelm Furtwängler; the
"Bruno Walter Concerts" with the Philharmonic Orchestra; a
wealth of choral concerts, chamber-music recitals, and concerts by
soloists; the State Opera, deserving of high praise because of *pre-
mières* such as that of Alban Berg's *Wozzeck* and Leoš Janáček's
Jenufa under Erich Kleiber's baton; the newly flourishing Municipal Opera under my guidance; the Kroll Opera under Klemperer;
and a number of other institutes matched the achievements of the

dramatic stage. The endeavors in the realm of the visible arts and the outstanding accomplishments of science — of which I cannot possibly speak here — completed the imposing picture of that epoch.

The Municipal Opera affected me from the beginning as being the most uninspiring and unmagical of all theaters. Its architectural style was expressive of nothing but prosaic stateliness. Besides, there had not as yet been any artistic achievements to make the house dear to its public. No solemn memories transfigured the unattractive auditorium or made those who entered leave drab reality behind them. The magic exerted by rooms and objects may be traced back to any number of causes. The artistic spirit expressed in their shape, their location, or their material may exert a certain magic influence. Gradually, however, it will be eclipsed by their history and their growing wealth of associations, in other words, by the symbolic force they have gained. I once saw at Stefan Zweig's Salzburg home Beethoven's wooden desk, to the eye a soberly uninteresting object without distinguishing features. But it caused a hardly bearable tumultuous onrush of imagination, pictures, memories, thoughts, and sentiments. In short, it exerted power. And it is a comforting thought, especially to the artist, that even in the most sober reality, material things frequently become romanticized, are changed from dull "existence" into a vital "significance." I have taken this roundabout way to motivate both my disappointment at the various aspects of the Municipal Opera and my hopes that the artistic achievements of the coming years might impart to the theater an emotional importance that thus far had been denied to it because of the sobriety of the interior and the surrounding street scene and because of its lack of historical background. But the very fact that the beautiful Munich theaters had so undeservedly presented me with many advantages as a kind of endowment made me eager to use my own powers in creating an atmosphere of its own in this new milieu. At the end of my Berlin activity, I had the impression that I had succeeded to a certain extent.

An endowment of a material kind, but of no mean value, was the technical apparatus of the stage. A fully equipped scene and its cast could be wheeled to the large side-stage at the left and changed there, while the next scene, completely built up, was shifted to the main stage from the right. This possibility of a quick change of scenery, the permanent massive backdrop, the splendidly equipped light-bridge, and an ingenious system of elevator stages and traps gratifyingly facilitated the solution of technical problems.

The stimulating spiritual atmosphere of Berlin was at that time favorable to a project such as mine; and so I hurled myself once more vigorously into the task of building up and developing an operatic institute.

The man associated with me in the guidance of the Municipal Opera, Heinz Tietjen, was one of the strangest persons with whom life has ever brought me into contact. In spite of our meeting almost daily for four years, I cannot say that I ever came to know this impenetrable man. Devoted though his attitude toward me was from the first day of our association to the last, and friendly though our intercourse was, he remained humanly distant and enigmatic to me.

"Did Tietjen ever live?" The jocular question, current among the members of the theater, had its origin in the strangely hidden existence of the official head. Our daily conferences notwithstanding, I should have hesitated to answer the question in the affirmative without certain reservations. Born in Tangier, the son of a German diplomat and a mother of English descent, he could speak German, English, and Spanish. He was moreover indebted to his origin for the quiet adroitness of his intercourse with all kinds of people. From his earliest days, his inclinations had made him turn his back upon his father's profession and social surroundings and espouse the cause of music and the theater. In his endeavors to obtain a thorough musical education, he had, as a budding conductor, had the benefit of Arthur Nikisch's tuition. He became a *Kapellmeister* and subsequently a theatrical director, attempting first in Trier and then in Breslau to combine these roles. At the Municipal Opera, he substituted one evening on short notice in *Siegfried* and was said to have conducted the work with surprising technical mastery. He also conducted occasionally at the Bayreuth Festival Plays, whose management he shared with Winifred Wagner. As a stage director, he was a reliable *routinier,* though lacking in imagination and individuality, but he proved thoroughly expert in questions of theatrical administration. In spite of all his efficiency and versatility, however, there was a certain gray drabness about him. He was a man of medium height, with drooping eyelids, a constantly sidewise look of his bespectacled eyes, a narrow-lipped and tightly compressed mouth, and a nervously twitching face. Never a spirited or spontaneous — to say nothing of an interesting — word came from his lips. His speech, soft, and well considered, was devoid of temperament. Suddenly, a friendly smile and an unmistakably good-natured, intimate expression would break through his natural reserve. He would indulge in cordial conversation — ah, Tietjen was actually living, one thought — when, just as suddenly, the attack would disappear behind a mask of blankness. This naturally provoked a disturbing impression of slyness, but also of restrained force. It no doubt contributed to the strong effect produced by the scheming and inordinately ambitious man. At any rate, though his was surely not a strong personality, there dwelt behind his strange immovability and self-possession a certain obstinate tension, able to outlast a long and patiently borne period of waiting and likely to manifest itself suddenly and at a cleverly chosen moment by well-ordered action. This quiet, long-term planning, combined with his faculty of being able to wait, was one of Tietjen's particularly characteristic traits. In that respect, he was the equal of men of great worldly effectiveness. The "breath control" of his determination may to a large extent explain his surprising rise and the permanence of his success.

In spite of the abysmal difference between the ambitious career-ist and myself, there was a bridge leading from one to the other. It finally collapsed under the excessive strain to which he exposed it, but even the parting of our ways, with all its serious professional and personal reasons, could not quite obliterate its former existence. I have not entirely given up the strange man. Greatly though he disappointed me, I continue to believe in a small oasis of good-naturedness in the desert of his all-consuming ambition, and I like to think that his much-avowed sympathy for me as an artist and a man has outlived our parting and the harsh words I wrote and said to him. Upon that sympathy our collaboration had been built, and he furnished me with proof of it by the sacrificial spirit with which he strove to have all my artistic wishes fulfilled, though they must frequently have been inconvenient to him. The trouble was that, after all, his ambition was greater than his devotion. He had often told me of his resolve to stand or fall with me. He adhered to but the first part of that: he stood with me. But then, I did not fall either — I just went. And as I said before, I am not angry at him. I like to recall the minutes of his frankness and am ready to forgive the hours of his opacity.

When the first months of our work had passed, Tietjen began to speak softly of great projects. What he had in mind was no less than a kind of fusion between our city-owned institute and the State Opera, which was under the jurisdiction of the Prussian Ministry of Culture. The plan of a junction of the state and municipal soloists, chorus, and orchestra, and of a well-ordered repertory for both houses, sounded wonderfully tempting, but I voiced my misgivings of the problems connected with so complicated a reorganization, not the least of which seemed a suitable adjustment between the state and the city. I also told him that I was quite satisfied with the extent of my present sphere of activity, that I was not desirous of adding to my authority, but that in the event of a fusion final decisions would have to be left to me even in the enlarged organization. Only then could I undertake the grave responsibilities that, both in the public's opinion and *de facto,* would rest upon me. I pointed out the difficulties I foresaw in that direction and advised him to drop the subject.

But what did all my reasoning and foresight mean when pitted against Tietjen's ambition? He explained that he considered the whole project attractive only because it would deservedly enlarge my sphere of activity. All he wanted was to prepare the way for me. The disaster I saw looming in the distance did not fail to materialize.

My fiftieth birthday came along, and Dr. Böss, Berlin's Chief Burgomaster, said that it must be celebrated. So, on September 15, 1926, he gave a splendid feast in my honor, and I was told the most flattering things. On the same day, I read in the newspapers that the Prussian State Ministry for Culture and Education had appointed Heinz Tietjen of the Municipal Opera to the post of General Manager of the Berlin State Opera. I called him up the next day and asked for an explanation. He came to see me, looked to one side, twitched nervously, and told my wife and myself that he had given his word to keep his negotiations with the ministry a secret and that he considered the present arrangements but the first step toward the realization of the great plans he had mentioned to me, the fusion of the Municipal and the State Operas under our supreme joint management. I replied that he should not have included me in his obligation of secrecy, as I was more vitally affected than anybody else by his assumption of a new sphere of activity. So far, our interests had been identical, but his affiliation with two institutes had enlarged his field of duties in a sense unfavorable to me. Suggestions made by me on behalf of the Municipal Opera would from now on have to be considered by him from the standpoint of whether or not they conflicted with the interests of the State Opera. I asked him if the Ministry, by his engagement, did not mean to put an end to the newly arisen competition furnished by the Municipal Opera. The result of that discussion and similar ones that followed was that he asked me again and again to have confidence in him and assured me that everything had been done solely in my interest.

My desire to believe him, my patience, and Tietjen's incredible skill in maneuvering succeeded in dragging out for almost three years the conflict between my endeavors centered upon the Municipal Opera and his divided interests. Whether he was still in earnest about his "great project," or whether, in spite of his professed devotion, he had had enough of my mild but stubborn "tyranny" and was eager to bring about a parting of our ways as soon as he felt strong enough — frankly, I do not know. After it had happened twice that young singers I had discovered were engaged by him for the State Opera instead of my institute — one of these instances involved the charming Jarmila Novotna, who had sung for me in Prague — I told him to make his decision: either an actual fusion of the institutes, which had been his project in the first place, and for whose organization I now submitted plans, or the severance of his relations with the State Opera. If that alternative were to be unacceptable to him, I would leave my position. To make me change my mind, Tietjen sent our mutual friend Preetorius to see me. A group of art devotees, led by Georg Bernhard, the editor-in-chief of *Vossische Zeitung*, begged me to stay. Berlin's Chief Burgomaster and a number of members of the City Council endeavored by any number of tempting offers to induce me to assume a more conciliatory attitude. But I proved to them all how impossible and unbearable were the conditions from which I had suffered too long. To the accompaniment of expressions of sympathy, surpassing almost the demonstrations at my leaving Munich, I parted from the Berlin Municipal Opera after an activity of four years. I again chose *Fidelio* for my farewell performance. While I kept my apartment and continued in charge of my concerts with the Philharmonic Orchestra, I conducted an opera in Berlin but once thereafter: Weber's *Oberon*, as a guest of the State Opera.

My decision to take over the Municipal Opera had been influenced by a very personal motive. My parents and my brother and sister lived in Berlin. Except for the concerts at Philharmonic Hall, they had not been able to enjoy much of my music and had only rarely come in contact with my own family. Both Father and Mother were past eighty. Public reports and my letters had kept them informed of my rise, and they had enjoyed the growth of my international reputation. Throughout the long years of my career, and as in my youth, Father's pockets were always crammed with the testimonials of my success. I was now greatly desirous of being near my parents once more and of enabling them to witness my performances. Father had grown entirely deaf, but he insisted that he could hear music. At any rate, he sat in the audience with a beaming face, but I presume the sight of the people and their applause made him happier than my performance. Mother's hearing was still good, but she was ailing a good deal and was therefore less able to enjoy things. Nevertheless, my parents, and naturally my brother and sister too, basked happily in the splendor that had never before come so near them, and I shared their joy with all my heart. The threatening disaster of the Hitler movement did not as yet trouble their thoughts, for in Berlin more than anywhere else it looked that year as if the danger were passing. My parents died before Nazism had a chance to affect their fate. So it was vouchsafed to me to enjoy their serene and peaceful presence and to be near them in their last days. They left this earth feeling that life had been beautiful.

Vienna had in the meantime changed a good deal. The great power, whose metropolitan center the city had been, was shattered, and the city of millions, having become the center of a small Austria, tried to adapt itself inwardly and outwardly to the changed conditions. Federal Chancellor Seipel was a clever statesman, a man of high moral standing, internationally respected. True, the two leading political parties, the Christian Socialists and the Social Democrats, were fighting each other, but not too violently. There was a feeling of recuperation and reconstruction in the air.

After Gregor's departure, the Opera had passed into the hands of Richard Strauss and Franz Schalk as co-directors. The two badly matched men were unable to understand each other, and so, in 1924, Strauss took his wrathful leave and Schalk remained in sole charge. He was a Viennese, filled with the local musical tradition, a pupil and disciple of Bruckner, an excellent musician, a man of spirit and culture — and he loved the Vienna Opera. Fully conscious of his grave responsibilities, he lived only for the beloved institute. Although his importance as a musician and a personality overshadowed that of the conductor, his effect at the desk — increasingly in the course of the years — was one of authority and seriousness. His achievements as director of the institute deserve to be held in high esteem. He was a man of fighting disposition, the possessor of an exceedingly nimble and mischievous wit, and he used his sharp weapons effectively in the interest of the State Opera and of art. When he took the ensemble of the Vienna Opera to Paris, he scored a decided success, especially with a performance of *Fidelio*.

During the eleven years of my first activity at the Vienna Court Opera, Schalk and I had not come in close personal contact with each other. The mocking tone of cool superiority, natural to him, had affected me rather disagreeably in my young years. I was not ready to concede to Schalk any superiority, except that of years and self-assurance, and kept away from him because of the feeling of aversion always caused me by persons of a mocking or sarcastic disposition. It is more than probable, too, that some of my qualities were disagreeable to him, but our relations were always marked by politeness and respect. There were even exceptional occasions when — probably to our mutual surprise — we found ourselves engaged in animated conversation. But we soon would withdraw again into our own selves. I do not know if I did an injustice to Schalk at the time by attributing to him emotional insufficiency accompanied by mental acuteness. In fact, the subsequent whole-hearted services he rendered the Vienna Opera, and his artistic growth during his final years would seem to indicate forces whose development had either been prevented by the mildew of his mocking coolness or whose presence had remained hidden to my youthful inexperience. At any rate, it turned out that, decades later, and shortly before his death, we suddenly found ourselves in an atmosphere of good will. I was touched by his unquestionable devotion to the Opera and by the increasingly deep seriousness of his musicianship, while he, on his part, was presumably pleased with my consistently maintained artistic attitude. So it happened that, when we met at his suggeston at a quiet café near Salzburg, we spent a cordially animated hour in each other's company. Later, when his serious illness prevented his conducting a certain work by Mozart at the Salzburg Festival Plays, he asked me in a letter to take over: it would be a comfort to him to know the work was in my hands.

The ties binding me to Vienna's musical life became ever closer in the course of the twenties. Musical Vienna seemed to be greatly attached to me and to stand by me. Every concert was marked by increased cordiality and furnished new proof of our intimate relationship. Then, too, I was able to see my friends on every visit to Vienna and to renew the old feeling of affinity that the wealth of our common spiritual and artistic inclinations kept green and flourishing.

At that time, a new person entered my life, enriching it with the gifts of his spirit. After I had conducted a performance of Mahler's Second Symphony, Alma made me acquainted with Franz Werfel. His name was not unfamiliar to me. I had read some of the poems that probably dated from the days of his association with a singular literary circle in Prague, and had discovered in them, in addition to a number of rather inaccessible obscurities, a noble, emotionally strong, and linguistically novel lyricism. When we became gradually better acquainted, his personality fully confirmed my first impressions of his poetic nature. I had to think of Staretz Sossima's friend in *The Brothers Karamazov*, whom Dostoyevsky called a "vibrating soul, as it were." Werfel, too, seemed to vibrate under the influence of every contact with life, with people, with events, and, perhaps to an even larger degree, with music. I recognized the wealth of formative thoughts made to gush forth by the compelling power of life's experiences.

Werfel was a true poet. When his genuine love of telling a tale —in which respect he reminded me of Hamsum and Lagerlöf— made him draw his word pictures in his great novels, it seemed that the essential element within him was an irresistible urge, vitalized by the richness of his vision, and that the shaping of his great forms was guided by that elemental, dreamlike impulse. Wonderful were the hours we spent at Alma's beautiful home in Steinfeldgasse on the Hohe Warte in Vienna, for Werfel possessed to a high degree the quality I value above all in intellectual persons: he gave of himself lavishly in conversation. He also had the gift of an oral expressiveness that made his every description into an actual experience. His love of music formed a special tie between us. I often noticed with admiration how thoroughly and profoundly he knew the music dear to his heart. Particularly remarkable was his familiarity with Verdi's operas, resulting in his German translations and adaptations of their librettos. Werfel's deep interest in the great Italian musician was manifested also in his Verdi novel, in which Venice is really the magnificently drawn main figure. I may say generally that never in my concerts and operatic performances have I had a more ardently sympathetic listener or one who was more earnestly devoted to music than Franz Werfel. He enjoyed music with his senses as much as with his soul; in short, he vibrated with music in conformity to his nature. I am of the opinion that his relations with Alma were based on her saturation with music and her enthusiastic playing of it as well as on her profound understanding of literature.

His *Barbara* had made a deep impression on me, I loved *The Pascarella Family,* and had been profoundly moved by the *Forty Days of Musa Dagh,* a book that, strange to say, was based upon his impressions of Damascus and was prophetically written before the persecutions of Jews in Germany took place. I enjoyed *Embezzled Heaven,* especially the masterfully written scenes of the deceitful nephew, and could understand how, in Lourdes, the terrible agitation of the poet in flight before the Nazi hordes longed to express itself in a yearning for a miracle and was captivated by the wondrous tale of the child Bernadette. I saw little of Werfel in those years in Vienna. I did not get there very often, and when I did, he was frequently working in Breitenstein on the Semmering. But we did not become lost to each other, and his work remained close to my heart. During the years immediately before the *Anschluss,* we saw more of each other in Vienna, and we met again later in America. I shall have more to say about him.

The Salzburg Festival Plays, which were destined to achieve world fame and of which I shall speak in detail later, had their inception in the twenties. I merely wish to mention here that I took part in them for the first time in 1925, when I was invited by the management to perform Donizetti's *Don Pasquale* in the handsome little Stadttheater — the Festival Playhouse had not yet come into existence — and that, in the following summer, I produced there Mozart's *Die Entführung aus dem Serail* and Johann Strauss's *Die Fledermaus.* That same summer, I conducted a symphony concert with the Vienna Philharmonic Orchestra in the beautiful hall of the Mozarteum, whose director was Bernhard Paumgartner, a former pupil of mine in Vienna.

Another memorable event of the year 1926 was my going to Russia once more. I conducted a number of concerts in Leningrad's Philharmonic Hall and one of several operatic performances in the former Maryinsky Theater; unless I am mistaken, it was Tchaikovsky's *Pique-Dame.* It was then, too, that Nicolai Malko spoke to me of the twenty-year-old Dmitri Shostakovich and asked me to let him play his First Symphony for me. I was strongly impressed by both the composition and the composer, and, as I mentioned before, I performed the work in Berlin soon thereafter. Egon Petri, the excellent pianist, was in Leningrad at the time. His several appearances as assisting artist at my concerts were highly successful. The city, crowded in my imagination with figures and events from Russian novels, aroused my passionate interest. I never grew tired, while wandering about, of conjuring up the St. Petersburg of that incomparable literature. But my preoccupation with the city's past cultural and social epoch, or rather with its poetical representation, did not prevent me from seeing the present. Magnificently present was the mighty city, so imposingly situated on the banks of the Neva, with its historically interesting and frequently picturesque buildings, squares, bridges, and avenues. And there were also the people of the present, conscious of the process of a social reorganization in which they were involved, their gaze and their plans directed toward the future, and accompanied and encouraged on their way into the new by the art of yesterday and today, the cultivation of which was close to the Russians' heart. The theaters and orchestras were giving of their best, and the magnificent collections of the Hermitage had been augmented by works of art from the private possessions of the former propertied classes. I paid a number of visits to the Hermitage and found it crowded every time with reverently gazing people. The streets still presented a rather doleful aspect, but there was a considerable improvement over what I had seen in Moscow three years before. The Leningrad Philharmonic Orchestra, the members of the Opera, and the audiences made me joyfully aware of that spirit of enthusiasm which imparts to Russia's musical life its pulsating force.

In the same winter, I accepted an invitation to conduct a concert with the orchestra of La Scala, Milan, and had the pleasure of meeting Arturo Toscanini for the first time. I had heard much of him, the first time from Mahler, who told me he had, in 1908, heard *Tristan* conducted by Toscanini. "He conducts it in a manner entirely different from ours," Mahler had added, "but magnificently in his way." A great many reports concerning Toscanini's work in Milan had reached me, but I had never had the opportunity to hear him. Now I had at least made his personal acquaintance. The meeting, casual though it was, made a deep and lasting impression on me. "Lucifer!" was the first thought called up by his striking resemblance to one of Franz Stuck's paintings. I wished I could come to know the man better and fathom the secret of so exceptional a being. My wish was to be fulfilled later. Our paths crossed, and I owe to the activity of the eminent musician and powerful man a wealth of valuable musical experiences.

V

MY work at the Municipal Opera House naturally prevented my going to America during the winter season. But when I was invited by Cleveland to conduct a number of symphony concerts in conjunction with a Music Festival of Choral Societies in the summer of 1927, and when soon thereafter the management of the Hollywood Bowl inquired if I was available for several concerts in that interesting amphitheater, I realized how greatly I, too, was susceptible to the old human urge toward the west. I decided to cross the ocean once more, accompanied by my wife and our younger daughter. We sailed for New York, beyond which the whole mighty continent now rose up before my tense expectation.

We were indebted to the warm season for a calm crossing, but also for unparalleled heat in New York. Cleveland was hardly more bearable. The Music Festival proved to be a super-dimensional event. Never had I seen anything of the kind in Europe. There must have been two thousand or more participants in the mammoth hall of the Public Auditorium, with its capacity of eight thousand. The orchestra was excellent and truly devoted to its task. Another enjoyable fact was the cordial American hospitality. Everything was done to make pleasant our stay in the city on Lake Erie. But my imagination was fired by the thought of the westward-moving frontier, the lines of pioneers, the covered wagons, the Spanish missions, and the gold-rush period and I looked forward with impatience to our journey from Ohio to California. It turned out to be quite a trial, for we literally jumped from the frying pan into the fire. Those were not yet the days of air-cooled cars and streamlined trains covering the distance between Chicago and Los Angeles in two nights and a day. The journey took about three nights and two days, and the heat in the compartments was almost suffocating. What good were the comforts of the drawing-room and compartment I had extravagantly engaged for the three of us? There was no escaping from the car's desert temperature. The main meals were taken at stations during sufficiently long stops of the train. I seem to recall distinctly that there was no dining car. From time to time, we tried to cool off by indulging in an ice cream cone, but it did not help. I can still see us in Dodge City stepping into the street from the station in search of a breath of fresh air, only to hurry back, startled and penitent, from the sizzling heat to the oven temperature of the car.

But how beautiful it was when we got to California and permitted ourselves to be captivated by the climate, the light, the colors, and the landscape! I was enraptured from the first moment. Often I thought I was in Spain or in southern France, until the fabulous motor highways and skyscrapers took me back to American reality, from which, again, I was transported into a world of fancy by the impressions I gained in the studios of the great film companies. When, during the first night at my Hollywood hotel, I stepped out on the balcony to enjoy the splendid coolness and the night wind, I saw in the light of the full moon on the roof of a nearby house a rifle-bearing soldier in a Turkish uniform walking up and down, sentry-like. I was at once impressed — as I was so often later — by the mixture of beauty and make-believe so characteristic of Hollywood.

I gladly accepted the invitation of a number of studios and set foot with interest in that artificial world. I made the acquaintance of Douglas Fairbanks and watched him direct scenes with fierce horsemen and old Spanish carriages. I saw charming Lillian Gish at work and met Paul Whiteman who, with his amazing jazz orchestra, happened to fulfill an engagement in Hollywood. I let Ramon Novarro and Conrad Veidt instruct me in the art of how to feel instantly in the proper mood during scenes it took barely two minutes to shoot, how to relax nonchalantly in sober surroundings for an hour, and how to flame up passionately again or grow icily rigid for another two minutes. I also watched Greta Garbo and John Gilbert in a scene from *Anna Karenina*. Everything was done silently, for the sound film had not as yet been invented. There was some sound, nevertheless, for at a number of scenes a harmonium started to drool out insignificant music that had not the slightest bearing upon the dramatic proceedings. I was told it was done to put the actors in the proper mood for their task. Many years later, when the spoken word had raised the film to a higher level, I again watched the filming of a few scenes and realized that my former amazement had been due to the erroneous expectation that I was to become acquainted with a branch of art related to the theater. It was the spoken word that made me realize that it was the only element the stage and the film had in common, that their ways must run in different directions, and that the enormous possibilities of the film, with laws of its own, could be achieved and developed only through an entire emancipation from the laws of the stage. To me, the essential difference seemed to be that in the theater living people had to present their parts in immovable surroundings and with an immovable audience before them, while in the film, with its surroundings changing at will, they became the object of the camera and its unlimited possibilities. They played not for an audience in front of them, but for the wide world. True, the living presence of the performer, his fruitful spontaneous vitality, and the mutual relationship between the audience and the artist were thus lost, but, to compensate for that and for the third dimension of substantiality, we had the whole limitless mobile fairy world of the camera and the facilities of a magic carpet able instantly to transport men and things anywhere. Moreover, the film will have gained the full supporting power of music as soon as it is able to reproduce tones more beautifully and faithfully than is now the case.

But will the reproduction by apparatuses, no matter how perfect, ever be able to achieve the blissfully elevating effect of spontaneous interpretative art produced by living people? Will the time come when mechanically contrived proceedings will no longer taste as if they had come out of a can? The answers to these questions will be furnished by the highly gifted people at work upon the discovery and development of the film style of tomorrow.

I was looking forward to my concerts in the Hollywood Bowl with some apprehension. I had never before conducted in the open, was afraid of the acoustic properties of the circular valley, of the incompatibility of the two infinites of music and space, of the effect of night dampness on the tuning of the strings, and of any number of other things. All aesthetic and practical apprehensions disappeared before the magic of that unique scene. So powerful was the effect on me that I could almost forget the acoustic insufficiencies of the space. It was uplifting indeed to conduct in that bowl while the orchestra strove devotedly and the many thousands filling the vast amphitheater way up into the mountains listened eagerly. What had happened to me to make me undisturbed by the night wind threatening the sheets on the musicians' desks, to make me overlook the insufficient brilliance of the *fortissimo* and the unreliability of the *pianissimo?* There was the splendor of the California night, of the starry sky, and of the dark mountains surrounding us; there was the touching silence of the immense throng. For once my musical conscience, stunned by so much beauty, yielded, and I felt overcome by a mood of happy exaltation, renewed at every future visit to the magic valley.

Opposite the Bowl's main entrance stood the house of our old friend Lili Petschnikoff. There she lived with two of her children — the eldest daughter was living in Munich — and two ancient women: her mother and the latter's sister. She had met us upon our arrival in Los Angeles with an outburst of exultation of which only she was capable and had given us the benefit of her familiarity with the surroundings. She took us bathing at Santa Monica and showed us La Venta near Palos Verdes and other paradisiac places. She loved and cared for her children, was devoted to her friends, and, with her exuberant vitality, lived a life of unselfishness and human sympathy. In the evening, when the endless stream of cars rolled past their house to the Hollywood Bowl, the two old women would sit peacefully side by side on the wooden veranda, turning the tranquillity of their aged gaze upon the violent agitation before them. I hardly ever omitted to say a word of greeting to them before I started out myself, hemmed in by the countless cars, which, at their destination, were directed by attendants to mammoth parking places. Lili had usually gone ahead to her place in the Bowl, her white curly head a plainly visible beacon in the vast multitude. After the concert, she would often take us back to her hospitable house for an hour of her joyful company and the amusing presence of "gran'ma" and "auntie."

I had to conduct a number of San Francisco concerts in the Auditorium, a giant hall holding ten thousand people, and at San Mateo. We went by way of charming Santa Barbara, still showing the effects of an earthquake, and enjoyed the magnificent countryside around Carmel, with its splendid Hotel Del Monte. San Francisco seemed to me the most beautiful American city I had seen. I never grew tired roaming its excitingly steep streets, exploring its wonderful surroundings, and having older people tell me of the earthquake and the fire that had gained so important a place in the city's history.

I vividly recall the Chinese theater I attended with my wife and daughter. The endless sequence of scenes, a strongly profiled histrionic performance now and then, the gorgeous colorful costumes, masterly fencing scenes, and the utter indifference to illusion — the stabbed man got up again at the end of the scene and the change of scenery took place before the eyes of the audience — all were strangely attractive to us. Only the "music," which formlessly and monotonously accompanied the proceedings on the stage almost without interruption was wholly incomprehensible to me. The frequent striking of a gong startled me again and again, and finally drove me from the theater. But the sight of the densely crowded streets of the Chinese quarter, of the shops with their precious, strange goods, of the exclusively Chinese audience in the theater, and of the performance itself left me with a deep and lasting impression and with a feeling of sadness caused by the realization of how little of his family and its habits of life man comes to know during his brief stay on this earth.

The beaming smile of the California sun does not protect one in San Francisco from the icy winds that suddenly sweep through the streets with wintry roughness. I felt increasingly ill at ease on my return east, spent the hours between our arrival at and departure from Chicago at the station, and went to bed as soon as I got on the steamer. I was fortunately too weak to heed the ship doctor's advice to walk about the deck and let the ocean air cure me. I lay motionless in my stateroom until the steamship docked, struggled aboard the Munich train, and was informed by our physician to my surprise and my family's horror that I was suffering from double pneumonia. Instead of conducting at the Salzburg Festival Plays, I had to lie in bed for weeks. It was my first serious illness, and it gave me the opportunity for a good deal of earnest thinking. So, in the end, it had a very salutary spiritual effect upon me.

A family event took place during the days of my convalescence. My elder daughter, who had started on her career as an opera singer in Hanover and had been engaged at the Würzburg Stadttheater for the past year, married the stage director of that theater. I had not as yet regained my normal health, and we celebrated the event quietly in our hotel rooms. At about that time, the circle of my friends was augmented by a new and valuable personality. In 1926, the writer and poet Bruno Frank had moved into my house in Mauerkircherstrasse, the ownership of which I had acquired during the days of my Munich activity. We now made each other's acquaintance. In fact, this highly gratifying meeting may have happened earlier, for I can see myself and Lisl Frank, Fritzi Massary's daughter, toiling from office to office of the Munich Lodging Department, trying to induce the guardians of the strict dwelling laws to permit the rental of my house to a single family of two members. Where my influence as the former General Musical Director of Bavaria proved insufficient, the impressive charm of the handsome and clever young woman did its share. The old officials relented, gave their approval, and Frank and his wife rented the house. Now, after my illness, we called on them and enjoyed their wonderfully cordial presence, the comfortable appointments of the familiar rooms, and their three jolly, but by no means noisy, dogs. I had been attracted before by Frank's poems, which had made his name favorably known. The performance of some of his plays, among them that of *Die Treue Magd* at the Vienna Burgtheater, had drawn attention to his dramatic talent. He also scored a great and far-reaching stage success with his delightful comedy, *Sturm im Wasserglas*, but what impressed me particularly were his tales about Frederick the Great. In his *Tage des Königs, Trenck,* and others of his writings I came to recognize a poet's unprecedented faculty of penetrating to the core of a historical figure. Bruno Frank had permitted his thoughts to dive so deeply into the problematical, complicated, and eminent nature of the king who hated and despised people and served his political and social aims with a kind of cold, fanatical idealism, that he seemed to speak in his tales with Frederick's own voice and the reader put down the book with the feeling of having made the personal acquaintance of the unhappy, brilliant, hard man, the lofty intellectual and lonely misanthrope. Frank's other novelettes and novels, too, were expressive of deep and affectionate human understanding. The narrative art pulsating through his warm heart was ennobled by a linguistic mastery that — consciously or unconsciously — had received its impulse from the mighty prose of Kleist's novelettes. In the Salzburg summers, only a lawn separated our house in Aigen from that of Frank, and so we saw much of each other. Later, we met again in Beverly Hills, California, and a friendly intercourse resulted, in the course of which I felt enriched by Frank's encyclopedic knowledge and uplifted by the flowing warmth of his pure heart.

In the meantime, the Covent Garden season in London had been repeated every year. Their spreading fame had induced M. Georges Caurier of Paris to come to London, in May 1927 to interest me in the project of a Mozart Cycle in Paris. He was planning to follow up the London season of 1928 by productions of Mozart's *Entführung, Nozze di Figaro, Don Giovanni, Così fan tutte,* and *Magic Flute* at the Théâtre des Champs Elysées. As he promised to fulfill my every wish concerning casts, orchestra, chorus, rehearsals, scenery, and costumes, I agreed to his proposition. I had thus far conducted only concerts in Paris. I think they were with the Orchestre

Philharmonique de Paris and with the Société des Concerts, the latter being the old orchestra of the Conservatoire, which had been so highly praised by Richard Wagner and which was now giving its concerts in the noble classic hall of the Conservatory under the guidance of Philippe Gaubert, the Opéra conductor. But my concerts had always taken place at the Salle Pleyel. Words fail me to express what Paris and France came to mean to me in those years and how uplifted and deeply moved I was by the realization that I was walking in the city of Berlioz, Auber, Bizet, Liszt, and Chopin, and of Stendhal, Balzac, and Maupassant. I had come to Paris late in my life, but late love is strong. It burned within me when I enjoyed the magnificent beauty of the city and the monuments of its prodigious history, and it overwhelmed me when France clasped me to her heart, in 1938 and made me her citizen.

Monsieur Caurier and I got up a cast composed of French and German artists, and he came to Berlin in the winter of that year, accompanied by Mme Ritter-Ciampi and Mme Destanges. They were to attend some of my Mozart performances at the Municipal Opera and rehearse with me in order to become acquainted with the style I required. The festive Paris performances took place in the early summer of 1928 and made a deep impression. *The Magic Flute*, especially, captivated the hearts of musical Paris. My memory has preserved a glowing picture of the superb Sarastro of my Munich basso Paul Bender, who looked like St. Francis, and of the girlish Pamina of the Viennese Lotte Schöne. I do not think that the sublime beauty of the moment when, after the message of love from the Sacred Halls, Sarastro places his arm protectingly on Pamina's shoulder has ever been more touchingly and solemnly revealed.

Moral support was given the performances by the circles around the idealist Firmin Gémier, whose aim it was to create a world theater. The Mozart Cycle with German and French artists under my guidance seemed to him a step toward his goal. He received me most warmly. Édouard Herriot, too, the then Minister of Education, upon whom I called at his Ministry, seemed to welcome this *rapprochement* in the realm of art.

My appearance as a guest conductor in Paris led to a new connection. A representative of the Palais des Beaux-Arts in Brussels called on me requesting that I appear at some concerts there. Ties of genuine friendship soon bound me to that charming and historically interesting city which, until the outbreak of the war, frequently called me to its beautiful hall and before its seriously musical and enthusiastic audience. I also came to know King Albert and Queen Elisabeth, a former Bavarian Princess. During an intermission, they asked me to their box through M. Leboeuf, a musical enthusiast and the founder of those concerts. I was gratified to find that the royal couple were high-minded as well as simple people, devoted to art.

Invitations to operatic festival plays also took me to Antwerp and Stockholm. In the latter city I conducted concerts in the architecturally magnificent Concert House, built by Tengbom, and operas in the Royal Opera House, which was influenced in its style by Austrian theatrical buildings.

I conducted some symphony concerts in Warsaw, too, and so the circle of my life took in an ever-increasing number of countries, cities, and people. Beyond my artistic activity, the concerts, operatic performances, and travels upon which I had to embark meant to me a welcome opportunity for gathering experiences, assimilating them, and coming to know mankind under infinitely varying circumstances.

While thus my outward *Lebensraum* expanded, I was vouchsafed the good fortune to discover new land in my very own domain, yes, in my own soul: I found Bruckner. Strange, that I had to grow almost fifty years before recognizing a genius who, at about the same age, had begun to create his great works. He wrote his Mass in F-minor when he was forty-four and the Third, which marks the beginning of his important symphonies, at the age of forty-nine. I had known Bruckner's works for many years without really coming close to them. I expended a good deal of zealous effort on occasional performances of his symphonies in Munich, Berlin, and Vienna. But with all my love of his themes, with all my admiration of the wealth and sublimity of his inspiration, I had felt "outside." His form had been unintelligible to me; I had considered it out of proportion, exaggerated, and primitive. The emotional substance of his music had stirred me by its soulful force and depth and delighted me by its occasional Austrian charm, but I had not been able to feel at home on his soil. To move without restraint within the monumental edifice of Bruckner's work had seemed to be denied me. All at once, a change came over me. The increased maturity and deeper tranquillity gained during my illness may have had something to do with it. For Bruckner, though he is a pure musician and though his symphonies, having their origin in elemental musical sources, are so far removed from thought associations, yet demands a certain fundamental spiritual frame of mind before he can be understood and loved. The Gothicism of the Cologne Cathedral had remained unfathomable to me; that of Bruckner's symphonies — for a kind of musical Gothicism is here involved — was now revealed to me. I recognized in the melodic substance, in the towering climaxes, and in the emotional world of his symphonies the great soul of their creator, pious and childlike. This stirring recognition, in turn, made me comprehend effortlessly the substance and form of his music. I can hardly express in words the importance Bruckner's work has since gained in my life, to what degree my admiration for the beauty and symphonic power of his music has increased, what ever more richly flowing source of exaltation it has grown to be.

In the spring of 1929, during the last months of my activity at the Berlin Municipal Opera, Toscanini came to Berlin with the artists of the La Scala. His masterly performances conveyed to the German public a higher conception of the older Italian operas, such as *Lucia, Trovatore,* and *Rigoletto,* and the very highest conception of Italian operatic culture generally. *Manon Lescaut, Aïda,* and *Falstaff* were added to the works mentioned above. Every detail of the performances I witnessed spoke of the life-work and the imperative moral feeling of responsibility of an eminent musician. The perfection and stylistic sureness of his performances were gratifyingly refreshing to me.

In the summer of 1929, I accepted another invitation from California. I was longing to renew the beautiful and warming impressions so deeply imprinted on my memory. I gave as little thought to the tormenting heat of the journey across the American continent as a woman in love does to former labor pains and to her determination never to have another child. This second visit was memorable because it afforded me the opportunity to see mighty Yosemite Valley and to pay a visit to the venerable redwoods. A San Francisco friend of mine who knew and loved the districts around his magnificent native city took me into the very heart of the grandiosely rugged mountainous site of that wild natural reservation. I marveled at the Indian-named hotel, outwardly adapted to its surroundings, but inwardly ultra-stylish. We spent the night there, but were longing for the wilderness ahead of us. We found it. While we were driving slowly through the forest in the dark of the night, a bear family suddenly burst through the trees immediately in front of us and trotted toward the water which, a short distance away, shone in the feeble light of the moon. The searchlight of our car showed us the gigantic parental couple and their droll offspring enjoying their night-cap.

Very different from this grandiose, and in its way moving, impression was the course of my experience in Bohemian Grove, formed by the thousand-year-old giant trees of the redwoods or sequoias. It was owned by the Bohemian Club of San Francisco. The then president of the city's symphony orchestra, a member of the club, had invited me to attend one of the annual festivities arranged in Bohemian Grove. A drive of several hours in his car, by way of the old town of Petaluma, took us north. Never had I experienced anything resembling my entry into that prehistoric forest. When I was a young man, the interior of the Gothic cathedral with its enormous pillars had seemed to me a forest of stone. Now I felt as if I were in a cathedral built by nature. Under these sky-high and entirely straight giant trees of fabulous circumference — the redwoods are said to be the oldest growing things in the world — walked a crowd of men, representing all walks of life. Most of them were past middle age. They hailed from all states of the Union, called one another by their first names, and gave free reign to their exuberant mood. They wished to spend a few days in the woods among congenial men, far from their business and families, sleeping out in the open under the clear blue sky of California in wooden shacks leaning against rocks or conforming to particularly bizarre shapes and positions of trees. Visits were exchanged. There was a good deal of talking and drinking, Prohibition being mainly responsible for the latter. There were music and songs. Not only stringed instruments could be heard, but occasionally there came from one of the fantastic dwellings the sound of a Steinway piano. In the evening there was opera, an opera specially written and composed for the occasion, sung and presented by men, and listened to by the whole crowd of visitors. There was a stage with a modern lighting plant. On the ground in front of it lay a considerable number of treetrunks on which the audience was seated. The by-laws of the Bohemian Club provided that the forest must have a prominent place in the opera's libretto. The subject of the work I listened to was the story of Robin Hood. I recall that there was a handsomely and colorfully costumed festival procession. It became visible between the trees, wended its way to the stage, and brought the performance to an effective conclusion. In addition to professional musicians, members of the club played in the orchestra. The performance over, everybody repaired to another clearing, in which a large fire was blazing. The coolness of the California night made its warmth quite agreeable. The participants in the festivity stood or lay about until far into the night. Driving once more through the forest on the following morning, we passed Russian River, in which the indefatigable men were already having their morning swim, and finally got back to San Francisco. Although I was somewhat confused by the strange combination of silently mighty primeval nature and the loud brisk stir of civilization, I was heartily interested in the festive occasion, called "High Jinks," as against the "Low Jinks" that had preceded it a week before. Its freshness, vigor, and originality have remained unforgettable in my mind.

Our second stay in California terminated more propitiously than that of two years before. The arrival of the Zeppelin on its round-the-world flight had been announced. Preceded by siren-sounding motor-cycle policemen, we drove to the airfield late at night. At sunrise, we witnessed the landing of the beautiful silvery airship, which had come from Japan. We were present at a super-dimensional dinner given by William Randolph Hearst to Hugo Eckener, the pilot of the Zeppelin. We met Eckener again on the ship that carried us back to Hamburg from New York. He asked me if I did not remember having been accosted after a Hamburg concert by a thin blond youth who had expressed his enthusiasm over my performance of the *"Eroica."* He had been the young man. I actually recalled the incident. We had a number of conversations during the voyage. He spoke about music, and I about aeronautics. When I asked about his great journey, he told me that the most imposing impression had been the flight over Siberia, where they had seen parts of the world never before trod by human feet or seen by human eyes. In mid-ocean, we were overtaken by the Zeppelin which, under another pilot, had left New York a few days after our departure. After some friendly greetings exchanged between above and below, the silvery sheen disappeared in the clouds.

VI

WHILE I was at the head of the Municipal Opera, I had accepted repeated invitations from the Leipzig Gewandhaus. At each of my appearances as a guest conductor I felt a close communion with this, the oldest and most celebrated of Germany's concert institutes. When my impending departure from the Berlin Opera became known, Max Brockhaus, president of the Gewandhaus Committee and head of the well-known publishing concern, inquired if I were willing to assume the position of Gewandhaus conductor. I consented with all my heart, for I felt a "selective affinity" with an institute unchangeably conscious of its responsibility to keep alive a great past and champion valuable contemporary creations. To care for its continued mission and its enduring importance in the musical life of Europe seemed to me, a man of fifty-three, a worthy task for the rest of my life. Like so many others, I expected to see Nazism decline, believed that Stresemann and Briand would be successful, and, with the Gewandhaus as the center of my work, looked forward to a flourishing activity in a progressively musical and decreasingly political world.

Theme and Variations

Wilhelm Furtwängler had been my immediate predecessor in Leipzig. Before him, Arthur Nikisch had held sway there for more than twenty-five years, and names like that of Carl Reinecke, Ferdinand Hiller, and Felix Mendelssohn bore testimony to the institute's old glory. It may be said that, as a center of music, Leipzig used to rank highest among the German cities. The Thomaskirche and Thomasschule owed their world importance to Bach, and Karl Straube, the present Thomaskantor, whose acquaintance I enjoyed during my years in Leipzig, knew how to add new luster to the school and the church by his sound musicianship. The Leipzig Conservatory, started by Felix Mendelssohn, had always been a powerful magnet to attract German and foreign students of music — Robert Schumann had been one of its teachers — and the music — and book-publishing activities of the city deserved its world-wide fame.

True, the city itself was singularly devoid of charm. No traces of the young student Goethe were able to lead me to interesting buildings, streets, or sites. Even Auerbach's Cellar hid its turbulent past — or at least its portrayal in *Faust* — under the appearance of a tame middle-class restaurant. I soon abandoned my efforts to see in Leipzig more than the sober frame for musical culture and booklore. It struck me that not even the university and the students' bustle seemed able to form a rebellious counterpoint against the *cantus firmus* of the city's Philistine character. Why, it appeared as if the Supreme Court, the highest judicial authority in Germany, and all its officials had taken on Leipzig's sober protective coloring rather than light up the city with the splendor of their transcendent authority as the dispenser of supreme judicial wisdom.

All this decided me to retain my Berlin domicile and content myself with going to Leipzig at regular intervals. I stopped there at the historically well-known Hotel Hauffe. Weather permitting, I could ride in my car from Berlin to Leipzig in about two hours and a half. My way took me past Potsdam, through the Brandenburg landscape and Wittenberg, where Martin Luther had nailed his combative theses to the doors of the castle church. Just when the countryside became wholly desolate and bereft of charm, I reached the outskirts of Leipzig and was fortified by the knowledge that I would soon conduct an orchestra rehearsal in the beautiful hall of the Gewandhaus. There was nothing I liked better, nothing that was more compatible with my musical nature than the atmosphere of that house and of those concerts. If the advent of the Antichrist in 1933 had not put an end to my activity after four years, I should surely have continued there, all the more so because my various outside guest appearances could have easily been accommodated to my Leipzig schedule.

In the spring of 1930, when Toscanini and the New York Philharmonic Orchestra were on their triumphal tour of the musical centers of Europe, Leipzig extended its welcome to them. It was interesting to be told by Toscanini that his one Gewandhaus concert, with its following social gathering, had made him, too, sensible of the institute's classic atmosphere, a quality that, in my more ample experience, had always impressed me as being the incomparable virtue of the Gewandhaus. I also attended Toscanini's Berlin concert with the New York orchestra. A splendid performance of Debussy's *La Mer* still sounds in my ear.

One of the peculiarities of the Gewandhaus concerts was the exemplary reverential attitude of the audience. There were no latecomers, and silence reigned even before the conductor appeared. The honest attendant used to summon me to the platform by announcing in unadulterated Saxon accents: "If you please, Herr *Kapellmeester,* silence has just set in."

Pleasant relations outside the institute began to develop. Gustav Brecher, whom I had met in the old days in Vienna and on a number of subsequent occasions, was now director of the Leipzig Opera. I was frequently in the company of this exceptionally clever and cultivated musician, and was soon on terms of friendship also with Max Brockhaus and his family. I felt attracted by Herr Kippenberg, the head of the Insel publishing concern and owner of a uniquely valuable collection of Goethe mementos. Ties of sympathy bound me to Chief Burgomaster Dr. Gördeler, the man who is said to have come to so horrible an end at the hands of the Nazis. I was especially gratified by the spirit manifested by Arthur Nikisch's family and deeply appreciative of their welcoming me to the position he had held for so many years.

The reputation of the Salzburg Festival Plays and my share in them had grown considerably in the meantime. When the Festival Playhouse was completed in 1928, I took part in its solemn inauguration by conducting the orchestra's first concert in the new hall. The Festival Plays later assumed so great an importance in my life and achieved so international a reputation that I shall speak more in detail of them when this record reaches the years of their world fame.

In addition to my Gewandhaus activities, my most important responsibilities between the year of hope, 1929, when Briand and Stresemann expended their political and moral powers on behalf of pan-European thought, and the year of disaster, 1933, which crushed every hope, were centered upon the Covent Garden season, though I conducted there for the last time in 1931, and on the constantly growing Salzburg Festival Plays. Moreover, I continued my steady connections with the Amsterdam Concertgebouw, the series of concerts in Berlin bearing my name, and — in addition to occasional guest appearances in European cities — my intensive participation in the musical life of Vienna. I also returned to America for a period of two months, in January 1932.

Toward the end of Schalk's directorial epoch, the voices of those who wanted to see me at the head of the Vienna State Opera became ever more urgent. Most weighty were the words of Dr. Julius Korngold, the musical critic of the *Neue Freie Presse*. As for myself, my natural impulses made me keep entirely aloof — I did not lift a finger. The loud call in a large part of the press and the enthusiastic demonstrations of the audiences at almost every one of my concerts gladdened and touched me, but it was quite clear to me that the Ministry of Education of a state ruled by the Christian Socialist Party would not likely view my appointment with favor, nor would it be at all convenient to me to have that Ministry as my superior authority. At any rate, the general demand for me was so urgent that the Minister could not very well ignore it. And so I received a letter, addressed to me at his request, inquiring if I were ready to enter into negotiations and suggesting that I state my terms. In a very guardedly written reply I confined myself to the statement that I would basically not be averse to discussing the matter, but I purposely refrained from saying a word about my terms. General Director Schneiderhan, who had been exercising the functions of the former General Manager since the last years of Schalk's incumbency, now wrote me requesting a secret personal discussion. I replied by suggesting the restaurant of the Western Railway Station as an inconspicuous place for our meeting. I was there, but nobody showed up. Quite some time later, I received a written apology from Schneiderhan, stating that my suggestion had reached him too late. I naturally made no further reply. When I had left Vienna again, a notice appeared in the papers to the effect that my excessive financial demands had prevented my appointment. This truly Viennese intrigue was launched by the same man who, almost thirty years before, had doubted my ability to "lead a riflemen's band" and had in the meantime advanced from musical reviewer to confidential man of the Ministry of Education. I wrote the Minister, asking for an official correction, but nothing came of it. Indignant though I was about the malicious treatment of the matter, I was quite content with its issue. It would have been hard for me to resist a serious call, in spite of the knowledge that to work under the prevailing conditions would have made me unhappy.

Years later, I met Schneiderhan in Salzburg. After leaving his position in Vienna, he had become president of the Mozarteum. My attitude toward him was naturally one of polar frigidity, but when he implored me in an equatorially couched letter to listen to him I agreed to a meeting. The man had aged considerably. Trembling and agitated, he assured me most solemnly that my first letter had mysteriously disappeared from the files soon after its arrival. The correction demanded by me could therefore not have had the benefit of that piece of evidence. Furthermore, my suggestion to meet at the Western Station restaurant had shown up on his desk only after about a week's delay. Anyway, the intrigue had succeeded in preventing my appointment. Clemens Krauss became director of the State Opera in 1929, and remained in his position until the end of 1934.

I conducted my eighth and last Covent Garden season in the spring of 1931. The theater passed into the hands of Sir Thomas Beecham, who also assumed its musical leadership. But my connection with English concert life naturally continued.

At one of my subsequent London concerts I was able to enjoy once more the assistance of Pablo Casals, who was to play the Schumann Concerto. The occasion dwells in my memory not only because of his glorious playing but also because of his fantastic immersion in the technical problems of his instrument. When I arrived at the conductor's room on the morning of the concert at Queen's Hall to lead the last orchestral rehearsal, I heard Casals practicing in the adjoining soloists' room. I walked over to him and expressed my regret at his having come so early, for I had requested the management to ask for his presence only during the second half of the program. He replied that that was quite all right, and continued his playing. He appeared on the platform at the appointed time and, to the orchestra's delight and mine, played the Schumann Concerto with all his saintly seriousness and perfection. When I changed my clothes after the rehearsal I heard him practicing again, and when my usual afternoon walk before a concert took me past Queen's Hall, where I inquired for mail, the well-known, noble sound of Casal's playing floated once more from the artists' room, affording me an impressive insight into the man's thorough absorption in his music and instrument. I listened to his intensive practicing for fully fifteen minutes. In the evening, after the concert, I could not help chiding him for not starting to practice again at once. My last meeting with Casals took place in Vienna, not long before Austria's collapse. He had in the meantime gone through a great deal in Spain, and he looked it. But he was as quiet, composed, and amiable as ever, and his playing of the Haydn Concerto with the Vienna Philharmonic Orchestra was of the perfection only he could achieve.

During my last Covent Garden season, I received an invitation from Prime Minister Ramsay MacDonald to have luncheon at Chequers, the summer weekend place of the chief of government. I accepted with alacrity, both because I hoped to catch some remark relating to the European situation and because I was interested in seeing the famous place. If I am not mistaken, Lotte Lehmann and Colonel Eustace Blois had also been invited. We were received by MacDonald and his daughter and shown over the beautiful house, with its interesting library. Among the guests was Lady Snowden, the wife of the Chancellor of the Exchequer, who called herself a "disciple" of MacDonald. She expressed to me her devotion to her master and, gratifyingly, also her enthusiastic approval of our Covent Garden performances. The conversation proved interesting but unpolitical, except for a remark that the Hitler movement was being overrated. Altogether, the England of those days showed but scant understanding of the dangerous situation in Germany.

There things had taken an evil turn after Stresemann's death. The growth of the economic crisis and of unemployment caused increasing numbers of dissatisfied people to espouse the cause of National Socialism. Then came the ominous Reichstag elections of 1930. I vividly remember the night preceding September 15. We spent it at our Berlin apartment, listening to the radio. Emanuel Feuermann was with us. Every few minutes, the triumphant voice of the announcer would tell of the progress of the election. We knew at about three in the morning that Hitler had polled about 6,500,000 votes and that the Nazis would be the new Reichstag's largest party. Feuermann, usually so gay, left us with the words: "It's all over with Germany; all over with Europe."

From that moment, even my stubborn optimism began to wane. Although I could not dimly foresee what was to come, I felt oppressed by the increased darkening of life. In 1931, I met Aristide Briand at a reception given in his honor by Reichschancellor Dr. Bruening. In the crowd surging round him, I barely managed to shake the great European's hand. The deep seriousness, the mournfulness of his attitude, impressed me all the more strongly because his reputation had made me expect to meet a man of fiery and enthusiastic temperament. His poor health may have caused the change — he died half a year later — but I thought I could recognize the fundamental mood of a man who saw his life's work dashed against the rocks.

In the same year, 1931, I got a letter from my old friend Harry

Harkness Flagler, inviting me in the name of the Philharmonic Symphony Society of New York to appear as a guest conductor during the 1931–2 season. The proposed dates conflicted with my Leipzig obligations, but the Gewandhaus management realized that in view of the threatening internal situation in Germany everything should be done to facilitate the resumption of my relations with American musical life. We succeeded in gaining the services of Karl Muck and Hermann Abendroth for the period of my American activity. New ties binding me to New York were now formed, and they were to become ever closer from then on. My first appearance within the framework of those New York concerts occurred in January 1932. I returned to Europe, and went back to New York again in January 1933. While I was there, Hitler was made Chancellor and the Nazis set the Reichstag building afire. The gates of hell had opened.

BOOK SIX

I

DURING the second half of March 1933, I had to appear at the Leipzig Gewandhaus and, later, at the Berlin Philharmonic Hall, and so my wife and I went back to Germany after the termination of my New York activity. The conversations at the captain's table gave us a suffocating foretaste of the atmosphere of disaster toward which our ship was carrying us. Hitler's name was not mentioned. No opinions, friendly or hostile, concerning recent events were expressed, but table companions watched one another, chose their words carefully, and turned the conversation whenever it approached politics, a topic uppermost in everybody's mind. People would sit about with inscrutable faces, hiding behind sedulous talk their cares and anxieties, or, in individual cases, their Nazi leanings. Unless we were among intimate friends, that was the only kind of conversation during my few remaining days in Germany, though it was complemented and spiced by that typical motion of the head, called by Berlin wags *Neue deutsche Rundschau* — New German Survey — an anxious gaze in every direction, fearful of eavesdroppers all the time.

When our ship approached its Cuxhaven pier, we saw two figures waving to us from a tall stone wall on shore: our two daughters had surprised us by driving up from Berlin in our car. The sight of them was to be my last joyful experience on German soil, or rather — symbolically — prior to my landing. For no sooner had I set foot on firm ground than I felt a chilling wave of strangeness flow toward me from the outwardly familiar surroundings. I experienced a ghostlike reversal of my one-time youthful impression of Vienna, when the first sight of what I had never seen before seemed so thoroughly familiar to me. Here an evil magic had turned a familiar world into a strange country. I cannot tell whence the impression came. I only know that it made my heart contract. I was in the Germany concerning whose change into the Reich of the Nazis I had read such copious accounts in newspapers and letters. But nothing I had learned abroad had been so revealing as were those first minutes after my arrival. The swastika flags, waving everywhere, did their share. They were raised at the pier, fluttered from the town hall in Cuxhaven, and were displayed at every inn on our way to Hamburg, effectively preventing our patronage. "If you aren't going to eat in any restaurant showing the swastika, we'll go hungry," my daughters said, and so we finally took a meal at the Hamburg hotel at which I had frequently stopped before. The receptionists welcomed us with the customary display of heartiness, though it had lost some of its spontaneity by the accompanying motion of the New German Survey. "Speak softly, hide your anxious fears; We're being watched by eyes and ears." The words of the prisoners in *Fidelio* came to my mind and kept recurring to me during the following days.

When we had arrived at our Berlin apartment, I was told that the Leipzig Gewandhaus had telephoned several times. I called up Max Brockhaus, whose faltering hints made me realize that "certain difficulties" had developed. He seemed greatly relieved when I promised to go to Leipzig next morning. I arrived early on a Sunday, and was told that the Leipzig Nazis were determined to prevent the concert scheduled for the following Thursday. Manfred von Killinger, Leipzig's Chief of Police, greatly in favor with the Nazi party because of his participation in the plot to kill Rathenau, had threatened officially to forbid the concert unless the management voluntarily cancelled it. The members of the managing committee, hurt in their civic pride, decided to offer resistance, counting upon the support of public opinion, which was wholly in my favor. There followed hectic times, filled with conferences and correspondence, with orchestra rehearsals and telephone conversations at night. It was Max Brockhaus who did the telephoning, reporting and begging, lamenting and imploring, while I assisted him as a whispering counselor and prompter. There the two of us would sit at night in the dimly lighted office of the Gewandhaus, the only wakeful room in the slumbering large building. Two watchmen were calling out for help against the creeping fire with which barbarians were threatening culture and its abodes. During the hours of waiting, which made long-distance conversations an agony in those days, we came to realize the symptomatic meaning of our fight. Its issue would decide infinitely more than the fate of the Leipzig Gewandhaus.

I had proposed at first to solve the difficulties of the directors by resigning voluntarily, but they refused to accept my proposition. They wanted to protect the musical tradition of the Gewandhaus and preserve their own independence. In those early days of Nazi rule, such dreams were still entertained. The Nazis proceeded cautiously at first, probably because they did not wish to frighten the older generation. Besides, there were wide circles in Germany that considered the party's cruel actions and outrageous utterances, even its anti-Semitism, symptoms of a short-lived youthful complaint, afflicting an inherently sound movement. They believed in an early return to decency and normality. Influenced by such thoughts, the Gewandhaus management intended, as a first step, to insist quietly but firmly that the concert take place. The next step would be to turn to competent quarters in an effort to bring about a definite decision concerning their independence. These respected Leipzig publishers, industrialists, scientists, and professional men looked forward to the future hopefully; little did they suspect what radical measures Nazism was determined to introduce in the realm of art and science. They believed that the Reich authorities could be induced to protect great institutes of art from undue interference by local powers. Tietjen was asked to intercede in Berlin, Winifred Wagner was begged to exert her influence with Göring. Everybody knew someone who would surely be ready to stand up for the old far-famed Gewandhaus, and so Brockhaus indefatigably telephoned "someone."

An unpleasant diversion from my rather passive, and yet continuous participation in those feverish endeavors was afforded me by the view from my windows at the Hotel Hauffe. With mingled disgust and fascination I stared down upon the marching Hitler Youth and Storm Troopers. Never in my life shall I forget the street meetings of those hordes, when all passers-by were forced to stand still and give the Hitler salute. I can still see the little baker's boy, pedaling his loaf-filled cart, and the gigantic booted Storm Trooper who tore him from his seat and drove him along with kicks in his back.

Thursday morning came, and the men at the Gewandhaus were still hopeful: many an influential person had promised to intercede. But when I started at about eleven to go to the public general rehearsal, groups of excited people who had been denied admission came surging my way. A placard at the entrance of the hall briefly announced that the performance would not take place. At the behest of the Saxon Ministry of the Interior, the police had, on Thursday morning, forbidden both the general rehearsal and the concert. Brockhaus and other members of the management were awaiting me. When the final injunction had reached them, it had been too late to notify me by telephone at the hotel. So confused and downcast was the little meeting that hardly anybody was able to speak. We shook hands and took leave of each other with a few murmured words. Members of the orchestra, dismay on their faces, stood about in the street and greeted me with deep respect as I passed them silently. Mournfully I gazed back at the noble edifice, whose entrance had for so many years been appropriately adorned by the statue of Felix Mendelssohn. I fetched my luggage from the hotel, the view from whose windows had so disturbed me, and rode to the station. Two ladies from the management, flowers in their hands and tears in their eyes, appeared at the train. Saddened by what had happened and apprehensive of what might be in store for me, I went back to Berlin where the next "Bruno Walter Concert" was scheduled to take place at Philharmonic Hall on the following Monday. Actual events were to surpass my forebodings.

"Louise Wolff has called up any number of times," my wife told me when I got home. "Wolff and Sachs want to know when you can join them in a conference." The Hermann Wolff concert management had changed its name to Wolff & Sachs, but it continued to be tyrannically ruled by the radiantly smiling "Queen Louise." In addition to Furtwängler's concerts, her loyal affections were particularly centered upon the "Bruno Walter Concerts," and me personally. Everything dear to her seemed now to be threatened: her social position, her professional activity, and my concerts. But when I came to the conference in the afternoon, I found the old lady in her usual regal attitude, entirely composed. Only her associates seemed excited and perplexed.

I was informed that the Propaganda Ministry of Dr. Goebbels had sent out a warning to cancel the concert lest there be unpleasant occurrences. Had my concert been forbidden? Louise said it had not. I said I was ready either to withdraw, if the management wished to avoid the threatened "unpleasant occurrences," or to conduct the concert if that were desired. When I saw that Louise and her associates, Messrs. Sachs and Simon, were undecided, I suggested that a direct inquiry be made at the Propaganda Ministry concerning the nature of the unpleasant occurrences we might have to expect. If they were to be particularly unpleasant, the official prohibition of the concert should be demanded. Sachs managed to get in touch at the Ministry with Dr. Funk, the man who later became president of the Deutsche Reichsbank. This was about his answer: "We don't wish to prohibit the concert, for we are not interested in getting you out of an awkward predicament or, let alone, in relieving you of your obligation to pay the orchestra. But if you insist on giving the concert you may be sure that everything in the hall will be smashed to pieces." To these remarks, interestingly revealing the frame of mind and tone of the new officials, the future Reichsbank president added the request that we inform him within the hour of the concert management's decision.

I learned later that the propelling power behind this exceptionally energetic treatment of my case and of the subsequent violence done to opera houses and concert institutions was a Herr Hans Hinckel, the Nazi government's specially empowered expert in musical matters. He had proved his aptitude for the job as editor of the *Miesbacher Anzeiger,* one of the oldest Nazi papers. His particularly aggressive and insulting anti-Semitic articles were said to have gained him the favor of the party bigwigs. So he had come to Berlin from rural Bavarian Miesbach, not far from charming Schliersee and its well-known peasant theater, and was now able to dethrone or instal musicians in eminent positions. After the information we had received, it was clear to us that I would not be able to conduct the concert. Sachs was instructed to inform Dr. Funk of our decision to cancel the concert. What was our surprise when we were told that it was desirable to have the concert take place, but under Richard Strauss's guidance instead of mine. Strauss would accept all right, Dr. Funk added. And so it turned out. The composer of *Ein Heldenleben* actually declared himself ready to conduct in place of a forcibly removed colleague. This made him especially popular with the upper ranks of Nazism. Later, to be sure, for reasons unknown to me, Strauss was said to have fallen out with the government.

Dr. Funk had closed his remarks with the strange words: "Besides, Herr Walter is politically suspicious." I had never taken an active part in politics, and so I had to assume that the authorities had decided to make things unpleasant for me personally by some infernal invention of theirs. My wife was waiting for me. She had been walking up and down in front of the concert management's office for an hour. She listened to my report with perfect calm, but when I told her of Dr. Funk's closing remark she stood still and said: "You'll have to leave Berlin this very day." I realized that she was right, and we decided that I'd leave that evening for Semmering with my elder daughter. My wife would prepare for our moving to Austria and follow later with the younger daughter.

Because it was inadvisable that I return home, my wife drove to our apartment alone. She was to pack the most necessary things for me and send them to me by my daughter. In the meantime, I got in touch with a trustworthy friend and requested him to have an intermediary lodge a protest at the Ministry against the suspicion cast on me. My friend, well versed in such matters, proposed that I ask Count Kanitz, the former Minister of Agriculture, to interest himself in my case. I did so a few days later from Semmering. Count Kanitz had long been devoted to me as a musician, stood aloof from Nazism, and enjoyed the general respect of the older government officials, many of whom were still active in the ministries.

I learned after some time that Kanitz had complied with my request and had been told that compromising letters written by me had been found in Liebknecht House, the Communist headquarters "captured" by the Nazis. Well, that looked quite serious and seemed to demand a vigorous denial, for it was hardly likely that the fairy-tale department of the Propaganda Ministry would refrain from making public use of the invention; nor did I underestimate the danger to which my family was exposed.

The *Deutsche Allgemeine Zeitung* was a liberal Berlin newspaper with Right tendencies. Its courageous attitude contrasted favorably with the unprincipled servility with which the German press generally submitted to the Nazi yoke, and was mainly due to its editor-in-chief, Dr. Fritz Klein, who erroneously believed that firmness of character would enable a person to assert himself in the new German Reich and even make him respected. I knew him from the Berlin Rotary Club, whose membership was composed of one representative of each profession and to which he belonged as a journalist and I as a musician. The weekly club luncheons had led to interesting conversations between us, revealing his artistic inclinations and his fondness for my musical activities. I wrote to him, too, from Semmering, enclosing a dignified but categorical rejection of that lie and requesting that he publish it. He had the courage to comply with my request and to continue to express his opinion in the editorials of the *Deutsche Allgemeine Zeitung* moderately, but with an unshakable loyalty to his convictions. An article on the Austrian question finally cost him his position. I have never again heard of the excellent man, to whom I bear a grateful memory.

I spent a day in Vienna on my way to Semmering, looking up friends and calling on Count Coudenhove-Kalergi, the founder of the Pan-European Movement, which I had joined. I expressed to him my amazement at the Nazis' aggressive attitude toward culture and their apparent determination to proceed radically. That was bound to lead to the destruction of the nations' cultural community, whose highly beneficial effect had made earth more habitable. The Nazis' belief in a superior master race, their opposition to religion, and their hostility to the world of the spirit had made them turn their backs to that community. I felt impelled to talk about these matters to the man whose life's work had been built upon an inter-European community and its development, so seriously threatened by recent events. Coudenhove's sagacity had at once recognized the menacing implication of that uninhibited vandalism in the realm of culture — leading later to the symbolic burning of books — and I recall his surprisingly clear perception of what these wild beginnings must inevitably lead to. Developments have proved the correctness of his political interpretations of events.

On the evening of the same day, I proceeded with my daughter to Semmering's pleasant Südbahn Hotel where, in the old days in Vienna, I had often spent days of relaxation. This time, I was not long to enjoy the woods and the mountain air, for on the second day Rudolf Mengelberg telegraphed me that his cousin Willem Mengelberg had fallen ill. He requested me to take over several concerts at the Amsterdam Concertgebouw. I accepted and, giving Germany a wide berth, drove to Holland by way of Switzerland, France, and Belgium. A number of journalists got into my car at the Dutch frontier. The Dutch papers had printed detailed reports of what had happened to me, but they wished to give their readers a personal account of my attitude. The cautiousness of my replies was dictated by my anxiety about my family, for it had happened that hostile utterances on foreign soil were visited cruelly on an anti-Nazi's family in Germany.

I arrived in Amsterdam and was met at the train by Rudolf Mengelberg. A surprise, hardly bearable because of the deep emotion it caused me, was in store for me. When I stepped out of the station, the immense square in front of it was black with people. They had come to express their sympathy to a musician whose name and activity were well known in Holland and who had suffered a grievous wrong. Their gathering was meant as a protest against the wrong and the frame of mind which had inspired it. Suddenly, they began to sing an old Netherlands song of freedom. The beautiful solemn sounds floating in the dusk across the wide square and the water imparted to the anti-Nazi demonstration of the Amsterdam Social Democrats — it was they, I later learned — the character of a manifestation of human fraternity.

From Holland and the fine concerts with the orchestra of the Amsterdam Concertgebouw, I returned to Vienna. My wife arrived there on the day following the boycott of the Jews ordered by the German government. She, who had hardly ever shed tears, fell on my neck crying bitterly when she alighted from the train. The sight of the unleashed mob, uniformed and be-swastikaed, the maltreatment of people in the Berlin streets, the wrecked shops, the fear and torment of the defenseless, and the howling delight of their persecutors had upset her entirely and kept torturing her for a long time to come. Her emotion was all the deeper because a number of her own relatives, who had been dear to her, had shown no sympathy with the persecuted, but had tried to exculpate the persecutors. There had been serious disputes, followed by her indignantly severing all ties.

During the following weeks, I performed Mahler's Eighth, the so-called "Symphony of the Thousand," at the Vienna Konzerthaus. The demonstrations before and after the concert assumed such proportions that I finally had to say a few words to the audience. I no longer recall what I said, but I am sure that I kept a check on myself and omitted any hint at possible extra-musical reasons for the demonstrations. It would have ill suited Mahler's and Goethe's message, which had just ebbed away. But the very fact that I had to speak proved that the events of the days had irresistibly penetrated into the circles of art. Wherever I went after those months following upon my banishment from German musical life, the honors paid me as a musician exceeded their usual warmth. They became an unspoken, passionate demonstration against my enemies, or rather against the enemies of culture, which, it was thought, had been violated by the affront to my person. On occasions, however, when a concert hall's atmosphere did not restrain me, and when the demonstrations assumed verbal form, as for instance at the Paris banquets in my honor, I did not hesitate to give voice to my unequivocal, indignant attitude toward the day's events and, to the best of my ability, to point out the general threat inherent in the happenings. At the first of those banquets, I shared honors with Emil Ludwig. We were considered fellow-sufferers. I also recall another Paris banquet, presided over by Painlevé, the former friend of Clemenceau and Picquart. After Painlevé's beautiful speech, Gabriel Pierné addressed me in the name of the French musicians. The cordiality of his words still warms my heart. I have a faint recollection of the conductor Rhené-Baton and the writer Tristan Bernard coming toward me after the banquet and calling attention to the surprising similarity of their gray-bearded faces. I also recall a friendly conversation with Paul Dukas, the composer of the *L'Apprenti-Sorcier* and the opera *Ariane et Barbe-Bleue,* and a brief, but highly stimulating exchange of thoughts with Maurice Ravel. A third banquet tendered me is worth mentioning in this connection. It took place in London during the same year, and was likewise intended to show how people devoted to me felt about my treatment by the Nazis. My pleasure and gratification at Sir Edward Elgar's having agreed to act as chairman gave way to disappointment and regret at news of his serious illness. His place was taken by Sir Thomas Beecham, with whom I had first come into artistic contact more than twenty-five years before. I had every reason to thank him and the assembled guests and to express my deep appreciation of the manifestation of their sentiments.

Operatic and concert work called me to Salzburg again in the summer of 1933. The Festival Plays, after their gradual organic growth, were entering upon their great days. Now, after my departure from Germany, I intended to devote myself to them, and to Austrian musical life generally, even more intensively than before. True, the political aspects were rather ominous in Austria, but the official trend was against National Socialism. Italy and the Western Powers were backing the country's national independence, and the Dollfuss government seemed to be master of the situation.

Dollfuss, Federal Chancellor since May 1932, had been governing Austria without benefit of parliament since March 1933. He had introduced the corporative authoritarian form of government in April 1934. Such a form of government was bound to be short-lived, even if the disturbances of February 1934, and the violence to the Social Democratic workers had not occurred. At that time, however, in 1933, even persons less optimistic than myself considered the situation rather favorable. The milder temperature of the Austrian nature made the undemocratic constitution more bearable in a general way, and when, after the assassination of Dollfuss in July 1934, Schuschnigg became Federal Chancellor, his lofty ideas and honest intentions managed to spread throughout the country a truly peacful atmosphere, in which music and the theater were able to develop unhindered and the Salzburg Festival Plays experienced their brightest period.

The Nazis had not stopped their demagogic intrigues even after the assassination of Dollfuss. They had merely become more cautious for some time. In July 1936, an agreement was reached in which Germany solemnly recognized Austria's independence. Thereafter, things gradually grew more unsettled again, but, for several years, Schuschnigg's intrepid attitude was able to protect Austria and her cultural life until Germany finally felt strong enough to dare the attack. Then, of course, everything was lost: Schuschnigg, his government, Austria, and the peace of the world.

II

THE SCHUSCHNIGG government had assumed the burden left to it by the Dollfuss régime. Its convictions made it uphold the authoritarian constitution, and it neither found nor earnestly sought a way to the working class. But no matter what we may hold against it, it proved friendly to the world of the spirit and tried to further Austria's cultural mission. The Salzburg Festival Plays' great splendor was reflected upon the Schuschnigg government, which was not merely a chance beneficiary of that wonderful institution that had once more gained for Austria the hearts of all serious friends of art, but had actually been helpful in bringing about the world fame of the Festival Plays.

Alexander von Humboldt classed the location and surroundings of Salzburg among the most beautiful on earth, equal to those of Naples and Constantinople. Its cultural atmosphere and that very charm of its landscape made the town a site eminently suitable for festival plays. What was more, its political connection with Vienna made available to it the still abundant resources of the State Opera, so rich in great traditions. But with the exception of its orchestra and chorus we were by no means restricted to the Vienna Opera when drawing up the lists of our artistic personnel. We freely chose from among the singers, conductors, stage directors, and other artists whose services we wished to enlist. Thus we succeeded in gaining Arturo Toscanini's consent to conduct several concerts in the summer of 1934 and, beginning in 1935, operatic performances too. His art and the glamour of his name greatly enhanced the effectiveness and prestige of the Festival Plays.

Besides, Salzburg was able to boast of a musical culture of its own, dating back to the days of Archbishop Hieronymus and, to a certain degree, to even earlier times. In our day, the Mozarteum, headed by Bernhard Paumgartner, had done much to preserve and intensify the local musical atmosphere. This highly meritorious musical institute proved helpful in many respects to our varied activities.

The history of Salzburg, expressed in the mute and yet so eloquent language of its streets, squares, and buildings, was not the least of the attractions that had made the small Austrian town into a festive world center. It was mainly a history of ecclesiastical predominance and of the cultivating forces of Catholicism. Symbolized by the beautiful churches and other clerical buildings, it gave its imprint to the picture of Salzburg and enveloped the town's charm in its religious atmosphere. The Hohensalzburg fortress, reigning high above the peaceful beauty of the old archepiscopal residence, was a powerful reminder of a harsh warlike past. In 1920, Max Reinhardt, intuitively aware of Salzburg's atmosphere, chose the Hofmannsthal version of the miracle play *Everyman* for the first festival-like performance. Salzburg proved an ideal frame for the religious piece. It became an integral part of every Festival-Play season. *Everyman,* the English-Dutch play of "the life and death of the rich man," is an immortal poem, effective wherever it is presented. I recall a performance in the courtyard of a medieval castle in Malmö. The small Swedish town had arranged a music festival, in which the Berlin Philharmonic Orchestra under my guidance participated. I listened to the Swedish-language performance in those rather unsuitable surroundings and was as deeply moved by it as the simple audience on its improvised tiers of seats.

In Salzburg *Everyman* was played in the square before the Cathedral's magnificent façade. The opening fanfares were sounded from the Porticus, the warning calls of "Everyman, Everyman!" came from the spires of the neighboring churches and even from the far-away fortress, and the time of the performance was so chosen that the death of Everyman was followed by the solemn peeling of the vesper bells of Salzburg's many churches. *Everyman* seemed created for Salzburg, and Salzburg for *Everyman.* The idea of Festival Plays had its source in those performances, and was thus due to Max Reinhardt's inspiration. True, the earliest suggestion of Festival Plays may be traced back to a Salzburg performance of *Figaro* at which Mahler was leading the forces of the Vienna Court Opera in 1906. He was conducting the opera as part of a Mozart cycle arranged by Lilli Lehmann. There were many who recognized the town's special suitability for such events at that time, but our Festival-Play epoch unquestionably had its inception in that performance of *Everyman.* Strauss and Schalk, the directors of the State Opera, performed a few Mozart operas in the handsome little Stadttheater in 1922, and Reinhardt added to the program his imaginative production of Calderón's *World Theater.* There were no Festival Plays during the following two summers, but the year 1925 witnessed Reinhardt's production of *Everyman,* Vollmöller's *Miracle,* and a repetition of the *World Theater,* while I conducted Donizetti's *Don Pasquale.* I was at the desk when Johann Strauss's *Die Fledermaus* and Mozart's *Entführung* were performed in 1926. After the modest beginnings had turned out so favorably, the Festival Playhouse was built. Now we had at our disposal a large house for operas in addition to the small one of the Stadttheater, Cathedral Square and the interestingly transformed courtyard of the Riding School for Reinhardt's dramatic performances — they were played indoors when the weather was inclement — and finally the beautiful hall of the Mozarteum for our orchestral concerts with the Vienna Philharmonic Orchestra.

The Festival Plays began to be known internationally in the thirties. The influx of art-lovers from all over the world increased from summer to summer. They came from other European countries and from across the seas. A heterogeneous, polyglot crowd filled the hotels, restaurants, and cafés, stood admiringly before the magnificent archepiscopal edifices, strolled through the Mirabell Garden, and made pilgrimages to the house in narrow Getreidegasse where Mozart had been born. In the daytime, their automobiles, whose license plates proclaimed their far-away homes, rushed over the dusty roads toward the paradisiac districts of the Salzkammergut, its mountains, lakes, and famous places, such as Ischl, St. Wolfgang, and Aussee, while in the evening unbroken lines passed over the beautiful bridge spanning the swiftly flowing Salzach and wended their way to the Festival Playhouse. And every evening, lines of curious Salzburgers and people from the surrounding district, clad in their characteristic native costumes, would watch the endless festive procession of the interesting foreigners.

Europe had seen similar scenes once before — in Bayreuth. But while there one of the world's most powerful creative geniuses gave a reception to humanity, uplifting it to the sublimities of his solemn work, we were inviting a variously inclined artistic community to witness a wide choice of works and performances with Mozart as their center. Moreover, what made the sense of the Bayreuth Festival Plays different from that of ours was not only the contrast between the loftiness of Wagner's creations and the beauty of the works of Mozart and the charms of many others we performed, but also the contrast between the spirit of yesterday and that of today. A style had been established and was being preserved in Bayreuth, while we were striving for an artistic realization of the diversified stylistic peculiarities of other musical dramatic works. Bayreuth's mission had been accomplished: Wagner's genius had conquered the world. We, on the other hand, endeavored to place all available resources and our highly developed operatic methods at the service of works which had never, or rarely, been treated with such care, and whose essential worth was therefore still to be recognized. The general approval bestowed on our work showed that we were on the right track.

There was the seething Festival-Play town; there was the solemn archepiscopal residence with its wealth of historical mementos built of stone; but there was still another Salzburg, which I knew and loved: it was the placid Austrian small town through whose sleepy streets I had rambled in former years and in whose quiet coffeehouses I had often sat. It was a Salzburg in undress, as it were, a Salzburg dear to my heart, a Salzburg with which I had been on intimate terms from the days of my youth. Often, during

Festival-Play days, it would give me a knowing smile such as a girl in the company of others gives her secret lover.

This was the Salzburg into whose tranquillity the aging Hermann Bahr had retired, in which Stefan Zweig lived with his interesting collections in his friendly house on Kapuzinerberg, and which, in winter, spring, or autumn, served as a *buen retiro* to many spiritually minded people who wished to spend there a few days or weeks of thoughtful relaxation. It looked essentially just as it had looked when it sheltered Leopold Mozart's family and when the adolescent Wolfgang Amadeus was driven to despair by its narrowness. Now it had become the noble dignified frame for a stirring artistic life and for worldly activities. While the majority of the visitors may not have been fully conscious of the magic of the old-Austrian small town, I am sure that they must instinctively have enjoyed the palatable flavor it added to the unique mixture of Festival Plays, eloquent historical sights, and natural beauties.

Dr. Erwin Kerber had been the administrative and organizational head of the Festival Plays from the beginning. It was he who was to join me in the management of the Vienna State Opera in 1936. A dyed-in-the-wool Salzburger, he spoke a dialect surpassed in purity by none, not even by Richard Mayr, nor did he have his equal in Alpine vivacity and humor. I remember with sympathy and esteem this honorable, efficient, and warmhearted man, to whom I became also personally indebted for his courageous help in a difficult situation. I shall have more to say about this later.

During one of the early Festival-Play summers I made the acquaintance of Oskar Strnad, of whose remarkable talent Roller had often spoken to me. Reinhardt's production of Gozzi's *Turandot* was responsible for my first sight of scenery and costumes designed by him. They made a lasting impression on me. Our personal acquaintance resulted from an excursion to one of the large Salzkammergut lakes. There followed a close artistic alliance between us, terminated only by his untimely death. Strnad had originally been an architect. He lived in space, in contrast to many stage designers whose scenic sets were nothing but flat paintings transposed into space. From the first sketch, his designs were three-dimensional. He was moreover gifted with a unique sense of color and with a glowing imagination that reacted quite sensitively to music. Remarkable was his staging of Weber's *Oberon* when I performed the work at the Berlin State Opera and, later, in Salzburg and Vienna; of Mozart's *Entführung* for my Florence and Salzburg performances; of *Figaro;* but above all of *Don Giovanni* in Salzburg. His designs for this *dramma giocoso,* outstanding because of their combination of Mozart-inspired general lightness and elements of Spanish baroque style, because of their technical possibilities for quick changes, and because of the suggestive power of the costumes, represent in my opinion the most successful solution thus far of the work's difficult scenic problems.

The repertory of the Festival Plays and its systematic development can only be touched upon here. We tried to keep away from works of a solemn character because they seemed unsuited to the milieu. The only exception was Wagner's *Tristan*, which, I think, I conducted during two summer seasons. Hugo Wolf's singularly charming *Der Corregidor*, which I had included in my Munich and Berlin repertoires, seemed to fit the Salzburg surroundings particularly well. Its festival performance was highly effective. A culminating point in my endeavors on behalf of the Festival Plays was the performance of Gluck's *Orfeo*, a work in which I have become engrossed again and again in the course of my long career and whose inexhaustible magnitude has richly repaid every new effort to fathom its depths.

The major part of my endeavors was naturally centered upon Mozart, whose *Le Nozze di Figaro* and *Don Giovanni* I performed in Salzburg for the first time in my life in the original language. I had always been troubled by the fact that many details of the German translation were incompatible with Mozart's music. At last I was able to enjoy the longed-for harmony between words and music. Some of my previous productions of *Figaro*, which presents no difficult problems, had turned out quite well. I had been less fortunate in my endeavors to cope with the problems of *Don Giovanni*. At any rate, my repeated experiences and disappointments had made me thoroughly acquainted with them, and now, in Salzburg, with the assistance of Strnad and Karlheinz Martin, I was ready to risk a well-planned attack upon the seemingly impregnable fortress. I had succeeded in coming to an understanding with my collaborators about the dramatic and scenic difficulties, and our plans for the performance held out the promise that this time we would overcome them. But of what avail was the best solution of all these problems as long as the most important question remained unanswered: where to find an artist for the title part? I knew of none. The best of those who had sung the part for me were lacking in some particular. Even the excellent D'Andrade of my recollections failed to measure up to the standard that a lifelong study of Mozart's figure had made to rise up before my vision. We made every preparation, but I warned Kerber that I would abandon the project unless a kind fate helped me to find a suitable Don.

Among the singers of Romance languages — for only they could be considered — I knew a number whose vocal accomplishments, diction, style, and even appearance called for serious consideration, but they were all lacking in that immediately convincing personal fascination which is an essential of the part. Then I learned that Ezio Pinza, of whose voice, talent, and appearance Artur Bodanzky had spoken to me enthusiastically several times, had scored a striking success as Don Giovanni at the New York Metropolitan Opera. An amusing incident inspired the hope that, in addition to his general artistic suitability of which all reports had made me convinced, he would also be endowed with the ability to produce that immediate personal effect. We had taken with us to New York our Bohemian cook, an efficient, but quite unimaginative middle-aged person. I called up Pinza and told him I should like to make his acquaintance. He kindly offered to call on me. There was a ring, and Anita went to answer it. She came rushing back, flushed, confused, and excited, and whispered to my wife: "Ma'am, there's such a beautiful man outside." I said to my wife: "I think I've found my Don Giovanni for Salzburg." I had.

There were a number of concerts in the course of every Festival-Play summer. As I said, they took place either at the Festival Playhouse or in the smaller hall of the Mozarteum. In addition to classic works, I played a good deal of Mahler and Bruckner. During the final years, a song recital by Lotte Lehmann, with myself at the piano, became an annual fixture.

It was admirable how Lotte Lehmann's dramatic feeling, to which she had formerly been inclined to yield almost to the point where she did violence to her voice, had gradually become restrained to fit the rendition of songs. Amazing, too, that her impetuous elemental personality should have found the way to the stylistic purity of the song by means of her own almost infallible instinct. The advice I gave her occasionally referred merely to details. She owed to herself the mastery of the essentials of Lieder-singing. Her deeply penetrating understanding made her conscious of the beauty of the melodic line as well as of the spiritual and emotional contents of the words. She managed to combine these two elements of Lieder-singing in a frequently ideal synthesis, and thus to fulfill the composer's intentions. And even in those weaker moments from which no instant-bound reproductive artist can escape, the purely vocal demands of a song or an operatic part may have suffered occasionally, but never their poetic essence.

Innate simplicity and tender sensitiveness are the poles of Lehmann's being. These qualities manifest themselves in her life as well as in her art, charmingly changeful at times, and often harmoniously blended. It is natural that so variously gifted a person

— she has a genuine gift for writing poetry and for painting —
should reveal certain erratic traits and be frequently guided by
impulses. But our friendship, in which she has cordially included
my family, has remained uninfluenced by atmospheric fluctuations
in her unchangeably young soul, for that friendship had had its
source in our essential artistic affinity.

From among Toscanini's operatic performances and concerts at
the Festival Playhouse, almost all of which I attended with the
utmost interest, Verdi's *Falstaff* and Requiem, and a superlative
rendition of Brahms Second Symphony are most vividly remembered by me. Our personal contacts, too, became closer in those
days. I am particularly fond of recalling a visit I paid him in Milan,
when we spent several hours in quiet conversation, a thing never
possible in the work-filled atmosphere of Salzburg.

The vacational tranquillity of my last days in Sils Maria in
the Engadine before the Festival Plays were to begin was disturbed
by news from Vienna that a conflict had arisen between Toscanini
and the Salzburg management, and that he had announced his
withdrawal. The Minister of Education telephoned me very ex-
citedly and asked me to intercede. I, in turn, called up Toscanini
and tried to make him change his mind. When he proved inflexible,
I said: "All right, I'll come to see you." I got into my car and rode
down the Bergell mountain road, past Lake Como, and, through a
terrible thunderstorm, to Milan. When I entered Toscanini's music room and asked: *"Come sta?"*, his gloomy *"Male!"* did not
sound particularly encouraging. He said very emphatically that
he would not go to Salzburg. We began to speak of his attitude
toward Wagner's work and of his personal relations with Bayreuth.
He searched among his memories, produced letters, and showed
me much that was dear to him. Our conversation made him un-
bend, and when the meal was served, an atmosphere of the most
animated communicativeness prevailed. Before returning to St.
Moritz, I had been able to assure myself of the helpful attitude
of Madame Toscanini. On leaving, I expressed the hope of soon
seeing him again in Salzburg. He actually went there the following morning. I have never learned whether his change of mind
was brought about by my visit, which had been so utterly lacking
in urgent persuasion, or by something within himself. I only know
that I was touchingly impressed by his deep devotion to Wagner,
by his warmhearted emotionalism, and by the glimpse I had caught
of his soul. The mighty upsurge of beautiful memories may possibly have banished his displeasure at some personal conflict.

Participation in Salzburg's increasingly busy social life was not
wholly avoidable, difficult though it was to reconcile it with the

wealth of work and responsibility. But there were the great receptions and dinners given by Max Reinhardt, the host at Castle Leopoldskron, at which everybody of rank and reputation was present. At one of these dinners, my neighbor at table was Mrs. Sarah Delano Roosevelt, the mother of the American president, and I was able to admire the vivacity and warmth with which the splendid old lady spoke of her great son. After the festive evenings in the almost too brilliant rooms, it was enjoyable to spend a more quiet hour in the magnificent library, where an intimate circle had gathered round Reinhardt and his wife, Helene Thimig. On such occasions, our host, who as a rule had little to say and was given to dreamily watching the smoke of his cigar, would become an enthusiastic conversationalist. There were times, too, when the charming little lake behind the castle, framed by clipped yew hedges, would lure me from the after-dinner company to its peaceful solitude.

Acceptance of the "official" invitations issued by the management or the local government was a "must." I have a particularly vivid recollection of the last reception given by Provincial Governor Dr. Rehrl. My wife and I were looking for a quiet place in which to find refuge from the hubbub of the crowd. We happened into the empty banquet hall of the Residence, where the laid tables were awaiting the guests. Searching for her place card, my wife discovered to her dismay that she had drawn for her neighbor at table Herr von Papen, the German envoy to Austria. She rejoined the party at once and asked Baron Pouthon, the general manager of the Festival Plays, to see that another place be assigned to her. He complied with some embarrassment, and so Herr von Papen was the only man at the banquet without a dinner partner. He was reasonable enough, though, to say to Dr. Rehrl: "I can well understand that Madame Walter does not care to sit at my side."

It goes without saying that there was no want of meetings of intimate friends. According to Austrian custom they often took place at a late hour at a coffeehouse or occasionally at somebody's home. Jakob Wassermann would drive over frequently from Altaussee, Bruno Frank come into town from his little house in Aigen. I made the acquaintance of Theodore Dreiser, and had an interesting conversation with him. I vividly remember the hours I spent in the company of Toscanini and other friends at Stefan Zweig's house looking into far distances and down upon Salzburg. I can still see the garden of my house in Aigen, watched over by the wood-covered Gaisberg and surrounded in a wide circle by the tall mountains of the Salzburg basin. There is a table around which a cheerful party is gathered. Thomas Mann, his wife Katja, and their children Erika and Klaus; Toscanini and his wife Carla; Lotte Lehmann; and myself and my family. My wife and daughters are wearing the charming dirndl dresses so universally in vogue there. And while we in Salzburg were producing Festival Plays, living a peaceful and pleasant life, entertaining lofty ideas, and gratefully enjoying the beauty of those days, immediately to the west of us was brewing the storm that was to destroy Europe with fire and brimstone.

Salzburg lay close to the German border. At the station, there was a Bavarian and an Austrian side, the customs office between them. An electric tramway led from Salzburg to Berchtesgaden. At night, a fiery swastika shone menacingly from a summit of the group of Berchtesgaden mountains. We were at all times conscious of the wicked neighbor, and he managed to make his presence felt. From the moment, especially, when Dollfuss had taken a determined stand against the barefaced Nazi propaganda in Austria, and when he had forbidden the Reichministers Kerrl and Dr. Frank to speak, Hitler's hostility toward Austria began to manifest itself with increasing violence, until it culminated in a catastrophe at the end of July 1934. The Salzburg Festival Plays were particularly hateful to the Nazis. Planes were dropping propaganda leaflets over Salzburg, and bombs were placed in telephone booths. I recall a *Don Giovanni* rehearsal at which the usually punctual Italians, Pinza, Lazzari, and Borgioli were half an hour late. Pale with terror, they reported to me that a bomb had destroyed a part of the Hotel Bristol.

There came July 25, 1934, with the terrible news of the assassination of Dollfuss. We were living in Hallein, a forty-five minute drive from Salzburg. It took us twice that long that evening. Our car was stopped again and again by armed men demanding to see our identification papers, while young fellows of the *Heimwehr,* the Austrian militia, kept their rifles pointed at us. At our beloved Castle Haunsperg, in which we spent about five Festival-Play summers — I did not rent the Aigen house until later years — we found the horror-stricken occupants gathered round our amiable hostess, Countess Thun, for it looked very much as if the Nazis were about to take possession of Austria. But Schuschnigg, the Minister of Education in the Dollfuss Cabinet, immediately grasped the helm, and we soon learned that the conspiracy had been suppressed. There ensued even a period of quiet for us. Hitler had realized that the conquest of Austria could not be accomplished by means of a surprise attack, but needed careful preparation. Thus we were granted a respite of almost three years, during which we worked and — underrating the danger — hoped.

III

THE NAZIS, as I said before, endeavored in certain directions to maintain a semblance of legality for some time after they had come to power. They no doubt wished to reassure those who still viewed the movement either with hostility or distrust. It was probably due to that fact that no difficulties were made when I transported my personal belongings to Vienna. To my surprise, a considerable part of my taxes was even refunded by the Reich a few months after my change of residence. True, many of the correct old officials still held their positions. They probably chose that way to manifest sentiments they no longer dared express in words. A middle-aged workman, who had often done odd jobs for us and had helped my wife in her hurried packing on the day of my departure, insisted on coming to the station and saying good-by to me. "Well, Herr Schulze," I said to the old Social Democrat, "I am afraid you will have to join the Nazi party, or else you'll find yourself out of work." "I suppose I'll have to do that," he replied mournfully. Then his honest face brightened and he added in broad Berlinese: "Well, I hope that all of Hitler's members will be of my kind." Similar sentiments were unquestionably entertained at the beginning not only by the middle classes but also by wide circles of the working class. But it seems that in the course of years the daily influencing of public opinion through the "politically co-ordinated" press and radio brought about a decided change of opinion on the part of even the older Germans of all classes. And as for the members of the younger generation, they heard nothing but the teachings of National Socialism from early childhood to their maturity. Thus a large proportion of the German people finally became accomplices in the Nazi atrocities, partly through active participation, partly through infection with the doctrine of German superiority, or at least through indifference to the terror and its victims.

In those early years, however, old and young frequently stood in opposite camps, a fact that shook the foundations of German family life. I was told of a typical case by one who was grievously affected. At the house of Swiss friends of mine I met a Protestant clergyman and his wife. They had just come from their home near Bremen. The more than seventy-year-old couple seemed deeply distressed. When I asked the man if he intended to return to his rural community, to which he seemed greatly attached, he said it was impossible. The Nazis had learned that his library contained some books they had banned, and he was faced with dire punishment. To my question if the books had been discovered by a searching party he answered in the negative. He had been betrayed: his own son had reported him to the Nazis. This tale and similar ones that came to my knowledge taught me that National Socialism had started its fight against the Decalogue with a successful attack upon the Fourth Commandment.

I had rented a Vienna apartment near the northern slopes of the Vienna Woods and resumed a quietly wandering mode of life. I went to Italy, France, England, Holland, Belgium, and the Scandinavian countries as a guest conductor, but was always glad to get back again to Vienna. My wife accompanied me to New York in October 1933. I stayed several months there, conducting concerts of the Philharmonic Society. Our younger daughter was married in London during that period. Her husband being a film architect in a German company, she had to live in Berlin, a fact that worried and distressed us a great deal. Still, she managed, during the following years, to visit us frequently in Vienna or, in the summertime, in the Engadine, and make us happy by her radiant presence on occasional visits to Paris, Florence, and Amsterdam. Incompatibility of views had in the meantime caused our elder daughter and her husband to separate.

My association with Italy's musical life was strengthened in those years. Some time after Toscanini had left the La Scala, I revived Mozart's *Don Giovanni* there. I had occasion to admire the efficiency of Toscanini's former secretary, Anita Colombo, who had assumed the management of the famous institution and was striving loyally to conduct its affairs in his spirit. I had also accepted invitations to appear again at the Accademia Santa Cecilia in Rome. But the classic old Augusteo had been torn down because the tomb of Augustus was supposed to be underneath it. It was thought that its restoration would furnish a further glowing proof of fascism's affinity with antique Romanism. The tomb was not found, however, and an ugly heap of ruins instead of the venerable Augusteo was the permanent though inglorious result of an insatiable thirst for glory. The Teatro Adriano, in which the Roman symphony concerts now took place, could not compare in atmosphere with the former hall, though the orchestra had developed splendidly under the guidance of Bernardino Molinari. The concerts gave me a great deal of pleasure.

Florence, spurred on probably by the success of the Salzburg Festival Plays, had in the meantime called into being the *Maggio Musicale Fiorentino*. An artistically minded management had known how to make clever use of the town's rich possibilities. I think that Mario Labroca, the able director of the Festival Plays,

had looked me up in Vienna. We had agreed upon my producing
Mozart's *Entführung* in the charming old Teatro della Pergola,
and the Requiem in the Teatro Communale. A new, pleasant connection was thus formed between me and a serious artistic enterprise. It was to be productive of particularly gratifying results later.

Florence itself was really too important to form a frame for Festival Plays in the manner of Salzburg. Here the miracles of the Renaissance had taken place and here the arts had attained their rich-
est flowering. How could the town have failed to overwhelm the
visitor by its own mighty existence and history — the town of
Dante, of the Medici, of Michelangelo, of Donatello, of Brunel-
leschi, and of Fra Angelico, the town of Boccaccio, the town of
Savonarola? Framed by its magnificent landscape, Florence was in
itself a feast to the eye and the spirit. It was bound to outshine anything the Florentine Festival Plays had to offer in animated living
art. True, the Festival-Play audiences, composed of Florentine
society and visitors from all over Italy, were stylefully and harmoniously effective. It was a joy to behold faces and figures such as one
liked to associate with the festivals in medieval Florence. The sight
of beautiful women, who might have been created by Ghirlandaio,
linked the great past with the charming present. And the Italian I
heard in Florence was undoubtedly the most beautiful of the many
variants of that musical language.

An open-air performance of a Savonarola drama in front of the
Palazzo Vecchio was well suited to the mighty frame. But when I
played Mozart's Piano Concerto in D-minor with the Florentine
orchestra in the hall of the great building, I felt that Mozart and
my modest self were strangers in those heroic surroundings. And
when, at night, I wandered through a gate in the Pitti Palace to
the Boboli Gardens and mounted to the wide moonlit lawns on
which choruses, groups of dancers, and soloists were rehearsing
Gluck's *Alceste,* I again felt that it was the vast palace, the magnificent garden, and the town below that fascinated me rather
than Gluck's work which, after all, had been transplanted somewhat arbitrarily into those surroundings.

Mozart's *Die Entführung aus dem Serail,* however, excellently
suited the charming old Teatro della Pergola. At my request,
Labroca had engaged as stage director Dr. Herbert Graf, with
whom I got along splendidly. Oskar Strnad's attractive settings
and costumes essentially contributed to the success of the performance. I produced the *Entführung* at the Salzburg Festival Plays
in the summer of the same year. Dr. Graf was then also the stage
director of *Don Giovanni,* for Karlheinz Martin, who had directed
it the previous year, had been forbidden by the Nazis further to

participate in the Salzburg Festival Plays. My congenial artistic relations with Graf proved lasting. He was in charge of the scenic arrangements of *Fidelio,* when I produced it with Lotte Lehmann as Leonore at the Paris Opéra in 1936. My collaboration with Graf became still more intensified when I met him again later at the Metropolitan Opera in New York.

Although the Nazi agitations could be felt in Austria at all times, life in Vienna during the thirties still had much of its old charm. The government's resolute attitude toward German and Austrian Nazism and the initial backing by Mussolini and the Western Powers were responsible for a certain feeling of security. Of my old friends, Albert and Nina Spiegler were still alive, and we were more closely united than ever before. But Nina's health was sadly impaired, and not even her unshakable lofty serenity was able to overcome our dejection caused by her physical suffering.

Alma and Franz Werfel's beautiful house on the Hohe Warte was the meeting place of an interesting group of politically important and spiritually eminent personages. I took part in the spirited gatherings as far as my work and my natural shrinking from social affairs permitted. The most interesting of the musicians there was Alban Berg, the composer of *Wozzeck.* I came to know him as a singular, introspective person. His wife, a natural daughter of Emperor Franz Joseph, was a clever, soulful woman, wholly devoted to her husband. I regret that my condemnation of atonality expressed in my essay *Of the Moral Forces of Music* deeply hurt the stubborn wanderer on labyrinthine paths.

A strangely moving experience, which seemed wholly dreamlike to me at the time and has lost none of its mysterious magic even today, is connected in my memory with that house. The glass doors of Alma's music room afforded a view of a beautiful terrace and of the garden beyond. I can still see the unearthly apparition we beheld when we sat there one day after luncheon. An angelically beautiful girl of about fifteen appeared in the door with a deer at her side. Her hand on the animal's slender neck, she gave us an unembarrassed little smile and disappeared again. It was Manon, called Muzi, Alma's daughter from her marriage with Gropius. I subsequently exchanged a few words with her, but was always under the impression that they never reached her, that she was far away. And she was still so far away when, after having been struck with infantile paralysis in Venice at the age of eighteen and brought back to Vienna, she lay in her bed, pale and heavenly serene. Her love of animals had extended to snakes, with which she liked to play. We frequently sat round her bed in the company of a young man who seemed to be greatly in love with her. As for myself, I was ever more strongly conscious of a feeling of distance. After a year of suffering and after patiently enduring a number of cures, she slipped away gently into that far-away distance. Alban Berg's Violin Concerto was dedicated to the parting of that angelic being.

It was through Alma that I came to make the acquaintance of Dr. Kurt von Schuschnigg. The then Minister of Education in the Dollfuss Cabinet was fond of music, and Alma wished us to meet. So a luncheon was arranged at the Grand Hotel in Vienna, attended by him and his charming young wife Herma, by Alma and Franz Werfel, and by my wife and myself. His quiet, serious, firm personality made a deeply sympathetic and powerful impression on me. It uniformly confirmed all I had read about the man, and was strengthened at every one of our infrequent future meetings. He may have been lacking in the political instinct that would have scented the terrible dangers of the international situation and possibly averted them. He may have been lacking also in the farsightedness and skill required for the solution of the internal Austrian difficulties. And he was surely lacking in that vital social feeling which would inevitably have drawn him toward the working class and formed a link between himself and the people generally. His outstanding virtues were absolute honesty, the ability to think clearly and quickly, and courageous determination. He was given strength and inspiration by his firm belief in Austria's political and cultural mission and the thought that it was he who was destined to prepare the way.

Schuschnigg became Federal Chancellor after the Nazis had assassinated Dollfuss. His very first radio proclamation testified to his strength of will and his belief in Austria, qualities that were reassuring as well as they were encouraging. He flung down the gauntlet to the Nazis and bravely kept up the fight until he succumbed to the enemy. Nobody perhaps was hated more fiercely by Hitler than this gallant idealist. In the end, he was struck most cruelly by the archfiend's revenge.

Seriously fond of music, Schuschnigg held Beethoven in particularly high affection. When I performed the *Missa Solemnis,* no official business, not even when the political situation was at the boiling point, could have kept him from attending the concert and listening with devout attention. I don't think he ever missed a performance of *Fidelio* either. As for Gluck's *Orfeo,* he was attached to it for personal reasons. His wife had become the victim of an automobile accident, and the loss had been a terrible blow to him. Months later, our Salzburg performance of *Orfeo* drew him into the theater. There he witnessed the lofty mourning ceremonies following upon Euridice's death, heard Orpheus' vow to snatch his wife from death, and saw him search for her through the horrors of Hades and the delights of Elysium, finally to regain her. I don't think that from that time I conducted a performance of the immortal work either in Salzburg or in Vienna that he did not attend.

In 1936, I received a letter from Dr. Hans Pernter, the Austrian Minister of Education. Referring to my life-long affinity with Vienna, he requested me to assume the artistic leadership of the State Opera. The administrative agenda were entrusted to Dr. Kerber, a man genuinely devoted to me. The sentiments of both the Federal Chancellor and the Minister of Education were beyond any doubt. I felt that I must accept the momentous offer. My acceptance was influenced by the fact that Kerber and I would be able to work out a smoothly functioning schedule for the Vienna State Opera and the Salzburg Festival Plays.

So I made my entry in the familiar noble rooms on the Opernring, or rather I shared them with Kerber, just as years before Strauss had shared them with Schalk. A man of almost sixty, I once more took upon myself the responsibilities of a great operahouse. I naturally had to give up my winter activity in New York. America did not see me again until January 1939. Salzburg and Vienna occupied my time and strength so fully that I had barely time for brief concert excursions to other European countries.

The government's amenable attitude in questions of art is aptly illustrated by the following example. The schedule for the State Opera worked out by Kerber and myself provided for a revival of Pfitzner's *Palestrina*. When we submitted our program to the Minister of Education, he requested that we abandon the *Palestrina* project because, several years before, Pfitzner had written a highly insulting letter in which he declined to conduct a concert at the Salzburg Festival Plays. A state institution could therefore not be expected to further his works. I had the letter taken from the files. ". . . as long as the present government is at the helm," was about what it said, "tyrannically suppressing the true inclinations of the population, a German musician cannot conduct in Austria." It was then that I recalled that Sigrid Onegin, the alto, had written a strangely similar letter declining to appear in Salzburg. I pointed out to Dr. Pernter that Pfitzner's letter as well as Onegin's had surely been dictated by the German authorities and should therefore not furnish the basis for a boycott. I was unable to convince him, and he finally referred me to the Chancellor. The latter's thoroughly unfavorable attitude toward Pfitzner, caused by that letter, made it impossible for him, Pernter, to yield to my wishes, though — he hinted — he might otherwise have been inclined to do so.

My meeting with Schuschnigg afforded me an unforgettable insight into the unique man's character. I had put off the *Palestrina* decision till the days of the Salzburg Festival Plays, when the chances for a quiet conversation with the Chancellor would be more favorable than in Vienna. He invited me to have supper with him at the Peterskeller. There, in a quiet *Extrazimmer,* the two of us spent an evening which will never fade from my memory. The aloofness attached to Schuschnigg's position as head of a state was actually quite suited to his shy and sensitive personality. He was wanting in the self-assured spontaneity that lends popularity to a man in the public eye. What was more, Schuschnigg, with all his courage and honesty, was too much of an introvert ever to be a man of the people. At that supper, however, official or personal aloofness was from the beginning swept away by a wave of communicativeness and a longing for knowledge. We spoke of Beethoven and his creative work, of *Fidelio,* and of the *Missa Solemnis.* He asked about Mahler, about his activity as the Opera's director, and about his personality. He visibly enjoyed participating for a few hours in a world so far removed from his own and so ardently yearned for by his heart. It was an easy matter to lead the conversation to the present-day cultivation of music in Austria and to my *Palestrina* woes. "All right," he said, "I shall see if I can get Minister Pernter to comply with your wish, but you will understand if we are not at the Opera that evening." I thanked him and wanted to take my leave. But, a true Austrian, he wished to conclude the evening at a coffeehouse. So we walked through the night-bound streets of Salzburg, crossed the beautiful Residenzplatz with its rippling fountain, and entered the Café Tomaselli, where excited waiters magically produced a table in the crowded space. We sat there for some time in quiet conversation, interrupted occasionally by autograph hunters. On my sixtieth birthday, in September 1936, which I spent with my family at Semmering's Südbahn Hotel — Alma and Franz Werfel had come over from Breitenstein for the occasion, and Lotte Lehmann and her husband from Vienna — I was gratified to receive a heartily worded message of congratulation from him. When — I think it was in the winter of 1937 — the French Envoy Gabriel Puaux tendered me a luncheon at which he handed me the order of Commander of the Legion of Honor, Schuschnigg was among those present. I saw him once more after that, on the occasion of my *Carmen* revival at about Christmas time of 1937.

Death robbed me of two beloved people in those years, and the world seemed gloomier to me after their departure from it. Ossip Gabrilowitsch died in Detroit of a dreadful disease in 1936, and Nina Spiegler finally succumbed to her years of suffering in Vienna. Thereafter, the baleful European developments became a daily experience. Hostile Nazism raised its head ever more flauntingly in Austria. German threats sounded from across the border. English sanctions during the Ethiopian campaign had made Italy turn toward Germany. We could no longer hope for Mussolini's protection against Hitler's designs upon Austria. One evening, at a performance of *Tristan and Isolde* stink-pots were thrown. They were not meant for me personally, for at the same time that evening, at eight-thirty, they befouled the air in all theaters and a number of cinemas in Vienna. The performance at the Burgtheater was stopped. I did not care to give the Nazis the satisfaction of having disrupted our performance, and kept on conducting, though a number of frightened or indignant people left the theater. I led the opera to its conclusion, but Isolde and Tristan — and especially the former — had become so hoarse through breathing in the vapors that the Love Death was played by the orchestra without vocal accompaniment. Before a Philharmonic Concert at Musikverein Hall I even received a much-signed letter conveying a threat of death. I handed the message over to the police, who seemed to take it seriously, for a number of stalwart men in shag suits and with chamois brushes on their hats — surprising that the detectives had not chosen a less conspicuous garb for their function at the street entrance, in the corridors, and at the door of the artists' room of a concert hall — surrounded me as a bodyguard on that evening.

There followed a number of happy events in the realm of music. I produced Pfitzner's *Palestrina* in Vienna toward the end of 1936, and Weber's *Euryanthe* in Salzburg in the summer of 1937. Mario Labroca engaged my singers and me for a repetition of the Weber work in Florence in May 1938. I also recall a rendition of Schönberg's *Gurrelieder* at the Vienna Konzerthaus toward the end of 1937. The main event of the season, however, was the aforementioned revival of *Carmen*. I had long been wrestling with the solution of that problem, and had always put it off because no fascinating songstress with a fiery temperament was available for the title part. I believed I had now found her in the person of a Danish singer. As for the rest of the cast, I had no misgivings. I had also succeeded with some difficulty in obtaining the services of Karl Ebert as stage director. We were all happy in our work, and I believe that the music and stage reproduction of Bizet's drama emerged in accordance with the composer's original intentions. I had asked members of the government, with Schuschnigg at their head, outstanding intellectuals, artists from the Opera, and representatives of the orchestra and the chorus to join me at the Hotel Imperial after the *première*. There we all stayed until far into the night, *gemütlich* as only Vienna knew how to make such occasions — even in those late days.

But now the sands in the hourglass were running low. On February 12, 1938, Schuschnigg went to meet Hitler in Berchtesgaden. He expected a courteous discussion of the situation, which would lead to improved relations with the Reich, but was instead subjected to unparalleled humiliations and threats. Most of Hitler's raging demands were unflinchingly rejected by Schuschnigg. Some of them he thought he ought to accept in the interest of neighborly peace, among them the disastrous inclusion of the Nazi Seyss-Inquart in the Austrian government. After Schuschnigg's return from Berchtesgaden, Ernst Lothar, the director of the Josefstädter Theater, called me up at the Chancellor's request, suggesting that I sign a new three-year contract with the State Opera before my impending departure for Amsterdam. The government desired to have a representative musician manifest his faith in Austria, a fact that would tend to reassure the excited population. "Is the government sure of its position and of Austria's future?" I asked Lothar, adding, "I have faith in Schuschnigg's word, and if he can answer my question in the affirmative I am ready to comply with the government's wish." Lothar called up again an hour later: "The Chancellor wants me to tell you that you need not hesitate to sign the contract. And Dr. Pernter would be thankful to you if you were to send a cable to Toscanini in New York, asking him to pledge his appearance at the 1938 Salzburg Festival Plays. That, too, would induce the Austrian public to draw favorable conclusions." I cabled Toscanini and was startled by his reply that he could not accept the invitation. While America was already aware of the hopelessness of the situation, we in Austria were still hopeful.

I conducted a performance of Weber's *Oberon* at the State Opera on the day of Toscanini's refusal. During the intermission, Bronislaw Hubermann, still suffering from the after-effects of an airplane accident in the Dutch Indies, entered my office. "I have come to thank you for the performance and to say good-by to you." When I looked at him questioningly, he added: "Why, can't you see that Austria is finished? You, too, ought to leave as soon as possible." I told him that I would consider it wrong on my part to leave Austria at so fateful a time: the government had informed me that it was master of the situation, Austria's independence was assured, and I had faith in the government.

After the next midday Philharmonic concert, whose program included a new composition by the Austrian Egon Wellesz and Bruckner's Romantic Symphony, my wife and I had luncheon with Wellesz. The meal over, we listened to Hitler's vulgar, grating voice on the radio, boasting about the incomparable increase in German industrial production brought about by the Nazis. The world of listeners was shaken by the mention of the "d'housands of dons" of material and moved by the sentimental and linguistically remarkable reference to "the country where stood the cradle of my home."

I went to Prague to conduct a concert with the Czech Philharmonic Orchestra. I still remember with what reluctance I left my hotel room to go to the Luzerna, where the concert was to take place. My daughter and I had been sitting at the radio, raptly listening to Schuschnigg's famous speech. It was full of the enthusiasm and wrath, the strength and defiance, to which the usually self-contained man had been inflamed by Hitler's threats and insults.

Schuschnigg's words had set the Austrian people afire as none of his previous utterances had been able to do. If the plebiscite announced by him in his subsequent Innsbruck speech had taken place, Nazism in Austria would have been swept away by the wave of enthusiasm for Schuschnigg. In the hour of peril, the Austrian Social Democrats extended their hands to the Chancellor. The resentment caused by the February events of 1934 and the dissatisfaction because of the Chancellor's aloofness from the working class did not keep them from placing themselves at his side. On one of the last February days of 1938, I produced Smetana's *Dalibor* at the State Opera. When Schuschnigg was seen to enter his box before the second act, the whole audience rose and tendered him a rousing ovation. After the performance, there was a festive and hopeful gathering in the magnificent *foyer* of the Opera. Representatives of the Czechoslovakian government attended. To the exuberance caused by Smetana's noble work was added the joyful assurance which the Chancellor's speeches and their enthusiastic echo had aroused in the hearts of all of us.

In that optimistic mood I left for Amsterdam the next day to comply with my guest obligations there. My wife and I took leave cheerfully of our daughter, expecting to be back in about two weeks. Little did we foresee what was in store for her; we did not foresee the fate of Austria; and we did not foresee that we were not to see the country again.

IV

WHEN we arrived in Amsterdam early in March of that fateful year 1938, we were struck by the icy blast of pessimism that had first frighteningly manifested itself in Toscanini's cable. Was it possible that only those most directly affected, the opponents of National Socialism in Austria, were ignorant of the true state of affairs? Like relatives in the sickroom of a dying person, we were clinging to hopeful symptoms, while outside there was no doubt about the hopelessness of his condition. Our eyes were opened suddenly. When, on March 9, Schuschnigg's Innsbruck speech announcing the plebiscite, scheduled for the 13, became known, we realized that it was a question of to be or not to be for Austria. Long-distance talks with our daughter informed us of street demonstrations for and against Schuschnigg. We urged her to leave the seething city and go to quiet Semmering.

But we had no idea of the imminence of the catastrophe, for we were looking forward trustingly to election day on the 13, and were fearful only of its possible consequences. When I got home from an orchestra rehearsal at the Concertgebouw on March 11, my wife received me with the terrible news that Hitler had just presented an ultimatum to Austria. Then we knew that no plebiscite would decide the country's future. The end had come.

From early afternoon until late into the night we sat at the radio, listening from afar to Austria's agony, to Schuschnigg's last hopeless fight, to his leave-taking, to the following confusion of the pathetic Austrian announcements, and to the Nazis' triumphant proclamations. And all this took place to the accompaniment of music, as if no historical tragedy were being enacted, the suffering and death of human beings were not involved, nor the victory of evil, but as if we were witnessing the insipid melodrama of a theatrical pen-pusher itching for a sensation. After Schuschnigg's farewell words "God protect Austria!" the country we had loved had passed away to the solemn strains of Haydn's national anthem played by a string quartet. And while the addresses of President Miklas and of Herr Seyss-Inquart, the calamitous news of German troop movements, and reports of the occupation of Austrian towns followed each other in rapid succession, every pause was filled by Viennese waltzes, only to be interrupted again by announcements of new disasters. Suddenly that mad mixture of death groans and dance music stopped. A new sound came to our ears. The announcements over the Vienna radio were made by a harsh Prussian voice. The listeners were told in terse brief sentences of the progress of Austria's conquest. Blaring Prussian military marches took the place of the waltzes, a musical symbol of what had happened. We listened to the Nazi jubilations until far into the night. They came to a grotesque end about midnight. "And now we shall show to our esteemed listeners," said the announcer triumphantly, "what the Austrian people think of these historical events. We shall ask chance passers-by for their opinion. Well, Miss, how do you like the new Austria?" The rather hoarse and common voice of a woman answered: "I am glad of the new Austria." After venal love had thus saluted Nazism, we turned off the radio. Hitler had started his campaign for world conquest with a great success; his power in the struggle against mankind and humanity had grown considerably, and there was no sign of resistance anywhere. Schuschnigg himself had ordered his inwardly torn country to submit to the aggressors.

The next morning brought news of the closing of the Austrian frontiers, of the despair of the fugitives who had been turned back, and of acts of violence in the streets. We were terribly fearful for our friends and for our daughter, although we could not at first imagine that she was in any danger. A telephone call informed us that she had returned from Semmering to her Vienna apartment on the morning after the invasion. It was agreed that she bide her time and wait until things had quieted down before attending to her departure.

My absorption in thoughts of the sufferings of those who were tortured by the "victors'" brutality was shattered by a crushing blow. During the intermission of a concert conducted by me, an official of the Amsterdam management came up to me and said: "I know that this is not the moment to excite you, but I think I ought to tell you what has happened. The radio has just announced that your daughter was arrested in Vienna." I asked that my wife be sent for, and we agreed that she was to call up certain friends in Vienna and request them to intercede at once. When I had conducted the concert to its end, I called up Kerber and implored him to let me know where my daughter had been taken to. I also asked my son-in-law in Berlin to go to Vienna without delay and consult with Kerber about steps that would lead to her speedy release. Kerber acted with courage and friendly sympathy. He telephoned me that very night that my daughter was held a prisoner at the Elisabeth Promenade police station. My son-in-law tried every day in vain to get in touch with her. We spent almost two weeks in a state of the most terrible anxiety.

I met Toscanini in The Hague, where we had moved in the meantime, and he shared our distress like a true friend. I could not go back to Austria, and neither could my wife. We might have been permitted to enter, but never to leave again. Not only would our intercession have been futile, but the enthusiastic telegram we had sent Schuschnigg after his great speech would likely have plunged us into the same disaster that had befallen others who had done as we had. So we had to rely on our friends in Vienna. All I could do was to guide their steps from afar. At the same time, I had to attend to my contractual duties. They took me from The Hague to Monte Carlo and Nice. My days and nights crawled along in a torment of waiting which would have been considered exaggerated cruelty even in Dante's infernal circles. When I returned from an orchestra rehearsal to our hotel in Nice, on March 28, my wife came rushing to meet me in the street. "I heard her voice," she called to me from a distance, "she told me on the 'phone that she was free." Unceremoniously as she had been arrested, she had been released from prison. It was now our task to make her departure from Austria possible.

My son-in-law had been informed that people without tax arrears were permitted to travel abroad, provided they could prove the professional necessity of their leaving. My daughter's passport still stated her profession to be that of a singer, and so I asked a concert manager in Prague with whom I was on friendly terms to engage her for a song recital in the Czech capital. The splendid fellow went so far as to have large placards announce the fictitious recital in the streets of Prague, so that any possible German investigation would reveal the professional necessity of my daughter's journey. I came to a similar understanding for a somewhat later date with a Zurich concert manager who was devoted to me. Thus both frontiers would be open to my daughter. Approval of her exit permit was delayed. She wrote the agent in Prague that she might be unable to fulfill her contract. To make the urgency or her petition credible, the agent now threatened that non-compliance with her obligations would have serious consequences. Besides, high Czech quarters had let me know that I could count on their support. I shall never as long as I live forget my Czech friends' readiness to help. At last, about the middle of April, our daughter's permit was issued. She chose the Swiss frontier because we were staying in Lugano at the time.

There was a quiet reunion at the station. We knew how severe was the Nazi control at the German-Swiss frontier and did not dare trust our good fortune until our child was actually with us. Besides, the trial of anxious waiting, made even more unbearable by her train being late, had thoroughly exhausted us. Our daughter plainly showed the effects of what she had gone through. She was unable for a long time to tell us the harrowing details of her experiences.

She was accompanied by our housekeeper, who had been able to smuggle into her trunks some clothes and linen belonging to us. Our other maid, who joined us later, had also managed to salvage a number of articles of daily use. A man greatly devoted to me succeeded in getting several valuable pieces of music across the Czech frontier. But on the whole I had to give up as lost almost everything in my apartment that had any value or to which I had become attached. In the face of what was happening generally and what I had experienced personally the loss did not greatly affect me. In fact, I was never able to think of the splendid career of my Cadillac without a certain feeling of humorous satisfaction. Years before, a jeweler by the name of Futterweit had been shot to death by one of a group of masked robbers. They had been apprehended and sentenced to long prison terms. I was told that the Nazis had released one of them — I think his name was Globotschnik — and made him *Gauleiter*. Now my car served the highly meritorious and qualified old party member and provided him with the comfort befitting his station.

To forestall the Nazis, I had, on the day after the invasion of Austria, sent Kerber a telegram requesting that my contract with the Vienna State Opera be rescinded and I be released from my Salzburg obligations. The planned Florence guest appearance of an ensemble from the Vienna Opera under my guidance was thus naturally made impossible. I wrote Labroca, the director of the Florentine Festival Plays, that he need not feel under any obligation to me in connection with the Florence performance of *Euryanthe* that coming May. He telegraphed back that he counted on me under all circumstances. We met in Monte Carlo, and he urged me not to leave Florence in the lurch — he'd do without the Vienna Opera and *Euryanthe*. So I had to choose works that could be performed by Florence artists. We substituted for our original program Beethoven's *Missa Solemnis* and Brahms' German Requiem.

While the political storm had thus far been unable seriously to harm me either professionally or personally, a problem now arose that threatened to become quite troublesome: that of my passport. As Austria no longer existed, our Austrian passports had lost their validity. The German imprint that made them valid, but also made Germans of their bearers, was out of the question for us. We had reached Switzerland and France before the invalidity of the Austrian documents had been proclaimed by Germany. While I had for several years had the right of domicile in Switzerland, the time thus far elapsed was insufficient for the acquisition of citizenship. We had lost our nationality and had no valid passports; and without a passport a person could neither travel nor stay permanently in any one place. For the time being, accommodating authorities still recognized the invalidated Austrian passport for the purpose of a limited stay, but it was useless for traveling, and my every effort must therefore be directed toward the procurement of a valid passport. A general spirit of helpfulness saved me from the sorrows of those without a nationality. A few months later, France magnanimously delivered me from my awkward predicament. But until then I was burdened by constant care. I made all kinds of attempts, all of them unavailing. I even entertained the thought of a so-called Nansen passport, the document of identification of those without a nationality, though I knew that the moment of hope inspired by its issuance would be followed by years of torment caused by the interminable waiting for visas.

I endeavored with a certain feeling of assurance to obtain the citizenship of Monaco. A passport from the principality would have given me full freedom of movement. I thought I could hope for a preferential treatment of my case because I was ready to offer an equivalent of no mean advantage to the small country. No sooner had Austria's fate been fulfilled than there were endeavors in any number of quarters to enter upon the inheritance of Salzburg. It was but natural that people should turn to me with their propositions. I advised against them in the majority of instances. But in the case of Monte Carlo I thought the plan merited special consideration because of the beauty of the location, the popularity of the French Riviera, and the possibility of an artistic co-operation with the Operas of Paris and Milan. The charming Opera Hall of the Casino would furnish an excellent frame for Italian and French *opéra buffa,* and the erection of a new great operahouse on the rocks of Monaco or in the fine grounds near the Casino would have made some of the sinful riches of the gambling establishment available for a noble use and, a moral atonement, presented to the world of culture a new center of artistic life. The idea was considered interesting in many quarters. At my suggestion, the Casino's management approached Karl Ebert, and there followed a thorough joint discussion of the plan. It finally came to naught, probably both because of the absence of an internal impelling force and the darkening of the political horizon. But at the time things looked favorable. When I departed, I hopefully left behind in the hands of a ministry official a definite project and a tentative budget I had worked out with Ebert — and my request for naturalization. I also considered it advisable to retain the services of a local lawyer who was vigorously to fan the feeble flame of ministerial activities.

Theme and Variations

The middle-aged Maitre X., together with his distinguished dusty offices in a four-storied quiet apartment house whose green shutters were permanently closed, seemed to have stepped into reality from a Balzac novel. He unfortunately lacked the temperament to inspire me with hope for an early settlement of my request, and so I returned to Lugano, perplexed. I was to resume my professional activity in October. If the question of my passport was not settled by that time, my every chance to work was gone.

We were, however, still able to go to Florence, for the Italian consulate in Paris had at the behest of Rome issued to us a permit to cross and re-cross the Italian border without passport control. I was greatly pleased by that bow to music on the part of bureaucracy. I returned from my fourth participation in the *Maggio Musicale* as satisfied as I had been by previous ones. The faithful attitude manifested by the management of the Festival Plays in a critical situation caused me to be more cordially attached than ever to the fine enterprise.

We went from Florence to Milan by rail. There we were awaited by our younger daughter and her husband. Their car was to take us to Lugano in Switzerland by way of the magnificent *autostrada*. During our absence, our daughters had hired for us a high-seated villa, whose windows and fine wide terrace afforded a splendid view of Lake Lugano below and the Tessin Mountains above. Anxious because of their feeling of responsibility, and yet proud of their choice, they took us through the house and the garden, until we stopped with a start of happy surprise before a trophy our elder daughter's cleverness had saved in Vienna from the Nazis' clutches and which now adorned our living room. It was a present the Vienna Singakademie had made me years before, after my performance of Mahler's Eighth: Rodin's bronze bust of my great friend.

No memory of past tormenting experiences, no anxiety caused by the thunderclouds on the European horizon, and no worry about the future could deprive us of our joy in our fine new domicile and in the picturesque little town with its narrow streets and colonnades, its splendid location on the lake, and its enchanting surroundings. Our elder daughter lived with us, while the younger one and her husband settled in Zurich, which was five hours by rail from Lugano. We had not abandoned all hope that a reasonable world would put a stop to Hitler's devilish plans. A few months of peaceful and confident life were still vouchsafed us.

We enjoyed to the full the brisk mornings on the terrace, gathered round the breakfast table near a beautiful old mimosa tree that clung to the corner of the house; quiet hours spent in my study; shopping in the pleasant stores in the town's old streets; meetings with friends in the coffeehouse on the lake; and evening walks down the slopes of the vineyard behind our house and through the surrounding villages, which were both picturesquely Italian and neatly and comfortably Swiss. And there were the two dogs: our highly sensitive shepherd bitch Asta and our daughter's overwhelmingly friendly boxer Tommy. They filled the house with manifestations of an elemental joy of living, a feeling that, in its two-legged occupants, had been gradually supplanted by a more tranquil mood. We liked to watch their curious antics in the dusk of the garden. I can still see Tommy returning to the living room from his late evening walk. From his mouth dangles a live hedgehog. He had acquired a technique all his own for seizing his spiny victims. With a heavy sigh of an onerous duty well performed, he drops the unfortunate beast at our feet.

In Lugano and in our beautiful home we spent our last comparatively quiet days. I believe we enjoyed them all the more because a feeling of farewell transfigured their tranquillity. Autumn came, and the terrible Munich meeting, after which there was no longer a quiet moment or a ray of hope. And then, during the following summer, the greatest personal disaster of our lives befell us.

V

THE FIRST Lucerne Festival Plays, in which Toscanini and I participated, took place in that summer of 1938. My memory has retained a remarkable event connected with them: a performance of Wagner's *Siegfried Idyll* conducted by Toscanini in front of the house near Triebschen where Siegfried Wagner had been born, where the piece had been composed, and where it had sounded forth for the first time.

Early in September, I went back to Monte Carlo to attend to the urgent matter of my naturalization. I found Maitre X. deeply somnolent and the Ministry disinterested. I had already made up my mind to become reconciled to the wretched thought of being condemned to stay permanently on the shoal on which I seemed to have run aground, when a saving miracle occurred. Georges Huismans, the Directeur Général des Beaux-Arts, wrote me from Paris stating that he had learned of my endeavors to acquire the citizenship of Monaco. If I wished, the French government would make me a citizen of France. Deeply moved, I telegraphed my sincere gratitude and enthusiastic acceptance. I immediately went to Paris, where I was most cordially received by Georges Huismans and the officials of the Ministry of Education. Everything proceeded with dreamlike ease. Doors and hearts were opened wherever I went. Two weeks after my arrival in Paris I was a French citizen. Most impressive was the visit of thanks I paid Paul Reynaud, the Minister of Justice and subsequent chief of government until the defeat of France in 1940. While I was being announced, my gaze was attracted by documents whose importance was emphasized by their being displayed under glass. I saw before me the *Declaration of Human Rights* of September 1791, that eternally glorious memento in the history of France. Its impressive preservation at the French Ministry of Justice cheered and comforted me at a moment when human rights were held in contempt and abrogated in Germany and when the world was again threatened with inhuman tyranny. Even I, on my peaceable way, had come in painful contact with it. Paul Reynaud met me with outstretched hands and expressed his joy at being able to welcome me as a French citizen. I assured him of my gratitude and of my hope to be useful to French musical life. Then, I believe, we discussed the events in Germany. Inasmuch as London concerts were closely impending and a French passport would be highly desirable in that connection, Monsieur Huismans did his utmost to expedite matters. I recall with particular pleasure the helpfulness of everybody concerned. Although the issuance of a passport took as a rule two days, two starry-eyed young women at the *préfecture* managed to have the one for Maitre Bruno Walter ready within two hours. The counter-clerk, to whom I presented the still crackling new document on my way to the plane, proved to me by his smile and his enthusiastic *"Bon voyage, Maitre!"* the satisfaction with which, it seemed, my naturalization was received also in wider circles. The French consulate in Lugano was told to issue a passport also to my wife, and so we had both of us become citizens of France and had acquired a new nationality and freedom of movement. Our anxiety was now centered upon our elder daughter. The younger one had become a German through her marriage, and much as we felt disturbed by the fact, she was at least spared the sinister fate of one without nationality.

When I had returned to Lugano from London, world events had become so oppressive that even the autumnal beauty of the landscape and the charm of our mode of living were unable to exert their magic spell. "Munich" had come, that self-abasement of the world before Hitler. To me it represented the most wretchedly shameful scene of the European drama. The gates leading to the realization of the wicked plans of the world-conqueror and his fellow-criminals stood wide open. Deeply depressed, I started upon a tour of the Balkans early in October. I had undertaken it at the urgent request of the Vienna impresario Dr. Hohenberg.

Theme and Variations

My tour took me to Zagreb, the capital of Croatia, which looked exactly like an old-Austrian town, and to Sofia, the capital of Bulgaria, which rather reminded one of Russia. My Sofia hotel, by the way, was unpleasantly alive with arrogant German Nazi emissaries. A plane carried me over the interesting mountain formations of the Balkans and, by way of Saloniki, to Athens.

My desire to see Greece, and especially Athens, had induced me to undertake this tour. The late, but therefore perhaps all the more moving, realization of my boyhood dream had come to pass. When my plane approached Saloniki for a brief stay, my senses began to be affected by a never-before-seen transparency of the sky and brightness of the light. Then we winged across the clear blue of the Mediterranean and past beautifully formed Greek islands, among which was the mighty, mountainous Eubœa. We finally got to Athens, where the Acropolis greeted me before we landed.

My days in Athens and those devoted to excursions into the city's immediate and farther surroundings were given up to visual delights such as I had never before experienced. My memory of the heroic monuments of Roman antiquity made them appear too humanly self-conscious and emphatic of their power when compared with the clear beauty and the quiet loftiness of the Greek forms, transfigured by the unearthly light of the skies above them. Every one of my leisure mornings was spent at the Parthenon, whose noble grandeur impressed me more deeply the more I saw of it. I gradually came to see it with the eyes of the French painter who had made himself known to me at one of my visits and told me that the temple had been the object of his studies and reproductions for years and that he was no longer able to part from it. The most powerful impression on my excursions to places and districts whose names had from childhood greatly excited my imagination was made by Delphi. Friends of mine took me there in their car. I was surprised at the gloomy grandeur of the landscape, which must have filled the minds of those who had anxiously come to consult the oracle with thoughts of dark powers and magic. I wandered about between the stone blocks of the mighty theater and drank from the Castalian spring. On our way back, I admired with truly reverential awe the towering shape of distant Mount Olympus whose summit had before been majestically shrouded in clouds by its heavenly occupants. I lived wholly in the atmosphere of a loftily distant past, and it was natural that I should have considered my contacts with modern Greece — including my concerts — an annoying interruption of my newly formed passionate relations with the classic home of European culture. A rather interesting contact with the present, however, was furnished by my call on Prime Minister Metaxas, who presented to me a Greek decoration and confessed in the course of the ensuing conversation that he was an admirer of German music.

The day of my departure had come all too quickly. I had made plane reservations for Brindisi and Milan, and had planned to proceed from there by rail to Paris, where I was to conduct some operas and concerts. My Athens friends saw me to the airport. When I thanked them for the delights experienced by my soul they remarked that I had unfortunately failed to become acquainted with an interesting part of the country, the Peloponnesus. A particularly wild whim of fate filled this gap in my Greek experiences, but it might easily have turned out to be my last experience on earth.

Bad weather had forced our plane to wait at the Athens airfield for hours, until finally the meteorological station reported an improvement, and we were permitted to start. After but a few minutes in the air, however, I knew that we were in for a bad time. Our plane was tossed about violently. Between hurrying clouds, the sun would now appear at the right, now at the left of us, which made me conclude that the pilot was up to some tricky maneuvering. My laboring heart and a member of the crew told me that we had risen to a high altitude. After two hours of vain endeavors the pilot decided to return to Athens, and so informed the passengers in a written message. Everything now began to grow black around us. Raging, the storm hurled itself upon our plane. Women cried. A young Italian mother, holding an infant, prayed. A young man at her side, a member of the crew, was splendidly helpful. He took the trembling woman's child into his arms and tried to comfort her. Suddenly, through the window on my left, I saw a bright flame leap up. Lightning had struck our left wing. The young humanitarian gestured to me: "We are lost!" I leaned back resignedly, waiting for the explosion and the end. But our pilot did not yield. He had at once disconnected the gasoline tank. Aided by his copilot and struggling with all his might to keep the plane balanced, he volplaned down. Below us I saw the sea. At the last moment, the pilot managed to reach the shore. The plane buried its nose deeply in the slime into which a sudden downpour of rain had turned everything. We leaped far down out of the quickly opened door at the damaged left side of the plane, which rested on its right. Distracted, we stood in the drenching rain. "Where are we?" I asked our pilot. "I don't know," he replied, "I've lost my bearings." Then it appeared as if my stormy trip had landed me, like much-traveled Gulliver, in a fantastic country. Strange figures were seen to approach: bearded little men, cripples, simple-looking boys, old women with streaming hair. Soon we were surrounded by a sinister crowd whose sight made me doubt that I was still alive. Could I have entered an unthought-of intermediary realm? There seemed to be no language in which to communicate with our unbidden visitors, who crowded around us or were moving with suspicious curiosity toward the plane containing our luggage. Then a woman came who had a smattering of French. From her I learned that we had landed not far from Missolonghi. I offered to go there. Help had to be provided for the removal of the women passengers and the salvaging of the luggage. The men were in the meantime to stay with the plane and protect it from undesirable interference on the part of the Greek gypsies. That was what these people turned out to be.

Guided by one of the young simpletons, I went, or rather waded to the place, distinguished by Byron's stay on his relief expedition during the Greek struggle for liberty. A casual glance convinced me that that was its only claim to glory. I carried with me a number of the passengers' and crew's home addresses, that I might by telegrams notify their relatives and mine of the long-overdue plane's emergency landing and our well-being. A helpfully inclined Missolonghi veterinarian who had some Italian aided me in my undertaking. He took me and my subsequently arrived fellow-travelers to an inn. While the prospect of getting spaghetti delighted our Italian crew, the spaghetti itself so depressed them that one of them declared the dish was his worst experience of the day. The pilot, to whom I said how greatly indebted we were to his courage and skill, replied with a serious look: "We must all thank God." Next day, the management of the airline sent a hydroplane to take us back to Athens. But in the meantime I had lost all desire to fly. I called up friends in Athens, and we agreed to meet in Patras, which I and a few other passengers reached by means of a branch railway line and a steamer. My friends went there by car. So my adventure had at least afforded me a glimpse of an interesting part of the Peloponnesus, through which our return trip to Athens took us.

I proceeded by rail to Paris, where I was scheduled to conduct a considerable number of events. I believe that Paris stay, too, was followed by a Swiss tour of the Orchestre Philharmonique de Paris under my guidance. Plans for my increased activity in France and a large-scale music festival in Paris were discussed with Monsieur Huismans and Director Rouché of the Opera. I conducted, I played Mozart sonatas with Jaques Thibaud in the magnificent Opéra, and I was bound ever more closely to French musical life. At the same time, I endeavored to have the authorities issue documents of identification to my elder daughter, to take the place of her invalidated Austrian passport. I actually succeeded in obtaining for her a *carte d'identité* and a *titre de voyage*, which relieved us of our most pressing cares. In the meantime, arrangements had been made for an official reception to celebrate my admission to the French state. The event took place in the festive rooms of a palace in the Faubourg St. Honoré. Little as I was suited to be the center of such a celebration, I was made most happy by the wave of goodwill and friendliness flowing toward me. Addresses by the Mayor of Paris, Director Rouché, and, I believe, a government representative, and a poem recited by a young actress from the Théatre Français bade me welcome as a citizen of France. It was probably because of the general cordiality that in my reply I felt suddenly free from my usual inhibiting shyness.

My obligations now called me once more to Amsterdam. A new mark of honor awaited me there. I was made Grand Officer of the Order of Orange-Nassau. When I had been General Musical Director in Munich, I had received a number of decorations which were owing to my position and therefore did not mean much to me. Every German prince visiting Munich habitually honored the head of the Opera in that manner. But I rejoiced in the distinctions bestowed on me by France, Austria, Holland, and Greece: they conferred honor on me personally and were meant to counteract the injuries inflicted on me.

From Holland, I was to have gone to Scanadinavia to conduct at Copenhagen, Stockholm, and Oslo. But how to get there without touching Germany? In addition to direct rail connections by way of Germany, there was a Dutch airline from Amsterdam to Stockholm, but the plane's route would take it over Germany, and an emergency landing might have placed me in a precarious position. I therefore decided to detour by way of London, from where a small Swedish steamer made weekly trips to Göteborg, in Sweden. I shall never forget the sight of the storm-flattened horizontal flags seen from our hotel windows. My daughter pointed at them, anxiously shaking her head. The approximately thirty-six hours at sea represented the most turbulent voyage of our lives. The coats hanging in our staterooms stood out as horizontally as the London flags. They would return to a limp verticality, only to return madly to their weird opposition to physical laws, especially during the night. And yet, how reassuring, how comfortable was that trip! At worst, we might have drowned, while an emergency landing in Germany would have put us in the hands of the Nazis.

The concerts in Stockholm and the bracing human atmosphere surrounding me again gave me a great deal of pleasure. I think it was on that occasion that I performed Mahler's "Resurrection"

Symphony. I am fond of recalling the splendid and carefully coached chorus, which deeply satisfied me by its sensitivity, strength, and vocal beauty, and the excellent performance of the orchestra. I have a particularly vivid recollection of a party at the home of Prince Eugene, the Swedish King's brother, which was connected with an important experience. I had met the Prince years before in Vienna at a luncheon at Bronislaw Hubermann's home. He had also been to see me in Salzburg, and on a previous visit to Stockholm had been kind enough to drive me and my wife to show us the city and its environs. It was a pleasure to be in the company of so intellectual a man. He seemed to exude seriousness and kindness. He led us on a tour of inspection of the impressive pictures he had painted, which adorned the lower floor of his house. They revealed the spirited young soul dwelling in the body of the aged man. He knew well how to assemble at his parties a harmonious circle of interesting people. I was indebted to him for the acquaintance of a man of whom I think with a sense of deep and lasting gratitude.

I was at that time greatly worried about the fate of my brother and sister. I had tried to get them out of Germany and into Holland, but seemed unable to obtain for them a Dutch entry permit. I had applied to several Dutch authorities. They were well-intentioned, but slow. So I decided to try my luck in Sweden. Chance came to my aid. After a party at Prince Eugene's, we were taken back to our hotel by a middle-aged man who occupied an important political position. The thought of the distress of my brother and sister made me overcome my reluctance to the extent that, with an apologetic reference to extraordinary circumstances, I ventured to ask his advice. He proved highly sympathetic at once and promised to inform himself in the matter. On the following day, he called at my hotel and suggested that I send a detailed written account of my wishes to a certain official department. He himself would endeavor to have the matter approved. Two or three days later, I believe, he called me up and said: "Everything is all right. The Swedish Legation in Berlin" — or was it the Consulate? — "has been instructed to issue a Swedish entry permit to your brother and sister." I owe to that humane man the elimination of the usual dangerous delays and the ultimate safety of my brother and sister. My heart was relieved of a heavy burden.

After having spent the month of December in Lugano, we went to London in January 1939. There I was to conduct concerts with the orchestra of the British Broadcasting Corporation and its chorus, and, I believe, also with the London Philharmonic Orchestra. Then I went again to New York, following an invitation from the orchestra of the National Broadcasting Company, newly created for Toscanini.

Letters from American friends had in the meantime informed me to my heartfelt satisfaction of the sympathetic interest with which my 1938 experiences had been followed there. There were cordial expressions of anxiety — unfounded, fortunately — concerning my personal circumstances. Hans Kindler, the conductor of the National Symphony Orchestra of Washington, wrote that he had suggested to our American colleagues that they be helpful to me by inviting me to lead concerts in the United States. He himself actively manifested his sentiments by offering to have me conduct one of his concerts. I thanked him most warmly for his truly brotherly attitude, assured him that my departure from German musical life, and later from the Austrian one too, had in no way harmed me professionally or economically, and stated that I was pleased and ready to accept his kind invitation during my next stay in America. So it came about that, after having fulfilled my obligations toward the N.B.C., I conducted a concert in Washington's Constitution Hall in April 1939.

German troops had in the meantime entered Prague. Even the most convinced advocates of appeasement realized now that war was inevitable. It even seemed to me to be just around the corner, and I was made to suffer from the thought that its outbreak would prevent our return to Europe and might separate us from our younger daughter for years. I made use of my stay in Washington to call at the State Department and asking that permission for the issuance of her American entry visa be cabled to the American Consulate in Zurich. I was received most cordially. Soon we were made happy by a cable from our daughter, informing us that the consul had summoned her by telephone and issued the visa. She was now in the position to take an early steamer for America. We returned to Europe early in May and met her in Paris, made radiant by all the charms of spring. There we discussed plans for the event of the outbreak of war, which was expected any moment. My daughter was once more able to attend my concerts — her musician's soul in harmony with my own, her clever enthusiastic remarks about what she had heard a joy to my heart, her mere presence a source of warmth and happiness.

In Lugano and Sils Maria, in the Engadine, we spent a last few fine weeks, made blissful by her presence. Then I had to go to Vichy to conduct a few concerts whose direction I had assumed at the request of some French friends. In August I arrived in Lucerne, where I was to perform Mahler's Second in conjunction with the Festival Plays. Soon after my arrival, my wife, my two daugh-

BRUNO WALTER, NEW YORK, 1941

(*photograph by Susan Hoeller*)

BRUNO WALTER ADDRESSING A PHILHARMONIC-
SYMPHONY SOCIETY AUDIENCE

*in Carnegie Hall, New York, on the occasion of his fiftieth
anniversary as a conductor, March 16, 1944*

ters, and I attended a performance of Verdi's Requiem, after which we had a meal with Thomas and Katja Mann. On the following day, we paid a visit to Toscanini at his house on Lake Lucerne.

I did not conduct the Mahler Symphony. The greatest affliction of our lives had befallen us, changing the whole aspect of the world for me. Our younger daughter had met a violent death. It was the horrible task of Toscanini's wife and daughter to acquaint me with the dreadful news. They did what they had to do with the utmost kindness, and then took me in their car to the place where I had agreed to meet my wife. She had been waiting anxiously for a long time. Now we had to tell her what had happened.

Into the night that covered our souls the news of the closely impending outbreak of war penetrated as from far away.

VI

THE ACCOUNT of my life is nearing its close. Not that the last years have passed uneventfully, but I still lack the perspective that turns experiences into memories. And I do not want the end of my tale to become a diary, characterized by its relation to the present. So I shall no longer consider continuity the law of my chronicle. I shall merely record details of experiences and impressions that have already assumed the patina of memory. Then, with a few words, such as may come into one's mind when the train is about to move and one looks back at those who are being left behind, I shall take my leave.

The German armies had invaded Poland on September 1, 1939. Again there was war. All I recall of those days after our horrible return to Lugano is that we all felt: Away from here! In my endeavors to have my European contracts rescinded, I met with general understanding and kindness. Accompanied by my wife and daughter, I sailed for New York from Genoa, on October 31. Because my duties with the N.B.C. would not begin until January, we decided to stay in California until then.

Anxiety concerning the fate of friends we had left behind in Europe and the welfare of those who were forced to build up a new existence in the United States was our constant companion during the first years of our settlement in America. And there was no day without our passionately questioning the papers and the radio: How goes the war? The war went badly. But in spite of Dunkerque and the tragic collapse of France in 1940, in spite of the threat to Alexandria and the invasion of Russia as far as Moscow and Stalingrad, I never had a moment of pessimism. Unshakable remained my assurance that evil could not be victorious. In February 1940,

Theme and Variations

I donated an ambulance for the French wounded. It was accepted with thanks by the Anglo-French Ambulance Corps. It was meant to express my gratitude to France and my general attitude.

The voice of hatred I had heard over the radio shortly before my departure from Vienna was to sound in my ear once more on this side of the ocean. In the garden in the rear of our house in Beverly Hills, California, stood the little magic apparatus around which we were gathered. A hysterical screaming came from it. The following words have remained in my memory: "I shall erase the English cities from the face of the earth." The raging voice broke at the end of the sentence. It took me a long time to get over my loathing of that jarring sound.

Another scene at the same place in Beverly Hills stands clearly before my vision: we were meeting Franz and Alma Werfel again. They told us of the terror of their last days in France; of the adventures of their flight; of Lourdes, where Werfel had been deeply impressed by the wonderful existence of the child Bernadette; of their hopeful arrival in Marseille; of disappointments and new roamings that took them past Cerbère and into the Pyrenees; finally, of an arduous night-bound mountain tour over goat paths up to the Spanish border and across it, Alma carrying the manuscript of Bruckner's Third Symphony under her arm. Werfel spoke, and Alma interrupted and corrected him, adding details. Their words made a picture rise up in my mind: masses of fugitives crowding the highways of European countries that were either enslaved or menaced, slinking along secret paths, hunted by the insane would-be world-conqueror's bloodhounds. So passionately filled with his subject was Werfel that, to himself as well as to us, his own past experiences and the monstrous suffering he had witnessed all about him became the living present. He had to leave our little circle for a while to recover from the excitement into which his own report had plunged him. A year later, we met him and Alma in their charming villa in Beverly Hills and were glad to see that in their case, at least, a repentant fate had seemingly endeavored to "make amends."

Our next meeting with Thomas Mann and his family took place in Princeton. We called on him at his handsome house, a short distance from the campus of the university at which he taught. He told me of the Indian fairy tale that was occupying his mind: the humorous and profound tale of *The Transposed Heads*. Later, Mann, too, moved to California, where both he and Werfel lived in the atmosphere of work they had created for themselves, enjoying the sun if anything could be enjoyed at all in those years shaken by the spasms and crises of world conflict.

Theme and Variations

We were to have the joy of meeting in California a third family of friends with whom ties of common experiences and thoughts united us: Bruno and Lisl Frank and the latter's mother, Fritzi Massary. I was made happy by knowing these old friends present at my concerts either at the Los Angeles Auditorium or the Hollywood Bowl. Lili Petschnikoff, too, was there, and again we were at her house opposite the Bowl's entrance. But the two old ladies were no longer there.

At times we would drive along the wonderful California seacoast to Santa Barbara to call on Lotte Lehmann at her fine house overlooking the ocean. Like my other friends, she, too, had acquired a new feeling of home. Painting, writing, singing, and teaching, she would leave with a feeling of regret whenever her professional activity demanded her presence elsewhere.

We met Adolf Busch in New York. The musical activity of this indomitable idealist was bound to give satisfaction and encouragement to all of a similar mind. His Bach performances have become an important and generally appreciated contribution to American musical life.

Bronislaw Hubermann, who had been dear to me in Europe for years as an artist and a man, though our paths had crossed only occasionally, now also joined the inner circle whose friendship enriched my life. I found within him a well co-ordinated combination of utter devotion to his noble art and an active participation in the events of the day, an enviable synthesis that has been denied me. His extremely busy musical life did not prevent his organizing the Palestine Orchestra, a deed by which he rendered an eminently practical service to an idea, to a state, and to art. In both his personal and his public life he gave utterance by clever words and a courageous attitude to what he considered his duty as a democratically thinking man and as one who felt a responsibility for world happenings.

I admit with deep regret that I have never attained to that happy balance between artistic and human duties. It ought to be one of the most important tasks, if not the most important one, of a democratic state to familiarize its citizens from childhood with the thought of sharing the responsibility for its internal and foreign actions and of making individual partisanship both their right and their duty. The course of my life in the parental home and at school did not bring me in contact with public affairs, nor were the comparatively quiet conditions prevailing during the years of my early manhood able to direct toward public duties a mind centered upon art and its own spiritual development. My life was surely wanting in the energetic public partisanship that would have corresponded to my later passionate inward participation in the burning questions of world happenings. Perhaps, too, the world citizen within me stood in the way of the state citizen. I should like to emphasize, however, that I cannot accuse myself of indolence, to say nothing of indifference, but rather of amateurism in the organization of my forces, which unresistingly yielded to the tyranny of art.

It is not surprising, in view of their accomplishments and importance, that the old-time friends of whom I have spoken and other acquaintances from the most varied professional circles should have reached a high standing here and find themselves in comfortable circumstances. Experience has shown me that even the average European has had little difficulty in building up a new existence in the United States, provided he was able from the beginning clearly to see the difference between here and "over there" and endeavored to adapt himself. On the other hand, there were any number of refugees who seemed wholly incapable of dissociating themselves from their former conditions. They were unable to become acclimated or to attain comfortable circumstances. Let me cite here from my personal experience a particularly striking example of that regrettable type. A young Austrian called on me and told me briskly that he had just arrived from Europe and was looking for an occupation. He had come directly from the steamer to see me because I had been on friendly terms with his father in Vienna. Well, it turned out in the course of our conversation, that that was a matter of thirty-five years ago. "You are conducting the concerts of the N.B.C. here, aren't you," he said, "and so I thought you might be able to get me a job there." "So you are a musician, are you?" I asked. "Oh, no!" he replied with radiant confidence and a hopeful smile, "I am a reciter, and there ought to be an opening for me with the radio." "What do you recite?" "Poems — I've become a specialist — I recite Austrian dialect poetry." The poor fellow was utterly disappointed and looked at me skeptically when I pointed out to him how little the American radio audience would appreciate his Austrian dialect poetry.

My own transplantation was accompanied by no crises. I am still conscious of the difference in tempo, which impressed itself on me during my first American visit, in 1923. American vitality has not ebbed, while, on the other hand, my own pace is governed by the "specific weight" of my nature. But in spite of my being different, or rather because of it, that mighty vitality has exerted upon me a fascination, perhaps because spiritually I am inclined less ego-centrically than is good for my self-assertion. In an earlier chapter I referred to my natural inclination to feel with "the other."

Theme and Variations

When I arrived in New York in November 1939 for permanent residence, America had already become familiar to me. I had no linguistic difficulties, not only because I was able to speak English, but also because as a musician I was able to express myself in the idiom that was my very own. But even if my circumstances had been far less favorable, the charm exerted upon me throughout my life by all that is new would have overcome the element of strangeness, for I am an optimist at heart. In spite of many painful experiences and the horror caused me by world happenings, I have always in moments of tranquillity been conscious of a feeling of harmony. And that disposition has surely nothing to do with the "execrable optimism" so indignantly referred to by Schopenhauer, but seems to me, rather, compatible with a full understanding of the world's sufferings.

Friends, too, have given to my life in America the warmth without which there can be no feeling of home. There are the people close to my heart, of whom I have spoken; there are dear friends made during my early years in America; and new ones have been added since. The country is becoming increasingly familiar to me through its literature, and I am acquiring a deeper understanding through my study of its history. To me, there stand out from the mighty epos the figures of Thomas Jefferson and Abraham Lincoln, whose lofty thoughts and immortal words have not only pointed the way to the American people, but are so wise, fruitful, and potent that they might well guide the whole world into a better future. To my discerning look, they were the first statesmen in responsible positions who used political wisdom and power for the attainment of humanity's goals. And I fervently admired Franklin D. Roosevelt, the clearness of his vision, the loftiness of his aims, his tremendous accomplishments as the supreme commander in war, and his warmhearted humanity. His death meant to me, as to countless others, the loss of a personal friend.

So I have gradually learned to live in the country and with the country without losing contact with myself or my past. A contributing factor naturally has been the landscape I viewed on my long travels or came to know closely on my wanderings. Of my many impressions, let me mention here but one, because it has indelibly stamped itself upon my mind: the Seventeen-Mile Drive near Monterey in California. From Del Monte, through forests and over a magnificent mountain road with a wide view of the Pacific Ocean, our daughter takes us down to the coast in our car. We walk along the shore with its usually turbulent surf. Inshore, beyond the undulating white dunes, the horizon is lined with pines whose grotesquely twisted and often ghostlike shapes are caused by the fierceness of storms. Among the rocks out in the ocean there is one that serves as a dwelling place to innumerable birds, and another alive with sea lions, whose whining barking we can hear from afar. Our field glasses reveal to us their games and fights, their skill in the water, and their lazy resting in the sun. Above our heads wing endless flights of birds with outstretched necks, their raucous cries piercing the magnificent expanse of ocean and sky into which they disappear.

My participation in America's musical life has spread and become intensified in the course of my permanent stay in the country. I returned to the Philharmonic-Symphony Society of New York in January 1941, and have remained its annual guest conductor ever since. On my first program I find Bruckner's Eighth. It is a source of heartfelt satisfaction that the sublime work made upon New York's Carnegie Hall audience the same powerful impression it had upon that of London's Queen's Hall, when I performed it there with the Vienna Philharmonic Orchestra. I harbor a profound faith, strengthened by every new experience, that the musical world of the future will recognize the importance of Bruckner's works. A performance of Mahler's *Das Lied von der Erde* took place during that epoch. As long as I can lift a baton, I shall persist in standing up for the works of Mahler and Bruckner. I consider it one of my life's tasks to uncover the sources of exaltation flowing from their music.

In 1942, I conducted *Fidelio* at the Metropolitan Opera, where I have since been active as guest conductor. Subsequent invitations from the splendid Philadelphia Orchestra have led to the formation of highly gratifying ties. Richly rewarding in both an artistic and a personal sense have been my occasional contacts with the Westminster Choir. When I think of America's musical culture and its future prospects, that choir, together with the accomplishments of the country's magnificent orchestras, inspires me with a sense of confidence. Raised and directed by the firm hand of Dr. John Finley Williamson, founder as well as head of the musical seminary whose pupils form the choir, it has succeeded by its vocal brilliance, its musicality, and its enthusiastic singing, in making a large number of oratorio performances deeply impressive. The secret of this impressiveness was revealed to me whenever I went for rehearsals to the university town of Princeton, almost English in its appearance. From the moment I was met at the station by Dr. Williamson till my departure I was gratifyingly conscious of the artistic idealism and cheerful faith emanating from him and inspiring his institution. I have never been able to work more easily, nor have I felt better understood than in the circle of these seriously enthusiastic youths.

There was an old sin for which I tried to atone: I decided to perform Bach's *St. Matthew Passion* in its entirety. I spent almost a year on the renewed clarification of the questions brought up by a conscientious penetration into the *Passion's* manifold nature, and I succeeded in creating the necessary conditions for thorough work with the performers. Of all the performances in my long life, this was probably the one that made me most thoroughly happy. Not because it was perfect — perfection is a goal to be striven for but never attained — but because I believe that, on the whole and in particulars, the performance fulfilled Bach's intentions as far as given circumstances permitted. My vital energy, which had threatened to flag at times, was renewed by Bach's immortal work, and so I had a personal reason, too, for retaining those performances in my memory.

In March 1944, fifty years had passed since I started my conducting career at the Cologne Opera. I had not been able to celebrate my twenty-fifth anniversary as a conductor: the year 1919 had not been propitious for that. The celebration of my fiftieth anniversary aroused the highly gratifying interest of fellow-artists throughout the country. Conductors and orchestras sent me messages of congratulation. On the day when I conducted Bruckner's *Te Deum* and Beethoven's Ninth with my old faithful friends of the New York Philharmonic, the management and orchestra did me the honor to unite after the concert in a touching celebration.

I had long yearned for a year of rest, a year far from the public eye. To remember, to reflect, to draw conclusions after fifty years of musical work, to write without being hurried by the moment, to render an accounting of my life to myself and to others — that was to be the sense of my sabbatical year. In August of the same year, however, my wife fell ill at the place where we spent the summer. We took her to New York. There she lingered for eight months in a hopeless condition. I was unable to help her, who had been a devoted helpmate to me throughout a lifelong partnership. She who had fought bravely and indefatigably on behalf of one who was not born to be a fighter was now for long and painful months engaged in the last fight — a fight we all must lose. After almost forty-four years of an all too exciting life at my side she left me and my daughter, to find in eternal life the peace she so richly deserved.

Looking back upon my life, I find much cause for mourning, more for gratitude. I had gained strength from people dear to me, from those who were near to me in life, and from others who, influencing me by their work and example, nourished within me the comforting assurance of a community of the human spirit, beyond centuries and mundane boundaries. It was this invisible church that had sheltered me from the innumerable attacks with which the events of daily life shake man's power of resistance. Strength was given me by nature, to which I am as devoted today as I ever was. Strength was given me by the sheltering affection of my family, but also by interest in the sufferings of others and by aid I was at times able to render. It was given me by the little joys of life. But above all it flowed into me from music. There flows from music, irrespective of its ever-changing emotional expression, an unchanging message of comfort: its dissonances strive toward consonance — they must be resolved; every musical piece ends in a consonance. Thus music as an element has an optimistic quality, and I believe that therein lies the source of my innate optimism. Still more important, however, and of decisive influence upon my life is the exalted message conveyed to us from the works of the great masters, a message most sacredly expressed in the symphonic adagio. The Church knows why it calls upon the power of music at its most solemn functions. Music's wordless gospel proclaims in a universal language what the thirsting soul of man is seeking beyond this life. I have been vouchsafed the grace to be a servant of music. It has been a beacon on my way and has kept me in the direction toward which I have been striving, darkly, when I was a child, consciously later. There lie my hope and my confidence — *non confundar in æternum.*

And so, on the whole, in spite of all weighty objections, life and the world get a fairly good testimonial from me. And what will be my testimonial once I leave this exceedingly strict and hard school? I think it will look somewhat like the reports I mentioned in the account of my childhood. I was not a model pupil, and I got no "Excellent" in any subject except in singing. I admit my serious deficiencies. I have often suffered from them. I admit the errors I have committed. But perhaps this picture of my life's doings will be brightened somewhat, if, in my final diploma, I come off with a favorable mark at least in music. Then I shall feel that I have been judged fairly, and I shall be satisfied.

INDEX

[i]

Index

Index

Index

Index

Index

Index

Index

Index

Index

Index

Index

Index

Index

Index

Index

Index

Index